The State
of
American History

The State
of
American History

Edited with an Introduction by

HERBERT J. BASS

QUADRANGLE BOOKS
Chicago
1970

Library of Congress Catalog Card Number: 77-101068

for Bob Wiebe
whose idea it was

Acknowledgments

I wish to acknowledge the contributions made to this volume by the members of the program committee of the Organization of American Historians for the year 1969: David H. Fischer, Lloyd C. Gardner, Stanley Katz, Leon Litwack, Alfred B. Rollins, Jr., Harry N. Scheiber, John L. Thomas, and, of course, Robert H. Wiebe, the committee's chairman. Thanks are due also to Herbert Ershkowitz, Mark Haller, James McClellan, William Cutler, and Allen F. Davis, all colleagues at Temple University, and Harry Scheiber of Dartmouth College for their help at various stages of this project.

The essay by Richard Wade appears in substantially the same form in George Billias and Gerald Grob, eds., *American History: Retrospect and Prospect* (New York, Free Press, 1970), and is reprinted here by permission of the author and the editors and publisher of that book.

Introduction

This book had its genesis in the spring of 1968 during the program planning for the 1969 meetings of the Organization of American Historians in Philadelphia. The program committee chairman, Robert Wiebe of Northwestern University, had earlier proposed that we depart from the traditional potpourri of papers in favor of a program with a single unifying theme, an assessment of the state of American history. Our committee invited scholars of various ages, levels of prestige, and intellectual styles to present statements on their own special areas in American history.

By spring we had enough acceptances to realize that a remarkable program was in the making. It occurred to several of us that these papers would deserve a larger audience than the relative few who would attend each session in Philadelphia. Published together, the papers would constitute an important appraisal of the state of American history as we near the bicentennial of the American republic. I agreed to edit such a book and asked those who were scheduled to present papers to revise them for consideration. The twenty essays printed here were selected for the importance of their statements about their fields of American history.

The result is a useful professional stocktaking. While most of the essays incorporate at least a brief review of recent literature, and some an extensive one, they eschew that kind of historiography in which an understanding of what happened is less important than an understanding of the historian who wrote about it. Though at times that approach provides useful insights, it has all too often yielded little more than a stale rehearsal of intellectual and social currents and schools or cycles of interpretation. At its worst, it has degenerated into a narcissistic fascination with the collective self of the profession.

Progressive historians, neoconservatives, and consensus schools do of course appear in these pages; but they do not determine the terms in which each field is discussed. Indeed, one is struck by the fact that the authors of these essays have little interest in tired debates. In a way, they take as a starting place some point beyond the now trite historiographical categories.

One value in printing a number of essays of this sort between two covers is that collectively they make some points that individually they cannot. The whole is, in truth, greater than the sum of the parts. For example, on viewing the essays together one gains an appreciation of the variety of the historical enterprise today. Pieces on traditional fields like political, economic, and diplomatic history are here, though the questions they ask and the methodologies they speak of are quite different from those of the past. There are also essays on such relatively new areas of interest to historians as urban, educational, and legal history, the history of social welfare, of American science, and of American technology. Robert Lifton's stimulating essay on psychohistory points to still another area we have only begun to exploit; and one can see a foreshadowing of future research in the call for more information on the history of children and of the family. Historians, in other words, are working in fields that until yesterday were the special reserves of other disciplines. Some regret this activity as a diffusion of energy, a fractionalization of historical experience. Yet it might as easily be argued that it is less a Balkanizing than an imperializing tendency that we are witnessing.

Whichever of these perceptions is correct, the more important question is whether in the end these new fields of historical inquiry will remain discrete, or will refresh each other with new insights and new perspectives. As to the ultimate aim, these essays leave no doubt. Running through most of them is precisely the argument that the enlargement of understanding in a given field will come only by approaching it anew with the insights, methods, and models of others. Thomas McCormick's essay on diplomatic history is a case in point.

What also strikes one, on reading these essays together, are the increasingly sophisticated methods of historical research—the greater awareness of underutilized sources of historical data, the application of quantitative approaches to the past, the disciplined use of comparative history, and the readiness to apply to historical studies the methods, models, and findings of the social sciences. The quest is clearly for ever greater precision in conceptualization, in method, in analysis, and in presentation of findings.

While in a larger sense all the essays bear the mark of our age, several respond particularly to the ferment of today. In a time when the persistence of our cultural pluralism is evident, Rudolph Vecoli argues for a greater attention to ethnicity in our history. Sydney Ahlstrom measures the impact of the moral and theological upheaval of the new generation upon religious history. In an era when even the reluctant are compelled to an awareness of the lower economic and social classes, David Tyack and Robert Bremner urge that the history of education and of social welfare pay more attention to the viewpoint of the client and less to that of those who operate, administer, and finance these activities. With Douglas Dowd, they seem to be calling for the history of the acted upon and not merely of the actors, a history from the bottom up rather than the top down.

Of course, the twenty contributors to this volume do not speak with one voice. Clearly, Edward Pessen is more skeptical about the potentialities of quantification than the several authors of the essay that assesses that methodology—though the latter themselves note many of its limitations. And Laurence Evans and Thomas McCormick see the way to an improved understanding of the history of our foreign relations rather differently. Yet more striking than the occasional differences among these authors is the coincidence of direction toward which most of them point.

This entire appraisal constitutes a formidable challenge for today's historians. Are we up to it? After one particularly stimulating session in Philadelphia I remarked to a colleague, one of the more traditionally oriented members of the guild, that I had found the speaker's call for a different approach to his field eminently sensible. With barely a moment's thought my colleague replied, in a phrase familiar to students of John Marshall and Andrew Jackson, "——— has proposed his new history; now let him write it."

That, of course, will be the test.

H. J. B.

Philadelphia
January 1970

Contents

The State
of
American History

Some Problems and Possibilities of American Legal History

LAWRENCE M. FRIEDMAN

When too many manifestos about research are published and people write *about* doing rather than attending to the doing, it is a sure sign that a field of knowledge is immature. American legal history is in something of this state. In print, and in speech, American legal historians complain about their field.[1] They ponder its uses to history, law, and the world; its untapped resources; and the reasons why it has not flourished. Of course there is a literature of American legal history, besides the complaints and manifestos; but there is cause for concern in the proportion between the two.

Another disturbing sign of immaturity is simply that there are few practitioners, alive or dead. Probably fewer than fifty persons in law schools and history departments could identify themselves as full-time historians of American law, or could realistically think of American legal history as their major intellectual effort. To these we may add an unknown but not staggering number of amateurs who hover about on the periphery. Not many persons even teach the subject. One hundred and fifteen law schools (out of 132 accredited by the American Bar Association) were surveyed on the subject in 1961. Only thirty-one had a legal history course in their curriculum.[2] Most of these courses, apparently, were exclusively English legal history, or were about something called Anglo-American legal history, in which the Anglo vastly overshadowed the American. Probably not more than ten law schools, then or now, offer a course in American legal history. I do not know how many history departments give offerings in this area;

aside from courses in constitutional history, the number is undoubtedly quite small.[3]

Since there are few who teach and few who practice this dark art, it should not be a matter of surprise that the secondary literature on American legal history is rather thin. Some of the writing is of extraordinary quality, and a great deal of it is very competent; but there is simply not enough of it around. Considering the current interest in criminal justice, it is something of a scandal that criminal law and the administration of criminal justice (aside from the Colonial period) [4] should be one of the blankest pages of all.[5] Even more serious is the lack of general histories of law. There is nothing in American legal history to compare with Holdsworth's *History of English Law,* a mammoth work of fifteen volumes.[6] There is nothing to compare with the solid one-volume surveys of English legal history; Plucknett's *Concise History of the Common Law*[7] is the leading modern example. At present there is no book in print with the title *A History of American Law,* or anything reasonably similar.[8]

Lack of general history is a serious detriment to the field. It means there is no tradition, no received learning, no conventional wisdom to define what is important and what is not for students, researchers, and historians in other areas. In American history generally, there is a great deal of common agreement on what trends and events are significant. Every general history speaks of the slavery controversy, the fall of the second Bank of the United States, the Progressive era, the New Deal. Wars and presidencies provide an obvious framework for chronology. Certain socio-economic processes are assumed as valid categories and as important: urbanization and industrialization after the Civil War; the rise of the labor movement; labor unrest in the late nineteenth century; the discovery of poverty in the 1960's. At all times there are of course disputes about relative importances, and in each historical generation a revisionist movement of some sort arises. But what a revisionist movement does is to revise. It does not totally discard or invent totally new categories; it reacts to a received learning. Since there is in general no framework in American legal history, and not even much of a chronology, there is hardly anything to revise. Some of its subsystems do have a conventional history and a conventional chronology—the United States Supreme Court, for example. Supreme Court history is richer than any other area of what is usually considered American legal history.[9] But the history as a whole lacks a skeleton. This is deplorable, and it stands as a major obstacle to further progress in the field.

The absence of framework and convention is not an accident, at least not entirely. Part of the problem is rooted in the conceptual baggage of the law schools, out of which a legal history might otherwise have emerged. The atmosphere of legal education has not been conducive to creative scholarship. History has not been the only stepchild of the law schools. Jurisprudence, Roman law, and the sociology of law have also been neglected. Law schools neglect, in short, everything more or less foreign to their dominant ideology. It is not necessary to belabor what that ideology is. Since the 1870's, since the days of the Langdell revolution (if not earlier), law schools have emphasized legal method, legal reasoning (teaching people how to think like a lawyer), and analytical skill in dissecting appellate cases (how to distill from these cases some precious doctrinal essence).[10] Doctrines were, in a way, treated historically, but only in the sense that scholars and teachers were interested in how the formulation of rules changed over time. Legal learning was never historical, if historical means to examine the law in any given period in its actual social context.

Some legal scholars in the late nineteenth century did develop a genuine fascination with the development of law over a rather longer time-series than other scholars and teachers. For these men, however, the relevant field was English legal history. Some of the most distinguished scholars in American law schools in the late nineteenth century were of this persuasion. James Barr Ames at Harvard,[11] for example, made real contributions to English legal history. But legal scholars left American law virtually untouched. There was some agitation over whether and when English law was "received" on these shores,[12] but hardly much more.

The fascination of American legal scholars with English legal history is, in a way, a most peculiar phenomenon. It would be an odd history department in the United States which offered more courses on English history than on American history. It would be an odd faculty in any country that did not stress its own history. What is even more peculiar is the *kind* of English legal history that was studied and taught—and still is, to some extent. One gets a good idea of its nature from examining Theodore Plucknett's book, *A Concise History of the Common Law*.[13] This admirable book was, according to the 1961 survey, the most widely used textbook in American legal history courses.[14] The fifth edition, published in 1956, is 746 pages long. The overwhelming bulk of it is concerned with medieval law. Less than a hundred pages are spent on the last three centuries of English life. The section on real property is typical; more than eighty pages of it treats the land law of the Middle Ages, ending with the Statute of Uses, which was enacted during the reign of Henry VIII.[15] Subsequent events are barely mentioned. There is not a single word about the twentieth century—a period in which English land tenure underwent great changes, in which land use controls were developed to a fantastic degree.

Textbooks or general accounts of American or English history are not usually organized this way. Very often the author hurries through the early periods, and slows down as he gets closer to modern times. The more contemporaneous the period, the richer the detail. Partly this occurs because of a greater storehouse of data; but it is true that modern life and its immediate antecedents seem more relevant than remote times to the concerns of students and teachers.[16]

Legal historians of Plucknett's persuasion must have some different standard or notion of relevance. And indeed they do. The clue is in Plucknett's title. What he has written is not a history of English law, but a history of the common law—a very different thing. The common law, as a system or entity, was presumably quite well formed by the sixteenth century. Since then, nothing seems to have happened to its basic structure, merely a further unfolding or flowering of its principles and institutions, whose characteristics were fixed in the formative period.[17] Besides, so much modern law is not common law at all, not the product of the judges but either statutory intrusions or the replacement or neutralization of judicial process by administrative law. Some such idea must lie behind the organization of Plucknett's book as well as behind the curious feature that many of the English legal history courses described in the 1961 survey, like Plucknett's book, end somewhere in the sixteenth century.[18] For those who stress what they consider the formative period of the common law, American legal history has nothing much to offer, just as Australia would have little to add to a brief history of the English language. If there is no great message in modern English law, how should we learn much about common law from America, which was not even settled until after the formative period?

This emphasis on common law in law schools explains some of the neglect of American legal history by law professors. Moreover, it leads the legal historian to conceive his task narrowly. That task, as expressed recently by one author, is to trace "the development of the concepts, doctrines, and rules which have been created and used to keep order in our society." [19] But this formulation takes a static view of the legal system. It begins by looking for something called "origins" —the first case to speak of the last clear-chance doctrine, the earliest example of docking the entail, and the like. It is also concerned with something it calls "development," that is, formal antecedents and middle stages on the road to more final formulation of specific "concepts, doctrines, and rules." Carried to an extreme, this means that nothing need be looked at in its full social context. The state of the law in 1700 is not treated as something vital and organic in itself, not as a part of the life of society in 1700, but only as a stage in the voyage toward some particular end-state. That end-state is not some complex social process but a doctrine, a concept, a rule. Now it is perfectly acceptable for a historian to be interested in 1700 only in so far as life then has some relevance for the life of his community today. But this kind of ulterior motive does not excuse him from the requirement of historical rigor. There is nothing to be learned from the past unless the past is taken in its context. It is a distortion to use history as some genealogists use records, searching for ancestors and discarding everything else as dross. Yet much so-called legal history has been exactly that.

The historians of common law, like Plucknett, have moreover focused most of their attention on the work of appellate courts. For them, only case-law is truly common law. Only case-law evolves "concepts, doctrines, and rules." Statutes do not, as a general rule, give rise to a concept, or a doctrine, or even a rule, in the sense used by those scholars. The Alien and Sedition Laws, the Internal Revenue Code, the Interstate Commerce law, laws about fugitive slaves, the estate tax, the Economic Opportunity Act—none of these has ever given rise to a "concept" with the dialectic beauty of "seaworthiness" in admiralty law or "proximate cause" in torts. From their standpoint of doctrine, the *Dred Scott*[20] case is trivial. Yet much of what passed and still passes for legal history is exactly this: a history of common law concepts, doctrines, and rules. This kind of history can explain very little. It can hardly explain even what it purports to. The dialectic of doctrine is not an insulated process; change in concepts is not immanent in the concepts themselves. Modern tort law was not hidden mystically inside the word negligence, waiting to be freed by the touch of a judicial wand. Every stage in the history of a "concept, doctrine, and rule" had a full, final meaning in the light of what was actually going on, either within the legal system or as a consequence of the external relations of the legal system with society. A legal history of concepts and rules cannot adequately explain how a society governs itself through law. What excites it most is the apparent dialectic of doctrine, subtly changing in a series of cases. From this standpoint, American legal history seems a dull, barren enterprise. Too many factors intrude on the common law process.

One should not paint too black a picture. American legal history is still an underdeveloped field, but it is growing. A generation ago there were almost no courses, no practitioners. It seems likely that within a few years, more American than English legal history will be taught in law schools and history departments. This development will be on the whole a healthy one. After all, there are more opportunities for original research on American law than on English law, whose sources are an ocean's width away. And students and faculty have a surer sense of American life than of British.

The literature of American law is also bound to grow. There are important strengths to build upon. Charles Warren's three-volume *History of the United States Supreme Court* was published more than forty years ago.[21] For all its failings, this was a richly suggestive work, far ahead of its time in its emphasis on the interplay between politics and the Court as a working institution. A vast new history of the Court is in process, carrying on the Warren tradition. Other legal historians have done, and continue to do, distinguished work on other aspects of American law. Probably the outstanding name is that of Willard Hurst, at the University of Wisconsin Law School. With great care and creativity, Hurst has explored the relationship between law and economic growth in the United States in the nineteenth century.[22] Even more significantly, Hurst has made a major contribution to the philosophy and theory of American legal history,[23] and he has founded something of a school of legal historians.[24] Other scholars have made excellent contributions to our knowledge of the Colonial period— George Haskins and Joseph Smith, for example.[25] Judicial biography continues to be relatively popular; some of these biographies have illuminated otherwise dark corners of institutional history.[26] In American history departments, too, there is more interest in American law,[27] despite a certain decline in the popularity of constitutional history. Finally, the *American Journal of Legal History*, now entering its thirteenth volume, devotes about half of its space to American legal history. In the academic world, no field that has its own journal, or part of one, can be given up for dead.

As the field expands, however, it faces problems of adolescence: and in particular it faces that twentieth-century curse, the identity crisis. The narrow point of view that looks upon legal history as a history of doctrine is easily rejected. But what shall replace it? A broader definition of boundaries is needed. This turns out to be no small problem. What *is* the legal system? No one can give a satisfactory answer. The legal historian in fact confronts a considerable intellectual dilemma. A narrow definition of law and the legal system is totally defective. To confine one's study to doctrines, concepts, and rules, or to concrete, bounded institutions yields a workable guide to particular studies—for example, of courts or the legal profession. But this falls far short of exhausting the whole of the legal system under any reasonable view. What, after all, is the purpose of research in legal history? Legal history is presumably only a means toward some end. That end may be to understand social control, how societies are governed. Or, as an American historian, one may wish to grasp the full meaning of the peculiar American way of government, as part of the job of knowing the American experience in general. What people call the legal system is a part of the larger system of social control, but only a part. The trouble is that an expanded view of the legal system melts the boundaries between law and the rest of society. The boundaries between the two become terribly fluid, or, to put it more charitably, imperfectly marked. How much of the government in general, how much of the total public effort in society should be considered part of the legal system for purposes of historical study? The legal historian easily excludes most foreign and diplomatic relations. Is this merely a convention, or is there some good reason why a legal historian should study what goes on in the Food and Drug Administration but not what goes on in the embassy in France? Moreover, how much nongovernmental activity should the legal historian concern himself with? Clearly, the activities of lawyers as lawyers; but what else? Rules of law—authoritative, institutionalized norms—sometimes govern people's lives, but they do so imperfectly and with a great deal of slippage. The social control system of any society is a network of attitudes and actions; public and private interact in hopeless confusion. Shall we consider as part of our job all actions influenced in any way by law? All avoidance of law? All substitutes for law?

There is a satisfying tidiness to any study which has definite limits— a biography is the best example. Institutional history seems to be another case. To study a court or courts over time can be illuminating, but it has its own frustrations and shortcomings. Courts perform different functions in different time periods. A history of courts (or of any other legal institution) can be wholly satisfactory only if the focus is on the institution itself, not on its impact or function. But often we want to study courts not for themselves but because their work is an index of a function—dispute-settlement, common law rule-making, execution of policy. Courts share these functions with other institutions; the relative share of each one in the total performance of the function is not a historical constant. What is constant is change. The historian of a function is dragged away from the courts into all the other things that law-trained people do and the places where they do them. He finds himself grappling with legislation and administrative regulation. He finds himself concerned with private lawmaking in law offices, where documents are drafted and forms of enterprise devised. If the point is to understand some aspect of the social control system, or all of it, the historian will have to look at a range of phenomena not bounded by what lawyers do at all. Yet when he steps out into the larger world, he faces two additional and enormous problems. If he is a lawyer, he must ask himself why this larger task is in his competence. There is no obvious answer. He is tempted then to retreat to more comfortable areas, where his special training gives him a competitive advantage. Lawyer and historian alike face a second problem: how can one quantify and deal with these more expansive phenomena, phenomena with no conventional limits and no conventional definition?

It is, of course, by no means a unique dilemma. Other specialized historians face it. It is hard to write a history of American education; and if the point is a history of how one generation transmits culture and technology to the next generation, the job is more intractable than a history of definite schools. The specialist feels his sureness of grasp slipping away from him; he does not know where to begin or end his search for data. A political historian is on safe ground if he studies voting patterns; if he wishes to study popular participation in public decisions and takes voting as only one index, he is suddenly alone and at sea.

All these problems of boundaries come about, in a way, when historians take up questions under the influence of social science theory rather than more conventional categories. Yet historical scholarship is bound to go in this direction; so, too, American legal history, if it aspires to be relevant to problems of modern government, or if it wishes to infuse fresh meaning into legal education, or to communicate significant insights to American historians in general. But legal history lacks general theory. No tradition of scholarship has defined its place in the sun and provided it with framework. The dilemma, then, is inescapable. Without general theory, American legal history will not solve its definitional problem. But so long as the problem is unsolved, legal history may have to accept a limited role and confine itself largely to the history of the profession and the courts.

On a more mundane level, the data of American legal history are also a fertile source of problems. What the data are depends on the ultimate definition of the field. But there are difficulties too with what all could agree on as data. In one sense there are data to burn—an immense bulk of primary documents. An American legal historian might secretly envy historians of the Hittites or the Dark Ages, where records are so scanty that the historian must make a great deal out of very little. The legal historian has to boil down to a little what begins as too much. His raw materials include a million or more reported cases, thousands of volumes of statutes and administrative materials, an infinitude of lower court records and public documents (almost all of them unpublished), uncatalogued and scattered private papers of lawyers, and all this in addition to nonlegal sources that bear on the operation of law. Legal records are a data bank of incredible richness. Some historians have made good use of it. Colonial history is unthinkable without court records, legislative acts, wills, and inventories. But on the whole, how to cope with this immense, intractable, trackless bulk is a problem of the first order.

It is sad but true, moreover, that the more visible and accessible the data, the less it can be trusted. Law does not speak its mind plainly and honestly. Legal language is clothed in a standardized, ritual dress. It is hard to tell what is real from what is show and form. Legal behavior may be formal or informal, public or private.[28] Obviously, the more formal and public the behavior, the more accessible it is to the historian. Appellate case-law, for example, is extremely accessible for most of the nineteenth century.[29] The historian interested in law and the economic system may be tempted to rely heavily upon it. This means ignoring the lower courts,[30] not to mention various bypass institutions. And the private behavior of businessmen and attorneys who, for example, worked out new commercial documents and forms of enterprise will be ignored until sporadic and belated echoes appear in the cases.

It is hard not to take the written record at face value. But it is dangerous to do so. Every modern student of criminal justice concedes the importance of research on police behavior to supplement the cases and statutes that purport to govern the police.[31] The gap between book law and living law is important for understanding the present; it must be equally true for the past. A full history of criminal justice cannot be written from cases and statutes alone. There is no reason to believe that the gap between the formal and the informal was any less important a century ago. Yet data problems are infinitely greater for the past. The urge to quantify, to take the path of scientific method comes from a commitment to solve historical problems whose theorems and hypotheses stem from or are influenced by the social sciences. At the same time social science theorems and hypotheses drive the historian to factors and realms of behavior that cannot be easily quantified, if they can be quantified at all.

Every kind of history faces this problem; it is certainly not unique to legal history. But legal history *is* particularly prone to be fooled by the formal. So much of this data seems so precise, so definite, so concrete. There is strong temptation to take it as literally true. As a result, one may assign an exact date to events that did not take place at all, or that took place at a very different time. Formal behavior is not necessarily pointless behavior. It is not unimportant if a man and a woman get married after living together for years. But marriage records alone cannot be used as an index of sexual behavior and family life.

Some formal legal acts truly set social process in motion; others merely codify behavior or ratify preexisting process. Yet it is not easy to tell one from the other. Mistaking formal ratification for innovation is one of the major traps of American legal history. For example, recent research makes reasonably clear that the meaning of the married women's property laws in the middle of the nineteenth century might be exaggerated or misunderstood. These laws did not set in motion any important changes in the status of women. They merely ratified and formalized a completed evolution.[32] The passage of Jim Crow laws is another example. What can be safely deduced from them about race relations in the South in the late nineteenth century? Often a flurry of legislation does not mean a new level of density in real social control over some area of life, but quite the opposite: break down of control, frantic efforts by one group to patch up controls that have decayed or met with more and more resistance.[33] It was no upsurge of patriotic fervor that led to recent laws against the burning of draft cards. If anything, these laws reflect the collapse of conventional patriotism among many of the young in America.

There is a glaring contrast, in American legal history, between the visible and the obscure. There is therefore a temptation to take the big case, the egregious example, and deal with it to the exclusion of more ordinary processes of law. One great virtue of Willard Hurst's explorations in legal history has been his willingness to handle great masses of information, each one in itself insignificant.[34] He has deliberately ignored big issues and front-page cases in order to build up his picture of legal process in the manner of a mosaic, creating a more complex and undoubtedly more accurate picture through the aggregation of bits of detail.

The nonlawyer who wanders into legal history is perhaps particularly vulnerable to the temptation to use only data that present the fewest technical problems. The trained lawyer admittedly has a head start in coping with the jargon, artifice, and verbosity of law. This advantage can be easily exaggerated. Many nineteenth-century lawyers, after all, had the gall to represent clients after the most perfunctory sort of legal training. If the nonlawyer is driven away from lawyer's law by a sense of insecurity, he may neglect legal process and take refuge in works of jurisprudence and rhetoric written by lawyers but not necessarily for a legal audience. The late Perry Miller used this kind of material in writing about the American "legal mind." [35] The results were not simply disappointing; they were downright misleading. Would it be presumptuous to say that American legal history is an area of scholarship where conventional materials for constructing intellectual history have even less to offer than is usually the case? Formal jurisprudential literature made a slim contribution at best to American culture, and it had little impact even on the work and thought of the profession. The materials that Perry Miller used tell us very little about what the average lawyer thought and did.

The legal profession was at all times a working legal profession. What it did was more significant than what some of its more pretentious leaders said it was doing. What the profession did, what it accomplished, however, is by no means self-evident. What, if anything, was the distinctive contribution of American legal life to the development of American society? Obviously, lawyers perform many tasks in the United States which are not done by lawyers in other societies. Americans litigate many matters not litigated in other societies. Administrative officers seem to have a freer hand in Great Britain and on the continent than they do in the United States. American law has carried judicial independence and judicial power further than the law in other countries. Whatever the origins of judicial review, some appellate courts have undoubtedly exerted pressure on legislatures and the executive to block them from acts which the courts consider wrong. In Great Britain and on the continent, judges do not have so much power or gall. But it does not follow that governmental outcomes are materially different in the United States, compared with other Western industrial countries. Judicial review is a very striking phenomenon, but on the whole it is rarely used and has always been rare. Can anyone *prove* whether the conservatism of the United States Supreme Court and some state courts in the freedom of contract cases around the turn of the century actually delayed, retarded, or warped the development of American social and economic policy? [36] Did the early anti-trust decisions, which tended to render the Sherman Act toothless, have any real impact on the organization of the economy? [37] For that matter, what, if anything, would have happened if the Sherman Act had not passed? What if it had been rigorously enforced from the very outset?

These questions point to the central question of American legal history, which is also its central opportunity. It is to devise ways to measure the impact of the legal system on the social order in general. To put it another way, how much of the quality of American life and American society can be ascribed to what one might call the structural variable?

Historical research on the legal system can be analytically divided into three main topics. One is the study of the background of law—the context out of which law in general develops, and the social forces leading to passage, enunciation, or enforcement of specific programs and rules. Two other topics deal with the impact of law on society, but one can distinguish, first, research on how public attitudes and actions warp and shape the application and enforcement of law; and, second, research on how structural and organizational choices affect the way law is (and can be) carried out. One could illustrate all the topics from studies of the Prohibition laws. The rise and passage of the Prohibition Amendment can be related to social movements that reached their culmination at the time of passage.[38] Research on the impact of Prohibition may focus on the population, drinkers, non-drinkers, salesmen and pushers of liquor, and its broader impact on the life of the nation as a whole. Or research could focus on the enforcement agents, the articulation of power between federal and state governments, the administrative organization of prohibition agencies, how the squeeze in money and men limited enforcement, and what Prohibition did to the court structure and police systems of the country.[39] It is impossible, of course, fully to separate the various strands of impact analysis, and all are important. But some sociologists, aided and abetted by some historians, might be prone to overemphasize how the behavior and attitudes of the general population affected the law, ignoring the intervening variables of organization and administration. This middle layer, the structural variable, is the special glory of legal history. After all, the Prohibition laws themselves were a structural variable, intervening between the proponent side of the public, and the population which was the target of these zealots. In a sense, the whole legal system is a structural variable in society.

That legal historians should stress the structural variable in research on general historical questions is not a law of nature. But lawyer-historians and historians who specialize in law are sensitive to structures. They also have the skill and the patience to examine structural data. I do not mean to suggest that the structural variable is the crucial one. It is precisely the research task of the legal historian to try to decide if it is or not, or when it is, or why, and what effect it has on society. Many of the specific problems mentioned here—married women's property laws, segregation laws, police behavior—can be analyzed as problems of the impact of the structural variable. So too can many classic problems of the history of American government. Has federalism—for example—made as much difference in the formation of modern American society as many people seem to think? Is it a cause, or an effect, or both? What of the separation of powers and judicial review?

A question like this one, whether judicial review makes any difference, has a double thrust. What courts do may make little difference to society for one of two very different reasons: first, because effective structures exist which neutralize or bypass the courts; second, because formal structures as a whole are not significant molders and shapers of society. Dockets of appellate courts, in general, have had little impact on the economic system for the last half-century, if not longer. This is precisely because bypass and neutralizing institutions have developed—arbitration, private lawmaking, executive and legislative action. But the legal system as a whole, and the structural forms it assumes do seem to make a difference to the economy. Exactly what the difference is cannot be easily expressed, certainly not in a pat formula. In a sense, the question of the structural variable is a problem for the sociology of law. But the sociology of law cannot now answer questions so broad. It needs, for one thing, a rich infusion of historical data. As history and the social sciences grow closer together, they will probably both come to look at the structural variable with increasing interest and sophistication. They will need the skills and the methods of the legal historian. Hopefully, enough of them will be on hand for the mutual endeavor of making sense of the American present and past.

NOTES

1. See Eldon R. James, "Some Diffiiculties in the Way of a History of American Law," 23 Ill. L. Rev. 683 (1929); Paul M. Hamlin, "A History of American Law: Possibilities, Progress, and Resources and Initial Requirements," 2 N.Y. Law Forum 76 (1956); Paul L. Murphy, "Time to Reclaim: The Current Challenge of American Constitutional History," *American Historical Review*, LXIX (October 1963), 64–79; Calvin Woodard, "History, Legal History, and Legal Education," 53 Virginia Law Review 89 (1967); Malcolm S. Mason, "On Teaching Legal History Backwards," 18 J. Leg. Ed. 155 (1966).

2. Edward D. Re, "Legal History Courses in American Law Schools," 13 American U.L.R. 45 (1963).

3. General histories of American historiography almost totally neglect legal history; perhaps one reason is that the subject is not interesting to intellectual

historians. Whatever the cause, legal history has been shunted aside in both of its potential havens.

In a private communication, Professor Mark Haller of Temple University makes the following observation: "For many years, the 'presidential synthesis' dominated the study of American political history. That is, political history was seen primarily as national politics and, particularly, as presidential politics. Similarly, legal history in history departments has been governed by a 'Supreme Court synthesis.' That is, legal history has been seen to be that which is done by the Supreme Court. In graduate schools, history graduate students have been taught almost no legal history except the history of constitutional law. Yet Supreme Court decisions are only a tiny part of appeals court decisions, appeals court decisions only a small part of court dispositions, and court dispositions only a small part of the decision-making of legal institutions. Because history graduate students have been taught nothing but a history of Supreme Court decisions, they have been prevented from seeing the possibilities of exploring broader questions about legal institutions and the role of law in structuring other institutions and patterning behavior."

I wish to express my thanks to Professor Haller for this observation, and also to Professor Harry Scheiber of Dartmouth College for his very helpful comments on the entire paper.

4. For example, Arthur P. Scott, *Criminal Law in Colonial Virginia* (Chicago, 1930); Julius Goebel, Jr., and T. Raymond Naughton, *Law Enforcement in Colonial New York: A Study in Criminal Procedure* (New York, 1944).

5. There are some monographic treatments of particular aspects of criminal law, for example, Jack Williams, *Vogues in Villainy: Crime and Retribution in Ante-Bellum South Carolina* (Columbia, S.C. 1959); and shorter essays such as David B. Davis, "The Movement to Abolish Capital Punishment in America, 1787–1861," *American Historical Review*, LXIII (October 1957), 23–46; on police history, Roger Lane, *Policing the City: Boston, 1822–1885* (Cambridge, Mass., 1967). Still the literature is amazingly small, considering the size and importance of the topic. Oddly enough, prison history has not been quite so neglected: see, for example, Negley K. Teeters and John D. Shearer, *The Prison at Philadelphia: Cherry Hill* (New York, 1957); W. David Lewis, *From Newgate to Dannemora: The Rise of the Penitentiary in New York, 1796–1848* (Ithaca, 1965); James Leiby, *Charity and Correction in New Jersey: A History of State Welfare Institutions* (New Brunswick, N.J., 1967).

6. Sir William Holdsworth died in 1944, without completing his *History of English Law*. Twelve volumes appeared during his lifetime, and three more have been brought out since his death.

7. Theodore T. F. Plucknett, *A Concise History of the Common Law*, 5th ed. (London, 1956).

8. Willard Hurst's *The Growth of American Law: The Lawmakers* (Boston, 1950) is perhaps the closest to a general treatment.

9. Charles Warren, *The Supreme Court in United States History*, 3 vols. (Boston, 1922); Charles G. Haines, *The Role of the Supreme Court in American Government and Politics, 1789–1835* (Berkeley, 1944–1957); there are also many judicial biographies and studies of particular doctrines, structures, crises, or periods, for example, Benjamin F. Wright, *The Contract Clause of the Constitution* (Cambridge, Mass., 1938); Harry N. Scheiber, *The Condition of American Federalism: An Historian's View* (Washington, D.C., 1966); Stanley I. Kutler, *Judicial Power and Reconstruction Politics* (Chicago, 1968).

10. On the Langdell revolution, see Arthur E. Sutherland, *The Law at Harvard: A History of Ideas and Men, 1817–1967* (Cambridge, Mass., 1967), pp. 162–205; Josef Redlich, *The Common Law and the Case Method in American University Law Schools* (New York, 1914), pp. 9–25.

11. See James Barr Ames, *Lectures on Legal History* (Cambridge, Mass., 1913). On Ames, see Sutherland, *The Law at Harvard,* pp. 206–225.

12. P. S. Reinsch, "The English Common Law in the Early American Colonies," in *Select Essays in Anglo-American Legal History* (Boston, 1907), I, 367; the matter is definitively treated by George Lee Haskins in *Law and Authority in Early Massachusetts: A Study in Tradition and Design* (New York, 1960), pp. 1–8.

13. Plucknett, *Concise History.* Alan Harding's *A Social History of English Law* (Baltimore, 1966) is an exception in the attention it gives to modern times.

14. Re, "Legal History Courses," 57.

15. 27 Hen. VIII, c. 10 (1536).

16. Many textbooks do trail off at some point just short of the present, to be sure, and for a variety of reasons.

17. There is a "formative era" concept in American legal history, too; Roscoe Pound, *The Formative Era of American Law* (Boston, 1938); see the trenchant criticism of this concept in Stanley N. Katz, "Looking Backward: The Early History of American Law," 33 U. Chi. L. Rev. 867, 873 (1966).

18. Since Plucknett is so widely used, this is not unexpected. But the professors could supplement Plucknett, if they wished, with more up-to-date material. For descriptions of these courses, see Re, "Legal History Courses," 52–56.

19. Frederick C. Kempin, Jr., *Legal History: Law and Social Change* (Englewood Cliffs, N.J., 1963), p. vii. For my critical review see 74 Yale L. J. 593 (1965). Another critique of the philosophy of legal history is Calvin Woodard's. See n. 1 supra.

20. Dred Scott v. Sandford, 10 How. 393, 15 L. Ed. 691 (1857). Whole books have been written about this case, for example, Vincent C. Hopkins, *Dred Scott's Case* (New York, 1951); Stanley I. Kutler, ed., *The Dred Scott Decision: Law or Politics?* (Boston, 1967). And historians continue to show an interest: see Walter Ehrlich, "Was the Dred Scott Case Valid?," *Journal of American History,* LV (September 1968), 256–265. But it usually gets short shrift in law school courses in constitutional law, partly because it is historical (which is itself box-office poison), but also because it has no particular importance in the evolution of doctrine. The extreme case must be the second edition of Barrett, Bruton, and Honnold, *Constitutional Law, Cases and Materials* (Brooklyn, 1963) which does not so much as mention Dred Scott, not even in the decent obscurity of a footnote.

21. Warren, *Supreme Court.*

22. Among Hurst's major works are *The Growth of American Law: The Lawmakers* (Boston, 1950); *Law and the Conditions of Freedom in the Nineteenth-Century United States* (Madison, Wisc., 1956); *Law and Social Process in United States History* (Madison, Wisc., 1960); and *Law and Economic Growth: The Legal History of the Lumber Industry in Wisconsin, 1836–1915* (Madison, Wisc., 1964).

23. On the significance of Hurst's work, see Earl Finbar Murphy, "The Jurisprudence of Legal History: Willard Hurst as Legal Historian." 39

N.Y.U.L. Rev. 900 (1964); Russell E. Brooks, "The Jurisprudence of Willard Hurst," 18 J. Leg. Ed. 257 (1966); John P. Frank, "American Legal History; The Hurst Approach," 18 J. Leg. Ed. 395 (1966); Harry N. Scheiber, "At the Borderlands of Law and Economic History," forthcoming, *American Historical Review.*

24. Among the works influenced by Hurst's ideas and methods—most of them case-studies in the legal-economic history of Wisconsin in the nineteenth century—are Robert S. Hunt, *Law and Locomotives* (Madison, Wisc., 1958); Spencer L. Kimball, *Insurance and Public Policy* (Madison, Wisc., 1960); Earl F. Murphy, *Water Purity* (Madison, Wisc., 1961); and Lawrence M. Friedman, *Contract Law in America* (Madison, Wisc., 1965).

25. Haskins, *Law and Authority in Early Massachusetts;* Joseph Henry Smith, *Appeals to the Privy Council from the American Plantation* (New York, 1950); Smith, *Colonial Justice in Western Massachusetts, 1639–1702: The Pynchon Court Record* (Cambridge, Mass., 1961). Another important work in colonial legal history is Richard B. Morris, *Studies in the History of American Law* (New York, 1930).

26. Most of the biographies are of justices of the Supreme Court, for example, Carl B. Swisher's *Stephen J. Field: Craftsman of the Law* (Washington, D.C., 1930), and his *Roger B. Taney* (New York, 1935); Charles Fairman, *Mr. Justice Miller and the Supreme Court, 1862–1890* (New York, 1939); Willard King, *Melville Weston Fuller: Chief Justice of the United States, 1888–1910* (New York, 1950); Donald Morgan, *Justice William Johnson: The First Dissenter* (Columbia, S.C., 1954); and C. Peter Magrath, *Morrison R. Waite: The Triumph of Character* (New York, 1963). But there is emerging also a literature on state court judges and lower federal judges: Leonard W. Levy, *The Law of the Commonwealth and Chief Justice Shaw* (Cambridge, Mass., 1957); Aurora Hunt, *Kirby Benedict: Frontier Federal Judge* (Glendale, Calif., 1961); John P. Reid, *Chief Justice: The Judicial World of Charles Doe* (Cambridge, Mass., 1967).

27. The University of Wisconsin, for example, with at least two practitioners, Stanley Katz and Stanley Kutler, in its Department of History. David Flaherty of the University of Virginia reports that a joint program in law and American history has been established there.

28. Thus there are four types of behavior to be studied: formal and public, for example, a reported case or statute; informal and public, for example, remarks made by a judge in chambers to the litigants; formal and private, for example, an unrecorded lease or deed; and informal and private, for example, a conversation between a man and his attorney.

29. American case-reports were not published, as a general rule, for the Colonial period. Even after the Revolution, most states did not publish case-reports for many years, though Ephraim Kirby brought out a volume of Connecticut Reports in 1789. In some states, manuscript collections of cases circulated among lawyers. Daniel Boorstin has collected and edited eleven of these for Delaware, covering the period 1792–1830. Daniel Boorstin, *et al.,* eds., *Delaware Cases, 1792–1830,* 3 vols. (St. Paul, Minn., 1943). By 1820 most states had begun their series of case-reports. Rhode Island was the last state to fall into line, in 1847.

30. Studies of lower-court behavior are rare. One interesting example is Francis W. Laurent, *The Business of a Trial Court* (Madison, Wisc., 1959), a study of one hundred years of cases in the lower courts in Chippewa County,

Wisconsin, between 1855 and 1954. This is, of course, another study emanating from Wisconsin and the school of Willard Hurst.

Colonial lower-court records exist in massive profusion, and there are any number of scholarly editions of records from some courts, for example, Smith's *Colonial Justice in Western Massachusetts,* and Leon deValinger, Jr., ed., *Court Records of Kent County, Delaware 1680–1702* (Washington, D.C., 1959).

31. Only recently have the police been systematically studied at all. Among the best known of these studies is Jerome Skolnick, *Justice Without Trial: Law Enforcement in Democratic Society* (New York, 1966). See also Wayne La Fave, *Arrest: The Decision to Take a Suspect into Custody* (Boston, 1965). Research on actual behavior in other sub-systems of the legal system, and on the legal profession, is beginning to develop in some quantity. Many of these studies deal with the criminal law, but some deal with civil law and administrative law, for example, Stewart Macaulay, *Law and the Balance of Power: The Automobile Manufacturers and Their Dealers* (New York, 1966). The literature on the legal profession is growing; see, for example, Jerome Carlin, *Lawyers on Their Own: A Study of Individual Practitioners in Chicago* (New Brunswick, N.J., 1962); Erwin O. Smigel, *The Wall Street Lawyer* (New York, 1964); Joel Handler, *The Lawyer and His Community* (Madison, Wisc., 1967).

32. For the married women's property laws, and the general absence of controversy surrounding their passage (the earliest was in Mississippi in 1839), I have drawn on Kay Ellen Thurman, "The Married Women's Property Acts," Unpublished M.LL. Thesis (University of Wisconsin Law School, 1966).

33. See August Meier and Elliott M. Rudwick, "The Boycott Movement Against Jim Crow Streetcars in the South, 1900–1906," *Journal of American History,* LV (March 1969), 756–775. C. Vann Woodward's *The Strange Career of Jim Crow* (New York, 1955) is an important contribution to the study of the relationship of law and culture in its historical context.

34. Hurst, *Law and Economic Growth.*

35. Perry Miller's book is *The Life of the Mind in America: From the Revolution to the Civil War* (New York, 1965); the second part of this posthumous work deals with the legal mind. Earlier, Miller edited a collecton of documents which he called *The Legal Mind in America: From Independence to the Civil War* (Garden City, 1962). Critical assessments of Miller's study of the "legal mind" include Lawrence M. Friedman, "Heart Against Head: Perry Miller and the Legal Mind," 77 Yale L. J. 1244 (1968); and Stanley N. Katz, "Looking Backward: The Early History of American Law," 33 U. Chi. L. Rev. 867 (1966).

36. The reference is to such cases as *Ritchie v. People,* 155 Ill. 98, 40 N.E. 454 (1895), which cast down a law limiting women to an eight-hour day and a forty-eight-hour week in factories and "workshops"; and the famous case of *Lochner v. New York,* 198 U.S. 45 (1905), which did the same for a New York law limiting the hours of bakery workers. The literature on the subject is immense, beginning perhaps with Roscoe Pound's well-known article, "Liberty of Contract," 18 Yale L.J. 454 (1909). See, for various points of view, Clyde Jacobs, *Law Writers and the Court* (Berkeley, 1954); Benjamin Twiss, *Lawyers and the Constitution,* 2nd ed. (Princeton, 1962); Arnold Paul, *Conservative Crisis and the Rule of Law* (Ithaca, 1960); Lawrence M. Friedman, "Freedom of Contract and Occupational Licensing, 1890–1910: A Legal and Social Study," 53 Cal. L. Rev. 487 (1965).

37. The background of the Sherman Act, and the early administrative and judicial history of the law, are treated in William Letwin, *Law and Economic Policy in America: The Evolution of the Sherman Antitrust Act* (New York, 1965).

38. See Joseph R. Gusfield, *Symbolic Crusade: Status Politics and the American Temperance Movement* (Urbana, Ill., 1963).

39. See Andrew Sinclair, *Prohibition: The Era of Excess* (Boston, 1962).

New Perspectives on the History of American Education

DAVID B. TYACK

Hear a student in a Harlem school:

> The early bird catches the worm. . . . Not always the worm get caught. Sometimes he is too fast for the early bird. I think that sometimes this is not true because the birds are not after worms, they might find something better to eat. One of these days the worm is going to eat the bird.[1]

It's a question of perspective. If one identifies with the worm instead of with the early bird, the world looks different. What we see here, as Ralph Ellison has remarked about the experience of blacks and whites, is a struggle over the nature of reality. Present crises are prompting educational historians to look with new perspectives at institutions long taken for granted, and to ask new questions about unfamiliar subjects. This reexamination is not so much another form of present-mindedness—a defect which has produced much anachronistic writing in the history of education—as it is an example of the "Age of Reinterpretation" described by C. Vann Woodward in 1960. As Woodward has reminded us, insistent and revolutionary changes today are forcing historians to understand the past in new ways.[2]

The dominant early genre in the history of education in this country was a version of house history comparable to the work of early denominational historians. Like ministers writing sectarian histories for their colleagues, educational historians often wrote to unite and inspire their co-workers in the schools. From the perspective of professional schoolmen, especially school administrators, they told a story of evolving institutions and increasing ideological consensus. Their narrative was linear, evolutionary, and often used states and other administrative units as a geographical focus; they divided the story chronologically according to the tenure of school officers. Commonly, superintendents themselves wrote these histories. When others recorded the past, they usually told the facts administrators chose to divulge: statistics of attendance and enrollment, laws affecting the schools, supervision, teachers' institutes, extensions of the curriculum, and related topics. In short, it was a promotional, optimistic account of progress achieved; any remaining problems could be handled within an improved establishment. This was an insider's view of the schools, seen from the top down.[3]

In the twentieth century some changes have appeared in this establishment view of American educational history. Historians have paid increasing attention to philosophical debates about the nature of learning and the learner, about curriculum, about the strategies of realizing the democratic purposes of the common school. Few have asked, as did Merle Curti, basic questions about the actual historical functioning, structures of control, and implicit results of schooling.[4] Commonly the history and philosophy of education have been closely linked in departments or colleges of education—indeed, often taught by the same people—and thus it is not coincidental that much of the writing in the field has centered on ideas about education rather than on empirical investigation of actual practice. Indeed, many of the ideologically minded have assumed that commitment to different theories of education automatically resulted in different behavior in the classroom. This point of view was well expressed by two scholars who wrote in the preface to their textbook that "we do not ignore events, but we do not enthrone them. Taking them as the *outcome* of thought and purpose, we record them with as much detail as seems necessary."[5]

As a result of this tradition, one which has produced useful analyses of ideas, we know a good deal about progressive theories of education, for example, but relatively little about the impact of these theories on students and society. Thus the history of education has sometimes resembled a history of politics based on political party platforms, a study of rhetoric rather than behavior. And tempering the debate over theories has been a common commitment to existing school systems, much as theological discourse among Anglicans has been mediated by a common membership in the Church.

In many respects, traditional educational historiography served its time and purpose well. It perpetuated and institutionalized Horace Mann's vision of a common school (a great social invention, however far the reality has fallen short of the ideal). It gave a miscellaneous procession of schoolmen a goal of becoming a united profession. It provided a simple linear model for institutional research, thus enlarging the body of empirical knowledge (even though it distorted history by seeing the past as "the present writ small"). It helped to explain and justify the public schools during the period of their most rapid growth, and, by expressing a consensus on certain values (for example, professionalism) and a selective inattention to others (for example, racism), it served to limit conflict within the professional guild. But in three important respects this historiography became dysfunctional: the history of education grew parochial and isolated from the main currents of historical and social research; the custom of seeing the schools from a schoolman's perspective helped to create a trained incapacity to see the schools from other viewpoints; and the view that educational practice was the result of the philosophical choices of professionals obscured the larger social forces and the overt or latent organizational pressures that constrained such choices.[6]

The present turmoil in education suggests that it is perilous to take familiar educational institutions and ideologies for granted. Today it is clear that many students and patrons have lost confidence in teachers and administrators, for the clients are rebelling against the professionals. Today there is increasing evidence that the schools are not—and were not—serving the egalitarian and democratic goals that justified them. Familiar facts need to be turned into puzzles. Today many do not want to ask "How did we achieve the public school triumphant?" but rather to question "Where did we ever get the idea that . . . ?"

Increasingly, historians have channeled the investigation of education into the historical mainstream. Scholars have sought insight into the wrenching policy issues of the present by asking new questions about the past. Naturally, such revisions have produced conflict between advocates of old and new interpretations. Much of this turmoil has really been academic status politics, a quarrel between members of educator and historical guilds. I do not intend to go into detail about these polemics beyond expressing the opinion that on both sides they have often obscured and stereotyped the issues rather than clarified them. The important question should not have been where a man taught or did his research, but whether his work was sound. Some educationists have been as critical of sloppy scholarship in the history of education as have the general historians.[7] Both groups have pointed out that new approaches are needed to give guidance to policy today. Irrelevance, lack of historical imagination, and defensiveness about established institutions and ideologies have hardly been a monopoly of educational history.

I also do not intend to offer a detailed systematic survey of studies in educational history in recent years, though I shall refer to a number of them. Paul Nash and Charles Burgess have done this well.[8] Actually, much of the terrain of educational history remains unexplored, and there has been comparatively little of the historiographical debate one finds in more popular fields such as Civil War history. I do not mean to suggest that recent writing in the field is insignificant. Quite the reverse: it shows what rich sources await those social or intellectual historians who turn to education for clues to perplexing problems in general history. But so heterogeneous in subject and approach has this recent writing been that it is not especially fruitful to treat it in conventional historiographical fashion. Rather, I should like to speculate about some of the directions that educational history may now be taking.

As a basis for my projection into this uncertain historiographical future, I want first to deal briefly with three influential essays: the pamphlet *The Role of Education in American History* (originally published in 1957 and revised in 1965); Bernard Bailyn's *Education in the Forming of American Society;* and Lawrence Cremin's *The Wonderful World of Ellwood Patterson Cubberley.*[9] In varying ways, these studies made two central points: (1) that education is far broader than schooling (indeed that "in a profound sense, it *is* the life of the young as they move toward maturity"); and (2) that historians should analyze the impact of education upon society, not simply "the character that education has acquired as a creation of society." The Committee on the Role of Education in American History put the latter conviction in this manner: "the historian may—and we trust he will— approach education saying: here is a constellation of institutions . . . what difference have they made in the life of the society around them?" The Committee urged scholars to investigate the influence of education upon such matters as the assimilation of immigrants, economic development, equality of opportunity, the development of political values and institutions, and "the growth of a distinctive American culture over a vast continental area." [10]

In his provocative essay, Bernard Bailyn suggested a hypothetical history of education in the Colonial and Revolutionary periods which would take into account changes in the family, religious life, race relations, and economic development as crucial determinants of the transmission of culture from generation to generation. Rather than tracing in linear fashion the institutions of the present from seeds in the distant past, Bailyn urged historians to regain a sense of surprise, a sense of discontinuity. The transformation of education in America, he wrote,

> becomes evident . . . when one assumes that the past was not in-
> cidentally but essentially different from the present; when one seeks
> as the points of greatest relevance those critical passages of history
> where elements of our familiar present, still parts of an unfamiliar
> past, begin to disentangle themselves, begin to emerge amid confu-
> sion and uncertainty. For these soft, ambiguous moments where the
> words we use and the institutions we know are notably present but
> are still enmeshed in older meanings and different purposes . . .
> these are the moments of true origination.[11]

Lawrence Cremin continued the historiographical dialogue in his essay on Cubberly published in 1965. In this study he traced the house history tradition as it flowed into and from Cubberley's influential *Public Education in the United States.* Acknowledging Cubberley's astounding industry, his clear organization, and his service in giving professionals an "unflagging commitment to universal education," Cremin nonetheless concluded that Cubberley's historiography had obscured the full character of education in America and "had helped to produce a generation of schoolmen unable to comprehend . . . much less contend with . . . the great educational controversies follow- ing World War II." He urged historians to examine educational agencies other than the school, to bring revisionist interpretations in general history to bear on educational questions, to exploit insights from the social sciences, and to place American educational history in comparative perspective.[12]

These three essays are excellent points of departure for historians who wish to investigate the role of education in American life. Each one sketches topics which could absorb a lifetime of research. The essays by Bailyn and Cremin include valuable bibliographical aids.

Since the appearance of the first pamphlet of the Committee on the Role of Education in American History, many important studies have appeared. In some respects the richest field has been the history of higher education, as illustrated by the work of Richard Hofstadter and Walter Metzger, John S. Brubacher and Willis Rudy, Laurence Veysey, Hugh Hawkins, Frederick Rudolph, Richard Storr, Winton Solberg, George Peterson, and several others.[13] Several studies of the content of academic teaching (notably the work of Jurgen Herbst, the studies edited by Paul Buck, and *Professors and Public Ethics* by Wilson Smith) suggest that the history of higher learning may be a useful framework for general intellectual history.[14] Ruth Elson, William Taylor, Rush Welter, Clarence Karier, and Charles Burgess, among others, have clarified the relation between political ideology and the schools.[15] Timothy Smith, Vincent Lannie, and Sol Cohen have shed light on the assimilation of immigrants.[16] Geraldine Joncich, Jack Campbell, Walter Drost, Jonathan Messerli, and several others have shown the continuing value of biography in educational history.[17] Various scholars have illuminated the way the schools have reacted to and influenced transformations in society: Edward Krug, Lawrence Cremin, Theodore Sizer, Robert Middlekauf, Berenice Fisher, Willis Rudy, and Patricia Graham, among many others.[18] New interpretations of the role of religion in public education have appeared in the research of Timothy Smith, Lloyd Jorgenson, Robert Lynn, Will Herberg, and the authors included in *Religion and Public Education.*[19] The Teachers College series, *Classics in Education,* has greatly expanded the range of readily available primary sources in educational history. Michael Katz and Charles Bidwell have explored the uses of quantification and the computer; Maxine Greene has looked at education from the angle of vision of creative writers; Daniel Calhoun has used sophisticated techniques of analysis from demography and behavioral science; William Brickman and others have enlarged the comparative perspective on American education.[20] In short, this brief and incomplete sampling of work during the last fifteen years reveals some of the variety of topics and methods of analysis emerging in the field.

This body of writing has demonstrated that the historical analysis of education can be intellectually respectable. Perhaps in the 1950's this was a point that needed reinforcement. Today, however, I suspect that a large group of educational historians will be moved by concerns not so prominent before the mid-1960's, especially the crisis in race relations and urban education and the signs of strain and conflict apparent in all educational institutions.

In the past, most critics of public education have come from the

right side of the political spectrum. Today critics on the left have been
pointing out that the facts of urban schooling belie democratic ideology:
to give each child equal opportunity, to mix all social groups under
one roof, and to place schools under public control. Writers like
Herbert Kohl, James Herndon, Jonathan Kozol, Peter Schrag, and
Nat Hentoff have been trying to tell the story of ghetto education
from the bottom up; titles like *Death at an Early Age* and *Our Children Are Dying* indicate that the prospect is not a cheerful one.[21]
Studies like *Racial Isolation in the Schools* and *Village School Downtown* show that education has become more and more segregated by
class and race, creating in effect two public school systems, one for the
white middle- and upper-class suburbanites and the other for the poor,
increasingly nonwhite residents of inner city tenements or rural
shacks.[22] Social scientists like James Coleman have revealed how far
we are today from genuine equality of educational opportunity. Surveys in ghettos like Harlem reveal that children there fall further behind in educational attainment each year they attend school, at the very
time when educational credentials have become essential for occupational mobility in our society.[23] And research by political scientists and
sociologists like Marilyn Gittell, Edward Hollander, James Anderson,
and David Rogers indicates that the public has only the remotest control over day-by-day school policies in the large urban bureaucracies.[24]

Teacher strikes, student unrest, and the push for community control
in black ghettos daily remind us of the seriousness of the current ferment in education. We read of new proposals which would fundamentally alter traditional educational ideology and structure: people
ask why free education need be a public monopoly and suggest tuition
vouchers for the children of the poor; blacks demand decentralization
of control; students and teachers reach for power over matters formerly
dominated by their superiors; scholars investigate what the mass media
and the education industries may do to our customary notions of education in the classroom; new definitions emerge of what genuine
equality of opportunity in education would cost in resources and effort.
Whether liberal or conservative, leaders in educational institutions
find it difficult to predict, contain, or coopt the new forces for change.
While it has been traditional in America to see education as *the
answer* to social problems, today many disfranchised groups regard
the schools as *part of the social problem*.[25]

These crises, and this new social research, prompt historians to recast the history of education, to analyze critical turning points leading to the present situation. David Cohen, the principal author of *Racial Isolation in the Schools,* puts the need this way:

> In every age there is an impulse to seek understanding of con-
> temporary dilemmas and accomplishments in the past. . . . This
> is strong at any time, and it must be particularly powerful in times
> such as ours, when it seems agreed on all hands that the society is
> undergoing wrenching transformations. Whatever we may think of
> the conflict, or of historical inquiry which arises immediately from
> such potent experience, it seems undeniable that for the next gen-
> eration at least, much work in the history of education will be
> given over to efforts to better grasp the experience we now live
> through by understanding how it all came to pass.[26]

It is possible, indeed likely, that research motivated by such concerns
will generate historiographical controversy over such issues as the
motives of school reformers; the use of compulsory education as an
agency of social control; the interests served by school bureaucracies;
the connection between education, nationalism, and militarism; the
role of the schools in promoting social mobility; and the nature of institutional racism. A basic issue is whether the American faith in reform through education has been a substitute for more far-reaching
social change. We are thus likely to see more historical analysis of the
mutual relationships between education and power, class, and race.
The definition of "schooling" will doubtless be expanded to include
further study of education in industry, the military, voluntary groups,
and in such governmental agencies as the National Youth Administration and the Civilian Conservation Corps. Educational historians will
also benefit from studies of institutions paralleling the schools, such as
Roy Lubove's examination of social work. Furthermore, educational
historians are becoming increasingly interested in the informal education that takes place in the family, through mass media, and in all
groups that socialize the young.[27]

These new perspectives are not without certain inherent dangers. Research arising from contemporary concerns may tempt scholars to read
the present into the past, and to concentrate only on those features of
our heritage which are pertinent to the problems of today. Disillusion-
ment with institutionalized education and discouragement with the
results of schooling in the present, especially for the dispossessed, may
prompt historians to tell a tale of woe as one-sided as the previous
story of the public school triumphant. Trying to see the schools from

the bottom up may become as monocular as the perspective from the top down. And broadening the scope of educational history to include informal agencies of socialization may cause researchers to lose the useful focus on society provided by institutions.[28] My hope is that we shall eventually see a sophisticated reaffirmation of the democratic purposes of free schooling, illuminated by greater understanding of how schools have actually functioned in the past and characterized by more flexible attitudes toward the means to reach these ends.

Historians must also use caution in using the essential tools provided by the social scientists. In his criticism of the Warner studies of Newburyport, Stephan Thernstrom has clearly demonstrated the perils of ahistorical social science with its facile assumptions about the past.[29] To the extent that previous attitudes, practices, or social systems may have been essentially different from those in the present—for example, the character of childhood and the family—it would also be dangerous for historians to generalize from current behavioral research.[30] Nonetheless, the social sciences offer useful concepts and categories of explanation, models of proof and generalization, and tools such as statistics which aid historians to extrapolate from necessarily limited data.[31] In addition, historians of the recent past have only begun to tap the empirical studies done in the past by social scientists. Students of black educational history, for example, can profit enormously from W. E. B. DuBois' book on the Philadelphia Negro of the 1890's, Frances Blascoer's treatise on the black schoolchildren of New York published in 1915, and Charles S. Johnson's study of education in the rural blackbelt during the 1930's.[32] It is not essential that such works be sophisticated as sociological research; it is necessary only that they portray their subjects honestly and in detail. Scholars wishing to use this type of evidence will benefit from an understanding of the history of social science which reveals the preconceptions, the values, and the techniques of the early researchers.[33]

I should like to discuss some possible approaches to three related topics which, it seems to me, would be central to a reinterpretation of our educational past: the history of childhood and the family; the history of the education of black people; and the history of urban education. I should stress again that much of what I have to say is speculative, for research on some of these questions is just beginning.

Recent behavioral and social research by men like James Coleman, Benjamin Bloom, and J. M. Stevens has supported the notion that formal schooling accounts for a relatively small part of the cognitive development of the child.[34] The historian Neil Sutherland has observed that "the child's attitude, personality, and his life in the family and its wider environment are more important factors in governing what he learns and how he uses what he learns than are curricula, textbooks, teachers, school administrators, and school boards." [35] A logical conclusion, then, is that historians should investigate the child as learner and the family context of his early years. Yet many historians have written as if children were to be neither seen nor heard.

There are reasons, of course, for this neglect of children. When written history was the study of politics, religion, and war, what was the point in speaking of the young (save exceptional events like the Children's Crusade)? Even when the scope of historical curiosity broadened, obstacles still blocked investigation into childhood and the family. What sources might one tap? Perhaps toilet training influenced the lives of the abolitionists, but how would one find out? Perhaps religious instruction in Puritan families was an intellectual as well as a religious Upward Bound program, giving these children a verbal edge over their contemporaries—but how would one find out? Just how would one estimate the emotional impact of a high rate of infant mortality on families? Historians normally deal with public events and written records; the private patterns of families and the vagaries of illiterate children seemed almost impossible to track by conventional means. And besides the lack of traditional sources, other puzzles intruded. What were the turning points in the history of childhood? Is the notion of "childhood" itself a recent invention?

The major historiographical break in the study of childhood, I believe, has been Philippe Ariès' *Centuries of Childhood*. Ariès has shown how new and varied sources—paintings and statues, architecture, games, clothes, guides on child care, diaries, autobiographies, medical records, and many others—can shed light on the dark corners of this history. More than that, he has offered bold new conceptualizations of the changing nature and social meaning of childhood and the family.[36] Others have indicated ways of studying these subjects: Bernard Bailyn; Bernard Wishy, in *The Child and the Republic,* a study of American views of child nurture and perceptive reading of childhood as seen in books written for and about children; Charles Strickland, in his forthcoming study of the family of Bronson Alcott; Robert Bremner and his associates in their project on the Child and the State.[37] Neil Sutherland has suggested a fruitful approach (exemplified by Michael Katz's study of a Massachusetts reform school in

The Irony of Early School Reform): "Since debate and conflict about dealing with the pathological often lays bare the unstated norms, our first centers of attention should be on children and families in trouble." [38] If we are to understand the role of schooling in the total pattern of education, and if we are ever to understand education from the client's point of view, it is clear that we must pursue vigorously this attempt to interpret the history of childhood and the family.

Today the black man is not invisible or nameless or silent, yet we are only beginning to understand the history of Negro education. Of Southern black education we know a fair amount, thanks to the research of Horace Mann Bond, Louis Harlan, and Henry Bullock.[39] But we have very few systematic historical studies of education in the dark ghettos of the North. Indeed, one of the important issues for historians to consider is precisely why scholars and educators have considered Negro education to be a Southern affair. Progressive educators in the North, prolific on almost every other subject, were strangely silent on the special problems of black communities. Gunnar Myrdal had this to say about Negro education in the North:

> There Negroes have practically the entire educational system flung open to them without much discrimination. They are often taught in mixed schools and by white teachers; some of the Negro teachers have white pupils. Little attempt is made to adjust the teaching specifically to the Negroes' existing status and future possibilities. The American Creed permeates instruction, and the Negro as well as the white youths are inculcated with the traditional American values of efficiency, thrift, and ambition.[40]

In both North and South the official rhetoric of education and the actual avenues of opportunity diverged sharply. It would be important to know what sorts of expectations black Americans had about education in different communities. Sensitive observers like Charles S. Johnson detected a curiously ambivalent attitude. On the one hand, one might call education the opiate of the black masses, for Negroes persisted in believing the educational dream of success even though society often frustrated this hope. But on the other hand, many blacks realized how whites were manipulating them. Richard Wright said in 1941:

> Deep down we distrust the schools that the Lords of the Land build for us and we do not really feel that they are ours. In many

states they edit the textbooks that our children study, for the most part deleting all references to government, citizenship, voting, and civil rights. . . . They say that "all the geography a nigger needs to know is how to get from his shack to the plow." [41]

Even where Myrdal's American Creed was taught as if relevant to blacks as well as whites, textbooks were often consciously or unconsciously racist.[42]

A related question needs investigation: how did Northern schools respond to the low job ceiling for black people, and what were the consequences? The traditional piety "America is the land of opportunity" and the self-help ideology of the curriculum may very well have increased self-hatred among black children who blamed themselves for failing to surmount almost impassable social barriers. We are all familiar with the dreary story of discrimination in employment. Schoolmen faced difficult choices. Should they train skilled people who would not be able to find jobs to match their ability? Should they accept the racism of the job market and give Negroes an education befitting janitors? Or should schoolmen try to enlarge opportunities for blacks? Despite the slogan of equal opportunity through education, I have found little evidence that educators tried the last course of action. They normally relegated blacks to the lowest rungs of the vocational curriculum, and some even produced "scientific" studies to prove that black folk had no aptitude for white folks' work.[43]

We need more detailed studies of intentional and unintentional segregation such as those done by August Meier and Elliott Rudwick. They have shown that the story is complicated, often involving struggles within black communities among different social classes. All across the North many cities and towns segregated Negro schools. Often black teachers were coopted by the promise of employment in all-black schools. In *The Learning Tree* Gordon Parks offers a fascinating glimpse of conflict over integration in a black community. Some white educators in the North argued that Negro children learned better in Jim Crow schools and gained a better self-concept there.[44] Ellwood Cubberley thought that schools should have the legal right "to so classify their schools as to separate those who are over-aged, defective, delinquent, or of the Negro race." [45]

Foreshadowing some of the present claims of black power advocates, W. E. B. DuBois claimed in 1935 that the Negro child needed segregated schools "to defend him against the growing animosity of the whites," and claimed that "there are many public school systems in the North where Negroes are admitted and tolerated, but they are not educated; they are crucified." [46] Earlier, Carter Woodson complained about miseducating the Negro by uprooting him from his heritage and making him ashamed of his race. The term "educational genocide" may be new, but not the concept. The notion of black-controlled schools may now be popular among militants for the first time, but the idea is old. Indeed, we need to look more closely than heretofore at the reasons for black support of integrated schools. I suspect that a major motive was profound distrust, not a desire for mixing of the races *per se*. Only if there were white children as hostages in classrooms would teachers really teach the black students, only then would there be adequate facilities and supplies.[47]

Obviously, one would need unusual historical sources to examine education from the perspectives of black people. One place to look is in the brilliant autobiographies of men like Malcolm X, Gordon Parks, Richard Wright, and Langston Hughes.[48] Another set of invaluable sources is the array of sociological studies by men like Charles S. Johnson, E. Franklin Frazier, W. E. B. DuBois, and Allison Davis.[49] To the extent that the problems of black people have been similar over long periods of time—a debatable issue—books like *Black Rage* by William Grier and Price Cobbs and Kenneth Clark's *Dark Ghetto* offer useful insights, as does Myrdal's *American Dilemma*.[50] Black newspapers and magazines demonstrate that black people, at least, knew that Negro education was not only a Southern problem. And a full story would analyze the role of black churches and lodges, settlement houses and missions, civil rights and separatist groups, and a host of other agencies supplementing the schools. It is essential to examine the ways in which black people themselves sought to make their lives bearable and meaningful.

By the time of the large-scale migration of black people to Northern cities, urban schools had mostly become bureaucratized and remote from the sort of neighborhood influence common in the nineteenth-century city. To look at this process of bureaucratization from the client's point of view as well as that of the professional is another task awaiting historians of education. In the decentralization controversy today we are witnessing the reform of a reform. In the nineteenth century in many cities there was decentralized control of schools in which large numbers of neighborhood school boards or committees supervised the hiring of teachers, the curriculum, the construction of buildings, and many other matters now handled by school administrators. Much work needs to be done before the pattern of interest groups favoring centralization will be clear, but it appears that a number of the movements to centralize schools and to turn their operation over to powerful superintendents were part and parcel of the Mugwump-Progressive cause. Protestant, native-born elites often saw school boards as their last refuge in politics, the schools as their opportunity to force their values on society.[51] Charles W. Eliot described the process in one city: "It was an extraordinarily small group of men acting under a single leader that obtained from the Massachusetts legislature the act which established the Boston School Committee of five members. The name of that leader was James J. Storrow. I am happy to believe that the group were all Harvard Men." [52] In many communities the predominantly WASP group of schoolmen, eager to build a nationalized profession, cooperated with this movement and justified it in terms of educational efficiency. During the middle decades of the first half of the twentieth century appeared a number of influential surveys of city systems, some of them highly critical of the school establishment. We need to know far more of the genesis and impact of these reform movements spearheaded by professionals and often sponsored by community influentials.

Michael Katz and I have made case studies of the processes of bureaucratization in Boston and Portland, Oregon. Sol Cohen and David Hammack have studied centralization in New York City. Raymond Callahan has dissected the use of models of business efficiency in education.[53] Many other studies of local practice and social models are needed (school administrators as easily turned to army or police models as to industrial ones, at least in the early stages of centralization). An integral part of bureaucratization was specialization of function, two aspects of which have been examined by Sol Cohen in his study of vocational education, and by Richard Stevens in his history of the vocational guidance movement.[54] Drawing on the work of George Counts, Robert Salisbury had raised important questions about the politics of urban education: Did the notion of a "unitary community" espoused by schoolmen actually mask important conflicts of interest both among the professionals and in the larger society? Has it been best in the long run to try to separate the control of schools from the political power structure in cities? Robert Wiebe has placed the movement to create a nationalized teaching profession in broad historical perspective.[55]

Such studies only begin to suggest the outlines of the histories of urban education that remain to be written. One important subject is how the city itself has been an educator, a topic imaginatively treated by Daniel Calhoun and by several of the authors in the collection of essays edited by Alvin Toffler.[56] Robert Dreeben has called attention to implicit norms taught in schools, standards of behavior inculcated by institutional rules, and habitual roles and expectations of teachers and administrators. Perhaps because of the influence of the rhetoric of progressivism, which often stressed individuality and democracy, such teachings in recent years have customarily been absent from official statements of purpose and curriculum guides. In 1874, however, a group of leading schoolmen stated candidly that city schools must stress "(1) punctuality, (2) regularity, (3) attention, and (4) silence, as habits necessary through life for successful combination with one's fellowmen in an industrial and commercial civilization." [57] One of the most important tasks of the historian of urban education is to gain a sense of sociological imagination, to try to see the ways in which the definition of roles, the educational reward system, and the formal and informal structure of the schools have shaped the behavior of children and adults. Such studies will perforce deal with unintended consequences and trained incapacity, with covert as well as explicit purposes, with matching the rhetoric of education against the actual performance of the schools in serving sub-groups and the larger society.

My observations on the historical study of urban education, Negro education, and childhood and the family might easily be extended to include other topics of interest to historians of education today. Unifying much current work in educational history is a broader definition of the scope of ideology and increased concern for actual behavioral changes in and out of classrooms. In a sense, a number of historians would like to break the boundaries of the house history of education in a manner comparable to the brilliant work of the religious historian Sydney Mead, who has illuminated denominationalism and the voluntary principle as major forces in American society, and who has expanded the parochial character of sectarian chronicles. But equally important, many historians of education today are trying to gain the perspective of a child who can identify with the worm, not the early bird.

NOTES

1. Stephen Joseph, ed., *The Me Nobody Knows* (New York, 1969), p. 113.

2. C. Vann Woodward, "The Age of Reinterpretation," *American Historical Review,* LXVI (October 1960), 1–19.

3. For example, see Richard Boone, *A History of Education in Indiana* (New York, 1892); Daniel Putnam, *The Development of Primary and Secondary Education in Michigan* (Ann Arbor, 1904); F. A. Cotton, *Education in Indiana* (Indianapolis, 1904); Thomas B. Stockwell, ed., *A History of Public Education in Rhode Island* (Providence, 1876). Lawrence Cremin discusses how this house history tradition flowed into and through the writings of Cubberley in *The Wonderful World of Ellwood Patterson Cubberley* (New York, 1965). In 1874 the U.S. Commissioner of Education requested states to prepare histories of education for the 1876 Centennial. The instructions issued by the Rhode Island Department of Instruction to local superintendents are revealing, asking each for "(1) educational facilities before establishment of public schools, (2) establishment of the public schools, (3) their growth and improvement, (4) their present condition, (5) supervision, (6) school libraries, apparatus, and other instrumentalities, and (7) special facts."

4. George S. Counts, *School and Society in Chicago* (New York, 1928); Merle Curti, *The Social Ideas of American Educators* (New York, 1935).

5. Ernest Bayles and Bruce Hood, *Growth of American Educational Thought and Practice* (New York, 1966), p. x.

6. For discussion of these disfunctions, see Bernard Bailyn, *Education in the Forming of American Society* (Chapel Hill, 1960), pp. 3–15, 54–59; and Cremin, *Wonderful World.*

7. See, for example, William W. Brickman, *Guide to Research in Educational History* (New York, 1949), p. iii.

8. Paul Nash, "History of Education," *Review of Educational Research,* XXXIV (February 1964), 5–21; Charles Burgess, "History of Education," *Review of Educational Research,* XXXVII (February 1967), 21–33.

9. Committee on the Role of Education in American History, *Education and American History* (New York, 1965). Also see the issue "Education and American History," *Harvard Educational Review,* XXXII (Spring 1961).

10. *Education and American History,* pp. 8, 9, 24.

11. Bailyn, *Education in the Forming of American Society,* p. 14.

12. Cremin, *Wonderful World,* pp. 42, 47, 46–52.

13. Richard Hofstadter and Walter Metzger, *The Development of Academic Freedom in the United States* (New York, 1955); John S. Brubacher and Willis Rudy, *Higher Education in Transition: An American History* (New York, 1958); Laurence R. Veysey, *The Emergence of the American University* (Chicago, 1965); Frederick Rudolph, *The American College and University: A His-*

tory (New York, 1962); Richard Storr, *Harper's University: The Beginnings. A History of the University of Chicago* (Chicago, 1966); Winton U. Solberg, *The University of Illinois, 1867–1894* (Urbana, Ill., 1968); George Peterson, *The New England College in the Age of the University* (Amherst, 1964).

14. Wilson Smith, *Professors and Public Ethics* (Ithaca, 1956); Paul Buck, ed., *Social Sciences at Harvard, 1860–1920* (Cambridge, Mass., 1965); and Jurgen Herbst, *The German Historical School in American Scholarship: A Study in the Transfer of Culture* (Ithaca, 1965).

15. Ruth Elson, *Guardians of Tradition: American Schoolbooks of the Nineteenth Century* (Lincoln, Nebr., 1964); William R. Taylor, "Toward a Definition of Orthodoxy: The Patrician South and the Common Schools," *Harvard Educational Review,* XXXVI (Fall 1966), 412–426; Rush Welter, *Popular Education and Democratic Thought in America* (New York, 1962); Clarence Karier, *Man, Society, and Education* (Glenview, Ill., 1967); Charles Burgess, "Two Tendencies of Educational Thought in the New Nation: America as a Presbyterian's City on a Hill or as a Deist's Island in the Sea," *Paedagogica Historica,* IV (1964), 326–342.

16. Timothy Smith, "New Approaches to the History of Immigration in Twentieth-Century America," *American Historical Review,* LXXI (July 1966), 1265–1279; Sol Cohen, "The Industrial Education Movement, 1906–17," *American Quarterly,* XX (Spring 1968), 95–110; Vincent P. Lannie, *Public Money and Parochial Education; Bishop Hughes, Governor Seward, and the New York School Controversy* (Cincinnati, 1968), and his forthcoming essay, "Alienation in America: The Immigrant Catholic Response to Public Education in Pre–Civil War America."

17. Geraldine M. Joncich, *The Sane Positivist: A Biography of Edward L. Thorndike* (Middletown, Conn., 1968); Walter H. Drost, *David Snedden and Education for Social Efficiency* (Madison, 1967); Jack Campbell, *Col. Francis W. Parker* (New York, 1967); Jonathan Messerli, "Horace Mann at Brown," *Harvard Educational Review* XXXIII (Summer 1963), 285–311; Messerli, "Localism and State Control in Horace Mann's Reform of the Common Schools," *American Quarterly,* XVII (Spring 1965), 104–118; Messerli, "Horace Mann's Childhood: Myth and Reality," *Educational Forum,* XXX (January 1966), 159–168; and his forthcoming biography of Mann.

18. Edward A. Krug, *The Shaping of the American High School* (New York, 1961); Theodore Sizer, *Secondary Schools at the Turn of the Century* (New Haven, 1964); Robert Middlekauf, *Ancients and Axioms: Secondary Education in Eighteenth-Century New England* (New Haven, 1963); Berenice Fisher, *Industrial Education: American Ideals and Institutions* (Madison, 1967); Patricia A. Graham, *Progressive Education, from Arcady to Academe: A History of the Progressive Education Association* (New York, 1964); Willis Rudy, *Schools in an Age of Mass Culture: An Exploration of Selected Themes in the History of Twentieth-Century American Education* (Englewood Cliffs, N.J., 1965).

19. Timothy L. Smith, "Protestant Schooling and American Nationality, 1800–1850," *Journal of American History,* LIII (March 1967), 679–695; Lloyd Jorgenson, *The Founding of Public Education in Wisconsin* (Madison, 1956); Robert W. Lynn, *Protestant Strategies in Education* (New York, 1965); Will Herberg, "Religion and Education," in James W. Smith and A. Leland Jamison, eds., *Religious Perspectives in American Culture* (Princeton, N.J., 1961).

20. Michael Katz, *The Irony of Early School Reform: Educational Innovation*

in Mid-Nineteenth-Century Massachusetts (Cambridge, Mass., 1968); Charles E. Bidwell, "The Moral Significance of the Common School: A Sociological Study of Local Patterns of School Control and Moral Education in Massachusetts and New York, 1837–1840," *History of Education Quarterly*, VI (Fall 1966), 50–91; Maxine Greene, *Public School and the Private Vision* (New York, 1965); Daniel Calhoun, "The City as Teacher: Historical Problems," *History of Education Quarterly*, IX (Fall 1969); William Brickman and Stewart Fraser, eds., *A History of International and Comparative Education: Nineteenth-Century Documents* (Glenview, Ill., 1968). Carefully to appraise each of these works would, of course, require several extended essays; my purpose here is simply to indicate the scope of important recent scholarship in the field.

21. Herbert Kohl, *36 Children* (New York, 1967); James Herndon, *The Way It Spozed to Be* (New York, 1968); Jonathan Kozol, *Death at an Early Age* (Boston, 1967); Peter Schrag, *Village School Downtown* (Boston, 1967); Nat Hentoff, *Our Children Are Dying* (New York, 1966).

22. James S. Coleman, *et al.*, *Equality of Educational Opportunity* (Washington, D.C., 1966); U.S. Commission on Civil Rights, *Racial Isolation in the Public Schools* (Washington, D.C., 1967).

23. *Harvard Educational Review*, XXXVIII (Winter 1968), Special Issue on Equal Educational Opportunity.

24. Marilyn Gittell, *Participants and Participation: A Study of Social Policy in New York City* (New York, 1966); Marilyn Gittell and T. Edward Hollander, *Six Urban School Districts* (New York, 1968); David Rogers, *110 Livingston Street* (New York, 1968); James G. Anderson, *Bureaucracy in Education* (Baltimore, 1968).

25. In the preface to his study, *The Imperfect Panacea: American Faith in Education, 1865–1965* (New York, 1968), Henry Perkinson wrote: "One day while she was typing the manuscript for this book, my secretary looked up and asked me, 'If the schools can't solve these problems, then who can?'"

26. David K. Cohen, "Education and Race: Research Needs and Opportunities," *History of Education Quarterly*, IX (Fall 1969).

27. For a provocative statement of new hypotheses in educational history, see Michael Katz's summary of a symposium, *History of Education Quarterly*, IX (Fall 1969); for an exploration of education outside of public school settings, as in industry and the mass media, see Lawrence Cremin, *The Genius of American Education* (Pittsburgh, 1965), chap. 3; in "Schools and War," *Teachers College Journal*, XXXVIII (May 1967), 256–265, Richard Stephens cites bibliography and poses important questions on the issue of militarism and education; Roy Lubove, *The Professional Altruist* (Cambridge, Mass., 1965).

28. Robert Wiebe has provided a suggestive model of broad institutional history in "The Social Functions of Public Education," *American Quarterly*, XXI (Summer 1969), 148–164.

29. Stephan Thernstrom, *Poverty and Progress* (Cambridge, Mass., 1964), chap. viii and Appendix.

30. Neil Sutherland, "History, Existentialism, and Education," *Educational Theory*, XVII (April 1967), 167–175.

31. Edward N. Saveth, ed., *American History and the Social Sciences* (Glencoe, Ill., 1964); a perceptive unpublished historical study of "Immigrants and the Schools" by David Cohen, social scientist at the Harvard Graduate School of Education, indicates the insight sociologists can bring to vexing historical questions, such as the past role of education in determining adult status.

32. W. E. B. DuBois, *The Philadelphia Negro* (Philadelphia, 1899); Frances Blascoer, *Colored School Children in New York* (New York, 1915); Charles S. Johnson, *Shadow of the Plantation* (Chicago, 1934).

33. For example, see Maurice Stein, *The Eclipse of Community* (Princeton, 1960).

34. Coleman, *Equality of Educational Opportunity;* B. S. Bloom, *Stability and Change in Human Characteristics* (New York, 1967).

35. Neil Sutherland, "The Urban Child," *History of Education Quarterly,* IX (Fall 1969).

36. Philippe Ariès, *Centuries of Childhood: A Social History of Family Life* (New York, 1962); Charles E. Strickland, "Review of *Centuries of Childhood,*" *History of Education Quarterly,* IV (December 1964), 307–309; Irene Q. Brown, "Philippe Ariès on Education and Society in Seventeenth- and Eighteenth-Century France," *History of Education Quarterly,* VII (Fall 1967), 357–368.

37. Bailyn, *Education in the Forming of American Society,* pp. 75–78; Bernard Wishy, *The Child and the Republic* (Philadelphia, 1968); Charles Strickland, "A Transcendentalist Father: The Child-Rearing Practice of Bronson Alcott," *Perspectives in American History,* III (1969); Robert Bremner, ed., The Child and State Project of the Charles Warren Center for Studies in American History; Richard L. Rapson, "The American Child as Seen by British Travelers, 1845–1935," *American Quarterly,* XVII (Fall 1965), 520–534. A number of older works are still useful, although they, like most of the newer studies, deal more with adult attitudes than with children's behavior *per se:* Edmund Morgan, *The Puritan Family* (Boston, 1949); Monica Kiefer, *American Children Through Their Books* (Philadelphia, 1948); Sanford Fleming, *Children and Puritanism* (New Haven, 1933). I am indebted especially to Charles Strickland and Neil Sutherland for suggestions about profitable methods of attack and for bibliography on the history of the child and the family; for Canadian attitudes toward child care see Sutherland's unpublished essay "The Social Context of Educational Reform in Canada: 1890–1920."

38. Katz, *Irony of Early School Reform,* part 4; Sutherland, "The Urban Child," p. 4.

39. Horace Mann Bond, *Education of the Negro in the American Social Order* (New York, 1934); Louis Harlan, *Separate and Unequal* (New York, 1968); Henry A. Bullock, *A History of Negro Education in the South* (Cambridge, Mass., 1967).

40. Gunnar Myrdal, *An American Dilemma,* II (New York, 1944), 879.

41. Richard Wright, *12 Million Black Voices* (New York, 1941), p. 64; Charles S. Johnson, *Growing Up in the Black Belt* (New York, 1940); Johnson, *Shadow of the Plantation.*

42. Elinor D. Sinette, "The Brownie's Book: A Pioneer Publication for Children," *Freedomways,* V (Winter 1965), 133–142.

43. See, for example, DuBois, *Philadelphia Negro;* St. Clair Drake and Horace Cayton, *Black Metropolis* (New York, 1945); Blascoer, *Colored School Children;* Richard Wright, *Black Boy* (Cleveland, 1947); Gilbert Osofsky, *Harlem: The Making of a Ghetto* (New York, 1966); E. L. Thorndike, "Intelligence Scores of Colored Pupils in High Schools," *School and Society,* XVIII (November 10, 1923), 569–570.

44. See, for example, L. A. Pechstein, "The Problem of Negro Education in Northern and Border Cities," *Elementary School Journal,* XXX (November 1929), 192–199; Gordon Parks, *The Learning Tree* (New York, 1963); August Meier and Elliott M. Rudwick, "Early Boycotts of Segregated Schools:

The East Orange, New Jersey, Experience, 1899–1906," *History of Education Quarterly*, VII (Spring 1967), 22–35; "Early Boycotts of Segregated Schools: The Case of Springfield, Ohio, 1922–1923," *American Quarterly*, XX (Winter 1968), 744–758; August Meier, "Early Boycotts of Segregated Schools: The Alton, Illinois, Case, 1897–1908," *Journal of Negro Education*, XXVI (Fall 1967), 394–402; L. D. Reddick, "The Education of Negroes in States Where Separate Schools Are Not Legal," *Journal of Negro Education*, XVI (Summer 1947), 290–300.

45. Ellwood P. Cubberly, *State and County Educational Reorganization* (New York, 1914), p. 4.

46. W. E. B. DuBois, "Does the Negro Need Separate Schools?," *Journal of Negro Education*, IV (July 1935), 328–335.

47. Carter G. Woodson, "The Miseducation of the Negro," *The Crisis*, XXXVIII (August 1931), 266–267; *The New York Age*, September 20, 1906.

48. Malcolm X, *The Autobiography of Malcolm X* (New York, 1964); Parks, *The Learning Tree;* Wright, *Black Boy;* Langston Hughes, *The Big Sea* (New York, 1940).

49. Johnson, *Growing Up in the Black Belt;* Johnson, *Shadow of the Plantation;* E. Franklin Frazier, *The Negro Family in the United States* (Chicago, 1939); E. Franklin Frazier, *Negro Youth at the Crossways* (Washington, D.C., 1940); DuBois, *Philadelphia Negro;* Allison Davis and John Dollard, *Children of Bondage* (Washington, D.C., 1947); Allison Davis, *et al., Deep South* (Chicago, 1941).

50. William H. Grier and Price Cobbs, *Black Rage* (New York, 1968); Kenneth Clark, *Dark Ghetto* (New York, 1965). On the question of the persistence of similar problems among black people, see Gilbert Osofsky, "The Enduring Ghetto," *Journal of American History*, LV (September 1968), 243–255. For a more extended treatment of these remarks and further bibliography, see my "Growing Up Black: Perspectives on the History of Education in Northern Ghettos," *History of Education Quarterly*, IX (Fall 1969).

51. Selma Berrol, "The Schools of New York in Transition, 1898–1914," *Urban Review*, I (December 1966), 15–20; Selma Berrol, "William Henry Maxwell and a New Educational New York," *History of Education Quarterly*, VIII (Summer 1968), 215–228; Colin Greer, "Immigrants, Negroes, and the Public Schools," *The Urban Review*, III (January 1969), 9–12; David Tyack, "Needed: The Reform of a Reform," in *New Dimensions in School Board Leadership* (Evanston, Ill., 1969).

52. Charles E. Eliot, "Educational Reform and the Social Order," *The School Review*, XVII (April 1909), 220.

53. Michael Katz, "The Emergence of Bureaucracy in Urban Education: The Boston Case, 1850–1884," *History of Education Quarterly*, VIII (Summer 1968), 155–188; Michael Katz, "The Emergence of Bureaucracy in Urban Education: The Boston Case, 1850–1884, Part II," *History of Education Quarterly*, VIII (Fall 1968), 319–357; David B. Tyack, "Bureaucracy and the Common School: The Example of Portland, Oregon, 1851–1913," *American Quarterly*, XIX (Fall 1967), 475–498; Sol Cohen, *Progressives and Urban School Reform* (New York, 1964), chaps. i–ii; David Hammack, "The Centralization of New York's Public School System, 1896: A Social Analysis of a Decision," Unpublished M.A. Thesis, Columbia University, 1969; Raymond Callahan, *Education and the Cult of Efficiency* (Chicago, 1962).

54. Cohen, "The Industrial Education Movement"; Richard Stevens, *Social Reform and the Origins of Vocational Guidance* (Washington, D.C., 1969);

Ronald Johnson is completing a Ph.D. dissertation at the University of Illinois on Andrew S. Draper, one of the main advocates of centralization.

55. Robert H. Wiebe, *The Search for Order, 1877–1920* (New York, 1967), pp. 117–120; Counts, *School and Society;* Robert H. Salisbury, "School and Politics in the Big City," *Harvard Educational Review,* XXXVII (Summer 1967), 408–424.

56. Alvin Toffler, ed., *Schoolhouse in the City* (New York, 1968).

57. Robert Dreeben, *On What Is Learned in School* (Reading, Mass., 1968); Duane Doty and William T. Harris, *A Statement of the Theory of Education in the United States, As Approved by Many Leading Educators* (Washington, D.C., 1874), p. 14.

An Agenda for
Urban History

RICHARD C. WADE

Historians have arrived at the study of the city by slow freight.
Almost every other discipline very quickly saw something of great
significance in the rise of the modern metropolis. American sociologists
took the lead in probing the nature of the new city, and the "Chicago
School" provided a framework and emphasis which continues to dominate urban analysis. To be sure, scholars in most fields were not very
happy about the consequences of the rise of the city, and they generally emphasized the "problems" urbanization occasioned. Some,
especially economists and geographers, dealt with its possibilities, yet
the view from the academy was essentially pejorative, and the response
by historians was largely indifference.

Nor was this neglect characteristic only of American historians.
H. J. Dyos, for example, raised the same question about British scholars. "Why has it taken so long for such a heavily urbanised country as
Britain to develop such a marked interest in the history of its cities
and towns?" he asked at a recent conference on urban history.[1] Attention on the continent, Dyos noted, has also been slight. In France,
"urban history has remained in its chrysalis . . . for a half century or
more." In Germany, "the activity going on also seems to have been
generated comparatively recently." The record is scarcely any better
in Australasia, where the primacy of cities has been the central fact
of historical experience since the first English settlement.

This neglect in the United States has not always been so obvious.
Many nineteenth-century historians had seen the importance of cities.

In 1854, for example, Richard Hildreth wrote that "density of population, and the existence of towns and cities are essential to any great degree of social progress." Observing that "scattered populations" lacked the interaction and competition needed for "improvement," he concluded that "cities are the central points from which knowledge, enterprise, and civilization stream out upon the surrounding country." [2] Hildreth developed this theme from the beginning, with the rivalry of Bristol and London for overseas hegemony in the early Colonial period, to the urban support Jackson enjoyed in his war .on the Second Bank of the United States.

There was also a promising beginning among local writers. In most cities amateur historians, fascinated by the urban explosion of the nineteenth century, wrote detailed accounts of the development of their own communities from early settlement to the year of publication. Though marred by excessive description, inadequate analysis, and a first-family bias, they were often written out of primary sources and after an exhaustive study of public records. Many contained the germ of a grand theme—the disproportionate influence of the city in regional and national expansion. J. Thomas Scharf, for example, not only invested his own city, Baltimore, with a three-volume history, but also produced extensive studies of Philadelphia and St. Louis. And he kept his vision broad. The historian, he wrote, "must always look with peculiar pleasure upon all that concerns the birth, growth, and development of cities, for it is in these congregated and crowded communities that man is seen working at most freedom from the restrictions and limitations of nature and evolving the greatest results from that complex and cooperative force which we call society." "The city," he concluded, "is the fountain of progress." [3]

What happened to this promising urban dimension? A part of the explanation can be found in the circumstances of the establishment of American history as a profession. During most of the nineteenth century, American history had been written by amateurs, though many were gifted and their work has an enduring importance. But the rise of the modern university and the growth of professionalization led to the organization of the discipline. Thus it was necessary to define "American" history. When did it begin, what were its major themes, and what were significant areas for investigation and research? Nor was this a simple matter. Was one to find the beginnings in the Revolution, or perhaps with the founding of Jamestown, or even the discovery of the New World? Indeed, what were the proper geographic areas to study? In the 1880's the nation quite clearly had not reached its ultimate territorial limits.

The scene was thus ripe for someone, or perhaps a few, to "define" American history—to provide the subject with a chronological and geographic framework. The men who did most in this regard were Frederick Jackson Turner and Charles A. Beard. Both saw American history in a broad and comprehensive way, indeed in almost poetic terms. Both developed a large theme which attempted to encompass the whole of American development. Both wrote with a learning and persuasiveness that made them figures of profound impact and lasting importance. Both have been continuously analyzed, attacked, and "revised." Yet, in a peculiar way, they commanded the strategic heights of historical writing for more than two generations.

Turner's framework contained the familiar elements. The continent was occupied in a series of waves. "It begins with the Indian and the hunter; it goes on to tell of the disintegration of savagery by the entrance of the trader, the pathfinder of civilization; we read the annals of the pastoral stage in ranch life; the exploitation of the soil by the raising of unrotated crops of corn and wheat in sparsely settled farming communities; the intensive culture of the denser farm settlement; and finally the manufacturing organization with city and factory system." The emphasis of the story rested at the thither edge of population movement where whites contended with the primitive life of wilderness and savage. Slowly, in this evolutionary scheme, the area was rescued from the red man and, from simple beginnings, a fully developed, complex society emerged. Thus, Turner concluded, "the true point of view in the history of this nation is not the Atlantic coast, it is the Great West."

Moreover, this "Great West" was agrarian. If, as Turner contended, "to study this advance, the men who grew up under these conditions, and the political, economic, and social results of it, is to study the really American part of our history," then the significant clues would be found in the cabins, sod huts, and farmhouses of the newly won country. In this Turnerian perspective, the distinctive phases of American development were seen as shaped by a rapidly growing rural West colliding with the older forces and institutions of the East.

Yet the Turner framework involved significant distortions. In its Western emphasis it overcompensated against the East; in its description of the occupation of the continent it depended on a sequence that only occasionally occurred; and, most importantly, in its insistence on the primacy of agrarian elements it neglected the importance of cities.

Turner himself felt this inadequacy. Not only did he write to Arthur Schlesinger in 1925 that perhaps the time had come for "an urban reinterpretation of our history," but his papers at the Huntington Library indicate he was interested in making a contribution of his own to this new perspective. "Do a paper on significance of the City in American History," he wrote to himself, and he listed some of the topics: "capital, labor, immign, mf., trade, Banks and currency, etc." Some of his questions went much further. "When and how did cities become densely populated, and why? How did urban, including alien ideas, interests, and ideals react on frontier and sectional items?" Still the city's role was to be confined within his famous framework. "The city dependent upon natural resources and markets furnished by extending frontiers," he put in his notes, "and by the talent supplied by areas recently (relatively) frontier areas." He wanted to examine "its [city's] counter influence in modifying frontier and sectional traits" but "still lean [to] sectionalism."

The other towering influence in the profession was Charles A. Beard, who also saw American history in a large unified way. He found the clue to the new Republic not on the frontier or in broad expanses of free land, but rather in industrialization. It was the factory, technological innovation, and modern organization that transformed a simple, rural nation into a highly complex industrial society. The keys to this rapid evolution were not to be sought in the fur trade, huts, and log cabins, or in the collision of European and Indian on the frontier, as in Turner's scheme, but in the establishment of the factory system, the development of an entrepreneurial class, the growth of trade unions, and the clash of competing industrial interests. Beard believed he was dealing with urbanization in this broad description as, indeed, did Turner, who wrote defensively that "I have written and lectured more on the subject [cities] than Beard recognizes. See my book and my notes." But Beard, too, looked upon the rise of the city as the culmination of an evolutionary process and located its importance in the modern period.

Urban development in the early years of the Republic was quickly dismissed. The towns of George Washington's day "differed so fundamentally in their industry and their markets from the modern American city," Beard wrote in 1912, "that they would really be called trading hamlets today." He agreed with Lincoln that on the eve of the Civil War the nation was "fundamentally rural." But he saw "a new force . . . composed of the captains of steel and steam and capital" whose power was located in the urban centers. By 1910 the "growth of municipalities" pointed "to the growing predominance of the city dwellers over the rural population and mark[s] the shifting of the balance of political power from the farm to the forge and market place." Urbanization was thus a function of an advanced industrialization—an historically recent rather than persistent phenomenon.[1]

Thus both Beard and Turner developed large views of American history, encompassing events from the discovery down to the twentieth century. But in each the significance of the city was seen as the culmination of a long historical process. And in each there was the fatal confusion of urbanization and industrialization—confusion which has afflicted urban analysis throughout the social sciences. Industrialization and urbanization were seen as closely related, indeed as almost two sides of the same coin of modernity. The customary shorthand emerged which characterizes the past century as a period of "urban industrial" or "industrial urban" domination. Thus things which are peculiarly industrial are attributed to urbanization; and things especially urban are called industrial. Yet the historian knows that these two forces, while related, are not the same thing. There were cities on a large scale long before there was an industrial revolution. In many areas of the contemporary world we can find extraordinary urbanization in essentially pre-industrial societies. In American history the movements were temporal companions, a fact which compounded, if it did not introduce, this mischievous astigmatism.

But the past decade has witnessed a dramatic recovery from this neglect. Urban history has suddenly become not only respectable but fashionable. Courses on urban history spring up all over the country. Urban institutes, once the particular preserve of planners, sociologists, and economists, now put history at the center of their activity. Federal commissions looking into the problems of our cities usually begin by corralling historians to provide a broad perspective for their investigation. And foundations, which earlier turned down opportunities for pioneering, are now busily making grants in the area. In short, rescued from near obscurity, urban history is in danger of becoming a fad.

What accounts for this astonishing tranformation? The answer lies both within the profession and in the urban crisis which afflicts the nation.

Post–World War II historians had become increasingly dissatisfied with previous explanations of major movements and events. In searching for more compelling analyses, they increasingly found themselves backing into cities.[5] It became commonplace, for example, to connect urbanization and progressivism. Yet the connecting links were vague; the terms "the urban impact," the "urban middle class," and "city reform" located the center of national change, but only generally.[6] Scholars found little in the monographs about specific cities which detailed this relationship. They were left, as Arthur Koestler once observed about Marxian analysis, with a sub-structure of urbanization and a superstructure of progressivism, but with no stairs or elevators between them. In dealing with other periods of American history the same dissatisfaction developed; scholars often looked at urbanization as one key to a more persuasive interpretation.

The second impulse to the development of urban history came from the emergence in the last two decades of what is now called the "urban crisis." The sudden and apparently unexpected appearance of a whole range of dangerous and intractable problems in our cities led to panic in both scholarly analysis and public policy. Sociologists, political scientists, planners, and "urban experts" from every discipline began to write of the "dying" city. Lewis Mumford grimly referred to the "necropolis" (the city of the dead) in his popular and influential *The City in History;* Jane Jacobs made a career out of *The Death and Life of Great American Cities;* [7] planners gave up the city for dead and spent their time designing "new towns" well away from the decaying metropolis. Indeed, the analogy between death and cities became so common that when *Newsweek* entitled a special issue "Our Sick, Sick Cities," many considered it the first breath of optimism to blow across the landscape in two decades. Policy-makers reflected this academic panic by enacting emergency measures which usually compounded rather than solved problems.

The inadequacy of scholarly analysis and the dissatisfaction with public policy in meeting contemporary questions led to a new interest in urban history. It was now clear that cities were not as plastic or tractable as people had imagined. Even when social scientists and planners were given wide latitude, the results were neither immediate nor reassuring. Hence many people asked elementary questions: How did these problems arise? And how did previous generations deal with similar questions? Were crime rates higher than before? Were relations with police worsening? Were there more poor? Were slums increasing? Was the pollution of air and water greater than before? Increasingly, both academic analysts and public officials turned to history for some perspective on the pressing problems of the day.

It cannot be said, however, that when the public turned to historians it got much help. For the immediate crisis, there was no good work on urban violence and disorders. Indeed, there was virtually nothing on the development of policing, much less on the broader question of the establishment of urban discipline.[8] The literature on race relations in the city was much more extensive, but that was more a tribute to those working in black history than to urban scholarship. And there are still no comprehensive works on such other elementary topics as housing, schools, mass transit, parks, city planning, or even public health.

Yet there is still time to rectify the situation. These problems will not go away, and they ought to be studied whether or not there is a crisis. There is some danger in isolating a question for immediate and intensive research simply to meet urgent contemporary needs, and there is no reason to believe that panic history will be any more satisfying or enduring than panic policy-making. What is required now is the patient reconstruction of our entire urban past. This task in the broadest sense is twofold: first, the analysis of how our cities have grown, from the smallest beginnings to the modern metropolis; and second, what difference this urban development has made to our national experience. To put it another way, one approach is to study the city from the inside; the other is to see the cities' role in American history.

The first task has the highest priority. There is no sense in talking about the larger meaning of something if it cannot be clearly described and analyzed. This is especially true when the literature is already too filled with loose generalizations about "the urban impact" and the importance of "the industrial city." Let us begin by finding out just how modern cities grow. We know they begin as small settlements, and in over a century or more become the homes of sometimes millions of people.[9] Yet we have so little precise knowledge of this process. Urban development is variously attributed to "commerce" or "industry" or "transportation" or, even more nebulously, "the urban spirit" or "the urban way of life."

Of course, we are not without some guidelines. Blake McKelvey's four volumes on Rochester, Constance McLaughlin Green's three volumes on Washington, and Bessie Pierce's books on nineteenth-century Chicago are detailed studies of the growth of important cities. These authors place their narratives within the context of national growth,[10] but the very comprehensiveness of the treatment makes intensive analysis at any point very difficult. Sam Bass Warner's *Streetcar Suburbs* suggests the utility of such a painstaking excursion.[11] Yet we are largely indebted to nonhistorians for theories of urban growth. Geographers especially have dealt most fully with this problem, and Homer Hoyt's *One Hundred Years of Land Values in Chicago* remains a lonely classic in the field.[12]

The crucial moment in the growth of American cities came with the introduction of mass transportation. Before this innovation the size of towns was confined to an area that could be covered on foot.[13] Residents had to walk to work, to shop, to visit, and to play. The "walking city" was thus compact. It was also characterized by a mixture of land uses—that is, residences, commercial facilities, and manufacturing installations were closer to each other than they would be again. The introduction of mass transit—the moving of numbers of people down a fixed route at set fares on schedules—broke the casements of the historic city and created the conditions for the modern one.

People could now live quite removed from their place of work; the population could spill outside its old confines. New areas, once unsettled or used for truck farming, came inside the widened municipal limits. When the horse-drawn streetcar was replaced by the cable car, then the trolley, then the elevated and the subway, and finally the automobile, the age of urban sprawl had begun. The outer edges of the metropolis were now defined by commuting time: any place within sixty minutes of downtown was drawn into the urban vortex. To be sure, every generation believed that the city could grow no larger; but every generation proved to be mistaken. And the physical expansion came at just the right time, for now the city could accommodate the great flood of immigrants from abroad that surged into the nation.

The introduction of mass transportation also created the social landscape of the American city. By providing residential options, it permitted a sorting out of people. Those who had the greatest resources, of course, had the widest choice. Almost from the beginning, they opted to leave the downtown areas and moved into larger homes on generous lots away from the noise, congestion, and confusion of the central city. The successful middle class could thus commute to work while it created new residential communities on the periphery of the built-up sections. Those with lesser incomes followed, but could not go out as far. They either built more modest homes or shared two-

and three-story flats closer to the center of the city. And those with still fewer resources did the best they could. They jammed into large old houses, converting them into apartments; they broke up abandoned warehousing for barracks; they transformed any sheltered space into residential uses. The result was the familiar social configuration of most American cities.[14]

Mass transportation also accelerated the essential instability of the whole urban structure. All of its parts were to be in constant movement. Residential change was the most obvious result. New neighborhoods were continually being created while old ones underwent astonishing changes. Everyone became, in a sense, a transient; all were uprooted. Even ethnic neighborhoods, which looked so stable from the outside, were scenes of constant turnover. They might remain Italian or German or Irish, but they were kept so only because the same kind of people moved in as moved out.[15]

The same centrifugal forces which created residential flux also were at work in the location of commerce and industry. They too moved away from the historic center of town.[16] Commercial installations were reluctant to leave because their function was to exchange goods and services in a central location. Yet as the customers moved out, new commercial activity followed, first to big nuclei around the core, and then to shopping centers near the municipal limits or into the suburbs beyond. Manufacturers abandoned the congestion and high land costs more readily, but the need for proximity to rail and water facilities limited choices and determined industrial patterns. The fundamental fact, however, for land use and spatial relationships was constant change and alteration.

It would be hard to overestimate the importance of internal transportation upon urban development. Yet the topic has no historian. It took George Rogers Taylor, who had already established transportation as a key to national development between 1800 and 1860,[17] to first explore the introduction of mass transit in the cities. But Taylor has dealt only with the first phase, and Sam Bass Warner with a later stage. The broader implications for the physical and social shape of the city remain largely untouched. As early as 1859, Sydney George Fisher, after taking a ride on a horse-drawn streetcar in Philadelphia, observed that the new device was "producing a complete revolution in our habits" since it permitted the "spread of the city over a vast space, with all the advantages of compactness and also the advantages of pure air, gardens, and rural pleasure." [18] Another contemporary caught its significance when he referred to the "moral significance" of mass transportation in reducing density and congestion.[19]

The new urban canvas was thus continually enlarged by mass transportation. No one has yet detailed the process by which these new communities were produced "instantly" outside the built-up areas. Large tracts of land fell to the developers and were quickly transformed for urban uses. Some of this building took place outside the formal limits of the city either along streetcar lines (present or expected) or along commuting railroads. As the population spilled over old boundaries, people were quickly incorporated into the city. Early suburbs thus became a part of the growing municipality. They had, of course, to give up their autonomy and often their identity, but the lure of receiving needed and expensive urban services made the decision seem wise to those suburbs which abutted the city's edge.

This process of annexation is still without extended treatment. Yet its importance is very great. So long as cities could continually widen their boundaries, they had within them the resources necessary to build their public plants—streets and bridges, water and sewer systems, schools and hospitals. They were in a position to provide an ever-widening range of urban conveniences. Industries and commercial property furnished an expanding tax base. The area's professional and managerial talent lay largely inside the city and hence had a residential as well as an economic stake in its well-being. It was the conjunction of the built-up area and municipal boundaries which accounts for that extraordinary surge of inventiveness between 1880 and 1920—a development which placed American cities in the forefront of urban change throughout the world.

This system broke down in the twentieth century, indeed in many places earlier. Somewhere around 1920 the tide had turned and annexation ceased to be a possibility in most American cities—though in the South and West the options often remained open. This watershed in American urban development went virtually unnoticed by contemporaries. Less understandably, historians have ignored it as well. But it is important to know why this process of orderly accretion stopped. Who opposed joining the city? Why did the suburbs begin to believe that separation was both feasible and desirable?

The consequences to the city of cutting off its natural hinterland were not immediately apparent. Most municipalities still had some room to expand before filling up their legal boundaries. But by the end of World War II, a crisis loomed. Not only did nearly all of the new

growth continue to take place outside city limits, but the normal centrifugal forces also included the movement of well-to-do citizens, commerce, and industry into the margins of the metropolis. Concurrently,
the cities filled up with more poor people, most of whom were black,
thus laying new and heavier responsibilities on local governments at
just the time their urban plants required renewal and replacement.
Most of the literature on this modern development omits the historical
dimension of the crisis and emphasizes only the final and most obvious phase.

Worse still, historians have left the growth of the suburbs to other
disciplines. This has meant an emphasis on contemporary analysis
with the assumption that suburban growth is new—that suburbs are all
alike, and that they are a permanent new type of community. Yet this
topic is too important to leave to others, for not only is it a legitimate
historical topic, but its importance in the future is bound to grow. The
1970 census will confirm that for the first time more people in the
standard metropolitan areas are living in the suburbs than in the cities.
We have become, in short, a suburban civilization. But this is the culmination of a long historical process that has its roots in the explosion
of the city over a hundred years ago.

At the turn of the century Adna Weber shrewdly saw the coming
importance of the suburb, noting that "the significance of this
tendency is that it denotes, not a cessation in the movement toward
concentration, but a diminution in the *intensity* of concentration. Such
a new distribution of population combines at once the open air and
spaciousness of the country with the sanitary improvements, comforts,
and associated life of the city." [20] In 1922, Harlan Paul Douglass wrote
an extraordinarily perceptive book entitled *The Suburban Trend,* in which
he more correctly assessed the new development than many recent authors.[21] By the 1950's the suburbs had begun to shape the postwar
society, and they will surely dominate it by the 1970's. Despite this
obvious importance, suburban history has scarcely been touched by
historians, and usually is not even an item in the index of most textbooks.

In all this metropolitan growth and expansion, real estate brokers
and developers were very active. Indeed, looked at in one way, urban
growth has been less a social system than a massive real estate lottery.
The process of urbanization has been the division of unoccupied land
into constantly new uses. The central intermediary in this exchange
has been the real estate "industry." This business, in most instances, has

been carried on by thousands of small operators dealing with individual buyers and sellers. Transactions are not easy to trace, and it is difficult to establish patterns of activity. When a local board makes a particularly significant statement—such as the Chicago association's decision in 1917 to sell to blacks only in contiguous blocks—it is possible to document the policies of a real estate group. But generally only the most intensive study can begin to reconstruct the work and assumptions of this group and its impact on the shape of our cities. Though we have many books on industrialists and large entrepreneurs, we have not found an historian willing to probe the most private and delicate transactions that have so fundamentally governed urban development.[22]

The expansion of the city created constant tensions inside the system. The persistent renewal of downtown areas, rapidly changing neighborhoods, and often convulsive alterations in land use produced persistent instability. The sharpest friction usually developed between the newer parts of the city and the old; between the central city and the periphery; between the congested core and the outlying residential wards. This pattern appeared early—by the turn of the century in most places—and it continues down to the present in the new city-suburban form. Because the boundaries between the contesting forces were always in flux, the line of division continually moved outward. But the tension was always there, for it was rooted in the ineluctable expansion of the metropolis.

The political consequences of this division also were clear. Each area developed an organizational style appropriate to the conditions of life in different parts of the city. The boss system, or machine, grew out of the teeming congestion, irregular employment, poor housing, and lower class life of the central city. Wherever there was, in addition, a large influx of immigrants, the machine gained added coherence from the discrimination felt by newcomers because of their language, religion, nationality, or customs. The boss arose out of the vulnerability and precariousness of downtown neighborhoods and the opportunities for advancement offered by a political system which placed premiums on numbers and organization. Lyle Dorsett, William Miller, Melvin Holli, and others have begun to explore some of the possibilities of the relationship between political leadership and urban conditions.[23] Yet we need intensive work on the social roots as well as the internal organization of machines in larger cities, especially of such sturdy performers as the Republican operation in Philadelphia. These studies would involve an examination of the saloon as a political and business institution, and particularly of the construction industry, which was always close to city hall and lived at the intersection of public and private enterprise.

If the boss system was the expression of downtown wards, the reform association was the expression of the pleasant residential sections lying at the outer edges of the city. Here social life revolved around schools, churches, and social clubs. These neighborhoods were connected by mass transit to the commercial core of the city, where middle-class commuters had their economic stake and their business and professional connections. Urban reform had its particular home in these outlying wards. And its customary organization was in the large committee—the "Committee of 81," the "Committee of 108," and so forth. This framework permitted the representation of scattered residential areas, lawyers, businessmen, editors, academics, clergymen, and other middle-class groups which comprised reform's customary leadership. The object of this political activity was to contain and control the centrifugal forces that were transforming the metropolis and to "Americanize" the inner neighborhoods.[24]

This process has not been yet fully described or analyzed. Zane Miller's *Boss Cox's Cincinnati* makes an important beginning, as does Allen Davis' *Spearheads for Reform,* which examines the political activity and implications of the settlement house movement. But we still await, for example, a good study of the growth of the public school system. Reformers placed immense confidence in this institution. It was not only to teach the rudimentary elements of learning, but also to instill into children, especially those of the poor, a discipline appropriate to the condition of the modern city.[25] We do not know how the newer concepts of districting developed. We have no profile of the schoolteacher, no persuasive analysis of what attitudes were conveyed in the classroom, and no comparison of slum schools with their middle-class counterparts in outlying areas. And if we know little about these important aspects of public schools, we know even less about the parochial system. Yet the Catholic school played a crucial role in adjusting many newcomers to the city and in forming for millions of urban dwellers an alternate loyalty to the public schools.

Another part of the attempt to transform the congested core of the city was the campaign against vice. This meant, above all, a crusade against the saloon which was the focus of gambling and prostitution. Since saloons were also the informal clubhouses of the political machine, this drive was often combined with an attack on the boss.

Hence one of the most characteristic aspects of reform regimes was the attempt to clamp down on such activities. Because these campaigns always failed and were usually accompanied by embarrassing ballyhoo and naive hopes, historians generally have brushed aside this dimension of urban reform as marginal.

The same is true of prohibition, though it was one of the most persistent interests of many urban reformers until the national experiment in the twenties. Moreover, they had been successful in many cities before the passage of the Eighteenth Amendment. By various systems of local option, residents could prevent the establishment of saloons or the sale of packaged liquor in a neighborhood. In Chicago almost all the middle-class residential communities at the edge of the city were thus protected before 1919. Indeed, there was even at one time an attempt by referendum to dry up Boston. Prohibition on a national level would not have come without substantial support in the cities. Some recent authors have noted the shortcomings of conventional views and pointed out that many urban reformers gave prohibition some kind of approval. But none has set the topic within the context of urban tensions.[26]

Sanitation was yet another concern, in some cases an obsession, of the urban reform movement. This movement also focused on the teeming blocks of the central city where the problem was most urgent and obvious. Overcrowded buildings, poor facilities, inadequate garbage collection, contaminated food and water, and bad personal habits combined to make congested neighborhoods areas of staggering disease and mortality rates. In Chicago, for example, three out of every five children born in a downtown ward in 1900 died before reaching the age of one. Since disease was no respecter of geographic divisions, middle-class communities felt threatened by these conditions. Thus reform vocabulary was filled with words like "clean" and "pure"; and reformers emphasized sanitation, good water, inspection of food and milk, fresh air, and, above all, clean government This concern was expressed so frequently that it was often difficult to tell whether reform was really a political program or simply hygiene. Despite its obvious importance, public health in this broad context has yet to attract an historian.[27]

Downtown wards were as unsafe as they were unclean. Just as maps of disease and infant mortality revealed a concentration at the center, so did the police blotter. And for urban reformers, few issues were as important as "law and order." Yet historians have generally left this

field to others, especially sociologists, with the result that concern has
been with crime rates and formal police organization. The topic is much
broader. Policing is not simply a matter of cops and robbers but rather
one part of an elaborate attempt to extend an urban discipline over a
loosely structured social system. Hence, policemen have always had a
wide range of duties which go well beyond apprehending criminals,
and have played a critical role in neighborhood life. Who were they?
We know the Irish early discovered police departments, but what kind
of career did they stake out? What kind of relationships existed between the precinct headquarters and the community? How did newcomers and the poor fare in "the good old days" when the man in blue
walked the beat? Roger Lane's study of Boston in the nineteenth century is a happy beginning on this subject, but the topic itself is large
and needs intensive cultivation.[28]

The central urge, then, of urban reformers was control of the
exploding modern city. Changes in the neighborhoods put their residential stake in jeopardy, and shifting land uses downtown often
threatened their economic investment. What reformers sought was
predictability in this otherwise apparently unstable system. Zoning
and planning were attempts to put a hand around the process, to create
some order out of a churning society. It was Fifth Avenue merchants
who campaigned for the first zoning ordinance in 1916 to protect that
exclusive street against incursions from nearby lower uses. But we know
almost nothing about zoning legislation elsewhere. In many ways zoning, with its control on the use of land, was a more radical interference
with private property than most Progressive measures. Nor do we have
the analogue for city planners of Merle Curti's *Social Ideas of American Educators*.

The modern city, then, bred deep divisions within the metropolis.
It should not be surprising that these differences were reflected in state
and federal governments as well as in city hall. But political scientists
and historians working within the old urban-rural dichotomy have emphasized that they cannot find the expected contrasts in the behavior
of legislatures and Congress. This is because the city merely exported
its divisions to state capitals and Washington. Urban representatives on
most questions, even when there seemed to be an urban interest at
stake, split their votes, just as rural legislators often did. We need
new studies on the relationships between various levels of government
which take into account these local conflicts, and which do not concern
themselves only with the classic dichotomy. The rise of the city did

have a profound and continuing impact on state and federal affairs, but the process was more complicated than conventional speculation assumes.

The second task of urban history is to indicate what difference this immense growth meant to national development. In the broadest sense this perspective can best be established by two simple facts: in 1790 less than 5 per cent of the American people lived under urban conditions; by 1969 more than 75 per cent did. This quantitative measurement is, however, misleading. The statistical watershed was not reached until 1920, when the census taker recorded that for the first time more people lived in "urban places" than rural ones. Yet it is obvious that the effective balance had swung to the cities well before that time. In short, the full urban impact cannot be appraised merely by computing the town's share of the national population. Cities have always played a disproportionate role in American history.

Carl Bridenbaugh's volumes on Colonial cities have most clearly made this point. Though these small urban communities accounted for only a fraction of the population, they dominated the commercial, social, and intellectual life of the British possessions. It was these exposed urban nerves that first reacted against the new British policy. And it was Boston, above all, that resisted Imperial reorganization and became the scene of the confrontation between colony and mother country. Independence was probably inevitable, but, as Arthur Schlesinger, Sr., argued, it came when it did and the way it did because of the peculiar conditions in Boston which made that city especially vulnerable to the new policies and which provided it also with the means of resistance.[29] The Hub had only sixteen thousand people (a statistical error by present calculations), yet it was enough to thrust the beleaguered city into a unique role in the coming of the American revolution.

This interpretation of the birth of the Republic seems well established, but the subsequent part played by cities in the early national period is not so clear. It would perhaps be worthwhile to take another look at the Constitutional Convention of 1787 and the nation's new governing document. The controversy over the Constitution has been cast as a contest over the class composition of the convention and the measure of democracy in the ratification of the result. An analysis of the famous fifty-five delegates shows a disproportionate urban representation. In the four critical delegations from Massachusetts, New York, Pennsylvania, and Virginia, for example, 87 per cent of the members had significant urban experience and connections. And in the struggle for ratification every city, North and South, East and West, voted for the Constitution. They did so with large majorities that included voters from a wide cross-section of people. Urban dwellers had become accustomed to municipal activity and were less suspicious of governmental power than those living in scattered settlements in the countryside. At any rate, an urban perspective on this period promises to redefine the traditional controversy and perhaps to provide a more satisfying explanation than a class or sectional framework.

George Rogers Taylor has convincingly developed the importance of transportation in the extraordinary growth of the country during its first half-century. Certain monographs have demonstrated the crucial role cities had in this whole process. For it was in the rivalry of seaboard ports for the trade of the West that scholars have found the impetus for the turnpike, canal, and railroad booms of the early nineteenth century. The felt need of commercial *entrepôts* provided the leadership, raised the money, and laid out the routes for what Taylor rightfully calls "the transportation revolution." [30]

What we need now is more work on the noneconomic aspects of this urban imperialism. For roads, canals, and railroads were only one dimension of these bitter contests; the same instinct generated cultural rivalry as well. Part of every city's statistical litany about its great past and its magnificent future were the numbers of schoolbooks in its libraries, trees on its streets, miles of sewers, gallons of pure water, numbers of museums, works of art in city hall, and so on. This boasting has seemed adolescent to historians, though it was indulged in by old and large cities as well as new and small ones.

Part of the explanation lies in a kind of pre-Darwinian Darwinism which assumed a life cycle of urban growth—unless the city grew (and as rapidly as others), it would stagnate and die. The constant repetition of favorable statistics and soaring prospects was a reassuring sign of vitality. Moreover, it met another deep private need. Almost all American cities were young, especially by Old World standards. Few residents had been there long, and many expected to move on again. Hence, if you did not have roots in the past, perhaps you could find some in the future. This "ideology" underlay the boosterism of the time. It may seem highly amusing to the historian, but contemporaries were serious about it. And those who were involved in this intense rivalry were not only merchants and editors; intellectuals, too, were urban patriots. When, for instance, the Chicago fire put that entire city in jeopardy, the St. Louis School of Philosophy privately exulted in the event. "We, with some public display, sent money for the homeless and provisions for the hungry, and even resolutions of sympathy for the unfortunate city—all of which was of right appearance; but privately everywhere could be heard without unhappy tears the pious scriptural ejaculation: 'Again the fire of heaven has fallen on Sodom and Gomorrah; may it complete its divinely appointed work!' " [31]

Another task that lies directly ahead for urban historians is a new look at the period between 1820 and 1860. These years witnessed the most rapid growth of cities in American history. Later, of course, large numbers of newcomers would swell municipal numbers, but never again would the rate of growth be quite so high. Yet it is here that the work is the slimmest and least satisfying. Historians have, for example, looked at Jacksonian Democracy from a wide variety of perspectives—the impact of industrialization, the emergence of the West, the new surge of immigration, the rise of a small capitalist class, and the importance of transportation—but none has taken into account directly the most significant change in the system, the extraordinary growth of the cities. This development affected all sections of the country, radically altered the rural-urban balance, and provided the scene of some of the most dynamic movements of the period.

The growth of cities also diversified the life of each section. In the East the urban dimension was quite old; yet it very quickly appeared in other regions as well. I have attempted to assess this importance in the Ohio Valley in *The Urban Frontier*. But two recent books are more revealing. Kenneth Wheeler's *To Wear a City's Crown* treats the origins of urbanization in Texas, and Robert Dykstra's *Cattle Towns* does the same thing for part of the Middle Border.[32] Rodman Paul and Earl Pomeroy have also sought this same emphasis in looking at the early period of Far Western history.[33] After reading these works it is impossible any longer to think of the West only in terms of pioneers, farmers, miners, and cowboys. Historians are thus slowly coming around to Josiah Strong's prophecy of eighty years ago that in the West the pattern of growth was "first the railroad, then the towns, then the farms. Settlement is, consequently, more rapid, and the city stamps the country instead of the country stamping the city. It is the cities and the towns," he continued, "which will frame state constitutions, make laws, create public opinion, establish social usages, and fix standards of morals in the West." [34]

The South, too, had its urban dimension. The importance of its cities was disguised at first because of the persistence of slavery with its concentration on cotton, tobacco, sugar, and plantations, and later because of the preoccupation of historians with Reconstruction and a new system of race relations. Yet urbanization in the South seems slow only when compared with the American North and West—the most rapidly urbanizing areas on the globe. Compared with other parts of the world, the pace of the process exceeded all of the Old World and was matched only by a few other regions. If secession had been successful, Southern historians would long ago have developed the city as a major theme in Dixie's life.

We have paid dearly for this omission. Not only have scholars neglected the economic and political significance of urban centers in the South, but they have missed their importance in the origins of racial segregation. In *Slavery in the Cities* I tried to suggest that the roots of segregation could be found in the crisis of the "peculiar institution" within an urban environment.[35] It is now clear that in the years following emancipation, segregation replaced slavery as the system of racial control in Southern cities. This development, which grew under both Reconstruction and Redemption governments, was ratified by the passage of state-wide Jim Crow laws.

The conjunction of urbanization and segregation often seems at odds with conventional expectations. Most people think (or used to think) of the metropolis as a place where people of all kinds mix, and that the historic "free air of the city" dissolves personal barriers. Yet it was just the fact that people did mix, rub elbows, and live in physical proximity that led whites to establish an elaborate system of public etiquette to maintain racial deference. A detailed analysis of this process still awaits an historian, but its importance can hardly be overstated.

Sectional studies have demonstrated that urbanization has not been confined historically to just a few parts of the country. This new scholarship paves the way for a discussion of the nationalizing influence of urban growth. In the first place, the rise of the cities everywhere muted regional differences. Though New Orleans and San Francisco and Chicago might take on a Southern, Western, or Midwestern flavor, they were still more like each other than any were like their own countryside a hundred miles away. Secondly, despite variations, American cities produced a similar environment for their residents. Nearly all began as commercial enterprises; most enjoyed their crucial growth in the nineteenth and early twentieth centuries; all shared the same urban technology; and, due to great interurban mobility and constant informal contacts, their leaders consciously exchanged techniques and solutions to common problems. In short, urbanization was a profoundly nationalizing force.

I have already mentioned progressivism and urbanization. In this perspective, national progressivism appears to be an extension of urban reform. Its roots lay in the expanding city and in the tensions produced by this extraordinary growth. Local reformers sought to control the rapidly changing metropolis and to process its future. Their power, however, was always frustrated by the boss and his control of city hall, and by business interests more concerned with short-term profits than long-range orderly and predictable growth. Little was said by national Progressives about predatory politics and selfish capitalists on the national level that had not been said many times on the local level in the last three decades of the nineteenth century.

What started as local campaigns to handle the problems of a single city soon became a national movement. In part this resulted from the tendency of the various groups involved in urban reform—social workers, professional people, business associations, civic clubs, and so forth—to establish their own national organizations. Here, once a year in conventions and constantly through the mail, those working on urban problems would talk of common concerns.

In part, too, broadening the political base resulted from difficulties on the local level. Contests with the machine were not always successful, and even when they were, most municipal governments proved to be unreliable instruments of change. Reformers soon turned to state legislation; a little later they carried the case to the federal government. Urban reformers usually found the wider constituency more congenial, just as the boss found the small unit of the precinct and ward more apt to his purposes than state legislatures or the federal government.[36]

If urban reform antedated the Progressive movement, it also continued afterward. Although the national mood became increasingly conservative in the twenties, much reform in the cities continued. The residual progressivism which Arthur Link tried to isolate in his article "What Happened to the Progressive Movement in the 1920's?"[37] was concentrated largely in the cities. The spread of zoning and planning across the country was only the most obvious illustration of the continued drive for urban reform. Blake McKelvey refers to the whole decade as "An Outburst of Metropolitan Initiative." [38]

But the urban impact in other areas of national life was less happy. The decade was, of course, characterized by the resurgence of the Ku Klux Klan, the experiment in prohibition, and the end of large-scale immigration. Historians have often viewed these movements as the last cry of small towns and rural America against the growing dominance of the city. Yet large numbers of urbanites were active in all three. Kenneth Jackson has compellingly demonstrated the urban dimension of the Klan.[39] Studies of the other two movements would also reveal large participation in the cities and find them connected with the tensions that were bred by the growth of the metropolis. Without this urban support it is unlikely that small towns and rural folk would have had the strength to acquire such national power.

Still another development in the city in the twenties needs fresh attention. It is commonplace now to emphasize the election of 1928. It is no longer thought to be unique simply because of a Catholic candidacy but rather as a harbinger of the future significance of the urban vote. Yet what created the "urban vote" was not just numbers but a growing consensus within the city. The deep divisions which characterized the reformer-boss struggles of the earlier period were now somewhat attenuated as the two antagonists discovered some areas of agreement, and as leaders such as Al Smith found techniques to create a new coalition.

It was this boss-reform coalition that lay at the heart of the New Deal. Historians and political scientists once talked of the "New Deal coalition" as a farmer-labor alliance, then later added "minorities" to this description. Yet the farmers were never really a part of the coalition (though the large ones ironically became one of its major beneficiaries); they had dropped out by 1940 and except for a fitful return in 1948 have remained out. What better accounts for the Roosevelt victories and explains the internal problems of the New Deal was the ability of the Democratic party to keep both machines and reformers in the same camp and, when in power, in the same cabinet.

What undid the boss-reform coalition was the rise of the suburbs. The pent-up demands for housing that had gathered during the depression and war suddenly burst, and new communities sprang up at the outer edges of every metropolis. The city-suburban cleavage became a crucial element in national politics. The fact that the cities were obviously in trouble (and the suburbs did not yet know that they were) deepened the old split between the center and the periphery. And the one-man, one-vote ruling of the Supreme Court meant that the rise of the suburbs would be felt almost instantly. At any rate, the historical reassessment of national politics from a metropolitan viewpoint is long overdue.

I should like to conclude with a few remarks about some special opportunities for research in urban history. The need for work in the black experience in cities is obvious. The rise of the Northern ghetto has already produced some especially useful books, and many more are nearing publication.[40] Yet the Negro ghetto was a Southern phenomenon before it was a Northern one. We need to know about Atlanta, New Orleans, and Richmond as well as Chicago, New York, and Detroit. Negro concentrations in the former cities are in the fifth and sixth generations; the institutions of the ghetto, therefore, are more fully developed and the consequences of the system can be more clearly studied. This emphasis would not only rescue a neglected area of historical concern but perhaps produce a better perspective for the formulation of public policy today.

Comparative urban history offers an equally important prospect. The temptations for the scholar to work in Paris, Rome, and London are strong, of course, and ought not to be discouraged. But the Soviet world is now over fifty years old; its cities have been governed by unique public power. By controlling housing, employment, and most everything else, government presumably has exercised control over the size and shape of the metropolis. What difference this has made in the physical and social texture of Soviet urban life is worth knowing.

In a different way, Australian cities offer an opportunity to test the influence of urbanization in a more comparable national experience. Despite the popular emphasis on the outback and bush, Australia has always been one of the most urbanized areas on the globe. Sydney and Melbourne are great metropolises by any standard; Canberra was one of the first planned capitals in modern times. The major cities in Australia are about the same age as our own. Since they are without large numbers of blacks or Eastern European immigrants, they provide an opportunity to assess more precisely the influence these forces have had on American urban growth.

Finally, a few words on urban resources seem appropriate. For those using quantitative methods, urban materials present particular opportunities. Cities have always been repositories of data on a large and systematic basis. When national censuses are not available, there is always the likelihood that the cities themselves kept records with similar information. School counts, for example, were made regularly and represent a rich but yet untapped source. Hospital records tell us more about family life than almost any other source, but they have not been used in any extensive way. Real estate conveyances, as I have already noted, reveal a critical dimension of urban development. The scale of this material is imposing, but new techniques may develop means of carving a way through the bulk and yielding results that escape more conventional longhand methods.

Then, too, the camera is coterminous with the rise of the modern city. The first American saw a daguerreotype at the same time mass transportation was introduced into New York. Yet historians have used photography as illustration rather than evidence, as ornament rather than document. The camera, however, provides the urban historian with peculiar advantages. From the beginning, photographers were fascinated by the many faces of the city. They went to the highest points and made panoramas—kinds of visual censuses. These documents show spatial relationships which traditional sources—census data, memoirs, and travelers' accounts—cannot catch. Local historical societies are beginning to save, and hopefully will soon start to catalog, invaluable pictures of neighborhoods, commercial centers, and street scenes. A pictorial account of a score of American cities would greatly enhance the reconstruction of our urban past.

It is clear, then, that the task before urban historians is a large one. There is no dearth of topics because there is virtually no end to the things that need to be done. Fortunately we do not start from scratch; we can build on the published labors of a growing number of competent and often imaginative scholars. In the jargon of our times, urban history is "relevant." Historians in more traditional fields are anxious to add an urban dimension to their analysis. And the public feels the need for an urban perspective to identify more clearly the nature of present problems and to gauge the extent of our contemporary crisis.

NOTES

1. H. J. Dyos, "Agenda for Urban Historians," in *The Study of Urban History* (London, 1968), p. 16.

2. Richard Hildreth, *Despotism in America: An Inquiry into the Nature, Results, and Legal Basis of the Slave-Holding System in the United States* (Boston, 1854), p. 139. Hildreth noted the rivalry between Bristol and London in his *History of the United States of America*, vol. I: *Colonial, 1497–1688* (New York, 1877), 35–37, 46, 94.

3. J. Thomas Scharf and Thompson Westcott, *History of Philadelphia, 1609–1884* (Philadelphia, 1884), I, 1.

4. Frederick Jackson Turner Papers, Henry E. Huntington Library; Charles A. Beard, *American City Government* (New York, 1912), pp. 1, 2.

5. An early historical examination of the city came from Arthur Schlesinger, Sr., author of *The Rise of the City, 1878–1898*, vol. X in *A History of American Life* (New York, 1933), and "The City in American History," *Mississippi Valley Historical Review*, XXVII (June 1940), 43–66.

6. A partial explanation for this is found in the great degree to which the Progressives addressed themselves to the peculiar problems of the city. See, for example, Jane Addams, *et al., Hull House Maps and Papers: A Presentation of Nationalities and Wages in a Congested District of Chicago* (New York, 1895); Lincoln Steffens, *The Shame of the Cities* (New York, 1904); Robert Hunter, *Tenement Conditions in Chicago* (Chicago, 1902); and Jacob A. Riis, *How the Other Half Lives: Studies Among the Tenements of New York* (New York, 1890). For a convenient checklist of the general concern about cities at the beginning of the Progressive period, see Robert C. Brooks, "A Bibliography of Municipal Problems and City Conditions," *Municipal Affairs*, I (March 1897), 1–234; revised version in *ibid.*, V (March 1901), 1–346.

7. Lewis Mumford, *The City in History: Its Origins, Its Transformations, and Its Prospects* (New York, 1961); Jane Jacobs, *The Death and Life of Great American Cities* (New York, 1961).

8. Recent concern over rioting and crime has spurred extensive research into these problems. Though the majority of reports based on this work are not historical in nature, one exception is the volume edited by Hugh Davis Graham and Ted Robert Gurr for the National Commission on the Causes and Prevention of Violence, *The History of Violence in America*.

9. Adna F. Weber, *The Growth of Cities in the Nineteenth Century: A Study in Statistics* (New York, 1899).

10. Blake McKelvey, *Rochester,* 4 vols. (Cambridge, Mass., and Rochester, N.Y., 1945–1951); Constance M. Green, *Washington: Village and Capital, 1800–1878* (Princeton, 1962), and *Washington: Capital City, 1879–1950*

(Princeton, 1963); Bessie L. Pierce, *A History of Chicago*, 3 vols. (New York, 1937–1957).

11. Sam B. Warner, Jr., *Streetcar Suburbs: The Process of Growth in Boston, 1870–1900* (Cambridge, Mass., 1962).

12. Homer Hoyt, *One Hundred Years of Land Values in Chicago* (Chicago, 1933).

13. There are very few secondary sources which deal with this phenomenon. In addition to Warner's work, one can turn to certain semi-historical studies such as John A. Miller's *Fares Please! From Horse Cars to Streamliners* (New York, 1941). A recent and invaluable start has been made by George Rogers Taylor, "The Beginnings of Mass Transportation in Urban America," *Smithsonian Journal of History*, I, parts 1 and 2 (Summer and Autumn 1966), 35–50, 31–54. An earlier but still valuable work is that of Edward Chase Kirkland, *Men, Cities and Transportation: A Study of New England History, 1820–1900*, 2 vols. (Cambridge, Mass., 1948). See also Harlan W. Gilmore, *Transportation and the Growth of Cities* (Glencoe, Ill., 1953).

14. Early attempts to outline this type of development were usually made by other disciplines. Most characteristic are the studies of members of the so-called "Chicago School." See Robert E. Park, *et al.*, *The City* (Chicago, 1925), and Ernest W. Burgess, ed., *The City* (Chicago, 1926). Under the general editorship of Morris Janowitz, selected papers of various Chicago sociologists are being published in a series titled *The Heritage of Sociology*. See, for example, Ralph H. Turner, ed., *Robert E. Park on Social Control and Collective Behavior* (Chicago, 1967), and G. Franklin Edwards, ed., *E. Franklin Frazier on Race Relations* (Chicago, 1968). Some of the earliest analysis was completed by Robert A. Woods, a leader of the settlement movement, whose experience gave him many special insights into the question. See Robert A. Woods, ed., *The City Wilderness* (Boston, 1898) and *The Neighborhood in Nation Building* (New York, 1923); Woods and Albert J. Kennedy, *The Zone of Emergence*, ed. by Sam B. Warner, Jr,. (Cambridge, Mass., 1962); Woods and Kennedy, *The Settlement Horizon* (New York, 1922).

15. Once again, scholarship in this particular area has been limited. One may begin, however, with two older but still important books: Homer Hoyt, *The Structure and Growth of Residential Neighborhoods in American Cities* (Washington, D.C., 1939); Woods and Kennedy, *Zone of Emergence*. G. A. Wissink, *American Cities in Perspective, with Special Reference to Their Fringe Areas* (Gassen, Holland, 1962) is more recent. The auxiliary question of social mobility has been given serious study by Stephan Thernstrom in his *Poverty and Progress: Social Mobility in the Nineteenth-Century City* (Cambridge, Mass., 1964).

16. A solid but short study of the changing physical landscape of cities over a long period is that of Christopher Tunnard and Henry H. Reed, *American Skyline: The Growth and Form of Our Cities and Towns* (Boston, 1955). Another helpful work is John E. Burchard and Albert Bush-Brown, *The Architecture of America: A Social and Cultural History* (Boston, 1961). We still lack historical studies of intra-city shifts in business. Geographers have provided a theoretical framework with such works as Edgar M. Hoover's *The Location of Economic Activity* (New York, 1948). For a brief survey of one city's changing commercial areas, see John E. Brush and Howard L. Gauthier, Jr., *Service Centers and Consumer Trips: Studies on the Philadelphia Metropolitan Fringe*, University of Chicago, Department of Geography, Research Paper #113 (Chicago, 1968), chap. 2.

17. George R. Taylor, *The Transportation Revolution, 1815–1860* (New York, 1951).

18. Nicholas B. Wainwright, ed., *A Philadelphia Perspective: The Diary of Sydney George Fisher Governing the Years 1834–1871* (Philadelphia, 1967), pp. 316, 327.

19. Miller, *Fares Please!*

20. Weber, *Growth of Cities in the Nineteenth Century,* p. 459.

21. Harlan Douglass, *The Suburban Trend* (New York, 1925). One of the few works on suburban areas is Robert C. Wood's *Suburbia: Its People and Their Politics* (Boston, 1959). For a study of a particular area, see Bennett M. Berger, *Working-Class Suburb: A Study of Auto Workers in Suburbia* (Berkeley, 1960).

22. As a beginning, one may look at Helen Monchow's *Seventy Years of Real Estate Subdividing in the City of Chicago* (Chicago, 1933).

23. Lyle W. Dorsett, *The Pendergast Machine* (New York, 1968); William Miller, *Memphis During the Progressive Era, 1900–1917* (Memphis, 1957); Melvin G. Holli, *Reform in Detroit: Hazen S. Pingree and Urban Politics* (New York, 1969). Some earlier studies such as Harold Zink's *City Bosses in the United States: A Study of Twenty Municipal Bosses* (Durham, N.C., 1930) treat the organizational side, but do little with the social roots of the machine. For instance, Edwin O'Connor, *The Last Hurrah* (New York, 1956); Joseph F. Dinneen, *Ward Eight* (New York, 1936); and Lloyd Wendt and Herman Kogan, *Lords of the Levee: The Story of Bathhouse John and Hinky Dink* (Indianapolis, 1943) do better than most histories in capturing the feel of machine politics. The ward bosses left few letters or documents, but one of the few written accounts is found in the amusing but important *Plunkitt of Tammany Hall,* recently issued in paperback, ed. by William Riordan, with an introduction by Arthur Mann (New York, 1963).

24. Zane Miller, *Boss Cox's Cincinnati: Urban Politics in the Progressive Era* (New York, 1968). One view of a local situation is that of Sol Cohen in *Progressives and Urban School Reform: The Public Education Association of New York City, 1895–1954* (New York, 1964).

25. "Above all, a well-behaved mind grows only in a well-treated body," wrote Hugo Munsterberg. "It is true that far seeing hygiene can prevent more crime than any law." Quoted in Beard, *American City Government,* p. 186.

26. James H. Timberlake, *Prohibition and the Progressive Movement, 1900–1920* (Cambridge, Mass., 1963), and Joseph Gusfield, *Symbolic Crusade: Status Politics and the American Temperance Movement* (Urbana, Ill., 1963).

27. Certain aspects of this topic are well covered in such works as Nelson Blake's *Water for the Cities* (Syracuse, 1956), and Charles Rosenberg's *Cholera Years: The United States in 1832, 1849, and 1866* (Chicago, 1962), but no one has put the public health issue in its larger urban context. Biographies of individuals are often helpful. James H. Cassedy's *Charles V. Chapin and the Public Health Movement* (Cambridge, Mass., 1962) and C. E. A. Winslow's *The Life of Hermann M. Biggs, M.D., D.S.C, LL.D., Physician and Statesman of the Public Health* (Philadelphia, 1929) are examples.

28. Roger Lane, *Policing the City: Boston, 1822–1885* (Cambridge, Mass., 1967).

29. Arthur Schlesinger, Sr., *Prelude to Independence: The Newspaper War on Britain, 1764–1776* (New York, 1958).

30. Taylor, *Transportation Revolution.* See also George R. Taylor and Irene D. Neu, *The American Railroad Network, 1861–1890* (Cambridge, Mass.,

1956). An important phase of this topic is covered by Wyatt W. Belcher's *The Economic Rivalry Between St. Louis and Chicago, 1850–1880* (New York, 1947). Other useful works are James W. Livingood's *The Philadelphia-Baltimore Trade Rivalry, 1780–1860* (Harrisburg, Pa., 1947), and Julius Rubin, *Canal or Railroad? Imitation and Innovation in Response to the Erie Canal in Philadelphia, Baltimore and Boston* (Philadelphia, 1961).

31. Denton J. Snider, *The St. Louis Movement* (St. Louis, 1920), p. 75n.

32. Richard C. Wade, *The Urban Frontier: The Rise of Western Cities, 1790–1830* (Cambridge, Mass., 1959); Kenneth Wheeler, *To Wear a City's Crown: The Beginnings of Urban Growth in Texas, 1836–1865* (Cambridge, Mass., 1968); Robert R. Dykstra, *The Cattle Towns* (New York, 1968).

33. Rodman Paul, *Mining Frontiers of the Far West, 1848–1880* (New York, 1963). Earl Pomeroy, *The Pacific Slope: A History of California, Oregon, Washington, Idaho, Utah, and Nevada* (New York, 1965).

34. Josiah Strong, *Our Country: Its Possible Future and Its Present Crisis* (New York, 1885), p. 206.

35. Richard C. Wade, *Slavery in the Cities: The South, 1820–1860* (New York, 1964).

36. Part of the story of the conflict between settlement-house reformers and the political machine is found in Jane Addams, *Twenty Years at Hull House* (New York, 1930). See also Louise C. Wade's *Graham Taylor: Pioneer for Social Justice* (Chicago, 1964), and Allen F. Davis, *Spearheads for Reform: The Social Settlements and the Progressive Movement, 1890–1914* (New York, 1967).

37. Arthur S. Link, "What Happened to the Progressive Movement in the 1920's?," *American Historical Review*, LXIV (July 1959), 833–851.

38. Blake McKelvey, *The Emergence of Metropolitan America, 1915–1966* (New Brunswick, N.J., 1968).

39. Kenneth T. Jackson, *The Ku Klux Klan in the City, 1915–1930* (New York, 1967).

40. *The Philadelphia Negro* by W. E. B. DuBois (Philadelphia, 1899), *Black Metropolis: A Study of Negro Life in a Northern City*, co-authored by St. Clair Drake and Horace R. Clayton (New York, 1945), and Robert A. Warner, *New Haven Negroes: A Social History* (New Haven, 1940) were pioneering works by nonhistorians. The recent escalation of interest in the Negro in our society has produced several detailed historical works on black history. For instance, Gilbert Osofsky's *Harlem: The Making of a Ghetto* (New York, 1966), and Alan Spear's *Black Chicago: The Making of a Negro Ghetto, 1890–1920* (Chicago, 1967).

Ethnicity:
A Neglected Dimension
of American History

RUDOLPH J. VECOLI

Twentieth-century sociological literature is replete with notices of the imminent demise of ethnicity in America. In 1945, W. Lloyd Warner declared: "The future of American ethnic groups seems to be limited; it is likely that they will be quickly absorbed." [1] A decade later, Will Herberg confirmed that ethnicity, if not dead, was rapidly dying.[2] These epitaphs to ethnicity, like Mark Twain's obituary, have turned out to be premature. Recent events have shattered the assumption that the melting pot has worked its cultural alchemy. Ethnicity, by which I mean group consciousness based on a sense of common origin, has demonstrated renewed vitality in the second half of the twentieth century.

Clearly this resurgence of ethnic consciousness, this "new tribalism," springs from deep-seated social and psychic needs. The "Black Revolution" appears to have served as a catalyst, energizing other groups to both defensive and emulative responses. Just as in Canada, where the French nationalist movement has spurred Slavs and others to assert themselves, so black militancy has elicited responding ethnic nationalisms. "Black Power" brings forth echoes of "Irish Power," "Polish Power," and so forth. Inspired by the example of black Americans, white ethnics tend to see themselves engaged in an analogous struggle for liberation from the stigma and burden of inferiority.[3]

Only the true believer can any longer sustain his vision of America as a "homogeneous society of undifferentiated men" where race, religion, or national origin do not matter. The inability to transmute twenty million blacks into the "historic American type" raised questions about how well the country's digestive system had worked in the past. Once the conspiracy of silence was broken, it became quickly apparent that it had worked only imperfectly if at all. Nathan Glazer and Daniel P. Moynihan were the first to say so: "The point about the melting pot is that it did not happen." [4] As behavioral scientists have renewed their explorations of ethnic America, they have found the historical literature on the subject to be thin indeed. Charging that historians have failed to do their job, social scientists grumble that they have to do their own historical research on ethnic groups.[5]

Sad to say, historians *have* neglected the dimension of ethnicity in the American past. We have been made dramatically aware of our deficiency in this respect by the sudden and widespread demand for minority history courses. The most pressing demand, of course, is for Afro-American history. History departments which would have scoffed at the notion a few years ago are now recruiting *black* Afro American historians. Unfortunately, much of the contemporary concern with minority group history is politically inspired rather than derived from an honest conviction of its inherent value as a field of study.

Clearly the historical profession has a responsibility to maintain the integrity of scholarly standards, to prevent the perversion of history into special pleading, and to seek the advancement of knowledge beyond the pragmatic needs of the moment. Our ability to meet our professional responsibility, however, is crippled by our knowledge that we are morally compromised. Who, if not the historian, is responsible for the fact that lily-white and racist history has been imbibed by generations of students? Our sense of guilt has stimulated more breast-beating than hard thinking.

I suggest that a searching examination of the reasons for our failure would be more fruitful. Why has the history of the United States *not* been written in terms of the enormous diversity of race, culture, and religion that has characterized the American people from the seventeenth century until today? My answer will be phrased in terms of the historiography of European immigration; others better able than I can address themselves to the neglect of the history of Afro-Americans and other racial groups. What I have to say on this score is not meant as castigation of our professional forebears; rather it is largely an exercise of self-criticism.

A joint committee of the American Historical Association and the Organization of American Historians recently issued a statement on

"The Writing and Teaching of American History in Textbooks," which declared that the diversity of the American people "must be faithfully portrayed." [6] By and large, the portrayal of this diversity has been an ideal to which we have paid lip service rather than a task to which we have addressed ourselves. A casual perusal of college and high school textbooks reveals that the factor of ethnic pluralism is not effectively presented. Aside from clichés about "a nation of immigrants" and "the melting pot," textbooks convey the impression of bland homogeneity. An unspoken assumption of American historiography has been that the important things have been said and done only by English-speaking whites. Negroes have not been the only "invisible men" in American history. Immigrants, Indians, and Hispanos have also usually appeared in the history books as faceless masses.

Nor are college students any more likely to be exposed to the "facts of life" about ethnicity. A survey of course offerings in one hundred colleges and universities revealed that thirty-eight offered courses touching some aspect of ethnic history; of these, twenty were general social and cultural history courses, nineteen Afro-American history courses, four American Indian history courses, and four immigration history courses.[7] More than 60 per cent of the institutions did not offer any course dealing directly with the history of group life in America. One cannot derive much comfort from the fact that sociology departments customarily offer courses in "American Minorities" or "Racial and Ethnic Relations." A recent review of such courses concluded that few of them provided a systematic analysis of group interaction, either historical or contemporary. Rather they tended to concentrate on prejudice and discrimination, and to substitute moral indignation for a critical assessment of the subject.[8]

But, I am assured, the field of immigration history appears to be flourishing today. After all, one can think at a moment's notice of ten or twenty excellent monographs which have appeared in recent years. I am not about to belittle the significant accomplishments of the historians of immigration, of which tribe I proudly claim membership, but my reading of the current state of health of this specialty is less sanguine. Despite the significant work of some very able historians, the study of immigration has been and remains an underdeveloped field of historical inquiry.

A generous estimate of the current number of American historians who have a major interest in immigration history would be two hundred, or perhaps 2 per cent of those now teaching American history at collegiate institutions.[9] An analysis of doctoral dissertations in immigration history further suggests that this theme has been peripheral to the concerns of most American historians.[10] Between 1893 (the year a student of Frederick Jackson Turner completed the first dissertation on an immigration topic) and 1965, a total of 127 Ph.D. dissertations related to American immigration have been written. Of these, 9 per cent were completed by 1925; another 35 per cent between 1926 and 1945; and 56 per cent between 1946 and 1965. That more than half of these dissertations have been written since 1946 might at first suggest that immigration study is booming, but the apparent upsurge merely reflects the general increase in the output of dissertations. Actually the percentage of history dissertations devoted to immigration-related topics has fluctuated around 1.5 per cent of the total for three-quarters of a century.

A topical analysis of the dissertations further reveals those large gaps in the literature of which immigration historians are only too aware. The great majority of the dissertations deal with the time period 1790–1920. Only four dissertations concentrate on the post-1920 era. This reflects the curious assumption that the history of immigration ends with the enactment of the restrictive legislation of the twenties. Most of the dissertations focus upon a particular immigrant group. The Jews, Irish, and Germans have received the most attention, with the Scandinavians, Italians, and Chinese lagging some distance behind. For dozens of other groups there is only a smattering of studies. As one might expect, the published literature reflects these lacunae.

Yet even if we had a library of competent studies of each of the immigrant groups, this would not add up to a history of ethnicity in America. To paraphrase Clemenceau, ethnicity is too important to be left to the immigration historians. If, as has been claimed, ethnicity is one of the strongest influences in America today, how much more true this must have been in the past. It is difficult to conceive of any institution which has not been profoundly affected by the ethnic factor. Still we have had histories of American cities, labor movements, religious denominations, politics, and schools [11] in which the immigrants and their children appear merely as residents, workers, parishioners, voters, and pupils. The fact that they also were, as the case might be, Polish Catholics, Welsh Methodists, Eastern Rite Ukrainians, Greek Orthodox, Swedish Lutherans, or one of a multitude of other ethnic identities is not treated as being significant. That the history of a society whose distinctive attribute has been its racial, cultural, linguistic, and religious pluralism should have been wrtten for the most part from an Anglo-American monistic perspective is indeed a paradox.

Two "explanations" are often advanced for the dearth of ethnic historical studies. One is the alleged language barrier. American students, it is said, lack the linguistic skills to undertake research on such exotic groups as Rumanians and Croatians. John K. Fairbank gave the proper response to this objection: "The problem here is not: What languages do we read? The problem is: What is our intellectual and historical horizon?" [12] When the profession places a correct evaluation upon ethnic studies, students will acquire the necessary linguistic facility.

The second objection has to do with the alleged lack of significant bodies of historical records for ethnic groups. Even historians who should know better speak of the "inarticulate nationalities." Such notions derive from the stereotype of the immigrants as uniformly illiterate peasants. Far from being inarticulate, the ethnic groups generated a vast amount of documentation. In 1910 more than a thousand newspapers and periodicals were being published in the United States in other than the English language.[13] Immigration probably raised the volume of communication among the "common people" to its highest level in history. Consider the hundreds of millions of letters that have crossed the ocean, both ways. Unfortunately, American libraries and archives have generally not troubled themselves with the collection of non-English-language materials. Only in recent years have systematic and successful efforts been made to gather the records of immigrant groups. Rich, untapped collections await the student of ethnic America.[14]

I believe there are two basic reasons why American historians have neglected the dimension of ethnicity. One has to do with the prevailing ideology of the academic profession; the other with its sociology.

A prime article of the American creed has been a profound confidence in the power of the New World to transform human nature. Even the "wretched refuse" of Europe was to be transmuted by the irresistible combination of the natural environment and republican institutions. The classic statement of the doctrine of Americanization was pronounced by the Frenchman Hector St. John Crèvecoeur:

He is an American, who, leaving behind him all his ancient prejudices and manners, receives new ones from the new mode of life he has embraced, the new government he obeys, and the new rank he holds. Here individuals of all nations are melted into a new race of men, whose labours and posterity will one day cause great changes in the world.[15]

The belief in a "new race of men" created in the crucible of democracy became axiomatic to the conception of an American nationality. How else were Americans to emerge from the confusion of tongues, faiths, and races? But as Crèvecoeur pointed out, the immigrant must be stripped of "all his ancient prejudices and manners" in order to become a "new man." Rapid and total assimilation thus came to be regarded as natural, inevitable, and desirable.

A review of immigration scholarship reveals how pervasive and powerful the grip of the assimilationist ideology has been. It was the generation of progressive historians that first addressed itself to the study of immigration as a significant factor in American history.[16] Imbued with the reform spirit of their time, they viewed American history as a process of struggle and growth toward a democratic order. Since, in such a society, differences of race, religion, and nationality were to be inconsequential, the progressive view demanded that the eradication of these "foreign" attributes be the theme of immigration history.

Frederick Jackson Turner and Charles A. Beard were the giants who towered over this generation of historians. Both were environmental determinists who stressed the primacy of economic forces, although, of course, with a difference. Turner was perhaps the first to call attention to the need for the study of immigration.[17] When Turner delivered his frontier thesis, in language reminiscent of Crèvecoeur, he described the impact of the wilderness upon the European: "In the crucible of the frontier the immigrants were Americanized, liberated, and fused into a mixed race, English in neither nationality or characteristics." [18] For Turner, the frontier was "the line of the most rapid and effective Americanization."

The historians who established immigration history as a field of study after World War I were almost to a man Turnerians. Their basic concepts were those of the frontier and the section, and their theme was that of the adaptation of Old World cultures to New World environments. Like Turner they were Midwesterners, but unlike him they were sons of German and Scandinavian immigrants. The works of Theodore Blegen on the Norwegians, George Stephenson on the Swedes, and Carl Wittke on the Germans are enduring accomplishments of this generation of immigration historians. But an aura of nostalgia lingers over their books; the "culture in immigrant chests" seemed destined to be buried with the first generation. "Americanization," Wittke observed, "moved irresistibly onward." [19]

Marcus Lee Hansen, while of similar background, was able to transcend some of the limitations which characterized the work of his contemporaries. Rather than focusing on a particular nationality, Hansen took all of European emigration as his province and related it to the full sweep of American history. A student of Turner, Hansen expanded the impact of the frontier to European society. He urged the study of the "immigrant communities in America that formed the human connecting link between the Old World and the New." [20] Despite such original insights, Hansen was fundamentally a Turnerian. In 1938 he told the Augustana Historical Society that "it is the ultimate fate of any national group to be amalgamated into the composite American race." [21]

While many aspects of Turner's frontier hypothesis have been criticized in recent years, his proposition that the American environment profoundly transformed the immigrant has gone practically unchallenged.[22] If the standard text on the westward movement now acknowledges the persistence of European traits as "equally" important with free land in shaping the nation, it also reiterates the Americanizing influence of the frontier and contains only a handful of references to specific ethnic groups. Certain recent elaborations of the Turner thesis, by David M. Potter, George W. Pierson, and Daniel Boorstin, are agreed upon an environmental explanation of national character.[23] Intent upon establishing the homogeneity of the American people, they share a common neglect of sources of diversity such as immigration.

It remained for Merle Curti, a student of Turner, to translate the frontier thesis from an ideological pronouncement into a verifiable historical statement. In his pioneering work, *The Making of an American Community*, Curti utilized quantitative as well as qualitative data to determine whether the frontier indeed made for democracy and Americanization.[24] Curti concluded that at least in Trempeleau County conditions did promote an equalization of opportunity and condition between the native- and the foreign-born. I think it significant, however, that no effort as such was made to measure the persistence of ethnicity.

That Turnerian determinism is far from being exhausted was demonstrated by the appearance in 1968 of a book entitled *The Immigrant Upraised*.[25] A history of Italians in the trans-Mississippi West, it depicts them as aspiring yeoman-farmers drawn by the magnet of virgin land. Contrasting their condition to that of degraded sweatshop workers and organ-grinders in the Eastern cities, the author asserts that the Western Italians achieved ready acceptance, rapid assimilation, and "success in the sun." In his foreword to the volume, Ray Allen Billington hails it as preparing the way for a completely new interpretation of immigration history.[26]

If the faith of the Turnerians in the liberating effects of the Western environment was unshakable, they were less optimistic about the future of the immigrant masses in the industrial cities. It is significant that no one of them, not even Hansen, effectively addressed himself to this phase of immigration history. Turner, himself, was distinctly uncomfortable in discussing the Irish and other immigrants in the Eastern cities. He doubted whether the melting pot could work under such circumstances and whether the denizens of the ethnic ghettos could be transformed into "the historic American type." [27]

For Charles Beard the triumph of industrial capitalism was the main theme of *The Rise of American Civilization*.[28] But Beard did not concern himself with the issues of assimilation or ethnicity. Viewed as "economic men," the immigrants simply played out their appointed roles in the scenarios of class conflict. As Lee Benson has pointed out, Beard did not even consider the variable of ethnic affiliation as a possible determinant of political behavior.[29] For the followers of the Beardian-Marxist interpretation of American history, economic class was the only meaningful social category. Such a crude economic determinism was not conducive to an appreciation of the subtle play of ethnic influences.

It remained for a sociologist to develop a theory of assimilation which would comprehend the immigrant in an urban setting. Robert Ezra Park was perhaps the most influential student of racial and ethnic relations in twentieth-century America. A close observer of immigrant life, Park was early persuaded that the country could digest "every sort of normal human difference, except the purely external ones, like the color of the skin." [30] Impressed by the ease and rapidity with which the immigrants acquired the language and customs, Park declared in 1913: "In America it has become proverbial that a Pole,

Lithuanian, or Norwegian cannot be distinguished, in the second generation, from an American born of native parents." In 1926, Park summed up his thinking about the process of acculturation:

> The race relations cycle which takes the form . . . of contacts, competition, accommodation, and eventual assimilation, is apparently progressive and irreversible. Customs regulations, immigration restrictions and racial barriers may slacken the tempo of the movement; may perhaps halt it altogether for a time; but cannot change its direction; cannot, at any rate, reverse it.[31]

Thus for Park and his followers assimilation was foreordained and unilinear.

Rather than posing an obstacle to assimilation, the city was Park's melting pot *par excellence*.[32] For Park the impact of the city was quite similar to that of Turner's frontier; it broke the "cake of custom" and emancipated the individual. If this experience was painful and traumatic, Park left no doubt that he thought this price for individual freedom was worth paying. Within his theoretical scheme of urban ecology, Park associated spatial movements with cultural change. The process of assimilation was conceptualized in terms of physical mobility through successive zones of settlement. The movement of the immigrants outward from the ghetto culminated in their final absorption into the larger society. Where Turner had faltered, Park succeeded in expanding the assimilationist ideology to encompass the immigants of urban industrial America.

Scholarship on racial and ethnic groups was also profoundly influenced by the rise of cultural anthropology—and particularly by the work of Franz Boas.[33] The rejection of "scientific racism" and the establishment of the primacy of culture as the determinant of human behavior were obviously of fundamental importance to the study of ethnicity. But when anthropologists turned to the study of ethnic groups in modern America, their much-vaunted "cultural relativism" failed to immunize them against the assimilationist faith. Margaret Mead, herself a student of Boas, depicted the generational changes between immigrants and their children as involving a complete break and acculturation to the "American Way of Life" on the part of the second generation.[34]

Fresh from field work among the Australian aborigines, W. Lloyd Warner descended upon Yankee City in the early 1930's. Among the subjects he investigated was ethnicity. His findings were reported in

The Social Systems of American Ethnic Groups. Although it contains detailed descriptions of ethnic sub-cultures, the data are arranged within a Parkian theoretical framework. The various immigrant groups are depicted as moving along a continuum from peasant village culture to modern urban culture. Residential, occupational, and social-class indices are used to measure their movement up the escalator of social mobility toward total assimilation.[35] Anthropologists thus proved to be just as susceptible to the ethnocentric appeal of the assimilation creed as other social scientists.

American historians, of course, were influenced by the significant work being done in the social sciences. In 1932 a committee of the American Historical Association on the planning of research urged historians to avail themselves of the new insights being developed in anthropology, psychology, and sociology. The report of the Eastern Conference on American History cited as one neglected area of research the history of race relations and of race acculturation.[36] Not until 1939, however, were social scientific concepts explicitly brought to bear on the historical study of ethnic groups. At the American Historical Association meeting that year, Caroline F. Ware presented a paper on "Cultural Groups in the United States." [37] She noted the neglect by American historians of ethnic groups that deviated from the dominant literate culture. Observing that the interaction of the immigrants with the modern city was creating a new industrial culture, she concluded: "In the still unexplored history of the non-dominant cultural groups of the industrial cities lies the story of an emerging industrial culture that represents the dynamic cultural frontier of modern America." [38] Unfortunately, Ware's manifesto was heeded by too few. Three decades later the industrial culture of modern America remains largely "unexplored history."

A significant breakthrough came with the publication in 1941 of Oscar Handlin's *Boston's Immigrants: A Study in Acculturation.*[39] Informed by the insights of anthropology and sociology, the book expertly delineated the impact of immigration upon the culture, economy, ecology, and social structure of Boston. With the exception of the Irish, the newcomers assimilated readily. But the group consciousness and cohesion of the Irish were intensified by the bitter conflicts between them and the "others." From contacts of dissimilar cultures emerged an ethnic pluralism which left Boston a divided city. Here then was no tale of rapid, easy assimilation.

For several decades, Handlin has been the primary exponent, ex-

emplar, and teacher of the history of American ethnicity. In essays
and books, he has chronicled and championed cultural pluralism in
American life.[40] While acknowledging the ugliness of group hostility
and prejudice, Handlin has contended that in a chaotic world, ethnic
identity provides a much-needed source of stability and order.

Handlin, however, is best known for *The Uprooted*,[41] and this
work has had the greatest influence on the thinking of historians and
social scientists. The theme of *The Uprooted* is the utter devastation
of culture by environment. The immigrant is deracinated because none
of his traditional forms of thought and behavior can be transplanted.[42]
Its grim environmental determinism places *The Uprooted* squarely in
the tradition of Turner and Park. For all of them, the physical voyage
from the Old World to the New was also a sociological journey from
the traditional to the modern, from the sacred to the secular, from
Gemeinschaft to *Gesellschaft*. Paradoxically, Handlin, who more than
any other historian has advanced the study of ethnicity, in his most
influential work reinforced the assimilationist ideology.

Ethnicity in American historiography has remained something of a
family scandal, to be kept a dark secret or explained away. Even those
historians who have dealt with the theme in a competent fashion have
felt obliged to apologize for its existence.[43] Ethnic studies thus have
long suffered from the blight of the assimilationist ideology. Because
of their expectations that assimilation was to be swift and irresistible,
historians and social scientists have looked for change rather than
continuity, acculturation rather than cultural maintenance. Since ethnicity was thought to be evanescent, it was not considered worth
studying.[44]

The sociology of the academic profession may provide yet another
clue to the neglect of ethnicity. Although the shift from the patrician
to the professional historian had a democratizing effect on historical
study, the first generation of Ph.D.'s still tended to be drawn from
middle-class Protestants of old stock. It is not surprising that interest
in immigration history during this period was minimal, or that a
nativist bias pervaded much that was written.[45]

The sons of northern and western European immigrants began to
enter the profession in the twenties and thirties. Some of them devoted themselves to writing the history of their particular ethnic
groups, but scholarly work on the "new immigration" was practically
nonexistent. Few offspring of southern and eastern European paren-

tage were as yet able to avail themselves of the academic profession as a ladder of upward mobility. One reason, as E. Digby Baltzell has noted, was that until the 1940's the major universities continued to be the preserve of old-stock Protestants.[46] It has not been very long since certain history departments as a matter of policy did not hire Catholics or Jews, to say nothing of Negroes.

Since World War II, with the boom in higher education, the walls of ethnic exclusion around the groves of academe have come tumbling down. As a result there has been a significant influx of second- and third-generation Americans, many of them of Catholic and Jewish origin, into the historical profession. Yet there has been no outpouring of ethnic studies by these sons and grandsons of immigrants. Why is this so?

Higher education in America has been one of the most effective agencies of acculturation (or, to use Joshua Fishman's term, de-ethnization). Its primary function, as Baltzell has observed, has been to assimilate talented youth from all segments of society to the Anglo-American core culture.[47] College students of ethnic background therefore are prime candidates to become marginal men. For those who choose academic careers, the university may represent an escape from ethnicity. Milton Gordon has suggested that these "marginally ethnic intellectuals" constitute a distinct "transethnic" sub-society.[48] Be that as it may, the second- and third-generation scholars do assimilate the academic ethos; they dedicate themselves to the life of the mind and the rule of reason. As emancipated intellectuals they reject the narrow parochialisms and tribal loyalties of their youth.[49] The responses of certain academic men of Italian descent to an invitation to participate in a study of the Italian-American ethnic group illustrate this state of mind:

> I am too concerned with trying to erase all national boundaries— and nationalisms—to be enthusiastic about activities delineating any national groups.

> I do not believe there is room for an Italian minority. I suggest that Italians or persons of Italian origin have no recourse but to merge into the majority.[50]

Here we have the interesting phenomenon of the intellectual who not only rejects ethnic membership for himself but denies the validity of ethnicity for all others as well.

The de-ethnization of scholars is related to the larger process whereby the most able individuals of ethnic origin have been systematically assimilated into the establishment.[51] This "brain drain" inevitably has had a major impact on the life of ethnic groups. Presumably it has deprived them of potential leadership and contributed to their cultural impoverishment. The estrangement of many intellectuals from their ethnic roots may have something to do with their alienation from popular culture, while the widespread anti-intellectualism among ethnic Americans may reflect their resentment of those aloof professors whom they regard as traitors and Uncle Toms. Many ethnic groups sponsor historical societies which attempt to record in a more-or-less scholarly fashion the role and contribution of their particular element to American history. These efforts have not been generally viewed in a kindly fashion by professional historians. But it has been the "standoffish" attitude of historians of ethnic origin which has been most resented. The Polish American Historical Association *Bulletin* recently complained about professional historians of Polish background who remained distant from the organization: "Why are they not members? Are they academic snobs who are so ambitious that they do not want identification with 'an ethnic group'?" [52] Such academic snobbery, if such it is, is regrettable. For the cultivation of ethnic history might serve as one of the much-needed bridges between the university ghetto and the ethnic ghetto.[53]

In addition, the academic milieu has generally not encouraged the pursuit of ethnic interests. How many graduate students have shied away from research topics for fear they would be suspected of ethnic chauvinism? And historians of ethnic origin have on occasion been reminded of their marginal status. A few years ago, the president of the American Historical Association commented: ". . . many of the younger practitioners of our craft, and those who are still apprentices, are products of lower middle-class or foreign origins, and their emotions not infrequently get in the way of historical reconstruction. They find themselves in a very real sense outsiders on *our past* and feel themselves shut out." [54] Filio-piety, as anyone who has read any American history knows, has not been peculiar to ethnic historians, yet they have been particularly suspect.

For a variety of reasons, therefore, the recruitment of scholars of ethnic background has not, by and large, had the fruitful consequences for historical study that one might have anticipated. Those who deliberately dissociate themselves from their group ties often reject at the conscious level any suggestion of lingering ethnic loyalty. But it has been suggested that their repressed ethnicity manifests itself in a sublimated fashion. Although we claim to be free of primordial ties based on race, religion, or nation, yet we have tended to identify with "the underdogs and disinherited in modern society." In our history as well as our politics, we have often championed the causes of "captive groups." A consideration of the ethnic backgrounds of white historians of black America lends substance to the notion of sublimation of ethnicity. Can it be, as Melvin M. Tumin has suggested, that we have "used our hard-won freedom from the enmeshment of our own primary groups with all their irrationalities only to be adopted into the equally disenabling and restricting network of other primary group loyalties? Can it be that we cannot bear to be without primary group loyalties, causes, and missions?" [55]

Whatever the answer to that particular question, it is not my intention to promote the study of ethnicity as a "cause" or "mission." I do not conceive of historical scholarship as a form of advocacy or therapy, nor am I suggesting that historians of ethnic origin should necessarily devote themselves to the study of their groups. I think the doctrine that only the individual of a particular ethnic or racial background can "understand" the history of "his people" is pernicious. Often the "outsider" can bring to the subject certain perspectives which are denied to the "insider." The historian of ethnicity, whatever his origin, must, if he would remain true to his calling, eschew the role of advocate, no matter how noble the cause, in order to pursue the truth wherever it may lead him.

There are signs that the long winter of neglect of ethnicity is coming to an end. Perhaps the surest indication of spring is that publishers are scurrying about seeking to sign up authors for ethnic and minority history series. More solid assurances have come from the increasing number of books and articles by historians and others which deal competently with the ethnic factor. There is evidence that the heightened pluralism of society is being mirrored in a new scholarly interest in the sources of diversity. American historians are beginning to free themselves from their compulsive obsession with assimilation.

At this particular juncture of our national history, we have an urgent need for a clear-eyed scholarship of ethnicity. What the historian can best contribute is a realistic perspective on the dynamics of ethnic group life and interaction. In place of a homogenized American history, he must portray the complex variety of racial, religious, and cultural groups living together in conflict and concord. Our current concern with Afro-American history should not be allowed to obscure the larger whole of which it is a part. Certainly the racial polarization of which the National Advisory Commission on Civil Disorders warned —"two societies, one black, one white"—should not be projected into the past. Such an interpretation of American history would be a serious distortion of reality, ignoring as it would the class as well as ethnic factors which have been and remain important sources of differences among whites. The historian of ethnicity has the responsibility of insisting upon a pluralistic rather than a dichotomized view of the past.

An appreciation of our own diversity should not only enable us to deal more intelligently with group conflict at home; it should also permit us to relate more realistically to the rest of the world. Professor Fairbank has recently suggested that our survival may hinge upon our ability "to get a truer and multivalued, because multicultural, perspective on the world crisis . . ." [56] The arrogant assumption of the unquestionable superiority of the "American way of life" which underlies the assimilationist ideology is, I submit, an insuperable obstacle to such a world-view. A recent statement by Senator Richard Russell of Georgia, for example, expressed the ethnocentric doctrine of 100 per cent Americanism in its starkest form. Commenting on the possibility of nuclear war, the Senator said: "If we have to start over again with another Adam and Eve, I want them to be Americans; and I want them on this continent and not in Europe." [57] A candid recognition that the melting pot did not work, that we remain a congeries of peoples, that there are *many* American ways of life rather than *one,* might help us to discard our notion of ourselves as a "chosen people" and to affirm our common humanity with the rest of mankind.

NOTES

1. W. Lloyd Warner and Leo Srole, *The Social Systems of American Ethnic Groups, Yankee City Studies,* III (New Haven, 1945), 295.

2. Will Herberg, *Protestant-Catholic-Jew,* Anchor Book ed. (Garden City, 1960), pp. 22–23. This view was echoed by the historian Maldwyn Allen Jones in *American Immigration* (Chicago, 1960), p. 307: "In the middle of the twentieth century ethnic distinctions might still persist. But they were less sharp, less conspicuous than before and they were fading rapidly from view."

3. American Jewish Committee, *The Reacting Americans* (New York, 1968); Royal Commission on Bilingualism and Biculturalism, *Report: Book I, The Official Languages* (Ottawa, 1967). In a letter to the editor, a Finnish-American wrote as follows: "Strides toward freedom can only come through being proud of their Finn-ness as it is essential for the blacks to become proud of their blackness." *Minneapolis Tribune,* March 30, 1969.

4. Nathan Glazer and Daniel P. Moynihan, *Beyond the Melting* Pot (Cambridge, Mass., 1963), p. 290; see also Milton Gordon, *Assimilation in American Life* (New York, 1964), p. 265; Joshua A. Fishman, *Language Loyalty in the United States* (The Hague, 1966), p. 31.

5. Peter I. Rose, *The Subject Is Race* (New York, 1968), p. 168; Charles S. Kamen, "On the Neglect of Immigrants by American Sociologists," unpublished paper (National Opinion Research Center, University of Chicago, 1967).

6. "The Writing and Teaching of American History in Textbooks," *AHA Newsletter,* VI (April 1968), 8–9.

7. Based on a survey of course descriptions in catalogs of colleges and universities in all parts of the country.

8. Rose, *Subject,* pp. 167–169.

9. There are fewer than one hundred American historians on the mailing list of the Immigration History Group.

10. The analysis was based on Warren Kuehl, *Dissertations in History* for the years 1873–1960 and on *Index to American Doctoral Dissertations* for 1961–1965. I am indebted to my former research assistant, Dr. Charles Clark, for assistance in preparing this analysis.

11. Examples of such histories would be: Blake McKelvey, *The Urbanization of America, 1860–1915* (New Brunswick, N.J., 1963); Joseph G. Rayback, *A History of American Labor* (New York, 1959); and John T. Ellis, *American Catholicism* (Chicago, 1965). The lack of studies of the impact of immigration on the schools is noted by Lawrence A. Cremin, *The Transformation of the School,* Vintage Book ed. (New York, 1961), p. 365. On the neglect of immigration in the historiography of the American Catholic Church, see Rudolph J. Vecoli, "Prelates and Peasants," *Journal of Social History,* II (Spring 1969), 217–268.

12. John K. Fairbank, "Assignment for the '70's," *American Historical Review,* LXXIV (February 1969), 869.

13. For a statistical analysis of ethnic publications, see Fishman, *Language Loyalty,* pp. 51–74.

14. For an elaboration of this argument, see Rudolph J. Vecoli, "The Immigration Studies Collection of the University of Minnesota," *American Archivist,* XXXII (April 1969), 139–145.

15. *Letters from an American Farmer,* paperback ed. (New York, 1957), p. 39.

16. John Higham, *History* (Englewood Cliffs, N.J., 1965), p. 192.

17. Turner wrote in 1891: "The story of the peopling of America has not yet been written. We do not understand ourselves." Quoted in Lee Benson, *Turner and Beard* (New York, 1960), p. 82.

18. Frederick Jackson Turner, *The Frontier in American History* (New York, 1920). In his later study of sectionalism, Turner recognized the role of cultural influences carried to the frontier by immigrants. He professed to see a "mixing bowl" rather than "melting pot" at work in the Old Northwest, but he was quite vague as to the outcome. He acknowledged the influence of Marcus Lee Hansen on his thinking about immigrant heritages. *The United States, 1830–1850* (New York, 1935), pp. 280–287.

19. Carl Wittke, *We Who Built America* (New York, 1939), p. 446, also chap. 13, "Culture in Immigrant Chests"; Theodore C. Blegen, *Grass Roots History* (Minneapolis, 1947).

20. M. L. Hansen, "The Third Generation in America," *Commentary,* XIV (November 1952), 500; *The Immigrant in American History* (New York, 1940); *The Atlantic Migration, 1607–1860* (Cambridge, Mass., 1940); Allan H. Spear, "Marcus Lee Hansen and the Historiography of Immigration," *Wisconsin Magazine of History,* XLIV (1961), 258–268.

21. Hansen, "Third Generation," p. 499.

22. In a little-known essay, Edward Mims, Jr., attributed American historians' indifference to the study of immigration to the nationalistic influence of the frontier thesis. The disciples of Turner, Mims asserted, emphasized the effects of environment to the neglect of European cultural backgrounds. Mims argued that the older Turner came to appreciate the role of immigrant influences, as did those of his followers who were exponents of "neo-Turnerism." *American History and Immigration* (Bronxville, N.Y., 1950). See also Marcus Lee Hansen's remarks in Dixon Ryan Fox, ed., *Sources of Culture in the Middle West* (New York, 1934), pp. 103–110.

23. Ray Allen Billington, *Westward Expansion,* 3rd ed. (New York, 1967), pp. 1–3, 308, 706, 746. David M. Potter, *People of Plenty* (Chicago, 1954); Daniel Boorstin, *The Americans: The National Experience* (New York, 1965); George W. Pierson, "The M-Factor in American History," *American Quarterly,* XIV (Summer 1962), 275–289.

24. Merle Curti, *The Making of an American Community* (Stanford, 1959).

25. Andrew Rolle, *The Immigrant Upraised* (Norman, Okla., 1968).

26. Rolle, *Immigrant,* p. x. Billington also commented that Rolle had demonstrated "for the first time that the Western environment could escalate the foreign- no less than the native-born"!

27. Turner, *United States,* pp. 53–55, 94–96. See also Turner's series of newspaper articles dealing with various immigrant groups, *Chicago Record-Herald,* June 19–October 16, 1901.

28. Charles and Mary Beard, *The Rise of American Civilization,* 2 vols.

(New York, 1927). Beard revealed an admiration for the politics and agricultural bent of the Germans and Scandinavians (II, 143); in this he shared the preferences of the Turnerians.

29. Benson, *Turner*, pp. 154–160.

30. Robert Ezra Park, *Race and Culture*, paperback ed. (New York, 1964), pp. 205–206.

31. Park, *Race*, p. 150. Park's colleague and associate, W. I. Thomas, the co-author with Florian Znaniecki of the influential work *The Polish Peasant in Europe and America* (Boston, 1918), shared this assimilationist perspective. He concluded: "Assimilation is . . . as inevitable as it is desirable; it is impossible for the immigrants we receive to remain permanently in separate groups." Edmund H. Volkart, ed., *Social Behavior and Personality: Contributions of W. I. Thomas to Theory and Social Research* (New York, 1951), p. 285.

32. I have benefited from Michael Passi's seminar paper, "Metropolis, Evolution, and Ethnicity: Robert Ezra Park," and discussions with him, in this analysis of Park.

33. George W. Stocking, Jr., *Race, Culture, and Evolution* (New York, 1968), pp. 195–233. Pointing to the persistence of the Lamarckian doctrine of inheritance of acquired characteristics, Stocking suggests it may have provided the rationale for the "melting pot" (p. 245). Boas himself, in his study of changes in bodily forms of descendants of immigrants, concluded that "the head form, which has always been considered one of the most stable and permanent characteristics of human races, undergoes far-reaching changes due to the transfer of the people from European to American soil." U.S. Immigration Commission, *Abstracts of Reports*, 2 vols. (Washington, D.C., 1911), II, 501–556. This conclusion, of course, reinforced the belief in the transforming power of the American environment.

34. Margaret Mead, *And Keep Your Powder Dry* (New York, 1965), p. 46. With obvious satisfaction, she wrote: "Almost miraculously the sons of the Polish day laborer and the Italian fruit grower, the Finnish miner and the Russian garment worker became Americans."

35. Warner, *Social Systems*. Writing in 1962, Warner was less dogmatic about the inevitability of assimilation. *American Life: Dream and Reality* (Chicago, 1962), p. 205.

36. Committee of the American Historical Association on the Planning of Research, *Historical Scholarship In America* (New York, 1932), pp. 92–93. "Race" as used here was the equivalent of ethnic.

37. Caroline F. Ware, "Cultural Groups in the United States," in Ware, ed., *The Cultural Approach to History* (New York, 1940), pp. 61–89.

38. Ware, "Cultural Groups," p. 73.

39. Rev. ed., Cambridge, Mass., 1959.

40. Oscar Handlin, *The American People in the Twentieth Century* (Cambridge, Mass., 1954); *Race and Nationality in American Life* (Boston, 1957); "Historical Perspectives on the American Ethnic Group," *Daedalus* (Spring 1961), pp. 220–232.

41. Boston, 1951.

42. *Ibid.*, pp. 170–171.

43. Robert Ernst, *Immigrant Life in New York City, 1825–1863* (New York, 1949), concludes with this reassurance: "Time, however, lessened the tenacious, old loyalties as the faces of immigrants turned west instead of east. Though the foreign born might rarely venture beyond the pale of New York's ghettos,

their children grew more like the Americans, and their children's children became an integral part of America" (p. 184).

44. Fishman, *Language Loyalty*, pp. 15, 21, 86; Kamen, "On Neglect," pp. 6–7.

45. Higham, *History*, pp. 52–67. See also Edward N. Saveth, *American Historians and European Immigrants, 1875–1925* (New York, 1948).

46. E. Digby Baltzell, *The Protestant Establishment*, Vintage ed. (New York, 1966), pp. 335–342.

47. *Ibid.*

48. Gordon, *Assimilation*, pp. 224–230.

49. Fishman, *Language Loyalty*, p. 372; Melvin M. Tumin, "In Dispraise of Loyalty," *Social Problems*, XV (Winter 1968), 267–279.

50. Personal communications.

51. Gordon, *Assimilation*, p. 256; Caroline F. Ware, "Immigration," *Encyclopaedia of the Social Sciences*, IV, 592.

52. Polish American Historical Association, *Bulletin*, XXIV (January–June 1968), 3.

53. Rudolph J. Vecoli, "Ethnic Historical Societies: From Filiopiety to Scholarship," an unpublished paper read at a joint session of the American Historical Association and the American Jewish Historical Society, Toronto, December 28, 1967.

54. Carl Bridenbaugh, "The Great Mutation," *American Historical Review* (January 1963), p. 322. My emphasis.

55. Tumin, "In Dispraise," p. 275.

56. Fairbank, "Assignment," p. 863.

57. Quoted in George Wald, "A Generation in Search of a Future," *New Yorker* (March 22, 1969), p. 31.

The State of
Social Welfare History

ROBERT H. BREMNER

Social welfare history is one of the newer areas of historical specialization. The subject, of course, is not new; it has a long history and a sizable literature. The only thing new about social welfare history is the professional historian's interest in it. In this respect it is like urban history, black history, medical history, business history, educational history, the history of science and technology, and the history of the family and children. In all of these areas historians are moving into fields which used to be considered the domains of other disciplines. In the case of social welfare history the writers were, until quite recently, social workers, sociologists, and economists. The growth of the professional historian's interest in such areas mirrors the concerns of our times. It also reflects the expansion of historical consciousness in the twentieth century. While each of us as individuals may be more and more specialized in our interests and competence, history as a whole has never been more comprehensive than today.

Our first problem is to define the boundaries of social welfare history. How inclusive or how restricted is its territory? What does it cover? What is its content? The broadest definition I know was advanced by William Graham Sumner in an essay entitled "Sociology" written in 1881. Sumner objected that social welfare was always treated as a novel issue. "In truth," Sumner declared, "the human race has never done anything else but struggle with the problem of social welfare. That struggle constitutes history, or the life of the human race on earth." But then Sumner went on to assert: "The only two things which really tell on the welfare of man on earth are hard work and self-denial . . . and these tell most when they are brought to bear directly upon the effort to earn an honest living, to accumulate capital, and to bring up a family of children to be industrious and self-denying in their turn. I repeat this is the way to work for the welfare of man on earth." [1]

Sumner's statement illustrates an oft-observed paradox: the more broadly a field is defined, the narrower its content. If we accept Sumner's definition and interpretation of welfare, we must omit the social aspects of the problem and concentrate on the history of economic individualism. But, in truth, to borrow Sumner's words, it is the organized character of welfare activities, the group auspices under which they are conducted, the social rather than the individual goals and rewards to which the programs are directed, and the social responsibility or accountability of the participants which distinguish social welfare from individual self-help. [2]

In 1880 one of Sumner's contemporaries, Theodore Dwight, professor of law at Columbia University, defined social welfare as "aid of the dependent classes in society . . . the care of paupers, habitual drunkards, the insane, the blind, the dumb, and vicious and neglected children." [3] Eighty years later Vaughn D. Bornet offered a more succinct definition: "special services supplied by all and material assistance given by all or part of society to a human being thought to be in need." [4] In the future we may amend Bornet's definition to read "services supplied to all and material assistance furnished *as a right* to human beings objectively determined to be in need." [5] Because the scope of social welfare has varied from time to time, its boundaries have contracted or expanded. Individual scholars or groups of scholars may attempt to define a field, but their definitions are always influenced and sometimes overtaken by the course of historical events. Instead of issuing flat statements on what social welfare history is or is not, should be or should not be, let us see what it has been.

A good place to begin is with Franklin B. Sanborn's articles on the historical development of public welfare in New England, which appeared in the *North American Review* between 1868 and 1872. Sanborn, who was secretary and later chairman of the Massachusetts Board of State Charities, also prepared a history of the public charities of Massachusetts for the 1876 centennial celebration. In the first of his articles, Sanborn observed that Daniel Defoe's pamphlet, *Giving Alms No Charity*, published in 1704, had set the fashion for much of the writing on poor relief in the eighteenth and nineteenth centuries. In a way, Sanborn's essays set the pattern for much of the social welfare history written in the last hundred years. Sanborn wrote as a participant, deeply involved in the struggle to improve the legal structure and administration of social welfare, dissatisfied with and critical of the current working of the system. His interest in history was dictated by his concern with the problems of his own day, and he looked to history for an explanation of how those problems had developed. Presentism has been one of the characteristics of American social welfare history because so much of it has been written by people like Sanborn who were as much makers as writers of history.[6]

The working relationship between historians and social workers can be traced back to the nineteenth century. In recent years historians and social workers have met at conferences to discuss poverty; in the 1880's they used to get together to discuss "charities," specifically to talk about the proper methods of organizing and administering aid to the poor. For one such conference, held in Baltimore in 1887, the historian Herbert Baxter Adams prepared a bibliographical essay, "Notes on the Literature of Charities," which was subsequently published in a volume of the Johns Hopkins University *Studies in Historical and Political Science.*[7] Adams was chairman of the department of history at Johns Hopkins, and a founder and the first secretary of the American Historical Association. One could not, he avowed, understand English and American institutions for the relief of pauperism "without some historical reading"; Adams regarded the historical point of view as the best of all approaches to the literature of charities. His essay, however, contained very few references to historical works. He mentioned Sanborn's writings and Sir George Nicholls' *History of the English Poor Law,* but for the most part the literature he discussed related to the problems and movements of his own day. One reason for Adams' neglect of history was his conviction that history had nothing of value to contribute to knowledge of charities except the negative lesson that largesse to the common people was terribly dangerous. "If one would really understand the movements of social science and organized charities in the nineteenth century," Adams wrote, "he should at the outset grasp the fundamental fact that, for eighteen centuries, the charitable and legislative efforts of society have been pauperizing instead of elevating men." It was only in the nineteenth century that the "great work of organizing charity into self-help" commenced.[8]

Probably the most important American contribution to the literature of charities in the late nineteenth century was Amos G. Warner's *American Charities: A Study in Philanthropy and Economics* (1894). Warner was a product of the department of history, politics, and economics of John Hopkins; he had served as superintendent of charities for the District of Columbia and as general agent of the Charity Organization Society of Baltimore; at the time *American Charities* was published he was professor of economics and social science at Stanford University. Warner's book is a synthesis of nineteenth-century knowledge of the science of "philanthropology." It is of immense value to historians as a source for attitudes toward and informed opinion about the "dependent classes" at the close of the nineteenth century. Yet it was not, and was not intended to be, a contribution to social welfare history. Warner, like Adams, thought the history of social welfare before the nineteenth century was a chronicle of errors.

The November 1899 issue of *The Charities Review* announced the forthcoming publication of "a historical study of American philanthropy of the nineteenth century." The announcement continued:

> The purpose in view has been to bring to bear on the present problems of American social workers a concise knowledge of the historical evolution through which the charities of this country have passed during the century.

According to the prospectus the work was to be divided into nine divisions:

Institutional care of destitute adults, by Robert W. Hebberd, secretary of the New York State Board of Charities;

Defectives: the insane, feeble-minded and epileptic, by Peter M. Wise, president of the New York State Commission on Lunacy;

Hospitals, dispensaries, and nursing, by Henry M. Hurd, superintendent of the Johns Hopkins Hospital;

Destitute, neglected, and delinquent children, by Homer Folks, secretary of the New York State Charities Aid Association;

Care and relief of needy families, by Edward T. Devine, general secretary of the New York Charity Organization Society;

The treatment of criminals, by Charlton T. Lewis, president of the Prison Association of New York;

Supervisory and educational movements by Jeffrey R. Brackett, lecturer on public aid, charity, and correction at Johns Hopkins University; and

Preventive work by Joseph Lee, Boston philanthropist and social worker.

Three of the studies were eventually published as books: Folks's history of child welfare, Brackett's study of supervision and education in charities, and Lee's volume on preventive work.[9] Each remains valuable as a reference work; the volume by Folks is a minor classic.

My point in recalling the series is not to discuss the individual volumes but to consider what the project indicates about the state of social welfare history seventy years ago. One of the things immediately apparent is that social welfare history was then written mainly by people who were not historians. Only one of the nine authors, Jeffrey Brackett, could be classified as a member of the historical profession. Brackett received a Ph.D. from Johns Hopkins in 1889; his dissertation was a history of the Negro in Maryland. The other authors were executives or administrators of important public or private agencies. The series also reveals the content of social welfare at the turn of the century: (1) public and private provision for the poor, the ill, the mentally and physically handicapped, the criminal, and the delinquent; (2) methods of administering and supervising public relief and private charity; and (3) "preventive work" such as improved housing, savings and loan banks, playgrounds, gymnasiums, and parks.

Let us suppose that a few years from now someone projects a series of volumes dealing with the history of philanthropy (using that word in its original and inclusive sense) in the twentieth century. How will that series differ from "American philanthropy in the nineteenth century"? In the first place it will not be necessary to rely on busy agency executives to write the books. Most, if not all, of the authors will be historians. More important than the change in authorship, however, will be the change in content. Like the series projected in 1899, the new one will have to deal with public and private provision for people "thought to be in need." But it will also have to include the people not currently in need who are nevertheless guarded against need by social security and other social insurance programs, the "preventive work" of our century. It will also have to take into consideration people of all ages and economic conditions who are increasingly making use of social services, not as a charity but as a right. In dealing with private giving, the work will have to examine the rise of foundations, their support of social research and demonstration, and their relations with government, universities, and public opinion.

The new social welfare history will have a much larger cast of char-
acters than the old. Instead of just the poor and unfortunate and their
helpers (the fortunate and the wise), the cast will include a very large
share of the population. It will grow even larger as we move from an
admittedly imperfect welfare state toward a welfare society. In the past,
social welfare history has been written from the standpoint of (and
usually by) the givers of assistance and service; in the future it will very
likely be written by and from the point of view of the recipients and
beneficiaries. If, as seems probable, social welfare becomes an increasingly important concern of society, it will become more and more
difficult to separate social welfare history from general political and
social history.

So much for the state of social welfare history in the past and in
the future. Where do we stand in social welfare history today? Thomas
J. Campbell, secretary of the Social Welfare History Group, estimates
that since 1964 more than two hundred doctoral dissertations have been
registered and 105 books published whose subjects bear on some aspects
of social welfare history. The scope and variety of these studies is indicated in the bibliographies of books and articles and the listings of
work in progress reported in recent issues of the swHG *Newsletter.*
They fall into six broad and overlapping categories:

1. Biographies of social welfare leaders.[10]
2. Histories and analyses of reform movements.[11]
3. Histories of public health.[12]
4. Histories and analyses of voluntary agencies, private philanthropy,
and philanthropic foundations.[13]
5. Histories of social work.[14]
6. Histories of public welfare.[15]

This, then, is what social welfare history now is. But what is that?
In looking over the list I am reminded of Roy Lubove's observation:
"Urban history, as understood today, is virtually synonymous with
everything that happened in cities." [16] Just so, social welfare history,
as currently practiced, is synonymous with everything that happened in
social welfare. We are still in the department-store stage of development, in which the individual historian can shop around and choose
from a wide variety of items according to his particular interests. I must
confess that I find this a congenial situation. But I can imagine some-
body saying about social welfare history what Eric Lampard said about
urban history. Lampard, you may recall, objected that urban history
had been largely concerned with the history of cities and their prob-

lems, not with the history of urbanization.[17] In similar fashion, someone may object that social welfare historians have dealt with the history of social welfare agencies, programs, and problems—but that they have ignored "welfarization," the broad societal process by which welfare has come to assume an increasingly important place in modern social arrangements. I would be prepared to argue, however, that what we are all trying to do, and what political, social, economic, and intellectual historians are also trying to do, is to trace the history of the processes that have made social welfare a leading concern of our times.

Dorothy Marshall, at the end of her chapter on "The Poor" in *Eighteenth-Century England,* concluded: "Political, social, and economic history are one and indivisible." [18] In similar fashion I would stress not the uniqueness but the closeness and connectedness of social welfare history to political, social, and economic history, as well as to medical, educational, and urban history.

The general needs of social welfare history are similar to—I am tempted to say identical with—the needs of other branches of history: we need to be more precise, and hence I think we will pay more attention to local history and to quantification. At the same time we need to be more comparative in our outlook. Social welfare, as Sumner told us, is the central problem of the life of the human race on earth. The fostering or neglect of social welfare in any society should be of interest to us whether the society is an ancient or a contemporary one. At the very least, we should consider similarities and dissimilarities between the extent and methods of welfare in different states and regions of the United States. If social welfare history has the advantage of relevancy, it also has the advantage of being largely unwritten. Everyone with whom I have discussed the unfinished business of social welfare history has commented on the thinness of biographical studies in this field. There is a need for biographies, not only individual biographies of social welfare leaders but collective biographies of such groups as the aged, orphans, widows, paupers, and the unemployed, who have been objects of social welfare concern or neglect. During the past fifteen years much has been written about the nature and sources of various American reform movements. New insights will no doubt lead to a reassessment of some social welfare reform movements. I think everyone is agreed that we need not more chronologies of poor laws but realistic accounts of how social welfare programs actually worked in given times and places. Other areas which remain to be explored include detailed and analytical studies of working agencies, both public and private; histories of professional associations; and in-depth studies of the processes of professionalization in public welfare and social work. Through the efforts of Clarke Chambers and his associates, important and extensive documentation for such studies is now available at the Social Welfare History Archives of the University of Minnesota.

Suppose we perform our tasks reasonably well. What purposes do we serve? What is the object of our labors? First, we serve each other and add to the store of knowledge of social welfare history by learning things we didn't know, didn't understand, or misunderstood. Second, we can serve social welfare policy-makers by providing accurate accounts of the circumstances, events, and considerations which led us to the present situation. I am sometimes abashed by the confidence policy-makers express in history as an aid in problem-solving. Thirty years ago Grace Abbott, in *The Child and the State,* wrote:

> For an understanding of our present situation and how the obstacles to progress may be overcome it is necessary to know the road we have travelled, the wrong turns that have been made because objectives were not clearly defined and because of fear to try a new road even when it was clear that the old one was only a *cul-de-sac.*[19]

Recently one of Miss Abbott's students, James Brown IV, made the same point in a review of a reprint of Charles Loring Brace's *The Dangerous Classes of New York:*

> One reason for reading history is to gain perspective and profit by earlier mistakes. *The Dangerous Classes* is an important item in the history of child welfare and abounds in examples of mistakes that should not be repeated. . . . Much of the money that has gone down the drain in the war on poverty might have been saved if the war strategists in the Office of Economic Opportunity had read some history.[20]

My own feeling is that what the historian can offer those who contend with current social issues is not historical precedents or information about right or wrong turns in the road map to the present—not knowledge, not solutions—but method, openness, and sensitivity.

Finally, the most valuable thing social welfare historians can do is to serve the other branches of the discipline of which we are a part. People, their problems, and their aspirations are the central concern of our research. In that respect we are not unique. But because of the special angle of vision from which we study the past, we have an opportunity and responsibility to lighten, enliven, and humanize the study of history.

NOTES

1. William Graham Sumner, "Sociology," in Albert Galloway Keller, ed., *War and Other Essays by William Graham Sumner* (New Haven, 1911), p. 186.

2. For current conceptions of social welfare, see Harold L. Wilensky and Charles N. Lebeaux, *Industrial Society and Social Welfare* (New York, 1965), pp. 138–147.

3. Theodore Dwight, "The Public Charities of the State of New York," *Journal of Social Science,* II (1870), 69.

4. Vaughn D. Bornet, "The Manuscripts of Social Welfare," *American Archivist,* XXIII (1960), 33.

5. See, for example, U.S. Department of Health, Education and Welfare, *Services for People, Report of the Task Force on Organization of Social Services* (Washington, D.C., 1968), and National Association of Social Workers, *So All May Live in Decency and Dignity* (New York, 1967).

6. Among other social welfare leaders who have contributed to its historical literature are Homer Folks, Edward T. Devine, Arthur Altmeyer, Edwin Witte, Wilbur Cohen, Charles Schottland, and Karl De Schweinitz. The tendency toward a pragmatic view of history was especially marked among members of the Chicago School, such as Sophonisba Breckinridge and Edith and Grace Abbott.

7. Fifth Series (Baltimore, 1887).

8. *Ibid.,* pp. 43–44.

9. Homer Folks, *The Care of Destitute, Neglected, and Delinquent Children* (New York, 1902); Jeffrey R. Brackett, *Supervision and Education in Charity* (New York, 1903); Joseph Lee, *Constructive and Preventive Philanthropy* (New York, 1906).

10. Walter I. Trattner, *Homer Folks, Pioneer in Social Welfare* (New York, 1968) does justice to the range and importance of Folks's activities in his long career. Dorothy Becker, "Social Welfare Leaders as Spokesmen for the Poor," *Social Casework,* XLIX (1968), 82–89, sketches composite pictures of social welfare leaders, male and female, in the period 1880–1914.

11. Two good recent examples are Jeremy Felt, *Child Labor Reform in New York State* (Syracuse, 1965), and Roy Lubove, *The Struggle for Social Security* (Cambridge, Mass., 1968).

12. See, for example, John Duffy, *Sword of Pestilence: The New Orleans*

Yellow Fever Epidemic of 1853 (Baton Rouge, 1966), and *The History of Public Health in New York City, 1625–1866* (New York, 1968).

13. A good starting point is *Report of the Princeton Conference on the History of Philanthropy in the United States* (New York, 1956). Recent works include Merle Curti, *American Philanthropy Abroad* (New Brunswick, N.J., 1963), and Curti and Roderick Nash, *Philanthropy in the Shaping of American Higher Education* (New Brunswick, N.J., 1965). Representative studies of local agencies are Jon A. Peterson, "From Social Settlement to Social Agency: Settlement Work in Columbus, Ohio, 1898–1958," *Social Service Review,* XXXIX (1965), 191–208, and Elizabeth Wisner, "The Howard Association of New Orleans," *Social Service Review,* XLI (1967), 411–418.

14. Roy Lubove, *The Professional Altruist* (Cambridge, Mass., 1965) traces the emergence of social work as a career, 1880–1930; Clarke Chambers, *Seedtime of Reform* (Minneapolis, 1963) is a sympathetic account of social workers in the 1920's.

15. Samuel Mencher, *Poor Law to Poverty Program* (Pittsburgh, 1967) treats the development of British and American policy toward the able-bodied poor. Grace Coll, *Perspectives on Public Welfare* (Washington, D.C., 1969) is a history of public assistance. On social security, see Edwin E. Witte, *Development of the Social Security Act* (Madison, Wisc., 1963), and Arthur Altmeyer, *The Formative Years of Social Security: A Chronicle of Social Security Legislation and Administration, 1934–1954* (Madison, Wisc., 1966). Two quantitative studies are Ida Merriam, "Social Welfare Expenditures, 1929–1967," *Social Security Bulletin,* December 1967, pp. 3–16, and James W. Wilkie, *The Mexican Revolution: Federal Expenditure and Social Change Since 1910* (Berkeley and Los Angeles, 1967). James Leiby, *Charity and Correction in New Jersey* (New Brunswick, N.J., 1967) is an excellent history of welfare at the state level.

16. Roy Lubove, "The Urbanization Process: An Approach to Historical Research," *Journal of the American Institute of Planners,* January 1967, p. 33.

17. Eric Lampard, "American Historians and the Study of Urbanization," *American Historical Review,* LXVII (1961–1962), 49.

18. (New York, 1962), p. 40.

19. Grace Abbott, *The Child and the State* (Chicago, 1938), I, vii.

20. *Social Service Review,* XLII (December 1968), 512.

The Moral and Theological Revolution of the 1960's and Its Implications for American Religious History

SYDNEY E. AHLSTROM

The essential mark of the truly modern historian—as against not only the panegyrist, the annalist, and the mythmaker, but even such giants of the past as Gibbon and Thucydides—is his awareness of a fundamental paradox that confounds the historian's task, an intrinsic difficulty that makes all history-writing a Sisyphean labor. This awareness was clearly stated at least as early as 1599, when Henri Lancelot Voisin, Sieur de la Popelinière, made the dual observation that, on the one hand, the historian is obliged to tell things as they actually happened (*reciter la chose comme elle est advenue*) but that, on the other hand, historians invariably represent events "not according to former times and customs but according to the age in which the writer lives." [1] For the mid-twentieth-century historian this double acknowledgment has come to be virtually axiomatic. Despite his commitment to veracity, he recognizes that the circumstances of his existence have a great deal to do with his apprehension of the past; he knows that a new present *always* creates a new past. If nothing else, it lengthens the extent of recorded time which he must interpret. The passage of the years 1965–1969, for example, added the Johnson administration to the world's collective past; and the historian must interpret not only these new events but their backward-moving reverberations.

At certain times, the course of events lays a particularly burdensome demand for reinterpretation upon the historian; and I would suggest that for the historian of religious developments the decade of the sixties has had this effect in several inescapable ways. These have been

years not only of peculiarly intense moral urgency and of rapid institutional change, but of radical transformation in precisely those realms
of sensibility and valuation which have the largest effect on our way
of understanding the intellectual tradition in which we live. This circumstance entails or will entail correlatively radical historical revisions. But before we get on to those problems we do well to consider
our own tumultuous decade more closely.

The period since 1960 has been revolutionary in its character as well
as its likely consequences. Like many of its elegant, gay, or roaring
predecessors, therefore, the Decade of the Death of God or the
Decade of the Great Moral Revolution will certainly get a name or
two. These names, moreover, will rest on actualities far more profound than, say, the gaiety of the troubled nineties or the elegance of
the eighties. The 1960s *did* experience a fundamental shift in the
aesthetic, moral, and religious attitudes of Americans. It will probably
be seen as a decisive turning point in American history.[2]
One salient feature of the sixties that may serve as an instance or
symbol of the more general phenomenon was the emergence of a
radical movement in theology. It has special significance for the religious historian because it has involved a major reappraisal of the
most assured elements of the historic Judeo-Christian consensus. From
beyond the grave, Dietrich Bonhoeffer's demand for a "secular interpretation" of biblical language has been answered by a deluge of
serious efforts to meet the needs of a "world come of age." [3] In
America it was H. Richard Niebuhr who delivered the crucial inaugural address to the sixties with his great essay on *Radical Monotheism* (1960), but it was perhaps Gabriel Vahanian who first brought
Nietzsche's famous phrase into currency with his book on *The Death
of God: The Culture of Our Post-Christian Era* (1961). Demonstrating
the widespread acceptance of the altered situation were three star-
tlingly popular best-sellers: Bishop J. A. T. Robinson's *Honest to God*
(1963) in Great Britain, Pierre Berton's *The Comfortable Pew* (1965)
in Canada, and Harvey Cox's *The Secular City* (1965) in the United
States. More abstruse theological and scholarly problems have in the
meantime been addressed by many impressive thinkers, some of them
taking cues from Karl Barth's assault on "religious" values, others following out Rudolf Bultmann's program for a "demythologized" biblical message.[4] In the Roman Catholic Church the call of Pope John
XXIII for *aggiornamento* and the decrees of the Second Vatican Coun-

cil are the most obvious signs of the times, but many distinguished Catholic theologians have shown even greater boldness in their willingness to invest old doctrines with new meanings.[5] Among Jews, too, radical theology has found spokesmen of great eloquence, with Rabbi Richard L. Rubenstein receiving perhaps the widest audience with his *After Auschwitz* (1966). Specific manifestations aside, the trend thus marked out constituted a significant shift in Western religious thinking, and like all such intellectual revolutions it was irreversible.[6]

Contemporaneous with this development and closely related to it was a veritable tidal wave of questioning of all the traditional structures of Christendom, above all the so-called "parish" church. After Peter Berger's sounding of an early tocsin with his *The Noise of Solemn Assemblies* (1961), "morphological fundamentalism" became the key word of the Protestant reformers. Roman Catholics and, to a lesser extent, Jews soon became involved in a similar process of institutional reformation. Concomitantly, old pietistic forms of the religious life as well as liturgical ceremonialism have been deeply eroded.[7] Traditional forms of evangelism both at home and on "foreign mission fields" have been seriously questioned by all but the most culturally alienated religious groups.[8]

In the realm of ethics and the moral life an equally significant shift of consensus can be noted.[9] Not only did the mass media devote much time or space to a "new morality," but even in doing so they often exploited a new permissiveness by dealing frankly with long-forbidden subjects. In schools, colleges, and universities this "moral revolution" took the form of opposition to the traditional doctrine that such institutions operate *in loco parentis*. Other critics, both black and white, applied the epithet of "morphological fundamentalism" to the structures of academic life. Questions of loyalty and obedience to constituted authority, meanwhile, have been reopened with an intensity that can be compared only to the American Revolution itself. Matching these trends was a distinct tendency among ethical thinkers to propose less legalistic, more situational modes of guiding the moral life. In the meantime, nearly every church body in America (as well as many in Europe, including the Roman Catholic in the person of Pope Paul VI) decided—after two millennia—that the time had come to appoint a commission to reexamine questions of sexual ethics. Almost every state in the union, in turn, has enacted or is considering reform legislation in the realms of marriage, divorce, adultery, abortion, and birth control.[10]

No account of the decade's radicalism, especially at the ethical level, is complete unless it also recognizes the ways in which a vast moral renewal has been taking place. The revolt against institutional hypocrisy, code morality, depersonalized life styles, and social inhumanity has in fact taken the form of a large and growing counter-culture, both in the black and other racial minorities, and in the student movements. But most of the organized protest of the sixties is not basically a "revolution of nihilism." It stems from moral indignation and expresses a desire for more exalted grounds of action than social success, greater affluence, and national self-interest. Safe, calculating prudentialism is not the order of the day.[11] In summary, one may safely say that for Americans of every type, whether thinking or unthinking, whether Catholic, Protestant, Jew, or Humanist, the 1960's have been a time of shaking foundations.

The impact of the decade's revolution is pervasive; it is by no means limited to church-going people or to religious affairs. The ultimate commitments and modes of understanding of almost all Americans—including those who give very little overt thought to religious matters—have been deeply shaken. One should not even talk in very strict terms of a generation gap. It is hardly a children's crusade that has corroded the country's civil religion and undermined its most venerable forms of patriotic reverence. The plan to integrate our national holy days—Independence Day, Memorial Day, and Armistice Day—into convenient long weekends is the work of superannuated congressmen.[12] Penn T. Kimball of Columbia University suggested something of this state of affairs in connection with a passing "narcotics scandal" in Westport, Connecticut. "Drug-taking by teen-agers has nothing to do with character," he observed. "It's more a symptom of a general malaise, a sadness which is sweeping our whole society." [13] Nearly every important social institution and many unimportant ones reveal the impact of dissatisfaction, disruption, and revolt. The National Committee for an Effective Congress in a report on Christmas Day, 1967, spoke of a "depression of the national spirit." Pointing out that terms such as malaise, frustration. alienation, and identity crisis had become part of the professional political vocabulary, the report went on to state that "at all levels of American life, people share similar fears, insecurities, and gnawing doubts to such an intense degree that the country may in fact be suffering from a kind of national nervous breakdown." The confessions of parched lives and spiritual pointlessness that dominated the audience response at a recent student protest meeting reminded a scientist at Yale of the Methodist prayer meetings of his youth. The 1968 Nobel Laureate George Wald put the matter poignantly in an address on March 4, 1969, at Massachusetts Institute of Technology. "Over the past few years, I have felt increasingly that something is terribly wrong—and this year ever so much more than last. Something has gone sour in teaching and in learning. It's almost as though there were a widespread feeling that education has become irrelevant." [14] Not only did the phrases post-Puritan, post-Protestant, and post-Christian gain popular currency, but intellectual historians began to speak with equally good reason and plausibility of post-historical man—half suggesting the obsolescence of their own discipline. The decade of the sixties, in short, was a time when the old grounds of not only historic Western theism were awash, but also the older forms of national confidence and social idealism—not to mention traditional moral sanctions and standards of public behavior. The effects of these changes pervade the assemblies of American historians just as decisively as they did the Second Vatican Council. Much that we say of the American experience, moreover, could be applied, *mutatis mutandis,* to Western civilization generally, or even to the whole world.

When an historian is confronted by such a disruption of the "normal" course of events, some questions force themselves almost irresistibly into the foreground. First of all, he asks why a moral and intellectual revolution that was centuries in the making should have been so suddenly precipitated in the sixties. Why, to shift the figure, did the fair weather, the complacency, moral composure, national self-confidence, and optimism of the fifties, of the Eisenhower years, and even of Kennedy's early New Frontier days become so quickly clouded? Why did *this* decade become the moment when the WASP's wings are clipped; when the Protestant Establishment collapses; when ancient standards of sexual morality are revised; when governments relax their equally ancient prerogative of censorship; when thousands resist or evade the country's call to arms; when ministers and thinking laity alike lose confidence in ecclesiastical institutions; when anti-supernaturalism makes deep inroads in both pulpit and seminary, and presumably also in the church historian's study; when a two-and-a-half-millennia tradition of religious opposition to "worldliness" and "secularism" is drastically weakened; when the religious category itself is profoundly questioned in the churches and synagogues; and when the New Morality and the Death of God become popular slogans? Why, in short, have so many long-term processes dropped their bomb load on the sixties?

In taking up this urgent question it would hardly be honorable for me to state the unvarnished truth: that any historical phenomenon of this scope could be "explained" only in terms of the whole past and the whole future of mankind—which is to say that we touch upon an edge of the *mysterium tremendum*.[15] Before making an audacious effort, however, let me state a corollary of this "truth," namely, that one's treatment of the decade's impact on the work of historians will inescapably reflect one's historical explanation of the crisis. In the discussion which follows, therefore, my historiographical observations will be linked to my explanations. When I do not utter warnings or speak of dangers, I wish to have it understood that I am not only describing new historical trends but that I regard the pressures being exerted by the times on the work of the historian as salutary, and in most cases long overdue. I have not dealt, however, with those historians who have been led by frustration and outrage to abandon disciplined research altogether or even to take up other occupations.

The developments that converge on the 1960's can, for clarity's sake, be understood as operating on two levels: first, at the intellectual or theological level where men formulate their conception of the cosmos; and, second, at the social level where men respond to the moral challenges precipitated by a changing social order. The two levels are, of course, interrelated, with confrontations at the social ethical level having powerful shock effects on prevailing conceptualizations of the world. But the fundamental source of the decade's spiritual crisis are those successive innovations in Western thought which have provoked the "rise of modern religious ideas." [16] What is referred to here is the gradual development of uniformitarian modes of explanation, first in the scientific ordering of the physical world, then in the more existentially relevant biological realm, and then still more urgently in the account of human processes (past and present) given by historians and behavioral scientists. Finally, one notes the continuing philosophical efforts to deal with the increasingly naturalistic world-view to which these scientific explanations conduce. In very recent times the "educational explosion" has tended to take these matters out of the hands of a relatively small intellectual elite and give them a broad popular base. This "explosion," one might add, results not only from the new order of magnitude in the size of college enrollments but also from the impact of the mass media—especially television—and the tutelary role of such things as the use and deployment of nuclear weapons and the launching of flights to the moon.[17]

Television and moon shots bring us the second or socio-ethical level of concern, for they symbolize another kind of transformatory process: the rationalization of human activities. Theorists such as Max Weber have linked this process at one end of the historical scale with Judeo-Christian civilization in general and the Protestant Reformation in particular, and, at the other end, with the rise of industrialism. During the twentieth century this process has been so accelerated by modern technology that it has long since swept beyond the bounds of Western civilization. It now threatens or has utterly disrupted primordial styles of life the world over, from Arkansas and Quebec to Ghana and China. It is gradually making "organization men" out of every member of the human race. Already in 1940 Waldo Frank published *A Chart for Rough Waters* in which he declared that "the collectivizing trend of society under machine production, whether that society calls itself democratic, fascist, or socialist, is irrevocable." [18] And the "rough water" of the 1960's may be the vindication of his theory. The Vietnam War, an inequitable Selective Service system, and the prominence of the military establishment have triggered much of America's discontent, but the problems of achieving genuine personal autonomy in an increasingly collectivized system are in fact far more basic sources of frustration and unrest. They are especially acute for those who are victims of discrimination and those ("under thirty") who are facing vocational questions. What makes matters still worse is the fact that escape from modern industrial society to more primitive forms of life does not even appeal to those who demand it, once the practical options are stated in terms of less food, fewer things, less leisure, and more human toil.

Modern conceptions of the world and modern industrial society—these are the two great creations of the Judeo-Christian West that underlie the trouble of the sixties. Both have emphasized the degree to which the most important historiographical effect of their "coming of age" in America is methodological: they have deepened the religious historian's commitment to "scientific" history in the broad sense of that much-disputed term. This is to say that more than ever the historian has been pressed to explain the past with the same canons of judgment by which he interprets and explains the world around him. He has come increasingly to see that only when he has exhausted the possibility for *natural* explanation has he done his best to *"reciter la chose comme elle est advenue."*

This may sound banal, but it has not always been deemed to be so. Most church historians were once of another mind, and many still are. In the United States in 1888 they organized the American Society of Church History separately from the American Historical Association in order to pursue their discipline in the context of Christian commitment. In 1897 the Society voted to disband and merge its efforts with the larger general association; but since 1906 the two groups of historians have again been formally separated.[19] In the very recent past, moreover, eminent American church historians have argued that true church history belongs to a specific genre that is methodologically distinct from the work of world historians generally.[20]

Yet historians of "secular" America can hardly look at this state of affairs too condescendingly, for they too have often practiced a kind of quasi-religious celebrationism in their treatments of this "nation with the soul of a church." [21] As would-be historians of American democracy, they have found it easy to ignore the terrible anomalies of slavery and racism in the land of the free. They have written paeans to the national glory and sung the nation's providentially guided destiny. They have extenuated sins and supported a veritable *theologia gloria* for the republic. The mood of the 1960's, with its indisposition for such forms of patriotic piety, has on the one hand brought a new kind of circumspection into the writing of American history, and, on the other, sent historians to a reexamination of the origins and consequences of the nation's sense of mission.[22]

When we move from questions rooted in methodological problems to the more direct historiographical implications of the country's "coming of age," the most obvious recourse is to consider the historiography of the radical tradition in American theology. The present-day attack on supernaturalism raises the need to clarify the rise of a critical movement in American religion and the thought of its chief architects. This new angle of vision could hardly be expected to lay bare thinkers who were heretofore unknown, but it is creating new contexts of relevance and exposing many neglected themes. The revolutionary implications of Puritanism, for example, are being uncovered. The same can be said in different ways of Jonathan Edwards and the Great Awakening—as will be pointed out later in this essay. Seen from this vantage point, Ralph Waldo Emerson also takes a somewhat different place in the history of American religious thought than has usually been assigned to him. No longer the parlor companion of Victorian America, he emerges as America's first profound critic of the churches and a radical theologian of genius. This does not mean that his was simply another harsh anti-clerical voice but that he perceived with uncommon acuteness the theological dilemmas that modern thought was casting up. When addressing a class of graduating seminarians at the Harvard Divinity School in 1838, Emerson spoke bluntly of the "death of faith" and the "famine of our churches," and proposed a creative religious alternative. The same could be said for many other transcendentalists who looked to Emerson for inspiration; in the fields of biblical criticism, philosophical theology, and the history of religions they took initiatives that led directly into the animating concerns of the twentieth century—even though a long period of abuse and misunderstanding was to intervene.[23]

In a similar manner, the rising interest in linguistic analysis and literary symbolism has given new vitality to our interest in the work of Horace Bushnell as a mediator between orthodoxy and romantic idealism. Sharing in this recovery, after even deeper neglect, is a considerable company of scholars and theologians who introduced various of the historically oriented schools of nineteenth-century German thought. A strong and at many points brilliant liberal movement that arose in most of the Northern churches is also beginning to recover its reputation after enduring long years of abuse at the hands of both orthodox and neo-orthodox critics.[24] By the same kind of perspectivist alchemy, the neo-Orthodox movement takes on new significance. It does so not because it rejuvenated orthodox doctrines but because in many ways it provided an essential education for future radicals by developing new nonliteralistic modes of interpreting Scriptures, finding a new place for secularity, stressing nonlegalistic ethics, calling into question liberalism's sentimental notion of the universe, and recognizing that cynics, atheists, and Marxists could bring a salutary note of realism into the church's thinking. One is reminded, for example, how two of the earliest theological secularizers, H. Richard Niebuhr and Joseph Haroutunian, were accomplishing a major revision in the 1930's. They saw Jonathan Edwards as "a religious philosopher of nature" whose "permanent" significance rested on his transcendence of the optimistic moralism that within five years of his death began to take its place as a basic element in the ideology of the emergent

American nation.[25] In short, the entire history of religious liberalism—
from Spinoza to the Niebuhrs—demands and is receiving intensified
study and reinterpretation.

The major ecclesiastical development of the 1960's has been the
dramatic transformation of Catholic-Protestant relations. First of all
came the events: John XXIII, Vatican Council II, a Roman Catholic
American President, an upheaval in the Roman Church, and a transformation of interfaith relations that reached out even into the remote villages of Western Christendom. Yet the fundamental fact is
the transformatory power of the intellectual trend we have been discussing. Historiographically speaking, therefore, Pope John's revolution assigns historians to heavy revisions of prevailing thought and
scholarship not only on interfaith controversy in the past but on the
history of the critical tradition in Catholic thought which has now
come to the surface.[26]

Taking their cue from the election of the first Roman Catholic
President of the United States in 1960 and the Supreme Court's controversial decisions on desegregation and religious ceremonies in public schools, historians are also being led to a closer study of changing
immigrant cultures and the deepening popular awareness of the
country's inescapably pluralistic character (a nation of minorities). It
is becoming steadily more clear that movements toward pluralism had
undermined the hegemony of the old white Protestant establishment.
Both the actions of the Court and the voice of the electorate raised
doubts about the credibility of the melting pot theory. In the train of
these discoveries, a new history of immigrant and migrant populations
was taking shape. Indeed, it was made manifest that the WASP himself was having identity problems. Entailed in these developments is
a vast and as yet unwritten history of ethnic religious history.[27]

Other revisions resulting from our decade's dominant mood become
clearer if we consider some of the specific factors which have precipitated the present spiritual crisis and hence prevented a gradual
adjustment to long-term social trends and an untraumatic assimilation of a thoroughly modern world-view. We certainly need no more
than a brief reminder of three familiar social sequences:

1. The *general* technological and demographic factors that have led
to a rapidly mounting environmental crisis in metropolitan areas.

2. The *special* technological and demographic factors that have
added educational and fiscal, but most basically racial crises to those
which urbanism itself was generating.

3. The war in Vietnam, if one may use four words to designate an incredibly complex national phenomenon which threatens to render the nation impotent and broken as it faces its tasks of domestic reconstruction.

In these three sequences we have at once the major catalytic forces of our decade and an agenda for the kind of revisionism that is creating a new American past.

Because it is paradigmatic, the transformation of Afro-American history is mentioned first. The absence of the black experience in American historiography is being rectified. What is so prominent in our present is entering our past, more convulsively than one would hope, yet irresistibly—because the major factor in the development of this "*Herrenvolk* democracy" has heretofore been so evasively, so incompletely, and so deceptively dealt with. In the realm of religious history the agenda is especially crowded simply because the Christian religion and the churches have been so vital a factor in each major phase of the black experience—from the days of Western Christendom's moral collapse when Africa was being discovered, on through the slave's "Americanization," to the rise and progress of the last century's emancipation movement which has, since 1965, become a veritable racial uprising.[28] Involved in these inquiries is the further question which church historians so far have rarely asked: What has been the long-term effect of black religion? Has it been for weal or woe? Equally implicated are most of the corollary phases in the history of the white churches and their long involvement in the mysteries of racism. In either case, even a simple itemization would require a paper by itself, especially because any kind of thoroughness would carry us also into the religious history of other racial minorities (chiefly Puerto Rican, Mexican, Indian, and Oriental). [29]

The major implications of the urban crisis for religious history are in large part suggested by the foregoing discussion. The present points to a new past, but not only one that lies in the city churches and their actual or potential constituencies. Perhaps more important is the long conflict between urban and rural (or agrarian) values that has featured American history, almost always to the detriment of the city. In this revisionary process religious history is especially important, for it must deal with the persistent tendency of American Protestants to conceive of the city not as the New Jerusalem but as Babylon.[30]

Also very instructive with regard to the urban theme is another symptom of the times that is full of historiographical promise: the love affair that has developed (for obvious reasons of elective affinity) between the 1960's and the 1920's. The fact has, of course, a two-way significance, but it directs us first of all to a momentous and marvelously demarcated decade in our religious past. So far the twenties have received from church historians too much deprecation and too little understanding. Evangelicals and Marxists have agreed to dismiss the decade as a time of folly, an age of excess, a postwar binge leading to economic catastrophe. That it was a dramatic confrontation between the old and the new America, above all between urban and rural America, and that Evangelicial Protestantism as a powerful national force expired on its battlefields, has been less appreciated—indeed scarcely noted. Historiographically speaking, therefore, the decade of the 1920's is ripe unto harvest.[31]

As for the historical fallout from the great disenchantment produced by the war in Vietnam, perhaps one could imagine Staughton Lynd's documentary history of *Nonviolence in America* (1966) and the report to the National Commission on *The History of Violence in America* (1969) as brackets for a large revisionist literature. As a symbol of the new trend toward a *dissensus* history of the United States, Lynd's *Intellectual Origins of American Radicalism* (1968) will serve. Though impressive neither for its research nor its logic, the book marks out the terrain. It examines the revolutionary elements of the American Revolution and then follows this radical tradition forward into the anti-slavery movement where it joins another urgent concern of the 1960's. Howard Zinn's documentary history of the New Deal exemplifies this same mood in a twentieth-century context, while his concluding essay in *The Antislavery Vanguard* (1965) makes the connections between past and present quite explicit.[32] Virtually all of these topics, as well as others more remote from religious history, are treated in *Towards a New Past* (1968), a volume of "dissenting essays in American history" edited by Barton J. Bernstein.

Even with this stimulation, there remains a great need for more intensive church-historical work on the relation of the American religious tradition to the domestication of violence and the celebration of war. With the exception of a few widely scattered works, church historians have tended to ignore the repeated efforts of the emissaries of the Prince of Peace to arouse the martial spirit—in the Revolutionary, Civil, Spanish-American, and First World wars, as well as the circumstances which made them far more moderate in World War II.[33] In a time of backlash politics there is also need (so far insubstantially answered) for study of the religio-political Extreme Right—from the days of its emergence in the revived Ku Klux Klan of the 1920's, on through several quasi-fascist movements of the 1930's, and up to the alliance of conservative religion (both Protestant and Catholic) with reactionary and chauvinistic movements in the 1960's.[34]

All three of the decade's chief precipitants of discontent (racial, urban, martial) have conspired to turn the dissenting spirit toward those master dissenters and nonconformists of Western Christendom, the Puritans. This has led to new interest in Puritanism's effect on the American social order, and most especially its seemingly (but not actually!) contradictory role in fostering revivalism on the one hand and in hastening the country's headlong abandonment of pre-modern social ideals on the other. This vital interest has been marked by a distinguished resumption of concern for the Weber thesis and its many subtle variants.[35]

Because of the Puritan accent on experiential religion, the field of revivalism has also been prepared for new explorations—with regard to its influence in the rise of the revolutionary spirit of the eighteenth century, to the humanitarian reformism of the nineteenth, and to the precipitation in both the South and the North of the final great struggle over slavery.[36] Perry Miller's *The Life of the Mind in America* (published posthumously in 1965) was one outstanding effort of this sort; it also served to link the author's lifelong Puritan studies to the great revival of evangelicalism in the early national period.[37] These "progressive" effects of revivals, however, have not blinded historians to their reactionary role in fostering anti-intellectualism. This is the baleful side-effect that helps account for the fact that "the first new nation" was one of the last nations in the Western world to come intellectually and religiously of age—as Richard Hofstadter's *Anti-Intellectualism in American Life* (1963) suggested. Another promising result of the study of revivalism has been the growth of interest in the religious history of the South and the relation of its unique evangelical heritage to the region's basic character. David Bertelson's raising of the specter of *The Lazy South,* Donald Mathews' study of *Methodism and Slavery,* William S. McFeely's sad tale of General O. O. Howard and the Freedmen's Bureau, and Samuel J. Hill's account of *Southern Churches in Crisis* (1967) indicate how crucial questions have arisen with regard to the very earliest, the intermediate, and the very latest phases of the region's religious history.[38]

By way of conclusion, one should perhaps answer a question which is almost automatically posed by the title of this paper: Is this essay in any sense an account of the historiographical New Left? The answer, almost inescapably, is "yes," but in a very broad sense of that as yet vague label. And for two reasons. First of all, the literature here adverted to *is* largely of the 1960's and hence "new." A definite program of revisionist concern has arisen and is growing, as a legitimate and probably inevitable response of historians to the restlessness that surrounds them. The tendency we observe, moreover, is of the new *Left* in that it is manifested chiefly by those who have been sympathetic with contemporary currents of intellectual and social criticism and responsive to the decade's unsettlement. Should any of those mentioned be surprised by this classification, or resent it, I would console them with the thought that the cunning of history is such that only after many years will it be clear who are the truly innovative historians of the 1960's. Many scholars can be assured that they helped to upset the somewhat illicit consensus that academic historians had been enjoying.

That religion and hence church history offer major clues to the moral climate of America and to the people's state of soul is no new discovery. Many of the greatest United States historians have recognized this. Interestingly, the point has been best underlined in recent times by the historian who drew attention to *The American Revolution as a Social Movement* (1926) and another who has done much to underline the revolutionary character of the 1920's.[39] In any event, it is clear that important new interests are arising. The agenda for continued study in the field is crowded.

NOTES

1. *L'Histoire des histoires avec l'idée de l'histoire accomplie* . . . (Paris, 1599), pp. 71–77; quoted in George Huppert, "The Renaissance Background of Historicism," *History and Theory*, V, No. 1 (1966), 49. Ranke's famous statement (*Er will bloss zeigen wie es eigentlich gewesen*) appeared in the Pref-

ace of his *Histories of the Latin and Germanic Nations* (1824). Georg G. Iggers, "The Image of Ranke in American and German Historical Thought," *History and Theory*, II, No. 1 (1962), 12–40. Historians often resist the notion that their writings do not transcend the historical context in which they work and think; yet few deny that each new generation not only adds to the factual store but revises the work of its predecessors.

2. Marcus Cunliffe gently chides American historians and sociologists for tending "to exaggerate the cataclysmic nature of the crisis in American history." Charles Dickens has *Martin Chuzzlewit* declaring that if its individual citizens are to be believed, "America always is at an alarming crisis, and never was otherwise." Not so applicable in the 1960's is Chuzzlewit's further observation that Americans nevertheless were insisting theirs to be "the most thriving and prosperous of all countries on the habitable globe." "American Watersheds," *American Quarterly*, XIII (Winter 1961), 489, 491. A judgment as to the present decade's importance is, of course, a venture in futurology if not eschatology, whether it be negative or positive. See note 15 below.

3. See especially *Letters and Papers from Prison* (New York, 1959), pp. 158–164, *et passim*.

4. Cf. Schubert M. Ogden, *Christ Without Myth* (New York, 1961); Paul Van Buren, *The Secular Meaning of the Gospel* (New York, 1963); Thomas J. Altizer and William Hamilton, *Radical Theology and the Death of God* (Indianapolis, 1966); Van A. Harvey, *The Historian and the Believer* (New York, 1966); William A. Beardslee, ed., *America and the Future of Theology* (Philadelphia, 1967); and, as indicative of related matters, William Braden, *The Private Sea: LSD and the Search for God* (Chicago, 1967). The only general essay on American church history to reflect this mood is William A. Clebsch, *From Sacred to Profane America: The Role of Religion in American History* (New York, 1968). I deal further with the theological mood of the sixties and related causal questions in *Annals of the American Academy of Political and Social Science*, January 1970.

5. See Edward Wakin and Joseph F. Scheuer, *The De-Romanization of the American Catholic Church* (New York, 1966); E. E. Y. Hales, *Pope John and His Revolution* (New York, 1966); Leslie Dewart, *The Future of Belief* (New York, 1966). See also the numerous theological works of Hans Küng, Karl Rahner, and Pierre Teilhard de Chardin.

6. History, of course, is never reversible. Even the great periodic repudiations are illusory. Romantic thinkers, for example, were products of the Enlightenment they attacked. Neo-Orthodoxy's relation to liberalism was similar. Theological radicalism will probably be a constitutive element in future modifications of belief and cannot be regarded as a passing mood or fad.

7. See Edward Farley, *Requiem for a Lost Piety* (Philadelphia, 1966); J. A. T. Robinson, *The New Reformation?* (Philadelphia, 1965), chap. IV.

8. In America, foreign missions have recently been most vigorously prosecuted by those churches which are most unsympathetic with contemporary cultural, intellectual, and ecclesiastical trends. Especially notable are the Pentecostalists and Jehovah's Witnesses.

9. See Joseph Fletcher, *Situation Ethics: The New Morality* (Philadelphia, 1966); Paul L. Lehmann, *Ethics in a Christian Context* (New York, 1963).

10. On July 29, 1968, Pope Paul VI published *Humanae Vitae* in which artificial methods of birth control were declared illicit. It was one of the most fateful papal pronouncements in the last 450 years.

11. As in other times of intense dislocation, extreme (even psychotic) behavior patterns gained public attention, but more pervasive was a sense of loss, unfulfillment, and powerlessness from which sprang a yearning that all but wore out the words "dialogue" and "community." My chief worry is that the student movement will be counter-productive. See Hermann Rauschning, *The Revolution of Nihilism* (New York, 1949), dealing with the rise of Nazism in Germany. See also Fritz Stern, *The Politics of Cultural Despair: A Study in the Rise of the Germanic Ideology* (New York, 1965), especially his quotation from Rauschning on the anti-capitalistic youth movements, p. 225.

12. The patriotic holy days, to be sure, have been losing their hold on the American imagination for a long time. But the process has been accelerated in the 1960's due to the incandescent ironies created by the juxtaposition of patriotic rhetoric and the national scriptures on the one hand, and the enormities of the present-day scene on the other. This is not to deny that the "generation gap" has been drastically widened in the 1960's, though both words in the term are highly metaphorical.

13. *New York Times*, November 3, 1967.

14. *The New Journal*, April 13, 1969.

15. Even an historian with a God's-eye view of the total past would be confounded by events of his own time unless he also had a God's-eye view of the total future. Voltaire (1694–1778) could not discern the significance of the birth of Robespierre (1758–1794). Jonathan Edwards seems to have sensed this characteristic of historical knowledge when he wrote his famous letter to the Princeton trustees, October 19, 1757. Without comprehension of "the admirable contexture and harmony of the whole," of the Alpha and the Omega, the Beginning and the End, the historian was doomed to very tentative enterprises. "Not a thing in our changing world," writes Teilhard de Chardin, "is really understandable except in so far as it has reached its terminus." *Panthéisme et Christianisme* (Paris, 1923), p. 8.

16. Countless historians have dealt with this intellectual trend and its religious implications. A. C. McGiffert's *The Rise of Modern Religious Ideas* (1915) was an influential account by a scholar who was forced from the Presbyterian ministry for his liberalism.

17. Those who observed Sputnik slipping through the stars during the fall of 1957 participated in a momentous spiritual event in human history. How it compares with Hiroshima in 1945 or the moon shots of 1969 is a nice question.

18. Roderick Seidenberg's *Post-historic Man* (Chapel Hill, 1950) recorded further developments; Michael Harrington's *The Accidental Century* (Baltimore, 1965) made a later sounding; and Theodore Roszak, *The Making of a Counter-Culture: Reflections on the Technocratic Society and Its Youthful Opposition* (New York, 1969) still another.

19. See Henry W. Bowden, "Science and the Idea of Church History," *Church History*, XXXVI (September 1967), 308–326.

20. J. A. Ross Mackenzie, in his inaugural address as professor of church history at Union Theological Seminary (Richmond), sought to define the norm of historians "whose outlook is fashioned and controlled by the event of Christ." "What are the cosmic presuppositions and implications of this incarnation of God?" He would not settle for a notion of double truth, but he did assert salvation history as a light by which secular history is to be interpreted. In this sense Mackenzie provided a rationale for the continued separation of church historians. "Recapitulation and Sacrifice: A Norm of Interpretation in

the History of the Church," *Affirmation*, I, No. 3 (November 1968), 6–7.
Cf. Sidney E. Mead, "Church History Explained," *Church History*, **XXXII**
(March 1963), 17–31.

21. G. K. Chesterton coined the term, but see Sidney E. Mead, "The
Nation with the Soul of a Church," *Church History*, **XXXVI** (September
1967), 262–283.

22. Ernest Lee Tuveson's *Redeemer Nation: The Idea of America's Millennial Role* (Chicago, 1968) is one admirable account of this concept. It underlines the profoundly theological basis of the concept and hence the degree to
which religion and American national feeling are intertwined. In this manner
the crisis of American *hubris* in the 1960's invigorates historical research all the
way back to Governor Winthrop's sermon on the *Arbella* in 1630.

23. Cf. Jerry W. Brown, *The Rise of Biblical Criticism in America, 1800–
1870: The New England Scholars* (Middletown, Conn., 1969), and my own
The American Protestant Encounter with World Religions (Beloit, Wisc., 1962).

24. Cf. James H Nichols, *Romanticism in American Theology* (Chicago,
1961); Kenneth Cauthen, *The Impact of American Religious Liberalism* (New
York, 1962); Jurgen Herbst, *The German Historical School in American Scholarship* (Ithaca, 1965); Lloyd J. Averill, *American Theology in the Liberal Tradition* (Philadelphia, 1967); and William R. Hutchison, ed., *American Protestant
Thought: The Liberal Era* (New York, 1968).

25. See Haroutunian's *Piety versus Moralism: The Passing of the New
England Theology* (New York, 1932), and Niebuhr's *The Kingdom of God in
America* (New York, 1937).

26. Histories of Modernism and the movements which led up to it, such as
Owen Chadwick's *From Bossuet to Newman: The Idea of Doctrinal Development* (Cambridge, Mass., 1957), became historically more important; and this
will lead to deeper study of these trends in America. Another sign of a much-
needed new approach is Myron A. Marty's valuable study of anti Catholic polemics in the Missouri Synod, *Lutherans and Roman Catholicism: The Changing
Conflict, 1917–1963* (South Bend, Ind., 1968).

27. Nathan Glazer and Daniel P. Moynihan, *Beyond the Melting Pot* (Cambridge, Mass., 1964) represents the concern for continuing patterns of ethnic
self-consciousness. But not even the 1960's have stimulated sufficient study of
the Eastern Orthodox churches in America (notably the Greek and Russian) or
the huge new constituencies (notably Italian and Polish) which the "new immigration" added to the Roman Catholic Church. Another facet of the new
pluralism was treated by E. Digby Baltzell in *The Protestant Establishment:
Aristocracy and Caste in America* (New York, 1964).

28. E. Franklin Frazier's brief, posthumous *The Negro Church in America*
(New York, 1964) is the only general history since Carter Woodson's pioneer-
ing survey almost forty years before. Each of the following, however, has made
a major contribution on some distinct aspect of this history: David B. Davis,
The Problem of Slavery in Western Culture (Ithaca, 1966); Winthrop D.
Jordan, *White over Black* (Chapel Hill, 1968); Clifton H. Johnson, ed., *God
Struck Me Dead: Religious Conversion Experiences and Autobiographies of
Ex-Slaves* (Boston, 1969); Edwin S. Redkey, *Black Exodus* (New Haven, 1969);
C. Eric Lincoln, *Black Muslims in America* (Boston, 1961); Andrew E. Murray,
Presbyterians and the Negro—A History (Philadelphia, 1966); David Reimers,
White Protestantism and the Negro (New York, 1965); Joseph C. Hough, Jr.,
Black Power and White Protestants (New York, 1968); and Vincent Harding,

"The Religion of Black Power," in *The Religious Situation: 1968* (Boston, 1968). Histories of nearly every sect, cult, and denomination are still lacking, as are biographies of many church leaders. Several controversial questions have been little more than broached: the survival of an African heritage, the effect of Christianization under slavery and after, the relationship of Christian belief and white racism, the effect of urbanization and the black awakening on the Negro church, the long-term interrelationship of "black religion" and evangelicalism in the Negro churches. This last question and several others have been considered, though not very convincingly, by Joseph R. Washington in *Black Religion: The Negro and Christianity in the United States* (Boston, 1964). On the concept of the United States as a *"Herrenvolk* democracy," see Pierre van den Berghe, *Race and Racism* (New York, 1967), a comparative study of race relations in South Africa, Brazil, Mexico, and the United States.

29. I am aware of virtually no significant work in this realm except in connection with Indian missions, and even here the last century has been neglected. But see Robert F. Berkhofer, Jr., *Salvation and Savages: An Analysis of Protestant Missions and American Indian Response, 1782–1862* (Lexington, Ky., 1965); Henry E. Fritz, *The Movement for Indian Assimilation, 1860–1890* (Philadelphia, 1963); Loring Benson Priest, *Uncle Sam's Stepchildren: The Reformation of United States Indian Policy, 1865–1887* (New Brunswick, N.J., 1942); Bernard W. Sheehan, "Indian-White Relations in Early America: A Review Essay," *William and Mary Quarterly,* 3rd ser., XXVI, No. 2 (April 1969), 267–286.

30. Robert D. Cross, ed., *The Church and the City, 1865–1910* (Indianapolis, 1967) surveys American thought on this subject. Present-day efforts to reorient the attitudes and strategies of American churches have led to a mountainous body of literature.

31. See John Braeman, *et al.,* eds., *Change and Continuity in Twentieth-Century America: The 1920's* (Columbus, Ohio, 1968), and Paul A. Carter, *The Twenties in America* (New York, 1968), a survey of scholarship.

32. Hugh D. Graham and Ted R. Gurr are the author/editors of this report to the National Commission on the Causes and Prevention of Violence (New York, 1969). *The Antislavery Vanguard* (Princeton, 1965) was edited by Martin Duberman. See also Irwin Unger's article, "The New Left and American History: Some Recent Trends in United States Historiography," *American Historical Review,* LXXII (July 1967), 1237–1263. The event of Erik Erikson's *Gandhi's Truth: On the Origins of Militant Nonviolence* (New York, 1969) should also be recorded here.

33. See Ray Abrams, *Preachers Present Arms* (New York, 1933) on World War I; Kenneth M. MacKenzie, *The Robe and the Sword: The Methodist Church and the Rise of American Imperialism* (Washington, D.C., 1961); James W. Silver, *Confederate Morale and Church Propaganda* (Tuscaloosa, Ala., 1957); and Frank T. Reuter, *Catholic Influence on American Colonial Policies, 1898–1904* (Austin, Tex., 1967).

34. Ralph Lloyd Roy, *Apostles of Discord: A Study of Organized Bigotry and Disruption on the Fringes of Protestantism* (Boston, 1953) is a helter-skelter mixture of facts and charges; but David H. Bennett, *Demagogues in Depression: American Radicals and the Union Party, 1932–1936* (New Brunswick, N.J., 1969), and Louis Gasper, *The Fundamentalist Movement* (The Hague, 1963) mark a beginning of more thorough study of extreme political and religious conservatism. The trend toward hyper-nationalism and militaristic at-

titudes among professed ultra-conservatives in religion needs more detailed research, however.

35. Representative of these new studies are Michael Walzer, *The Revolution of the Saints: A Study in the Origins of Radical Politics* (Cambridge, Mass., 1965); David Little, *Religion, Order and Law: Religious and Social Conflict in Pre-Revolutionary England* (New York, 1969); and Edmund S. Morgan, "The Puritan Ethic and the American Revolution," *William and Mary Quarterly*, 3rd ser., XXIV (1967), 3–43. Richard Bushman, *From Puritan to Yankee: Character and Social Order in Connecticut, 1690–1765* (Cambridge, Mass., 1967); and, most magisterially, Bernard Bailyn, *The Ideological Origins of the American Revolution* (Cambridge, Mass., 1967). See also my own "The Puritan Ethic and the Spirit of American Democracy," in George L. Hunt, ed., *Calvinism and the Political Order* (Philadelphia, 1965).

36. Accenting the radical implications of the Great Awakening for both political and ecclesiastical structures are Clarence C. Goen, *Revivalism and Separatism in New England, 1740–1800* (New Haven, 1962); William G. McLoughlin, *Isaac Backus, 1724–1806* (Boston, 1967); Alan Heimert, *Religion and American Life: From the Great Awakening to the Revolution* (Cambridge, Mass., 1966).

37. George Stephenson, Gilbert H. Barnes, Sidney E. Mead, Timothy L. Smith, and several others pioneered in this sort of revisionism; but more recent explorations include Robert Merideth's biography of Edward Beecher, *The Politics of the Universe: Edward Beecher, Abolition and Orthodoxy* (Nashville, 1968), and Richard Wolf's study of Abraham Lincoln's theology, *The Almost Chosen People* (New York, 1959). The old Southern view of abolitionists as meddling troublemakers has in the meantime gained support from Stanley Elkins, *Slavery* (Chicago, 1959); Clarence S. Griffin, *Their Brothers' Keeper* (New Brunswick, N.J., 1960), and others. Griffin provides a valuable survey of scholarship on ante-bellum reform in *The Ferment of Reform, 1830–1860* (New York, 1967).

38. Bertelson's work raises the question of the significance, for the rise of the slave-system, of the *absence* of thoroughly institutionalized Puritan nurture; from another perspective so does Hill's effort to describe the South's unique place in Western Christendom. See also C. Vann Woodward's meditation on Bertelson's question: "The Southern Ethic in a Puritan World," *William and Mary Quarterly*, 3rd ser., XXV (July 1968). Mathews' work underlines the relation of evangelicalism to the anti-slavery movement. Eugene Genovese's *The Political Economy of Slavery* (New York, 1965), though not immediately concerned with religion, is important for its stress on the radiating implications of slavery for the Southern social order as a whole—an emphasis, incidentally, that makes one more appreciative of the analysis of both Edward Beecher (see note 37 above) and his sister Harriet. The very first ten pages of *Uncle Tom's Cabin* depict the corrupting effects of "organic sin," and the original subtitle of the novel was "The Man That Was a Thing." Northern complicity in this "organic sin" has also received recent emphasis in William A. Clebsch, "Christian Interpretations of the Civil War," in *Church History*, XXX (June 1961). The lineaments and consequences of Northern complicity in slavery and the underlying racism have been too little explored. McFeely's work, *Yankee Stepfather: General O. O. Howard and the Freedmen* (New Haven, 1968) illustrates the limitations of Northern commitment. All in all, nothing the 1960's have done for religious history is more important than sharpening the focus on

American racism. The importance of Jordan's *White over Black* is apparent.

39. J. Franklin Jamison, "The American Acta Sanctorum," *American Historical Review*, XIII (January 1908), 286–302; Henry F. May, "The Recovery of American Religious History," *ibid.*, LXX (October 1964), 79–92. See also May's *The End of American Innocence: A Study of the First Years of Our Own Time, 1912–1917* (New York, 1959) and *The Discontent of the Intellectuals: A Problem of the Twenties* (Chicago, 1963).

The State of
American Diplomatic History

THOMAS J. McCORMICK

The study of American diplomatic history as a distinct field is a relatively recent development. It is young enough that many of its first practitioners are not only alive but, in terms of continuing scholarly production, quite well. Yet there are few fields which stand more in need of a critical rethinking than does this one.

As a field embracing not just one society but two or more in interaction, diplomatic history offers a unique opportunity for comparative, cosmopolitan, culturally relative analysis; in terms of subjects studied and interpretations offered, however, few fields of historical study have been more subject to presentism and national bias. While resisting, in general, the stimulation, insights, and methodology of the other social sciences, diplomatic history has permitted itself to succumb, in the particular, to a metaphysical debate over "realism" versus "idealism" first generated by political scientists. In an age when more Americans than ever are global-minded, and when more non-Americans than ever are aware of the American impact on their lives, no other subject of inquiry has more contemporary importance; yet diplomatic historians are often disparaged by other students of history for their alleged amateurism, imprecision, and lack of social context. They are, in the word of one of my colleagues, "sports."

Before making my own effort to assess the state of American diplomatic history,[1] I set about to gain a more accurate and comprehensive picture of the raw material I wish to analyze: contemporary writings in American diplomatic history—or, as I prefer, American foreign relations. I decided to review the entire corpus of American diplomatic history written and published in the past two and a half decades of the epoch we call the Cold War. Rather than make a subjective judgment as to which books fell into the category of scholarly respectability, I let the profession make that judgment for me, restricting my attention to those monographs reviewed by the *Mississippi Valley Historical Review,* the *Journal of American History,* and the *American Historical Review* that by the most liberal definition could be regarded as contributions to the study of American foreign relations.

I emerged from that laborious and masochistic exercise with a conviction of the pressing need for different conceptual frameworks to reshape our research in more imaginative ways. American diplomatic history, for all the notable accomplishments of its earlier practitioners, is trapped in increasingly sterile modes. Only a rethinking of the processes and the very meaning of diplomatic history will rescue it.

Characteristically, most recent writings in American diplomatic history have done one of two things. Some so-called "think" pieces have tried to describe American foreign relations in the aggregate. They variously describe our policies as "moralistic" or "realistic"; "isolationist" or "internationalist"; "legalistic" or "nationalistic." Our foreign relations are sometimes presumed to reflect an endemic "American approach" or "American tradition," and it is a rare monograph and a rarer textbook that does not mirror these types of judgments. So, one historian's Woodrow Wilson is a naive moralist surrounded by hardheaded, realistic advisers, while another's has an astute appreciation of *Realpolitik* and the balance of power. Franklin Roosevelt's conversion to collective security comes in 1935, or in 1937, or perhaps he was really an internationalist all along. In the 1920's, American policy in Europe was the product of a revived "isolationist impulse," but American policy in the Far East was not. The point is that these aggregate characterizations are exceedingly vague and amorphous; they are not so much descriptive terms that enable us to understand the past as they are rhetorical conveniences for historians to impose their normative judgments on the past.

Most recent products on American diplomatic history, however, are diametrically different from the aggregate generalization, though they often adopt those generalizations and superficially incorporate them. What they do instead is to stress the isolated event, with inadequate regard for the evolving, long-term social setting within which that event took place. That is, the "event" is studied intensively through primary research, while the larger context is simply inferred or intuited, often on the basis of very debatable assumptions. The process reminds one of the liberal historiography of the Progressive period, where each political historian studied his event—be it the Interstate Commerce Act or the Country Life Movement—and then properly and sometimes piously presented his event as a case of "the people" (meaning the middle class), with the benevolent aid of a liberal federal government, chastising the malpractices of corporate "interests." In like fashion, liberal diplomatic historians have taken their events and both placed them and judged them in terms of the unfolding drama of America's two-steps-forward/one-step-backward effort in the twentieth century to extricate herself from the atavism of nationalistic isolation and to shoulder, however reluctantly, the burdens and responsibilities of liberal internationalism: *The Price of Power* as Herbert Agar phrased it. In this value-laden setting, the Spanish-American War becomes "the great aberration"; the rejection of the League of Nations "the great betrayal"; and the Washington Conference treaty system the "parchment peace."

Not satisfied with just any event, contemporary diplomatic historians often study the *crisis*-event. Let me illustrate. In an effort to be reasonably systematic, I made a crude effort to plot a graph of time periods emphasized by American diplomatic historians who have published since 1945. What emerged was a picture of sharp mountains and erratic troughs that graphically depicted the tendency of American diplomatic history—at least that treating the twentieth century—to cluster around the crisis years of 1898–1900, 1917–1919, 1937–1941, and 1945–present. Now, the difficulty with overemphasizing crisis-events is very much like the difficulty inherent in overusing the problem approach. The very definition of the problem tends to predetermine and constrict the data to be mobilized and the questions to be asked. Witness our century-long fixation about the Civil War. Certainly something so traumatic and wrenching deserves study. But by treating it as isolated crisis-event instead of viewing it in the context of social change both before and after the event, we managed to obscure the vital facts that the war probably did not provide the stimulus for accelerated industrialization and did not effect the realignment of popular voting as we assumed.

In like fashion in diplomatic history, our isolated preoccupation with the Spanish-American War and the dramatic debate associated with formal, political imperialism masked for too long the movement for informal empire and economic hegemony that both predated the Spanish-American War and continued apace throughout this century. And our preoccupation with the League of Nations issue prevented us from perceiving that the 1920's, far from being a retreat to isolationism and "normalcy," in fact continued and in some ways accelerated the expansion and internationalization of America already begun. In short, an inordinate amount of American diplomatic history has been involved in the interpreting and the reinterpreting of America's wars, hot and cold, in an unending syndrome of traditionalism and revisionism. And while one likes to think that this dialectical process leads eventually to something approximating historical truth, the question remains whether the insights have been worth the inputs. Has this crisis orientation retarded the placing of American foreign relations, both events and nonevents, in a social setting that is not inferred and overgeneralized, but precise and systematic?

One would hope that new research methods or refinements of older ones might lead to less conventional diplomatic history, but I doubt that this hope is being fulfilled. For example, it is my impression that more and more diplomatic historians are using multi-archival research. This is, to be sure, hardly an innovation in method. Senior diplomatic historians like Samuel F. Bemis long ago pioneered in multi-archival research; Richard Leopold's book reviews in the late 1940's and early 1950's frequently admonished less scholarly diplomatic historians for failure to use such techniques; and Ernest R. May's essay in *The Reconstruction of American History* was, among other things, an exhortation to make more systematic and comprehensive use of such methods. I think such examples and injunctions are finally beginning to bear full fruit, and unquestionably this has added to our fund of knowledge and insights and tended to ameliorate some of the past parochialism and national bias of our writings.

Nevertheless, this development generally has represented only a horizontal expansion of traditional and narrow diplomatic history. All too many of its practitioners have assumed that foreign relations is the end product of elite decision-makers, operating in a relative social vacuum, interacting with other nations' elite decision-makers. Hence the excessive emphasis on diplomatic archives and selected manuscript collections to the relative exclusion of other types of sources. Thus, while it may be a trifle unfair, there seems to me some essential truth in G. M. Young's classic characterization of diplomatic history as simply the discursive account of "what one clerk said to another." So, in one sense, multi-archival history, for all its obvious value, simply enlarges the number of clerks talking to each other. It does not liberate the historian's perspectives from its focus on the isolated decision-maker operating on the isolated event. It either ignores or overgeneralizes about the social context of policy formulation, and it fails to place the event systematically in the continuum of change over time. There are some notable exceptions to my generalization, but they tend in fact to reinforce my point. That is, the more sophisticated and successful examples of multi-national research have gone beyond the use of foreign official, diplomatic materials and used many different foreign sources, including some generally associated with domestic social and political history I have in mind, for example, Ernest May's superb treatment of German politics and its impact on German foreign policy in his *The World War and American Isolation,* or Akira Iriye's excellent integration of Japanese foreign policy, social forces, and polity in his *After Imperialism: The Search for a New Order in the Far East.*

More recently a few diplomatic historians, borrowing from the social sciences, have begun to use quantitative methods in an effort to analyze foreign relations in a nonintuitive, nonnormative way. If I may interject this note, it does seem to me that the general reaction of most diplomatic historians to these innovative efforts has been akin to the papal response to Galileo. Now there undoubtedly are grounds for skepticism. Some of the social sciences *have* been sidetracked into a preoccupation with constructing ever more complex and sophisticated mathematical models, with little or no regard for reality. And it might be argued that quantifiers have a built-in bias to study *only* those events and phenomena that can be counted and measured, and to denigrate or ignore those that cannot. On the other hand, a method is only that—a *means* to an end. An historian, after all, has an obligation to use any and all relevant data, be it diplomatic correspondence or census tracts, and to employ whatever methods best enable him to manipulate and make sense out of his raw information. In fulfilling that obligation, the historian—with his consciousness of the past and his empirical training—is in a most enviable position to pick and choose from the social sciences those methods, as well as concepts, that relate to the changing human condition over time. For example, I have personally found several types of roll-call analyses of congressional voting extraordinarily useful in giving me what an impressionistic analysis of traditional literature could not. In studies of American expansionism in both the 1850's and 1890's, students of mine, employing the Gutmann Scalogram analysis of congressional voting, have been able to give a far more differentiated and precise profile of group divisions than the usual imperialist/anti-imperialist bipolarity would ever suggest; and they have been able to make interesting correlations between expansionist sentiment and other variables like party, section, slaveholding, and attitudes on other issues such as tariff, banking, money, and Southern reconstruction. So I would hope that, as regards quantification, we could move from an anti-innovational "throw the baby out with the bath" response to a more eclectic, utilitarian one.

Having made my ecumenical call, let me add my judgment that unhappily the quantitative diplomatic historians and political scientists have not yet given us very much from which to choose. Specifically, I do not feel quantitative international relations has yet provided any radically new concepts, questions, or insights. It seems to me no more than traditional diplomatic history with *numbers,* for it has erred in the same ways. Typically, quantitative studies have done one of two things. First, they have tried to perform an aggregate data analysis on what, in fact, are often disaggregate events and processes. For example, a growing number have tried to break down the transactional flows between nations into component parts—such as trade, investment, tourism, student exchanges, cultural forms, national attributes, and the like—and then to use them as indicators to explain and sometimes predict the waxing and waning of alliances, or the waxing and waning of client-state dependency of backward nations upon advanced ones.[2] Others have used either multi- or single-variant analysis of aggregate data to test the relationship between internal "psychic crises" and international aggression, or between the formation of alliances and the outbreak of war. There is value in many of these studies, but their value and validity often seem in direct proportion to their level of abstraction and generalization. The more one studies specific sets of relationships in specified time spans, using highly detailed and specialized information, the less useful such aggregate studies seem.

For example, an aggregate study might demonstrate a strong correlation between the flow of American dollars overseas and the tendency of recipient nations to identify their interests with the United States and, perhaps more specifically, to vote with it in the United Nations. As a description of general trends, this may be perfectly adequate. But it is extraordinarily difficult to infer, much less predict, anything from this generalization when one is dealing with more specific, concrete relationships. And I think this is so precisely because the flow of dollars is not an aggregate phenomenon; it is disaggregate. Capital, after all, does not flow from one economic entity such as the United States to another entity such as Brazil. Specific groups with specific placement in the American social structure direct that investment; it flows from specific segments in the American political economy through specific overseas intermediaries into specific segments in the Brazilian economy; it then directly affects only specific elements in the Brazilian social structure and indirectly, in a spin-off way, others. Its concrete effect on the Brazilian economy will vary enormously, depending not only on the terms of investment but on enormously complicated preconditions in Brazil itself, preconditions that gross data typically used by quantitative scholars simply cannot pinpoint. This complicated mix will determine how many Brazilians will be economically affected by American investment; whether that investment tends to move Brazil toward an integrated economy or a dual economy; or whether it leads to greater technological innovations and change or simply to another "equilibrium trap."

Differentiated economic impact may also lead to differentiated perceptions and attitudes in Brazil. Commercial modernizers may view the impact of American capital as innovative and desirable; traditional elements may view it as disruptive of traditional values, modes, and organizations; ambivalent intellectuals, who want to modernize but in an independent, nationalist way, may respond with Hobsonian-Leninist sets of perceptions. Which attitudes dominate operationally will depend upon indigenous social conditions, but clearly the aggregate data analysis may point in one direction while the specific response goes another. One need only note the number of anti-American rebels in Latin America who made good use of the tactics they learned at Fort Bragg; or the important role played in anti-foreign movements in China by Chinese students educated overseas. In sum, aggregate analysis must, at the very least, recognize the highly different social structures involved in the flow of international transactions; and it must use more refined data that lend themselves to more sophisticated analysis. It must not restrict itself to the manipulation of easily obtainable but relatively gross data, like GNP figures, but must get on with the time-consuming but necessary business of scouring the world for more detailed, statistical information. Unless it does, it will remain in a position analogous to that of a political historian trying to generalize about American politics from election returns broken down by states instead of precincts and wards.

The second characteristic type of quantitative studies can be classified as perceptual investigations. Their frequent object of inquiry has been the decision-making process itself; the methods most often used are simulation, retrospective interviews, and content analysis; the stress has been upon those variables that shape perceptions and consequent choices—for example, the inner dynamics of small-group behavior; the importance of each individual's "role" (i.e., the job shapes the man); and personal idiosyncrasies such as an authoritarian personality. Now, one could hardly deny the importance of the decision-making process and the role of individual perceptions in it. It is a subject that demands more attention in the twentieth century with the constant enlargement, bureaucratization, and professionalism of the foreign policy apparatus. So I think these perceptual studies are to be applauded for their effort to go beyond the conventional method (or nonmethod) of common-sense intuition and to make a more systematic analysis.

Nevertheless, like conventional diplomatic history, their focus has been on isolated elites and isolated events; for what clearly interests most perceptual analysts is the decision-maker operating in a crisis: what one popularly calls today "crisis management." This may reflect the greater accessibility of data on crises that led to war; but my impression is that it also reflects a desire to make quantitative international studies a policy-science: that is, the capacity to use historical studies to *predict* what configuration might lead to war in the present and future and to *prescribe* the proper antidotes. Laudable as this may be, these studies, for all their innovative methods, have not escaped the conceptual weaknesses that I earlier ascribed to traditional crisis-oriented history. Indeed, in one sense they have compounded them by assuming that the crisis-managers are largely unaffected by the domestic sources of foreign policy; that they simply interact, in a stimulus-response way, with their international adversaries; therefore, perceptual analysis of crises need not deal with those domestic sources at all, much less infer them. Which leads me to the truism that a method is only as good as its concepts.[3]

If this critique is correct, then American diplomatic history, like an underdeveloped one-staple economy, is in an "equilibrium trap": while our technology and the quality of what we produce gets better, our conventional conceptual categories act as a mental straitjacket which retards expansion and diversification. Where, then, can we go from here? As a point of departure, let me offer a few simple and by no means wholly original suggestions. In order not to be too diffuse, I shall limit my illustrations to American diplomatic history since the 1890's.

The first and most essential point to make is the need to fill the gap between isolated events and aggregate generalizations; and the way to fill the gap is to appreciate the degree to which America's foreign relations are the product of domestic social structure. But before one arrives at that appreciation he must have a precise and systematic picture of that social structure.

The conceptualization of American social structure that I find most persuasive and which lends itself most to the diplomatic historian is one developed in a number of recent articles by Samuel P. Hays.[4] Its basic premise is that industrialization, urbanization, and bureaucratization created a highly expanded vertical social structure that became ever more differentiated and finely divided; that while there was constant mobility within this expanding vertical structure, mobility did not lead to homogeneity in occupation, income, or levels of consumption. Using terms first popularized in America by the sociologist Robert Merton, Hays sees the resultant differentiation in terms of a local-cosmopolitan continuum. Those grouped at the local end of the continuum have a range of activities and interests spatially confined to the geographic unit of the local community; their contacts and relationships are immediate, personal, face-to-face; their human consciousness is restricted in scope and variety; in the corporate orders of the private business world and the public administrative state, they are largely managed and manipulated by others.

Those in the middle ranges of this continuum have activities, interests, and a level of consciousness that transcend the inclusive community; instead of being organized spatially, they tend to develop a more exclusive organization on the basis of function. Typically, these would include interest groups in business, agriculture, and labor that collectively try to influence markets and prices.

Those at the cosmopolitan end of the continuum have contacts and relationships that are more impersonal and widespread; their educational experience has expanded their "scale of awareness" and their "tolerated variety of experiences"; their interests, activities, and consciousness transcend space and function. In short, the cosmopolitans are system-makers. They integrate many functional interest groups from widely different geographic areas; they systematize human relationships on a large scale; they centralize decision-making from the top down; they manage the corporate order in both the private and public world and increasingly integrate and coordinate the two. According to Hays and others, the main innovative impulses in modern America come increasingly from cosmopolitans (or what William Appleman Williams called many years ago "corporatists"), while local and middle strata either resist innovation, or try to shape it to their own needs, or simply acquiesce in it.[5]

The usefulness of this structural framework, both as an analytical and descriptive tool, is almost boundless for the diplomatic historian. For one thing, it helps him pinpoint and describe coherently the interested clientele of American foreign policy. Diplomatic historians in talking about public opinion on foreign policy have tended to analyze it in terms of grass-roots, man-in-the-street aggregates, or the role of special-interest groups—the NAM, the AFL, the mission board, hyphenate organizations, and the like. But the contemporary work of political scientists has suggested that these approaches are unrealistic; that the mass public is never informed and rarely interested in foreign policy save under extraordinary circumstances where some temporary, emotional involvement is generated; and that functional groups, while somewhat better informed, are primarily interested in those international aspects that directly affect their well-being (when they get what they want on a concrete issue, it is often because their goals coincided fortuitously with the perceptions and attitudes of the cosmopolitans). If one applies the local-cosmopolitan continuum to recent public opinion studies, it is clear that the large, so-called "inattentive public" are "locals," the smaller "attentive public" are "functionals," and their "opinion-makers" are "cosmopolitans."[6] Or similarly, James N. Rosenau, in his case study of the 1958 foreign aid bill, discovered that his interested public was divided into two groups which he called "segmented" and "continentals." 7 The "segmented," with their ties chiefly to the legislative branch, are described in terms quite similar to Hays's description of the middle-strata types, while the "continentals," with links directly to the administration policy machine, are most certainly "cosmopolitans." In like fashion, the nearly omnipotent foreign policy elite analyzed by Gabriel Almond in his *The American People and Foreign Policy* is primarily composed of cosmopolitans—only secondarily of functional leaders. The same holds for the power elite that G. William Dumhoff, the psychologist, discovers in the Council on Foreign Relations, the Council on Economic Development, the "think" tanks, and the major foundations. Buttressing evidence comes also from the work of Bernard C. Cohen and Samuel P. Huntington.8

Admittedly, this process of identifying and relating specific social elements to attitudes and behavior on foreign policy becomes more difficult as one pushes back in time. We simply do not have satisfactory survey data, if indeed any; and there is a rapid diminution of the number of "interested" organizations, like the Council on Foreign Relations, from which one can extract lists of directors, membership rolls, and the like. One could, of course, make an inferential leap and simply project contemporary studies back into time, and for all its hazards there is merit in doing exactly that. Nevertheless, the optimum use of this approach can only come with a relatively precise delineation of foreign policy elites at every point on the time span. One historian, Ernest May, recently made such an effort for the years 1898–1899 in his speculative essay *American Imperialism*. While I question both the accuracy of his methods and the validity of his interpretations, I do think it is an important step in the right direction. I hope it will provoke some effort to sophisticate techniques of elite identification, though this would undoubtedly mean that diplomatic historians would have to enter the unfamiliar realm of Social Registers, Blue Books, newspaper content analysis, and collective biographies.

Once one has placed the interested foreign policy public in specific spots in our vertical social structure, then all sorts of interesting questions open up, questions that ought to be asked not simply for fixed static points—for 1898 or 1914 or 1941 or 1969—but always with an eye to discovering possible change over time. Where, for example, does one fit the policy-makers themselves into this social continuum? Are the managers of the administrative state "cosmopolitans" in the same sense as those who manage the complex, conglomerate, corporate world? How much interchangeable movement of personnel is there between cosmopolitans in the parallel structures of business and government? What sort of linkages, both institutional and informal, exist between public and private elites, and how do they change quantitatively and qualitatively over time? To what degree and in what ways do elites, in and out of government, share the same values and perceptions; and to what degree may it be said, as Gabriel Almond did in different context, that policy-making "involves a constant search for the most adequate means to realize the values of their clienteles . . . ?" If this is true, is it not also true even for the decision-maker who operates in a crisis situation where direct communication with his clientele may not be feasible, but where shared values and perceptions continue to operate powerfully upon his choices?

Beyond the implications for governmental policy-making, several other questions follow from the effort to relate foreign relations to domestic social structure. Basically, they are all variants of the same question: what is the source of innovational impulses? Is an overproduction theory and a commitment to marketplace expansionism the product of functional leaders who think their special interests would benefit by such expansion? Or does the main impulse come from cosmopolitan corporatists who think in more integrative, systematic terms about the social order as a whole, and who worry about making it more rational, predictable, stable, and prosperous? In the movement to reform the banking laws and liberalize the tariff for more efficient marketplace expansion, does the major innovational thrust come from a sort of horizontal give-and-take between interest groups with a stake in the world market and those without one? Or does the thrust come vertically downward from a cosmopolitan elite that defines overseas markets as a marginal but important multiplier for the political economy? In the effort of the 1920's to systematize and coordinate the public and private roles in overseas investment and lending, did the resistance to that innovation come from middle-strata interest groups who felt constrained by the not-so-"hidden hand" of the Commerce Department? And did the main stimulus for that innovation come from the corporatists of the Herbert Hoover stripe? Is foreign policy ideology, as we have often assumed, the reflection of shared grass-roots values that permeate equally every level of the social structure? Or does it often reflect simply the leadership strategy of cosmopolitans seeking to use ideology to "mobilize local impulses for national" and international objectives? (Hays has argued the latter view, and in his own way Frederick Merk has done so in his *Manifest Destiny and Mission in American History*.) Finally, are elitist *Weltanschauungen* figments of the fertile imaginations of William A. Williams and Arno Mayer? Or are they, as our picture of social structure suggests, real and indeed crucial to the understanding of America's foreign relations? After all, does the domestic input for American foreign policy consist of no more than the accumulated interplay of guns-and-butter interest groups? Or is a vital ingredient the penchant and capacity of cosmopolitan corporatists to think in integrative, systematic terms—not only about their domestic social order but about the international order as well; not only in the short-run present but in the long-term future as well?

Those who lean to the latter view can take heart from N. Gordon Levin's fine monograph, *Woodrow Wilson and World Politics*. It has successfully done what many of us have attempted but rarely managed: It has avoided the tendency to interpret diplomatic history in an unintegrated, fragmented, pluralistic way. As Levin so beautifully explains, Woodrow Wilson's mind is not divided like the chapters of a diplomatic history textbook into economics, politics, and ideology; it is not, in Dean Acheson's words, "the intellectual equivalent of a cream separator"; it is not something that can be carved up into chunks and factors without lobotomizing and making senseless the whole. In Levin's Wilson there is, for example, utterly no contradiction between economic expansion and the American mission to expand the area of freedom. Commercial expansion—as William McKinley had earlier noted—was a pacifying and civilizing force; wherever commerce went —as John Dewey was to state—the consequent changes in values, social structure, and institutions invariably made for greater democracy. War and traditional imperialism were—as Joseph Schumpeter was to view them—simply atavisms in a modern, commercial, industrial world, throwbacks to earlier, nomadic warrior stages of human existence, while the natural condition of modern, international capitalism was peace and cooperation. Ultimately, of course, it was as inconceivable to Woodrow Wilson as it had been to Adam Smith to see personal freedom and liberty in any other social context than that of private property—so that for Wilson, as for the American military in Vietnam that Mary McCarthy describes, expanding the area of freedom and expanding the area of free enterprise were inextricably one and the same.[9]

I have focused thus far on specific segments in the social structure as domestic sources for foreign policy innovation. But there is an external dimension involving that same social structure which must not be overlooked: that is, the expansive internationalization of American society. By that I do not mean simply the expansion of our government's global responsibilities, or the enlargement and extension of its military power and presence, or American involvement in this century's wars—what Howard Beale euphemistically entitled "America's Rise to World Power." That is part of what I mean by internationalization, but that part is already receiving adequate treatment from diplomatic historians. What has been neglected is the concurrent and almost geometric expansion of private, nongovernmental segments of American society—through their overseas agents—into specific segments of nearly every other national society on the face of this planet. Just as the cosmopolitans of an urban metropolis like Chicago have expanded into its regional hinterland in search of comparative economic advantages, recreational facilities, and greater social order, so have the cosmopolitans of the national metropolis of the United States expanded into its global hinterland—and for largely the same reason. I do not mean to denigrate the coordinate role of the American government and of the formal diplomatic bureaucracy. But our fascination with policy-makers using power to manipulate others has, I believe, prevented us from appreciating the role played by corporations, universities, foundations, labor unions, mission boards, and the like in the exportation of American ideas, values, life styles, capital, goods, and services. Our concern for the crisis event, moreover, has obscured the degree to which this expansion of America has become institutionalized. That is, the American presence overseas has become more or less integrated into the daily life and social fabric of "host" countries, so that American interests in a given country are no longer (as perhaps they were in the past) on a specific, crisis-to-crisis basis, but are habitual, daily, continuous, and routinized.

This private, institutionalized internalization of American society has had profound consequences—of which we are largely ignorant—for America and the societies with which she interacts. One has been its impact upon American governmental policy itself. In the narrow sense —that involving the specific event—the American community overseas, through its feedback role in communicating information, or in its capacity to alter the definition of a situation, becomes a crucial ingredient. Whether or not America decides to build a rail system in Manchuria competitive to Japan's in 1909; whether or not America decides to break the world rubber pool in the 1920's; whether or not America seeks to alter Middle Eastern oil arrangements in the 1940's—all that depends not simply (though obviously in part) upon corporatists' conceptions of the Open Door, or the "community of interests, aims, and ideals," or national security—but also upon the happiness or unhappiness of American textile merchants in Manchuria, or rubber people in Malaya, or oil men in Saudi Arabia with their working relationships with Japanese, British, French, and Dutch capitalists and bureaucrats. At the same time, in the broader sense, this institutionalization of American interests overseas has demanded an enlargement of government responsibilities. No longer can they be limited to occasional promotion, protection, or crisis-management. Since the American presence abroad is continuous and habitual, so must be governmental policy: thus the increasing need of the government to develop permanent institutions like the Export-Import Bank, the International Monetary Fund, or the World Bank; or the need for long-term programs like the Marshall Plan, Point Four, or the Alliance for Progress. Just as the domestic arena had to be systematized and rationalized when the dominant social elements became (in Ida Tarbell's words) "nationalized" in consciousness and operations, so the international theater has had to be similarly altered when some of those same social elements became "internationalized."

The second chief set of consequences of this expansion and institutionalization of American society abroad has been its impact upon other societies. In our egocentricity, our emphasis has been upon the motivation of American policy; and for all our multi-national research, little stress has been placed upon the concrete consequences of American overseas expansion. My own *China Market* deals exclusively with the dynamics of American involvement in China, and treats China as a kind of passive entity. Paul Varg's *Missionaries, Chinese, and Diplomats* . . . , for all its great value, seems to tell us much about missionaries and diplomats, and precious little about Chinese. To be sure, as diplomatic historians we have a concern for the consequences of American policy overseas. But almost invariably, what is really meant is only the consequence of formal governmental policy (the Open Door Notes, the Consortium, the Neutralization Scheme, and so forth); and almost invariably it is limited to anticipated consequences. To wit: policymaker X anticipated that his policy Y would lead to consequence Z. If it does, it is a good policy; otherwise not. But there is no systematic concern for unanticipated consequences—upon social mobility, cultural values, political structure, or economic change in the foreign society. In this sense, one might well bear in mind K-C Liu's opening remarks in his *Americans and Chinese* that "in certain large areas of the world such as Asia, contacts with the United States at the nongovernmental level—through traders and entrepreneurs, missionaries, educators, and scientists, and through students and other visitors—had greater effects, on the whole, than any direct activity of the American government. In China, America's cultural and economic influence was undoubtedly more important than the impact of her power."

How, as diplomatic historians, do we come to grips with this internationalization of American society and the resultant institutionalization of our relationships with other countries? I would suggest that the first step is simply to be more aware of the important role in the process played by the exportation of *human capital:* i.e., missionaries, students, tourists, military personnel, consular officials, sales representatives, managers, skilled labor, insurance agents, bankers, and expatriates, as well as returning students, teachers, and military officers educated in the United States. Once our awareness is sharpened, then we have an obligation to reconstruct, over time, the American "universe" and presence overseas; or, if you will, the American "colony" abroad—the state within states. And then we must reconstruct the specific linkages between specific groups of overseas Americans and specific social groups in the "host" country; that is, we must see where and how these Americans fit into the indigenous social structure. And then we must reconstruct the consequences of the American presence for that foreign society.

Take Mexico as an example. We would first need some elemental demographic and social data about the American community. How large is it, and what percentage of it is transient and what is reasonably permanent? What has been the historical pattern of its growth? Who are these Americans in social and occupational terms? Where do they live? In urban areas like Mexico City, or in mining camps and ranches in the North? If they live in Mexico City, for example, do they reside in outlying upper-class suburbs, or in closer-in, middle-class "in" places near supermarkets, coffeehouses, specialty stores, and entertainment? Are they self-segregated with other Americans or foreign residents, or are they intermixed with Mexicans? And if the latter, which specific Mexicans? Do they send their teen-agers to Mexican high schools; or to the "American School" just across the street from the expensive American-British Hospital; or to the prestigious British tutorial schools? And if they do send them to American or British schools, do Mexicans also attend there, and in what proportion? And more especially, which Mexicans—poor children on scholarships, or the children of wealthy politicians and businessmen who see both practical and status value in learning English? What precisely do they do in their jobs? With which Mexicans does their work bring them into contact, and what sort of working or social relationships grow out of that contact? In short, we need some idea as to how much the American community is integrated into Mexican life—and, more especially, into which slices of Mexican life.

Now, let me generalize by suggesting that the net impact of that American presence is innovational. I do not mean to imply that what is innovational or modern is necessarily better and progressive. I simply mean that the American presence means newness and change. The American, after all, brings into Mexico an alien version of Christianity; an unfamiliar music; personal mannerisms like punctuality and bluntness; bourgeois values that stress risk-taking, achievement, and efficiency; and innovations in managerial and organizational techniques. The interaction of these innovational thrusts with Mexican life will, in turn, have impact on Mexican perceptions and feelings about the source of this innovation—namely, the metropolitan United States itself. And since Mexican foreign policy—like ours and everyone else's —is in part the product of domestic sources, this will have impact on Mexican diplomatic policy toward this country.

I do not think, for example, that one can understand the ambivalence of Mexico's American policy without insight into the relationships between Mexican society and the American community living in its midst. How does one explain, after all, the Mexican policy of maintaining direct, bilateral relations with the United States on an extraordinarily friendly basis while at the same time sustaining ties with Castro's Cuba, voting against American resolutions in the OAS, and pursuing a sometimes independent course in the UN? Are the latter merely the perfunctory acts of an established regime paying rhetorical allegiance to a revolutionary heritage? Partly, to be sure. But as the Mexican diplomatic historian Mario Ojeda-Gómez has recently suggested, this seeming ambivalence represents also a conscious balancing act by the Mexican Foreign Ministry to satisfy contending social and political groups that have very different feelings about the United States.[10] And these widely differing feelings grew not simply out of abstract ideology—of an anti-American left or a pro-American right; they grew out of concrete experiences with an ever-present overseas America that often had profound impact upon the daily activities and life styles of Mexicans.

The oft-quoted remark, "Poor Mexico—so far from God, so close to America," has a nice ring and undoubtedly much truth. But it obscures the fact that some segments of Mexican society were penetrable and tended to respond quite favorably to the innovational intrusions of the United States; other segments were impenetrable and tended to resist innovation and protect traditional modes and values; and a whole range of grays existed between those blacks and whites. How, for example, do Mexican businessmen respond to American capitalism? Those who help the Americans run the large, multi-national, Mexican-American joint companies—like the automobile assembly plants—may well be pro-American; and the pronouncements and politics of their powerful organization, the Mexican Chamber of Commerce, would reflect this fact. Junior executives employed in wholly owned American companies obviously owe their income and mobility to American penetration. At the same time they may be merely tolerated by their American counterparts, given less social status, and denied equal decision-making power. So their attitudes may be mixed. Small-to-medium Mexican businessmen may feel themselves competitively threatened by American economic inroads, and their reaction may be hostile. Indeed, many such businessmen were instrumental in organizing the CNIT and in making common cause with left-wing intellectuals in an anti-American capital movement.

Without belaboring the point further, I would suggest that the same kinds of vertical differentiation could be found among Mexican labor leaders, politicians, and the like. And one can at least hypothesize that if one could construct a vertical social structure for Mexico, one might discover positive correlations between points on their local-cosmopolitan continuum and tendencies to approve or disapprove the innovational penetration of overseas Americans. This hypothesis, in turn, suggests the need for comparative studies to determine why some nations, like the United Kingdom, had so little capacity or inclination to resist

American penetration, and why others, like contemporary France, continue to have so much. I think at least part of the answer is to be found in differing social structures and in the quantity and quality and kinds of linkages established with overseas Americans.

I have been writing about the need to investigate the role of human capital, of people, in the internationalization of American society and the institutionalization of American relationships with the rest of the world. One final and concluding element remains to be pursued, about which diplomatic historians have been remiss. That is *material* capital. To be sure, we have not been as negligent in talking about economic expansion as we have been about cultural and social expansion. But the primary concern has been egocentrically upon the relative importance of domestic economic factors in American foreign policy. Is American expansion a form of Open Door, informal imperialism that seeks to keep the underdeveloped world in neo-mercantilist bondage? Or, as John Braeman put it two years ago in a paper on the so-called Wisconsin school of diplomatic history: "After all, what's wrong with wanting to trade?" This question of internal motivation is an important concern, and it relates intimately to my earlier discussion of the ties between American foreign policy and American social change. But that is no longer enough. We must get out of our culture-bound preoccupations with Self and examine the concrete consequences of the American exportation of capital upon the growth and diversification of the rest of the world—particularly of the underdeveloped world. This we have not done. We have tossed around a lot of gross, raw statistics, and then proceeded to make our respective—and mostly intuitive—value judgments. The liberal traditionalist may see the economic impact as essentially beneficial (as intended) and, although the benefits (as with the Alliance for Progress) may be slow in coming, they are as inexorable as they are gradual. The radical revisionist may see the impact as simply calamitous (as intended), and any rhetoric to the contrary as simply cant. No doubt these judgments provide satisfaction in reinforcing personal ideologies. But I would like to suggest that as diplomatic historians we do not know enough about the complex business of economic growth to make these kinds of overgeneralized pronouncements; and I suggest we suspend them until we do.

The shame of it is that there is no reason for such ignorance. There is an exciting body of literature on economic development, and all we need to use it is the capacity to read and enough intelligence to learn some new terms and to master a few relatively simple economic concepts. I think, for example, of Gunnar Myrdal's *Rich Lands and Poor,* Clifford Geertz's *Agricultural Involution,* and Jonathan Levin's *The Export Economies.* Especially enlightening is the model developed by Robert E. Baldwin in his article on "Export Technology and Development from a Subsistence Level" in the *Economic Journal.*

Baldwin's model suggests to me that most American overseas investment is prompted less by grand policy considerations, either imperialistic or altruistic, than by the unrelenting effort of American capitalists to make use of comparative economic advantage to maximize their rate of profit. It suggests that there is not one pattern of economic growth (or retardation) that flows from American investment, but several. And it suggests that only under rare circumstances will private foreign investment generated by private foreign capitalists lead to industrialization.

For example, if American investment goes into "plantation economies" like tea, tobacco, rubber, coffee, and sugar, its general tendency will be to promote what Baldwin calls a "staple trap." The demand created by wages to field hands will lead to a larger market for simple consumer goods like textiles and cooking utensils; but because of cost advantages, these will be chiefly supplied by American and other advanced manufacturers. Demands for foodstuffs by plantation workers will produce more commercialized and innovative farming; but after an initial rise, demand inelasticity will force farm income to level off. And because investment in plantation economies makes such little use of skilled labor and complex, capital goods, the objective basis for expansion into nonagricultural activities is quite unsatisfactory.

On the other hand, investment in a "mining economy" like oil, copper, bauxite, and iron tends to produce a "dual economy." Because the number of workers employed is relatively small, there is insufficient demand generated to produce a more commercialized agriculture; it tends to remain at a subsistence level. On the other hand, the pool of skilled labor created by the mining sector may make it possible for local manufacturers—again in such simple things as consumer goods—to compete with foreigners. But the general tendency is to produce a dual economy in which the small mining sector is integrated into a foreign metropolis and the much larger agricultural sector remains at a backward subsistence level.

On occasion, however, foreign investment in a mining economy can

lead to more significant growth, diversification, and even industrialization. This depends on two things. One is that the needs of the mining
economy must lead to an integrated transportation system that lowers
costs enough to stimulate *other* industries. (And not just any transportation system—a single-use oil pipeline may have absolutely no
value for other industries; a railroad that leads only from a single
mining area to some seacoast city without branching out geographically
may have little multiplier effect.) The other variable is that the mining economy must process the raw material in the underdeveloped country itself. And this, in turn, depends upon a number of things:
comparative labor costs, the weight reduction in processing, available
electrical power, the economies of scale, and the existence of a local
market for the processed raw material.

So there is Mr. Baldwin's model. It is deficient in the sense that it
does not include the government's role through foreign aid and the
like in socializing risks and subsidizing costs—much as the government did a century ago with the transcontinental railroads. It ignores
the government's function in providing military protection and promoting political stability for overseas investment. It assumes that
comparative cost advantages are the sole determinant of what is invested where, without sufficient regard for long-term policy-planning
generated by governmental and corporate cosmopolitans. But for all
its inadequacy, it does suggest the kind of conceptual thinking that
diplomatic historians must do if they are to get beyond historiographical
squabbling over the motivations of America's economic expansion to
some realistic assessment of its consequences.

I have argued for a conception of diplomatic history—or whatever
name you might wish to apply—as the study of the *total impact* of
societies upon other societies. The emphasis has been upon American
social structure and its linkages to American governmental policy and,
as well, to the social structures of other nations; upon the importance
of private as well as governmental foreign relations; and upon unanticipated cultural and economic consequences as well as political ones. I
am aware that implicitly I am asking diplomatic historians to also be
social historians, and not only of our national society but the others we
treat as well. I am aware of the implications this has for our own
methodological retooling; for the exploration of new and unfamiliar
materials; for our modes of training graduate students. I am aware that

little of what I suggest can be done without the collection and dissemination of now unavailable data, and without the building of monographic blocks not now in existence. I know only too well from personal experience the difficulties involved. But the penalties for not doing these things are too great to pay. For I fear that without redefinition and reconceptualization, American diplomatic history will simply become a kind of atavistic, esoteric enclave, performing its traditional tasks—undoubtedly well, but with less and less relevance for and communication with the more systematic studies of non-diplomatic American historians.

NOTES

1. I wish to thank two of my colleagues, Samuel P. Hays and Dennis Kelly, and two former colleagues, Joel Silbey of Cornell University and Paul Kleppner of Northern Illinois University, for extensive conversations which greatly aided my conceptualization of this paper. Several fellow diplomatic historians also offered stylistic and substantive criticism. Especially helpful were Ernest R. May of Harvard University, John DeNovo of the University of Wisconsin, and Akira Iriye of the University of Chicago.

2. For an excellent example of such transactional studies, see Bruce M. Russett, *Continuity and Contention: Britain and America in the Twentieth Century* (Cambridge, Mass., 1963).

3. The best general introduction to such quantitative studies is Joel David Singer, ed., *Quantitative International Politics: Insights and Evidence* (New York, 1968).

4. Some of Hays's articles remain unpublished. The most available and relevant article is Samuel P. Hays, "Political Parties and the Community-Society Continuum" in William N. Chambers and Walter D. Burnham, eds., *The American Party Systems: Stages of Political Development* (New York, 1967).

5. The concept of corporatism is best developed in William A. Williams, *The Contours of American History* (Cleveland, 1961). See also Gabriel Kolko, *The Triumph of Conservatism* (New York, 1963), and Robert H. Wiebe, *The Search for Order* (New York, 1967).

6. For example, see Lester Markel, *et al., Public Opinion and Foreign Policy* (New York, 1949).

7. James N. Rosenau, *National Leadership and Foreign Policy: A Case Study of the Mobilization of Public Support* (Princeton, 1963).

8. For example, see Bernard C. Cohen, *The Political Process and Foreign Policy: The Making of the Japanese Settlement* (Princeton, 1957).

9. See Mary McCarthy's series of articles on Vietnam in the *New York Review of Books,* 1968.

10. Mario Ojeda-Gómez developed this analysis in a talk at the University of Pittsburgh in early 1969.

The Dangers of
Diplomatic History

LAURENCE EVANS

I

Today, when so much of the nation's attention is turned to international questions, it must surely be disturbing to historians to note what a small part history plays in the attempts of our society to understand and master the problems we face in our relations with the rest of the world. Vast resources are brought to bear on these problems by the government, universities, and private interests in support of investigations ranging from anthropological studies of emerging peoples to computer mathematics, from economics to psychology, not to mention the enormous sums spent on improving our military capabilities. But in the midst of all this activity, history, measured by the use to which it is put by policy-makers and the public, and measured by the coarse but ready yardstick of the cash the country is willing to invest in historical studies of foreign policy, would appear to have as much relevance to international politics as theology, and rather less than tourism.

I think we owe it to ourselves as historians and to society at large to consider why history seems to have so little to say to our fellow men about the problems that beset us; why we seem to be antiquaries scratching about in an irrelevant past. Of course, it may be true that history has little to teach mankind about international politics today; the study of the past may indeed be irrelevant to our present difficulties. I for one do not believe it. Santayana's warning is as true in the realm of international affairs as it is in any other sphere of human activity—that the community that does not know its own history is condemned to repeat it. Further, history is directly relevant to our present difficulties if for no other reason than that every decision and commitment made in the past limits our options in the present.

I am far from believing that the only or even the prime justification for historical study is immediate relevance to present trouble, but I do believe that the present irrelevance of our discipline is very strong evidence of a fundamental weakness in it, and that our present methods of studying and writing about the relations between states are fundamentally flawed. They are based on a misunderstanding of the nature of these relations. Consequently they have contributed to a vast misunderstanding of America's role in the world in the past, and they offer no guidance to her role in the present and the future. We have in fact failed as practitioners of our profession to accomplish what any discipline must do or perish: to expand man's awareness of reality and thus increase his ability to control his own destiny. If it is true that history is not playing the role it ought to play in this crisis in human affairs, we must not blame others for that failure. It is an essential part of the historian's responsibility to make sure that what he has to contribute does in fact make a contribution, and if it is not doing so, to acknowledge that the failure is his and attempt to rectify it.

We need look no further for a clue to this state of affairs than the name we generally use for the historical analysis of the relations between sovereign states—diplomatic history, with its implication that diplomacy and its ramifications are the most important (and some historians write as though they were the only) aspect of foreign relations. But diplomacy is only a part of a very complex process called policy-making, that is, the formulation and implementation of the goals of foreign policy. Foreign policy may be defined as the determination of what is necessary and possible to protect and advance the national interest, or, in concrete terms, the attempt to control the political relations between one's own state and another to one's own advantage. Diplomacy is the conduct of these relations and includes every action short of war taken by a state to influence these relations, and is not confined to the activities of ambassadors. It is concerned not with ends but with means, as war is a means to an end or, as Clausewitz put it, the continuation of policy by other means.

This exclusive concern with political relations may seem excessively narrow, particularly to those historians whose interests lie in the study of economic and social relations between states. My approach is based on the claims to primacy of political over other forms of relations. The overriding goal of foreign policy is survival, and this depends on relative power. Political relations are the product of relative power between states, and until the nature of these political relations has been determined it is impossible to assign any order of importance to other relations; all of a state's interests—economic, social, cultural—will be sacrificed to ensure the existence of the state. One has only to consider the relations between Britain and Germany before the First World War to see this point. Each was the other's greatest trading partner; they shared a long tradition of friendship and alliance; their royal families were related; intellectual, social, and cultural relations were close. But all of this counted for nothing when the political interests of the two countries clashed.

Now I realize that historians are talking less about diplomacy and more about foreign policy than they used to. I do not think this marks a real change, however, but rather a shift in emphasis from formal and legal relationships to power relationships between states. With few exceptions, the historian concerned with the international community is studying and writing and teaching diplomatic history and not the history of foreign policy. Unfortunately, again with few exceptions, he is unaware of it.

This overemphasis on diplomacy and its history is easy to understand. Traditionally, the historian dealing with foreign policy has been forced to confine his studies to diplomacy because diplomatic papers were the only sources available. Diplomacy being the overt aspect of foreign policy and by its nature visible, states were less reluctant to make public those documents dealing with diplomatic actions. Except for the United States, it is only very recently that governments have begun gingerly to open their files on the policy-making process. Thus habits of thought and standards of performance developed over the years in Europe and in this country have hardened into an unconscious application of the standards of diplomatic history to the study of foreign policy as a whole. This has had particularly unfortunate effects in the United States, where the traditions developed in writing domestic history under a relatively open governmental system have led to the assumption that the government is equally open in matters connected with foreign relations.

II

The history of the conduct of foreign policy, or diplomatic history, as an independent field of study has several weaknesses, some intrinsic and some in turn deriving from the historian's failure to recognize these weaknesses. The first of the intrinsic weaknesses is that diplomatic history deals with only a part of a complex process and is concerned not with ends but with means. The goals of a country's foreign policy remain stable, but the means will vary as the political situation varies. Lord Salisbury put it best seventy-odd years ago when he said that England had no permanent friends and no permanent enemies, only permanent interests. In short, diplomatic history can have nothing to say in its own right about motive and purpose. The second weakness is that when diplomatic history deals with the relations between one country and another, it is again treating as an end in itself what is merely one element of the total political situation comprising relations with all the states in the international community. Unless one considers how policy-makers are limited by competing claims for a country's power, influence, and attention in other parts of the world, how can one discuss the meaning and significance of any particular aspect of the relations between one country and another? In short, diplomatic history does not form what Arnold Toynbee called, in another context, an intelligible field of study.

Let me draw upon my own special interest, American Middle East policy, for an example of the difficulties inherent in relying on diplomatic action as a guide to motive and purpose in foreign policy, as well as an example of the danger of ignoring the total political situation in assessing the significance of a particular political move. In August 1919, Woodrow Wilson made scarcely veiled threats—which he was quite ready to carry out—to pull out of the Versailles settlement and the League of Nations in response to Italian and Greek deals over certain areas in Anatolia and the question of French control of Syria.[1] Considering the enormous efforts Wilson had made to establish the League of Nations and was yet to make to get the American people to support the League, the United States' interest in Western Anatolia and Syria must have been of momentous importance, and Allied actions threatened these interests. But no amount of research in the field of American relations with the Middle East will uncover any such interest. So we must conclude that Wilson was (a) stupid, or (b) emotionally un-stable, or (c) stubborn, or (d) all of these.

But once we look beyond the Middle East a different picture appears. What was the American interest in the Middle East after World War I that caused Wilson to react so strongly? It was the American interest in the League of Nations, which in turn derived from American inter-est in the stability of Europe. By dint of much hard work and the sacrifice of lesser interests, Wilson had made the League an integral part of the peace settlement. This meant that the Covenant would be written into each of the treaties including that with Turkey. The United States, though not at war with Turkey, would sign the Turkish treaty, and through the League would in fact be guaranteeing the Middle East settlement. What the Allies were doing in the Middle East in the summer of 1919 was to grab what they could before the Turkish treaty was negotiated. They were able to do this because in signing the Treaty of Versailles Wilson had already lost his chief diplomatic weapon, his freedom to refuse to join in a common treaty of peace with Germany. If the Allies were permitted to continue their activities, the Middle Eastern settlement would be so blatantly out of tune with what the League purported to be as to make it a mockery; and more, the United States would have guaranteed that settlement. We can imagine the political holiday the enemies of the League would have had with such a mess. Now I am not making a case for the validity of the policy followed by the United States. This policy may in fact have been wrong. My point is that it is not possible to come to any conclusion at all by studying the diplomacy of these political moves in isolation.

These intrinsic weaknesses of diplomatic history are compounded by the failure of historians to recognize them, and by the natural dis-inclination of scholars to accept the fact that their investigations have only a limited significance—or perhaps I should say their natural ten-dency to think that their studies contain the key to understanding the field they are investigating.

Another weakness is that the historian of state diplomacy is almost forced by the limitations of his source material to take at face value the statements of diplomats or public officials, for these statements are his prime source of information on motive. But, in the first place, it is impossible to ascertain from the material being used whether these statements are true or false. Diplomacy being what it is, it is most unlikely that the people engaged in it expose their true motives. Then again, the agents of diplomacy are not always, as a matter of course, informed about the motive behind a particular policy or course of action. It is not essential to the performance of their duties that they be informed. An example is the cloud of unknowing in which Mr. Winant operated as Ambassador to Great Britain during World War II. Ambassadors of course object to this, as did Winant and more recently Ambassador Kennan during his embassy to Yugoslavia. Kennan in fact insisted on a significant role in determining our policy toward Yugoslavia, as though Yugoslavia were the major factor in American Yugoslav policy.

III

Let me demonstrate how these inherent limitations of our present approach to the study of foreign policy have affected historical writing. I have chosen two textbooks for examples. Written by distinguished scholars, they represent the distilled essence, as it were, of received scholarly opinion. The first, Julius Pratt's *History of United States Foreign Policy*,[2] which I use myself in my courses, illustrates in its treatment of World War I the weakness of an analysis which cannot come to grips with purpose. In the chapters dealing with this period it is almost impossible to discover any motive behind American policy, or to find any discussion of American interests: how they were affected by the war; the role, if any, these interests played in the decisions made by the policy-makers; whether these decisions were correct. There is no consideration of the significance of the various stages of the war—for instance, whether the policy and attitudes of the government changed when it became apparent in 1915 that the war would not be over quickly, or whether the United States had any direct interest in the state of Europe after the war had been won. Of course, it may be argued that we are dealing with a textbook, and it is unfair to expect it to offer definitive answers in its own right. But this reinforces my argument. The state of the art in these matters is so vague and lacking in definition that they are better left out of a text, though they are the heart of any study of American foreign policy. What is left? A chronicle. The entire policy-making process is recorded in the State Department Archives, the Wilson Papers, the House Papers, and elsewhere; and yet, after fifty years' accumulation of research and writing on this subject, a textbook cannot include a discussion of motive. Pratt's book also illustrates the problems one runs into when one begins with diplomatic actions and then looks for motives behind them, instead of the other way about. In the first procedure, one is faced with an infinity of possibilities with little or no guidance from one's material. In the second case, if one begins with the goals of foreign policy, the research and analysis of these goals and the means used to achieve them are almost automatically defined. It is practically impossible for the writer of a study such as Pratt's to begin to demonstrate purpose and motive in foreign policy if the literature in the field has not already done so, and Pratt has shown admirable restraint in rejecting the temptation to be striking.

In addition to substantive weaknesses, diplomatic history also has built-in weaknesses of emphasis and organization that tend to obscure and distort the story. My example here is a case from the honored text, Samuel Flagg Bemis' *Diplomatic History of the United States,* Chapter 23, "The Great Anglo-American Arbitrations." [3] Even considered as an analysis of the phase of Anglo-American relations, this grouping together of a sequence of arbitrations, from the post–Civil War period to shortly before World War I, is quite artificial. The organization of data in itself is a method of communicating ideas by implying certain relationships between the data. What do these arbitrations have in common? Only that one method was used to solve certain differences between Britain and the United States. The fact that arbitration rather than some other method was used to settle all of these differences has of course some significance, but this is not great enough to warrant including them in a single chapter in a book on American diplomatic history. This implies that the fact that they were arbitrated was the most important thing one can say about them in terms of the diplomacy of the United States, and, going a step further, that the arbitration of the fisheries dispute was on the same level of significance for American interests as the Alabama claims or the Venezuela incident. A glance at the shifting political situation as it affected Anglo-American relations shows also how artificial Bemis' organization is. The forty years or so covered by the chapter break down into several distinct periods. In the first period after the Civil War, the United States had just fought a war which had revealed to the world her military capacity. The Civil War was the greatest war fought in the history of the Western world, and the national effort called up to fight it the greatest ever mustered, outweighing even the national effort of France during the Napoleonic war. A nation able to mount this level of military force acquires a certain standing in international affairs, and Anglo-American relations in the period show it. The second period runs from the middle seventies to the eighties and is a period of relative quiet. The third period covers the last great expansion of Europe and runs from the partition of Africa to the Russo-Japanese War; we see the United States protecting its outlying flanks by solidifying its position in Samoa and Hawaii, building a first-class navy, establishing its primacy in the Caribbean, fighting the Spanish-American War—moving with decision, in other words, to protect its interests from the challenge of the expansion of European powers. The last phase is the time of waiting for the outbreak of general war in Europe. Any conflict of interest, however minor, with political significance has a different meaning in each of these periods. To classify them together ignores these enormously important shifts in the involvement of the United States in world affairs.

This then is the case against diplomatic history, and against the history of international relations generally as it is pursued today: its weakest point is that very characteristic that defines history and distinguishes it from other disciplines concerned with the human past— antiquarianism, for instance. This characteristic is, of course, human purpose and motive. Perhaps we have been all along antiquaries scratching about in an irrelevant past. But this is far from being the worst of it. Antiquarian studies are valuable in their own right; they are not history to be sure, but a very strong case can be made for studies of the past which leave out motive and purpose when they cannot be demonstrated by the available evidence, or where the evidence is too weak to form the basis of valid hypotheses about motive. They can build up a corpus of information on which, eventually, historical studies can be based, as Darwin based his theories on a long tradition of natural history. But historians are not content to perform this service. We must analyze, judge, demonstrate our insights, and supply motive and judgment whether our material warrants it or not. Only rarely do we find restraint.

These weaknesses in concept and scope lead to a further weakness. Much of the historical data available are never investigated, sometimes because the researcher doesn't think they are important, but more frequently, I think, because he doesn't know they are there. Whatever the reason, the history of American foreign policy is the only specialty within our discipline that permits its practitioners to ignore almost systematically most of the significant sources. The diplomatic materials on which most studies of American foreign policy are based are only a small fraction of the data available.

Let me illustrate with a recent study written by a leading scholar and well received by the profession. The book is *Politics and Diplomacy of Peacemaking* by A. J. Mayer.[4] Here is a study based on material relating to the implementation of policy, the diplomacy of the Paris Peace Conference, which does not touch on the formulation of policy as distinguished from its implementation, which does not relate the problem under investigation to other problems faced by American policy-makers, and which practically ignores the enormous amount of significant documentary material in the files of the American Mission to Negotiate Peace, except the tiny fraction published. At the same time the author does not hesitate to draw large conclusions about American foreign policy from the material he does use, nor to judge the actors in the drama. Now, I do not know whether or not the author is correct in his conclusions and judgments, but then neither does he. Not having investigated all the available material, he is not justified as a historian in substituting hypothesis for historical data as he would be if, having searched all the sources, his data were insufficient to explain the subject he was investigating.[5]

The results of our failings we can see. Here in the United States, with unmatched opportunities for research in foreign policy, it is considered respectable to write books with daring and challenging hypotheses and judgments about the meaning of American foreign policy without setting foot in the archives. (These are paralleled by studies of contemporary foreign policy, also with daring and challenging hypotheses and judgments, based on the *New York Times* and other fragmentary sources.)

IV

If, as I maintain, what diplomatic historians have been concerning themselves with is not an intelligible field of historical study, what would constitute such a field? I suggest that it can only be the policy-making process as a whole, including the implementation of policy, or diplomacy. This is not to say that individual aspects of this field, including diplomacy, cannot be studied, but not out of context. Any study of a part of this complex process must always be studied and written about in relation to the whole, or it can be no more than a narrative or descriptive account. One thing it should not do is deduce motive solely from the data it is considering.

Some may object that diplomatic papers, for example, are often the only sources available. True, but does this mean that one can then proceed to ignore the lack of adequate data and write history that either explicitly or implicitly claims to have all the necessary information to judge motive and purpose, and to assign praise or blame accordingly? A favorite device of historians caught without adequate data, and unwilling or unable to recognize their problem when their material does not present a coherent or logical sequence, is to call the policy-makers naive or stupid or something worse. They may be so, but not from the evidence presented.

But the most popular device used to fill in the gap between motive and act is the use of a priori reasoning. One assumes from the outset that policy is motivated by some overriding purpose—imperial delusions, economic expansion, paranoia—and if the pattern doesn't fit here and there one can always fall back on the other device of calling the President a fool.

Diplomacy, including by my definition all aspects of the conduct of political relations between states, is a significant part of the policy-making process, but so are many other things. Navies, armies, money, and trade, for example, all have a part in policy-making, for they all have an effect on the relations between one state and the outside world. So do the policies of other states. The historian must ask many questions. What information do the policy-makers have about the problem? Is it accurate? How is the problem analyzed? What limitations exist on the freedom of action of the policy-makers, such as competing claims of other problems, or military and naval commitments elsewhere if the problem involves the possibility of the use of force? What is the state of public opinion on the issue? What can other countries do to frustrate the solution to the problem? The policy-makers ask these questions and must attempt to answer them before a policy is decided on, and it is here that the historian's investigation must begin, not after judgments have been made and a policy initiated.

I can best illustrate these points by examining a specific diplomatic act and probing beneath the public manifestation of policy to the motives underlying it. Woodrow Wilson's Fourteen Points address, the most famous or perhaps the second most famous foreign policy statement in American history, is seen as a monument to Wilson's idealism, stupidity, Calvinism, inexperience—according to your taste. On the face of it, the President is laying down the war aims of the United States, touching on problems far beyond the direct interests of the United States and involving it in matters beyond its control. Why did Wilson make the speech, and why did he make the kind of speech he did?

From the evidence available—mostly from Colonel House—its purpose was to seize the psychological initiative not merely from the Bolsheviks but also from the Allies, and establish the United States as the leader of the anti-German coalition. So far so good. But what about the contents of the address, the Fourteen Points themselves? If we do a little more research we discover that the points were based—literally, for the original draft was written in its margin—on a memorandum drawn up by Walter Lippmann and others giving a detailed analysis of the political-military situation and what the coalition must do to contain German-controlled Mittel Europa after the war. Now how important was the memorandum? Was it merely the brainchild of an adviser? Was Lippmann the author of the Fourteen Points? Further research discloses that this memorandum was based in its turn on doctrine already well established in the administration. It formed the basis of Wilson's Flag Day address. I have traced it back so far to an unsigned memorandum attributed to Robert Lansing written in May 1917. The Fourteen Points are an expression of a basic policy, the containment of Germany after the war. The individual points are in fact proposals for action designed specifically to break up Mittel Europa and inhibit the exercise of German power toward several highly strategic areas. Wilson casts them in phraseology in keeping with American political tradition and in keeping with the psychological purposes of the address.

What did the Fourteen Points mean individually? Do they state American policy on the subjects mentioned in the points? Was the United States in the war to give the peoples of Central Europe and the Ottoman Empire self-determination, or to restore Alsace-Lorraine to France? If we continue our research and compare the final draft of the address with the version actually delivered, we see a significant change. Wilson had written that all the points "must" be implemented; as he gave the address we see that they now "should" be implemented, except for restoring Belgium and the League of Nations. House says that this change was made in those situations where justice was not clear cut, but it also meant that the United States was not committed to these points. And this is emphasized by further research. Shortly after the address was made, the Italians were making no secret of their dissatisfaction with the contradiction between the Treaty of London and Wilson's proposals, and also between these proposals and those of Lloyd George made three days before the Fourteen Points speech. Wilson told the Italian Ambassador personally that the territorial proposals depended on effective guarantees of territory being established through a League of Nations, and if this were not achieved, "my mind would be open on all such matters to new judgments."

As we know, Italy did get a commitment on the Brenner Pass from Wilson in October. Wilson also agreed to French claims to Syria in the analysis of the Fourteen Points drawn up by Lippmann and Frank Cobb for the pre-armistice talks. Why? Because Wilson was already selling out? Or because he was bamboozled by wily European politicians? No, because though Germany had asked for peace, it was still doctrine in the administration that Germany and Mittel Europa had to be contained after the war, and it was officially accepted that Germany, though militarily defeated, still retained the potential to regroup her forces in the future.[6]

But soon all this changed. Mittel Europa was breaking up and Germany was cut off from the east and southeast by new nations. So what was the role of the Fourteen Points now? I have seen little evidence that Wilson referred to them systematically as a guide to policy during the Peace Conference, except for the two American commitments, the restoration of Belgium and the League. Wilson admitted during a discussion of Turkey in the Council of Four that he had forgotten he had mentioned in Point 12 the sovereignty of the Turks over the Turkish-speaking areas of the Ottoman Empire.[7]

Here we see very clearly the difference between ends and means. Were the Fourteen Points a statement of applied morality, a naive solution to the world's ills, a clear concise statement of the goals of American foreign policy? They were none of these. The Fourteen Points were a means to an end and could be changed, modified, or discarded as circumstances required. Having reached this point in our analysis, we can now, and not before, ask the fundamental question. How important are the Fourteen Points to the historian as evidence of American foreign policy? Having answered that, we can then proceed to a second question. How important were they as part of American policy toward Germany?

V

The examples I have given underline several important considerations which should govern research and writing in the historical study of any aspect of foreign policy. The first, of course, is the necessity of distinguishing between means and ends, and then relating means to ends. The second is that all policies adopted by a state revolve around the most important problem facing that state. The Fourteen Points, though they touched on problems in many parts of the world, related all of them to the major problem facing the United States in January 1918—the defeat and containment of Imperial Germany. A vivid current example is our present Middle East difficulties. That any course of action we may take in the Middle East must be subordinate to our relations with the Soviet Union is clearly demonstrated by the overriding necessity of an American-Soviet agreement on the Middle East, and by the level on which American-Soviet negotiations on the Middle East have been and are being conducted.

This is significant also in the third point, that in investigating any aspect of foreign policy it is necessary to start where the basic decisions are made. These decisions are frequently made in reponse to factors not connected with the particular problem the historian is researching. One's most important sources will often be found among the materials on the country's major problem, as most of the material on the Fourteen Points is filed in the major files on the war. Wilson's statement to the Italian Ambassador on war aims is not filed under Italy or Italian relations with Austria but in the file on the termination of the war.

Of course, a good deal of the time it is not possible to document the whole policy-making process, and the historian must perforce fill in the gaps by inference and guesswork. This brings up the fourth point. When it is necessary to reconstruct a policy, as a paleontologist reconstructs a skeleton from a piece of a jawbone, it is as necessary for the historian to have a knowledge of how policy is made as it is for the paleontologist to have a knowledge of anatomy. Too often we forget that in a subject as complicated as foreign policy, in which many conflicting interests must be reconciled or assigned an order of priority, appropriate machinery must be developed to handle the flow of information comprising analyses, instructions, records of recommendations, and decisions, all made by agencies or sub-divisions of agencies, each with a different point of view and with different objectives. Each embassy has its own job to do, each bureau in the State Department, each department of government; they all see a part of the picture and frequently see it in a different light from everybody else. Thus the historian must be able to judge the approximate significance of an individual document by its provenance. A historian has a memorandum by an Assistant Secretary of State analyzing a problem and proposing a solution; how important is the document? It helps to know that it must be considered by the other Assistant Secretaries, then by the Under Secretary, then by the Secretary of State, and, if the subject is important enough, by the National Security Council and the President, which brings in the Departments of Defense, Treasury, and anybody else involved. So this lowly memorandum is most unlikely to be by itself reliable evidence of what American foreign policy was. A case in point would be the value of Professor Schlesinger's book on the Kennedy Administration as a guide to American foreign policy.[8] Where does a presidential adviser fit into the policy-making machinery?

That is the situation as I see it. Here we are, with unmatched opportunities for research in the National Archives, presidential collections, and other depositories where the complete policy-making process is documented in detail for some of the most important decisions ever made in American history. One would think that battalions of historians would be swarming over these collections, but there is always plenty of room in the National Archives. Why bother to toil and sweat in dusty documents when the profession accepts less arduous standards, when a guess about the motives behind a policy is as good as going to the sources and finding out what it really was? This is the first danger: that the historical study of foreign policy will become nothing more than a launching pad for opinions, rather than the intelligent analysis of the human past.

But we must worry not merely about not being as good at our job as we should be, though that is worry enough. There is a second danger, and here the stakes are much higher. The major threat to democratic societies today is that they have not demonstrated to their own satisfaction—or to the dissatisfaction of their opponents—that they can conduct an effective foreign policy while maintaining intact their democratic institutions. The danger is twofold: that society remains in ignorance, and that what it does know is wrong. A democratic society is not viable under these conditions. The effectiveness of democratic institutions in solving domestic problems is the product of a widespread knowledge in a society of the procedures and limits of government, a sophistication about government based on a long experience of and participation in the processes of government. The nature of foreign policy makes it almost impossible for most people to gain the same sophistication about foreign affairs directly through their own experience. They can gain it only if the record of past decisions and policies is laid before them so that they can see foreign policy whole, so that it ceases to be a mystery and becomes familiar. I suggest we start to do that.

NOTES

1. Laurence Evans, *United States Policy and the Partition of Turkey, 1914–1924* (Baltimore, 1965), pp. 198ff.

2. Julius W. Pratt, *A History of United States Foreign Policy,* 2nd ed. (Englewood Cliffs, N.J., 1965).

3. Samuel F. Bemis, *A Diplomatic History of the United States,* 4th ed. (New York, 1965).

4. A. J. Mayer, *Politics and Diplomacy of Peacemaking: Containment and Counterrevolution at Versailles, 1918–1919* (New York, 1967).

5. This is not to say at all that Mayer's research was skimped; he in fact conducted intensive research in a wide variety of sources in this country and Europe, and his bibliography is definitive. My point is that until the policy-making process had been definitively researched, there wasn't any point in researching anything else, because the significance of other sources could not not be assessed. The policy-making process of the United States at the Paris Peace Conference is documented in full in the hundreds of thousands of documents in the files of the Department of State, the American Mission to Negotiate Peace, the Wilson Papers, the House Papers, and elsewhere. There is no evidence of any systematic research in any of these collections apart from half a dozen unimportant files relating to the activities of some of the advisory staff of the American Delegation and several references to documents in the Wilson and House Papers. It may be objected that to investigate all of these sources would take a lifetime. Perhaps it would, but we should not blind ourselves to the fact that until it is done, none of our studies mean very much except for the new data they may incidentally uncover.

6. Evans, *United States Policy and the Partition of Turkey,* pp. 32–37, 71–81, 89–92.

7. At the Council meeting of May 19, 1919, 11:30 A.M.; *Foreign Relations, Paris Peace Conference,* V, 708.

8. Arthur M. Schlesinger, Jr., *A Thousand Days: John F. Kennedy in the White House* (Boston, 1965).

American Military History: Over the Top

ALLAN R. MILLETT

At least since Charles Francis Adams made his plea for military history to the American Historical Association in 1899, scholars have put a fog as great as "the fog of war" about research in this specialty. It has suffered from the liberal, often pacifistic, narrow-mindedness of historians, the lack of graduate programs, the paucity of research support, and the capture of the field by the armed forces' historical programs, journalists, publicists, and political scientists. Some of these influences still affect research in the specialty, especially the limited number of courses, programs, and teaching positions. I would modestly propose, however, that military history research is now reorganizing and consolidating, not struggling to the line of departure. Scholarly activity since World War II has elevated military history to full intellectual status.[1]

Part of the difficulty in assessing American military history research rests in definition. Scholars who have examined the specialty have complained that it pandered to the military, either by overemphasizing the study of command and combat or by celebrating military institutions in order to foster their cohesiveness. This is a real concern.[2] We have the testimony of Generals Eisenhower, Patton, and "Chesty" Puller (the Marine Corps' Beowulf) that military history has psychedelic impact. In a recent army novel we find "Sad Sam" Damon reading Clausewitz and Jomini; no doubt it would have been Freeman's *Lee* if he could have afforded it on lieutenant's pay. There is a persistent military belief that historical study opens the future, as revealed in an immutable set of rules known as the "principles of war." This professional definition gives military history an aura of timelessness and universality by turning tactical truisms into laws governing the conduct of all wars.

This military definition of military history is best exemplified by the Mahanite concept of "Sea Power," that quaintly nineteenth-century grouping of battleships, merchantmen, colonies, and Providence which shaped the genre known as "naval history." As James M. Merrill pointed out in an essay in 1960, most writing on naval affairs still bears the influence of Mahan.[3] The mature authors who wrote immediately after World War II were most concerned with describing the naval contribution to America's wars. This "history-as-strategy" approach also satisfied the professionals' interest in didactic operational narratives. Represented by the writings of the Sprouts, Samuel Eliot Morison, Dudley W. Knox, and the faculty of the Naval Academy, this type of history emphasized the U.S. Navy's strategic value and wartime functions.[4] Furthermore, it described in sympathetic terms the contributions of the Navy to science, exploration, and the protection of commerce, but subordinated these missions to the struggle to prepare for war. Operational history demonstrated the utility of the Navy, thus continuing Mahan's scholarly special pleading for an ocean-based security system.[5] What emerged was a version of naval history which emphasized the efforts of the Navy to get a concept (Command of the Sea) and an agency (the battlefleet) accepted as the nation's deterrent in peace and first line of defense in war. The same institutional self-consciousness characterized studies of the Marine Corps, for which we still do not have a history free of paranoia.[6]

Most of us, however, have abandoned the military's definition of military history as "lessons" of command and strategy, the definition which has so agitated Walter Millis, Alfred Vagts, and Arthur Ekirch. Nor do we believe, as Quincy Wright and his associates did, that the study of war might reveal the way to universal peace. Rather we study the conduct of America's wars and the development of its military institutions in the unique political, economic, social, ideological, and technological milieu which shaped them. I would guess we hope such study will give us a fuller understanding of American history rather than make us strategists. While we may have trouble convincing our colleagues that the historical study of military affairs is useful, there is near consensus that our major task is to rewrite American military history from a civilian viewpoint, to counter the military claim that professional interests are the only criteria for studying our military past.[7]

What are the major characteristics of American military history research since World War II? Some generalizations are in order. First, the armed forces' historians still dominate the study of World War II, although their perspective has been progressively civilianized. Second, the monographic stockpile on military affairs which the Social Science Research Council's Committee on National Security Policy Research could not find in 1954 now exists in the form of both published studies and unpublished dissertations—as the footnotes accompanying this text attest. Unfortunately, except for the diplomatic historians, scholars usually leave the specialty to teach and write in a periodized field. But their work remains (much of it published), and it represents study in America's best graduate history departments.

Other major characteristics include the weak contribution military historians have made to interdisciplinary national security research programs and their reluctance to apply social science concepts and methodology in their research.[8] The barriers to social science techniques have been lowered in the last five years, but the absence of historians in security research has allowed research support and writing on post–World War II defense policy to fall into the hands of the political scientists. Nor has American military history generated the historiographical controversies about causation upon which reputations in our profession feed. There are signs, however, that this characteristic is disappearing.

But the major development in American military history research since World War II has been the erosion of the concept that military history should either illuminate strategic principles or contribute to the cohesiveness and political legitimacy of the armed forces. This demilitarization of military history has altered our understanding of America's wars, diplomacy, and armed forces. It has blurred the division between "military history" and "naval history." It has freed scholarship from a rigidly nationalist framework. Historians are in fact producing the reinterpretation of American military history suggested by C. Vann Woodward in 1959.[9]

If military history has been demilitarized since World War II, has the new scholarship produced insights sufficiently important to justify American military history as a scholarly specialty? I think it has. Contemplating our military past, I find it impressive testimony to the ambivalence of Americans about the morality of force and to the pluralism of our military institutions, which is a reflection of this ambivalence. The discovery of our martial past has been especially shocking, for a traditional part of the American dream was that this "new nation" would escape the wars and militarism of decadent Europe. When Americans discovered that the Western Hemisphere was not Eden, their compromise was to have their wars without allowing their professional soldiers and sailors to dominate their military institutions. This is the phenomenon Russell Weigley has described as America's "two armies" and Samuel Huntington has called the interplay of military professionalism, technicism, and popularism in American military policy.[10] Noted by Alexis de Tocqueville, martialism without militarism has been further pondered by Sir Denis Brogan, Walter Millis, Arthur Ekirch, and, most recently, Marcus Cunliffe.[11] It is this national experience that much of our military history scholarship now examines.

American military pluralism has its origins in the Colonial period and has persisted to our own time. As Daniel Boorstin has pointed out, the Colonial militia was an assertion of American uniqueness and expressed a contempt for regular forces that also exaggerated the colonials' own military prowess.[12] Yet the militia itself varied enough by region, era, and circumstance to make the colonials' trainbands and punitive expeditions themselves plural military organizations.[13] Even after the Revolution, the conviction that the citizen-soldier was a moral ideal continued to be a cornerstone of military policy.[14] And one need only read Jim Dan Hill and Martha Derthick to realize that the National Guard still sees itself as an essential political and military institution.[15]

Scholars who have investigated the institutional life of the United States Army have also discovered American military pluralism. For at least its first century of existence, the Regular Army was not designed for major war at all but instead policed, explored, and developed the national domain. As the books of James Ripley Jacobs, Robert Athearn, Francis Prucha, William Goetzmann, Forest Hill, William Leckie, and Robert Utley have shown, the Army, the least democratic of institutions, was a product of Turner's frontier. Only by performing useful services tangentially related to defense could the Army survive in a basically hostile political environment.[16]

Yet the mission of the Regular Army was the defense of the continent from external attack; at least this was the mission accepted by regular officers by the 1890's. The Army, then, by definition was to perform a function for which it had neither authority nor resources. As Stephen Ambrose, Jack Lane, and Forrest Pogue have told us, this dilemma drove Emory Upton to suicide, made Leonard Wood a political evangelist for military preparedness, and was barely resolved by George C. Marshall in the mobilization of World War II.[17] The civil leadership of the United States not only dominated military policy-making but made few concessions to military priorities.[18]

Besides a traditional reluctance to spend money on the Army and Navy, civilian leaders were interested in using the services as agencies of social reform. From the moral reformers of the Jacksonian era to the many-splendored healers of the New Deal, the easily ordered, usually compliant Army and Navy offered a perfect target for those change-minded pressure groups who could capture a President or Congress.[19] Despite an officer corps most sympathetic to cultural Anglo-conformity, minority groups have used military service, both regular and militia, in war and peace, as an avenue to fuller equality.[20] Because of the writings of Benjamin Quarles, Dudley Cornish, William Leckie, Ulysses Lee, and Richard Dalfiume, the military history of black Americans is best known, but, as O'Flaherty's study of the Sixty-ninth New York shows, other minorities have seized arms for political purposes.[21]

In the rewritten institutional history of the United States Navy, diplomacy, domestic politics, and technology make "strategic lessons" more relative and ambiguous than they ever could be for Mahan. Marshall Smelser, for example, has properly placed naval policy in the hands of mortal congressmen concerned with patronage, fiscal policy, and entangling alliances rather than with frigate captains fighting the Barbary pirates.[22] Naval historians like Edward Billingsley, Robert Johnson, Lance Buhl, and Peter Karsten have demonstrated that the nineteenth-century Navy was not so much designed for commerce raiding in wartime (anathema to Mahan) as for commerce protection and expansion in peacetime. In other words, the Navy was not organized for war of any sort, let alone committed to a particular strategy.[23]

It took, in fact, significant changes in naval architecture and administration, both copied from European powers, to create a Navy designed for wartime service. The formative influence of technology, emphasized in Baxter's study of the ironclad, Bernard Brodie's *Sea Power in the Machine Age,* and E. E. Morison's biography of Admiral Sims, is now a major theme in naval history.[24] But naval technology and administrative reform were not forces *deus ex machina.* They were the products of political bargaining within a pluralistic officer corps and competing civilian interest groups, neither with a closely reasoned strategy to sell.[25] And no sooner would some consensus be achieved, as it was for the battleship by 1914, than some infernal machine like the airplane emerged to challenge the established order.[26]

While coping with technological change, the Navy after 1898 was confronted with a strategic revolution as well, and it is the Navy's role in twentieth-century American diplomacy that has attracted many post-Mahanite historians. More specifically, O. J. Clinard, William Braisted, Earl Pomeroy, Gerald Wheeler, Thad Tuleja, and Robert Hart have gone full astern from Pearl Harbor to study Japanese-American naval relations in the Pacific. The general sense of their findings is that after 1898 both navies considered war with each other inevitable and made that future conflict their *raison d'être*.[27] Yet American diplomacy was more than "one ocean," and the admirals did not vote their own budgets. Despite the real threat of Japan and the pseudo-threat of the Royal Navy, the United States after World War I experimented with naval disarmament. This experience has also received considerable attention. While diplomatic historians have followed the path of Anglo-American relations through the arms conferences, military historians have outlined the Navy's participation and influence as well.[28]

The history of America's wars as it has been rewritten since World War II now reflects an American ambivalence about war and professional soldiers. In itself this is not a new development. No one had to tell Upton, Wood, Steele, Spaulding, Ganoe, and the Colonels Dupuy about the domestic constraints upon military policy. But the academic histories are not policy prescriptive nor professional as were the writings of these officer-historians. The result is a more accurate picture of the social roots of America's military experiences and, therefore, a fuller view of our nation's history.

Until the Civil War, America's military experience was pre-national, that is, it was determined by local and sectional political values. This pre-nationalism explains the division of authority and responsibility not only between plural military and political organizations, but also between geographically separated polities. As the British government learned to its dismay, localism and civilianism in the North American colonies gave the Crown's officers the choice of using expensive regulars or vigilante-like militia expeditions in the Imperial wars. Fortunately the French had equal troubles with their Indians and colonials.

What a relief Quebec must have been for Wolfe and Montcalm.[29]

The military histories of the American Revolution for the most part underemphasize the pre-national character of that conflict. Instead the fighting by national troops has most often been recounted—the Continentals, led by national leaders-in-the-making, such as Freeman and Flexner's George Washington.[30] It has taken several studies of British strategy (such as Paul Smith's of Loyalism) and the war in Vietnam to remind us of the difficulties of creating legitimate civil government by military occupation during an internal war.[31] In other words, the deplorable lack of support for the Continental Army that so grieved Upton reflected not weakness but strategic strength in a people's war. Fortunately we have enough biographies of Revolutionary leaders and accounts of the war in the South and along the frontier to see the invertebrate nature of the rebels' resistance.[32] Hopefully the bicentennial histories of the Revolution now being written will not make the War for Independence a Whiggish World War II. What one needs most to understand the war is an acquaintanceship with the military writings of Mao Tse-tung.

Perhaps because they are not so useful in instructing officers or indoctrinating schoolchildren, the War of 1812 and the Mexican War have retained their pre-national character. Neither, of course, suffers from overexamination. In accounts of the two conflicts, Harry Coles's *The War of 1812* best explains the political localism and geographic barriers that frustrated the American national government.[33] For the Mexican War, the three-cornered confrontation of Polk, Taylor, and Scott over strategy, manpower, and political credit is well known; what needs more investigation is the sectional and partisan enthusiasm which sustained "Mr. Polk's War." [34]

If the pre-national wars have been relatively neglected, the Civil War was a national, total experience which from the last shot has captivated military historians. Two features of Civil War historiography are unique in military history scholarship: the interest in the conflict has been continuous, and the war has never been the sole property of soldier-authors, especially when one considers the influence of E. Merton Coulter, James G. Randall, William B. Hesseltine, Clement Eaton, Douglas Southall Freeman, and Lloyd Lewis on the current army of Civil War scholars. There are discernible trends since World War II. First, the conduct of the war now vies evenly with the causes of the war and Reconstruction for scholarly attention. Accounts of the war no longer concentrate on the battles or the Eastern theater, but consider all operations on land and sea, strategy, military organization and doctrine, and command problems. And there is a growing interest in the economic, manpower, scientific, and political mobilization North and South.[35] Most representative of these trends are Bruce Catton's centennial trilogy and Allan Nevins' *The War for the Union*.[36]

The studies of command, strategy, and military organization which have accurately portrayed the Civil War's national character have most often been done as biographies. While Robert E. Lee still wins attention, the influence of Joseph E. Johnston, Bragg, Beauregard, Albert Sidney Johnston, and Kirby Smith on the Confederate war effort have been explained. For the Union, the story of Lincoln and his generals, east and west, is well known.[37] The history of an army or a campaign, done in conventional narrative, is a vehicle of increasing popularity.[38] Considering the flow of writing, I often wonder how Civil War "buffs" escape book fatigue. Yet the fighting and the planning can be reanalyzed profitably, as dissertations on Confederate coast defense, cavalry doctrine, infantry tactics, trench warfare, and the socio-psychological impact of the war on the common soldier show.[39]

What is sometimes lost in Civil War history is that the Union armies not only had to destroy Confederate organized resistance but occupy the South long enough to restore loyal government. The difficulty of this task (after all, it defeated the British in the Revolution) is not always recognized outside of the border states where it produced partisan warfare unhidden by conventional battles.[40] Perhaps only since World War II have we recognized the problems of military government. At any rate, the Civil War as a social revolution began for the occupied South in 1862 and was won by it in counterrevolution in 1877, though clearly at great cost. If the North had barely avoided war-weariness by 1865, it and the Regular Army succumbed to occupation-weariness by 1877. It is this experience which John Carpenter, George Bentley, and James Sefton have described, but which bears further study, especially for the war years.[41]

Fought by massed armies over a wide area for the loyalty and productivity of a large civilian population, the Civil War demanded a mobilization of national dimensions North and South. War in the industrial age called not only for generals, but for managers and scientists like Edwin Stanton, Montgomery Meigs, Stephen Mallory, Joseph R. Anderson, Matthew Fontaine Maury, and Josiah Gorgas, and for military bureaucracies that could reduce invention, procurement, and distribution to routine.[42] It demanded of the belligerents that they make their trains run on time.[43] And it meant that the governments had to guard the health and souls of their soldiers and regulate the opinions and behavior of civilians.[44] This is total war, impossible without a high degree of national and democratic integration, however civil the conflict.

The military history of Manifest Destiny-turned-amphibious in 1898 pales in comparison with the Civil War, both in extent of effort and volume of writing. The "Hot Time in the Old Town Tonight" aura given the War with Spain by Walter Millis obscures the seriousness of our self-assumed responsibility to liquidate the Spanish Empire. Undeniably, the mobilization of 1898 had a comic character; the interventions and pacifications that began in that year and extended into the 1930's did not. Of the war itself, we know that TR was not alone in Cuba and that Gridley was ready to fire, but the war awaits fuller treatment.[45] This should be forthcoming in Graham Cosmas' dissertation and David Trask's and John Grenville's book in the "Wars of the United States" series.[46] The subsequent occupations in the Philippines and Latin America have been more adequately and recently studied and demonstrate the ambiguities of limited intervention in American diplomatic usage. This is especially so when American military forces protect property, sponsor native constabularies, and encourage social change in other cultures.[47]

For the United States and its professional soldiers, World War I was a military puberty rite, for it marked the acceptance of the wartime primacy of the regular officer corps and the participation in war with and against the armies of Europe. Reading the letters and diaries of the AEF's senior officers, it is clear they believed the war in France would sorely test them and their nation's capacity for mass, technological warfare. The stress of the American war effort in 1917 and 1918 and the qualified achievements of the Army and the War Department still offer an arresting field for original study, as most recently demonstrated by Edward M. Coffman's *The War to End All Wars*.[48] Practically any phase of our coming of age on the Western Front is worth more examination. There are, nevertheless, books which, like duckboards in a trench, have elevated the study of the war above the muck of the memoirs. For the AEF there is Laurence Stallings' *The Doughboys*, an admirable blend of recall and reflection.[49] David Trask has outlined the military influence on Wilsonian diplomacy, and Daniel

Beaver, David A. Lockmiller, and Coffman have examined the War Department's trials in their biographies of Newton Baker, Enoch Crowder, and Peyton C. March.[50]

For all the obviousness of the impact of the machine on World War I, only the airplane has received major scholarly attention. The interdependence of machines, strategic doctrine, and organizational politics, revealed in the studies of Army aviation by I. B. Holley, Alfred F. Hurley, James Hudson, and Edwin Rutkowski, should be equally intriguing in studies of the adoption of the radio, tank, truck, and machine gun.[51] Yet the motorization and mechanization the Army prescribed as an antidote for future Western Fronts has not yet been exhaustively studied, especially outside the armed forces' historical programs.[52]

The most unique feature of scholarship in American military history is that the academic historian not only competes in his specialty with scholars in alien disciplines, military officers, and enthusiastic amateurs, but also shares his subject with fellow professionals in the armed forces' historical agencies. Indeed, the writing on American participation in World War II and the Korean War is dominated by the latter. While the military's historical research is intended primarily for internal use, its divisions have produced in the last twenty years a staggering amount of scholarly writing for public consumption. They will continue to do so, and their contribution is of incalculable importance. One sometimes feels that the rest of us are the historical divisions' country cousins, birds of passage flitting through the records guarded in Washington, Maxwell Air Force Base, St. Louis, and Kansas City.

The truth is that the historical divisions willingly assist outside scholars, and their own publications are honest and skilled history. Official history has come a long way from the days when Leonard Wood wanted Professor R. M. Johnston for his staff Boswell, and the AEF's Historical Section could write that the American effort in World War I was "on a colossal scale, dwarfing that of Germany, England and France, when the facts are looked at in their true perspective"— the perspective being John J. Pershing's.[53] Professionals under government sponsorship have produced works on World War II which must be the starting point for rational discussion of that conflict: the multi-volumed *United States Army in World War II*, Morison's *History of United States Naval Operations in World War II*, *The Army Air Forces in World War II*, and *History of Marine Corps Operations in World War II*.[54] Furthermore, the historical divisions are doing or assisting in the writing of comprehensive administrative and logistical studies and histories of the Korean War. They are already at work on Vietnam as well.[55]

The official historians are justly proud of their accomplishments; they have in the imperfect world of military politics come close to the objectivity, balance, and interpretive diversity they sought, and they have written for posterity as well as the Pentagon.[56] They know the documents, and they are willing to share with the rest of us. Many of them are now in the academic world or are writing independently on military subjects.

The present professional directors of the armed forces' historical programs—Stetson Conn, Albert F. Simpson, and E. M. Eller—are aware that their agencies cannot completely exploit the records at their disposal, especially for publication.[57] They admit that their departments are most interested in operational narratives and the internally usable past, in the "lessons learned" upon which the military thrives. They are unanimous in suggesting that academic historians apply their knowledge of political, social, intellectual, and economic history to military affairs. I would go further and suggest that even the possibilities of doing operational history for World War II and Korea have not been exhausted by the official historians, especially when operations involve interservice doctrinal disputes and service prestige. Let us look at a couple of examples.

The capture of Saipan in 1944 not only was a crucial American victory in the Pacific but raised several issues about the conduct of amphibious operations, primarily the relative capacity of the Army and the Marine Corps to conduct a multi-divisional landing followed by extended ground combat. At Saipan this doctrinal problem involved supporting arms coordination, staff and task organization, and logistics. Surely there were many lessons to be learned—and they were. But the official histories do not fully and freely discuss the lessons of the campaign, although the Army's historian in 1951 wrote the best published discussion of Saipan for the Marine Corps. The most balanced, extended analysis of Saipan is, instead, a doctoral dissertation: Gordon Turner's "The Amphibious Complex: A Study of Operations at Saipan," written from the same records available to the official historians.[58]

Another example of the sort of revision some of the official histories need is the account of the long-range fighter issue and the combined bomber offensive. The account in the Army Air Forces series explains that the failure to develop an escort was technical and strategic, not doctrinal. This is the record the public has. Yet the Air Force itself knows better, for its own Historical Division has written and the Air Force Academy teaches that prewar air doctrine played a decisive part in sending unescorted B-17's against the Luftwaffe. This interpretation is further strengthened by another dissertation, Bernard Boylan's "The Development of the American Long Range Escort Fighter," written from Air Force archives.[59]

There are, I am sure, other weaknesses in the official and semi-official histories; all it proves is that the service historians have no more captured truth than we have. The official histories, nonetheless, stand high in American military history scholarship. If one wants to discuss World War II and Korea with the official historians, he had better do his homework. But their work has not closed off our military history since 1939 from other scholars, nor should it—as the official historians themselves agree.

There has in fact been a growing academic interest in our military experience in World War II. This is perhaps best symbolized by the formation in 1968 of the American Committee on the History of the Second World War, a constituent part of an international committee to further research on the war. The American Committee's first two newsletters, listing studies completed or in progress, amply document scholarly activity on the war. Research thus far has come most rapidly on those parts of our war effort most comfortable for academics: Allied diplomacy and the Home Front. The general thrust has been to remove the glow of wartime propaganda from inter-Allied relations and domestic mobilization, neither a model of selfless cooperation.[60] In addition, there is a growing willingness to examine critically more specialized military subjects. I have already mentioned two examples, to which can be added studies of logistics and air warfare doctrine.[61] Among military historians, though, there is not yet a major school which suggests that World War II was not worth fighting, or that the war was really directed against someone other than the Germans and Japanese. Studies of occupation policies, however, point out that once the shooting stopped the old ambiguity about the use of troops to change whole societies reemerged, even at the end of a crusade against Evil.[62]

The No Man's Land of American military history is the post–World War II period. Few of us would deny the criticality of United States military policy in contemporary history. Yet only a handful have probed the subject. At the moment American military history became most relevant, historians ignored it. Fortunately the political scientists, in their rush to discover the relationship between elite groups, process, and organization, have filled the gap. When one eliminates their prefaces, italicized passages, and rhetorical questions, one finds that the political scientists have written what history we have of American defense policy and military institutions since 1945.

I am somewhat at a loss to explain this phenomenon. Perhaps it is a traditional distrust of contemporary history; perhaps it is an assumption that this history cannot be or should not be written without access to documents now classified. Yet even the extant material in oral history repositories, declassified archives, presidential libraries, and the voluminous public record have barely been exploited.[63]

Take the interrelated problems of defense organization, budgeting, and strategy, clearly a central concern in our postwar military history. The most thorough and influential accounts have been done not by historians but by political scientists: Samuel Huntington, Paul Hammond, Demetrios Caraley, Warner Schilling, Glenn Snyder, Vincent Davis, Edward Kolodziej, William Kintner, and John Ries.[64] Stripped of their most esoteric language and policy prescriptions, these scholars' books are essentially historical. The only significant contributions made by historians in unraveling our defense policy since 1945 are Albion's and Connery's sympathetic biography of James V. Forrestal and two dissertations, Murray Green's study of Stuart Symington and the B 36, and Curtis Tarr's account of the unification controversy.[65]

The same pattern of neglect characterizes other aspects of our writing about postwar military affairs other than the Korean War. Political scientists have made the preemptive strikes in civil-military relations, military education, military public relations, strategic intelligence policy, the politics of military science, and the history of military assistance.[66] While it appears that there is increasing scholarly interest in these areas, especially by students at the Fletcher School of Law and Diplomacy, historians have not made much of a contribution to our knowledge of recent military affairs, certainly not as much as they have to diplomacy and domestic politics. But neither of the latter subjects, ironically, makes much sense without some appreciation of defense policies. The few historical studies we have are late entries and must be considered poor relations to the works of both political scientists and military sociologists, the latter sired by *The American Soldier*, Morris Janowitz, Eli Ginzberg, and C. Wright Mills. Historians have

done some useful work, such as studies of the business careers of retired officers and civil defense planning.[67] But this piece of historical
terrain is still held by the behaviorists.

Regretfully, I must add that a general understanding of military
history does not exist in our universities and armed forces. Assuming
that America's wars and military institutions have influenced our national history, such ignorance is inexcusable. Hopefully the books in
the "Wars of the United States" series will make the substance of
the new scholarship more available. But American military historians
have a continuing obligation to educate our students and readers about
the character of America's wars and military institutions. Such knowledge clearly would make them more intelligent judges of military
policy and foreign affairs, and the historical arguments used to justify
both. In addition, we must point out to career officers the ineluctable
societal influences they will meet in the institutional development of
their services and the conduct of war.

For our own part I propose two reforms: that we more openly
expose ourselves to research in military affairs in other disciplines and
the methodologies they use, and that we stop apologizing for our interest in military history as if it were a boyish enthusiasm we had
never outgrown.

NOTES

1. Charles Francis Adams, "A Plea for Military History," in *Lee at Appomattox and Other Papers* (Boston and New York, 1903), pp. 337–375; Stetson
Conn, "The Pursuit of Military History," *Military Affairs*, XXX (Spring
1966), 1–8; Robert C. Brown, *The Teaching of Military History in Colleges
and Universities of the United States*, USAF Historical Division Study No. 124
(Air University, 1955); W. Stull Holt, "Historical Scholarship," in Merle
Curti, ed., *American Scholarship in the Twentieth Century* (Cambridge, Mass.,
1953), p. 105; Dexter Perkins and John L. Snell and the Committee on Graduate Education of the American Historical Association, *The Education of Historians in the United States* (New York, 1962), pp. 74–77, 123; Louis Morton,
"The Historian and the Study of War," *Mississippi Valley Historical Review*,
XLIX (March 1962), 599–613. For a more optimistic assessment: Stetson Conn

to the author, September 13, 1968, and Harry L. Coles, "Reinterpretations of World War I and World War II," paper delivered at the First Annual Military History Symposium, USAF Academy, May 1967.

2. Arthur A. Ekirch, Jr., "Military History: A Civilian Caveat," *Military Affairs*, XXI (Summer 1957), 49–54; Alfred Vagts, *A History of Militarism* (New York, 1937), pp. 21–36; Walter Millis, *Military History*, AHA Service Center for Teachers of History Publication No. 39 (Washington, D.C., 1961). For a defense of the military's history, see Stefan T. Possony and Dale O. Smith, "The Utility of Military History," *Military Affairs*, XXII (Winter 1958–1959), 216–218; Department of the Army Pamphlet 20–200, *The Writing of American Military History: A Guide* (Washington, D.C., 1956), pp. i–v, 1–25; Marine Corps Order P5750. 1A: *Manual for the Marine Corps Historical Program* (1968), pp. 1–3, 1–4.

3. James M. Merrill, "Successors to Mahan: A Survey of Writings in American Naval History, 1914–1960," *Mississippi Valley Historical Review*, L (June 1963), 79–99.

4. Harold and Margaret Sprout, *The Rise of American Naval Power, 1776–1918* (Princeton, 1939) and *Toward a New Order of Sea Power* (Princeton, 1940); William E. Livezey, *Mahan on Sea Power* (Norman, Okla., 1947); Samuel Eliot Morison, *John Paul Jones* (New York, 1959); Charles Lee Lewis, *David Glasgow Farragut*, 2 vols. (Annapolis, 1941, 1943); Richard S. West, Jr., *Admirals of American Empire* (Indianapolis, 1948) and *Mr. Lincoln's Navy* (New York, 1957); Dudley W. Knox, *A History of the United States Navy* (New York, 1948); E. B. Potter and Chester W. Nimitz, et al., *Sea Power* (Englewood Cliffs, N.J., 1960).

5. For discussions of a war Mahan never wrote about, see Karl J. Bauer, "United States Naval Operations During the Mexican War," Unpublished Ph.D. Dissertation (Indiana University, 1953); John L. Betts, "The United States Navy in the Mexican War," Unpublished Ph. D. Dissertation (University of Chicago, 1955); and Francis J. Manno, "History of United States Naval Operations, 1846–1848," Unpublished Ph.D. Dissertation (Georgetown University, 1954). See also Benjamin F. Gilbert, "Naval Operations in the Pacific, 1861–1865," Unpublished Ph. D. Dissertation (University of California, Berkeley, 1951), and James M. Merrill, "Naval Operations Along the South Atlantic Coast, 1861–1865," Unpublished Ph. D. Dissertation (University of California at Los Angeles, 1954).

6. For the latest defense, see Robert D. Heinl, *Soldiers of the Sea* (Annapolis, 1962) and *Victory at High Tide* (New York, 1968).

7. Tyson Wilson, "The Case for Military History and Research," *Military Affairs*, XXI (Summer 1957), 54–60; Maury Feld, "The Writing of Military History," *Military Affairs*, XXII (Spring 1958), 38–39; Louis Morton, "Historia Mentem Armet: Lessons of the Past," *World Politics*, XXII (January 1960), 155–164; John K. Mahon, "Teaching and Research on Military History in the United States," *Historian*, XXVII (February 1965), 170–184; Russell F. Weigley to the author, October 9, 1968; Louis Morton, *Writings on World War II*, AHA Service Center for Teachers of History Publication No. 66 (Washington, D.C., 1967).

8. Theodore Ropp, "Military History and the Social Sciences," *Military Affairs*, XXX (Spring 1966), 8–13; Social Science Research Council, *Annual Reports, 1952–1965* (New York, 1953–1966); Brown, *The Teaching of Military History*, pp. 25–28; Gene M. Lyons and Louis Morton, *Schools for Strategy* (New York, 1965), pp. 52–57, 135–136, 143, 149, 239, 260.

9. C. Vann Woodward, "The Age of Reinterpretation," *American Historical Review,* LXVI (October 1960), 8–13.

10. Russell F. Weigley, *Towards an American Army* (New York, 1962) and *History of the United States Army* (New York, 1967); Samuel P. Huntington, *The Soldier and the State* (New York, 1958).

11. D. W. Brogan, *The American Character* (New York, 1944), pp. 149–165; Walter Millis, *Arms and Men* (New York, 1956); Arthur A. Ekirch, Jr., *The Civilian and the Military* (New York, 1956); Marcus Cunliffe, *Soldiers and Civilians: The Martial Spirit in America, 1775–1865* (Boston, 1968).

12. Daniel J. Boorstin, *The Americans: The Colonial Experience* (New York, 1958), pp. 341–372. On the last point, see John K. Mahon, "Anglo-American Methods of Indian Warfare, 1676–1794," *Mississippi Valley Historical Review,* XLV (September 1958), 254–275.

13. John W. Shy, "A New Look at Colonial Militia," *William and Mary Quarterly,* XX (April 1963), 175–185; Douglas E. Leach, *Flintlock and Tomahawk: New England in King Philip's War* (New York, 1958); Frederick S. Aldridge, "Organization and Administration of the Militia System of Colonial Virginia," Unpublished Ph.D. Dissertation (American University, 1964); Richard H. Marcus, "The Militia of Colonial Connecticut, 1639–1775: An Institutional Study," Unpublished Ph. D. Dissertation (University of Colorado, 1965); David R. Millar, "The Militia, the Army and the Independency in Colonial Massachusetts," Unpublished Ph.D. Dissertation (Cornell University, 1967); Jack S. Radabaugh, "The Military System of Colonial Massachusetts, 1690–1740," Unpublished Ph.D. Dissertation (University of Southern California, 1965); Darrett B. Rutman, "A Militant New World, 1607–1640," Unpublished Ph.D. Dissertation (University of Virginia, 1959).

14. John K. Mahon, *The American Militia: Decade of Decision, 1789–1800* (Gainesville, Fla., 1960); George C. Bittle, "In Defense of Florida: The Organized Florida Militia from 1821 to 1920," Unpublished Ph.D. Dissertation (Florida State University, 1965); Lyle D. Brundage, "The Organization, Administration, and Training of the United States Ordinary and Volunteer Militia, 1792–1861," Unpublished Ph.D. Dissertation (University of Michigan, 1959); John G. Westover, "The Evolution of the Missouri Militia, 1804–1919," Unpublished Ph.D. Dissertation (University of Missouri, 1948).

15. Jim Dan Hill, *The Minute Men in Peace and War: A History of the National Guard* (Harrisburg, Pa., 1964); Martha Derthick. *The National Guard in Politics* (Cambridge, Mass., 1965) and "Militia Lobby in the Missile Age: The Politics of the National Guard," in Samuel P. Huntington, ed., *Changing Patterns of Military Politics* (New York, 1962). See also Louis Cantor, "The Creation of the Modern National Guard: The Dick Militia Act of 1903," Unpublished Ph.D. Dissertation (Duke University, 1963); James J. Hudson, "The California National Guard, 1903–1940," Unpublished Ph.D. Dissertation (University of California, Berkeley, 1953); William H. Riker, *Soldiers of the States: The Role of the National Guard in American Democracy* (Washington, D.C., 1957).

16. James Ripley Jacobs, *The Beginning of the U. S. Army, 1783–1812* (Princeton, 1947); Robert G. Athearn, *William Tecumseh Sherman and the Settlement of the West* (Norman, Okla., 1956); Francis Paul Prucha, *Broadax and Bayonet: The Role of the U.S. Army in the Development of the Northwest, 1815–1860* (Madison, Wisc., 1953) and *The Sword of the Republic: The United States Army on the Frontier, 1783–1846* (New York, 1969); William

H. Goetzmann, *Army Exploration in the American West, 1803–1863* (New Haven, 1959); Forest G. Hill, *Roads, Rails and Waterways: The Army Engineers and Early Transportation* (Norman, Okla., 1957); Robert M. Utley, *Frontiersmen in Blue: The United States Army and the Indian, 1848–1865* (New York, 1967); William H. Leckie, *The Military Conquest of the Southern Plains* (Norman, Okla., 1963). See also Stephen E. Ambrose, *Duty, Honor, Country: A History of West Point* (Baltimore, 1966); Leo E. Oliva, *Soldiers on the Santa Fe Trail* (Norman, Okla., 1967); Edward S. Wallace, *The Great Reconnaissance: Soldiers, Artists and Scientists on the Frontier* (Boston, 1955); Henry C. Borger, "The Role of the Army Engineers in the Westward Movement in the Lake Huron-Michigan Basin Before the Civil War," Unpublished Ph.D. Dissertation (Columbia University, 1954); Patrick L. Halley, "The Western Experiences of Major Stephen H. Long, 1816–1821," Unpublished Ph.D. Dissertation (University of Oklahoma, 1951); Willis B. Hughes, "The Army and Stephen Watts Kearny in the West, 1819–1846," Unpublished Ph.D. Dissertation (University of Minnesota, 1955); Harold D. Hampton, "Conservation and Cavalry: A Study of the Role of the United States Army in the Development of a National Park System, 1886–1917," Unpublished Ph.D. Dissertation (University of Colorado, 1965).

17. Stephen E. Ambrose, *Upton and the Army* (Baton Rouge, 1964); Jack C. Lane, "Leonard Wood and the Shaping of American Defense Policy, 1900–1920," Unpublished Ph.D. Dissertation (University of Georgia, 1963); Forrest C. Pogue, *George C. Marshall: Education of a General, 1880–1939* (New York, 1963) and *George C. Marshall: Ordeal and Hope, 1939–1942* (New York, 1966). See also Fred Greene, "The Military View of American National Policy, 1904–1940," *American Historical Review,* LXVI (January 1961), 354–377.

18. See, for example, Edward H. Brooks, "The National Defense Policy of the Wilson Administration, 1913–1917," Unpublished Ph.D. Dissertation (Stanford University, 1950); Paul Y. Hammond, "The Secretary-ships of War and Navy; A Study of Civilian Control of the Military," Unpublished Ph.D. Dissertation (Harvard University, 1953); Paul A. C. Koistinen, "The Hammer and the Sword. Labor, the Military and Industrial Mobilization, 1920–1945," Unpublished Ph.D. Dissertation (University of California, Berkeley, 1964); James W. Pohl, "The General Staff and American Military Policy: The Formative Period, 1898–1917," Unpublished Ph.D. Dissertation (University of Texas, 1967).

19. Harold D. Langley, *Social Reform in the United States Navy, 1798–1862* (Urbana, Ill., 1967); Fred D. Baldwin, "The American Enlisted Man in World War I," Unpublished Ph.D. Dissertation (Princeton University, 1964); Innis La Roche Jenkins, "Josephus Daniels and the Navy Department, 1913–1916: A Study in Military Administration," Unpublished Ph.D. Dissertation (University of Maryland, 1960); John W. Killigrew, "The Impact of the Great Depression on the Army, 1929–1936," Unpublished Ph.D. Dissertation (Indiana University, 1960); Bill C. Reid, "Proposed American Plans for Soldier Settlement During the World War I Period," Unpublished Ph.D. Dissertation (University of Oklahoma, 1963); Carlton B. Smith, "The United States War Department, 1815–1842," Unpublished Ph.D. Dissertation (University of Virginia, 1967).

20. Richard C. Brown, "The Social Attitudes of American Generals, 1898–1940," Unpublished Ph.D. Dissertation (University of Wisconsin, 1951);

William B. White, "The Military and the Melting Pot: The American Army and Minority Groups, 1865–1924," Unpublished Ph.D. Dissertation (University of Wisconsin, 1968).

21. Benjamin Quarles, *The Negro in the Civil War* (Boston, 1953) and *The Negro in the American Revolution* (Chapel Hill, 1961); Dudley Taylor Cornish, *The Sable Arm* (New York, 1956); William H. Leckie, *The Buffalo Soldiers: A Narrative of the Negro Cavalry in the West* (Norman, Okla., 1966); Ulysses Lee, *United States Army in World War II: The Employment of Negro Troops* (Washington, D.C., 1966); Richard M. Dalfiume, *Fighting on Two Fronts: Desegregation of the United States Armed Forces, 1930–1953* (Columbia, Mo., 1969); Patrick Daniel O'Flaherty, "The History of the Sixty-Ninth Regiment of the New York State Militia, 1852–1861," Unpublished Ph.D. Dissertation (Fordham University, 1963). See also Robert S. Bahney, "Generals and Negroes: Education of Negroes by the Union Army, 1861–1865," Unpublished Ph.D. Dissertation (University of Michigan, 1965); Mary Frances Berry, "The Negro Soldier Movement and the Adoption of National Conscription, 1652–1865," Unpublished Ph.D. Dissertation (University of Michigan, 1966); Roland C. McConnell, *Negro Troops in Antebellum Louisiana* (Baton Rouge, 1968); Otis Singletary, *Negro Militia and Reconstruction* (Austin, Tex., 1957); Marvin E. Fletcher, "The Negro Soldier and the United States Army, 1891–1917," Unpublished Ph.D. Dissertation (University of Wisconsin, 1968).

22. Marshall Smelser, *The Congress Founds the Navy, 1787–1798* (South Bend, Ind., 1959). See also John J. Carrigg, "Benjamin Stoddert and the Foundation of the American Navy," Unpublished Ph.D. Dissertation (Georgetown University, 1953), and Stephen T. Powers, "The Decline and Extinction of American Naval Power, 1781–1787," Unpublished Ph.D. Dissertation (Notre Dame University, 1965).

23. Edward B. Billingsley, *In Defense of Neutral Rights: The United States Navy and the Wars of Independence in Chile and Peru* (Chapel Hill, 1967); Robert E. Johnson, *Thence Round Cape Horn: The Story of U.S. Naval Forces on the Pacific Station, 1818–1923* (Annapolis, 1963); Lance C. Buhl, "The Smooth Water Navy: American Naval Policy and Politics, 1865–1876," Unpublished Ph.D. Dissertation (Harvard University, 1968); Peter Karsten, "The Naval Aristocracy: U.S. Naval Officers from the 1840's to the 1920's: Mahan's Messmates," Unpublished Ph.D. Dissertation (University of Wisconsin, 1968). See also Samuel Eliot Morison, *"Old Bruin": Commodore Matthew C. Perry, 1794–1858* (Boston, 1967); Maury D. Baker, Jr., "The United States and Piracy During the Spanish-American Wars of Independence," Unpublished Ph.D. Dissertation (Duke University, 1947); Curtis T. Henson, "The United States Navy and China, 1839–1861," Unpublished Ph.D. Dissertation (Tulane University, 1965); Richard W. Turk, "United States Naval Policy in the Caribbean, 1865–1915," Unpublished Ph.D. Dissertation (Fletcher School of Law and Diplomacy, 1968).

24. James Phinney Baxter III, *The Introduction of the Ironclad Warship* (Cambridge, Mass., 1933); Bernard Brodie, *Sea Power in the Machine Age* (Princeton, 1941); E. E. Morison, *Admiral Sims and the Modern American Navy* (Boston, 1942).

25. Walter R. Herrick, Jr., *The American Naval Revolution* (Baton Rouge, 1967); J. A. S. Grenville and George B. Young, *Politics, Strategy and American Diplomacy* (New Haven, 1966); Richard K. Morris, *John P. Holland, 1841–1914: Inventor of the Modern Submarine* (Annapolis, 1966); Edward W. Sloan

III, *Benjamin Isherwood; Naval Engineer: The Years as Engineer-in-Chief* (Annapolis, 1965); Vincent Davis, *The Admirals Lobby* (Chapel Hill, 1967); Leonard A. Swann, Jr., *John Roach: Maritime Entrepreneur* (Annapolis, 1965); Armin Rappoport, *The Navy League of the United States* (Detroit, 1962); Warner R. Schilling, "Admirals and Foreign Policy, 1913–1919," Unpublished Ph.D. Dissertation (Yale University, 1953); Ronald H. Spector, "Professors of War: The Naval War College and the Modern American Navy," Unpublished Ph.D. Dissertation (Yale University, 1967).

26. A. D. Turnbull and C. L. Lord, *History of United States Naval Aviation* (New Haven, 1949); Ashbrook Lincoln, "The United States Navy and Air Power: A History of Naval Aviation, 1920–1934," Unpublished Ph.D. Dissertation (University of California, 1946).

27. O. J. Clinard, *Japan's Influence on American Naval Power, 1897–1917* (Berkeley, 1947); William R. Braisted, *The United States Navy in the Pacific, 1897–1909* (Austin, Tex., 1958); Earl S. Pomeroy, *Pacific Outpost: American Strategy in Guam and Micronesia* (Stanford, 1951); Gerald E. Wheeler, *Prelude to Pearl Harbor: The U.S. Navy and the Far East, 1921–1931* (Columbia, Mo., 1963); T. V. Tuleja, *Statesmen and Admirals: Quest for a Far Eastern Naval Policy* (New York, 1963); Robert A. Hart, *The Great White Fleet* (New York, 1965). See also Willis E. Snowbarger, "The Development of Pearl Harbor," Unpublished Ph.D. Dissertation (University of California, Berkeley, 1951); Lynwood E. Oyos, "The Navy and the United States Far Eastern Policy, 1930–1939," Unpublished Ph.D. Dissertation (University of Nebraska, 1958); James H. Herzog, "The Role of the United States Navy in the Evolution and Execution of American Foreign Policy Relative to Japan, 1936–1941," Unpublished Ph.D. Dissertation (Brown University, 1963); Emmanuel T. Koginos, *The Panay Incident: Prelude to War* (West Lafayette, Ind., 1967).

28. Raymond G. O'Connor, *Perilous Equilibrium: The United States and the London Naval Conference* (Lawrence, Kans., 1962); Ernest Andrade, Jr., "United States Naval Policy in the Disarmament Era, 1921–1937," Unpublished Ph.D. Dissertation (Michigan State University, 1966); Thomas H. Buckley, "The United States and the Washington Conference, 1921–1922," Unpublished Ph.D. Dissertation (Indiana University, 1961); George V. Fagan, "Anglo-American Naval Relations, 1927–1937," Unpublished Ph.D. Dissertation (University of Pennsylvania, 1954); Dorothy T. Groeling, "Submarines, Disarmament and Modern Warfare," Unpublished Ph.D. Dissertation (Columbia University, 1950); Paul E. Million, Jr., "The Influence of the Washington Naval Conference upon American Sea Power," Unpublished Ph.D. Dissertation (Georgetown University, 1956).

29. Laurence Harvey Gipson, *The Great War for the Empire,* vols. VI–VIII in *The British Empire Before the American Revolution* (New York, 1946–1953); Howard H. Peckham, *The Colonial Wars, 1689–1762* (Chicago, 1964); John W. Shy, *Toward Lexington: The Role of the British Army in the Coming of the American Revolution* (Princeton, 1965); William A. Foote, "The American Independent Companies of the British Army, 1664–1764," Unpublished Ph.D. Dissertation (University of California at Los Angeles, 1966).

30. For accounts emphasizing the national character of the war, see Howard Peckham, *The War for Independence* (Chicago, 1958); Christopher Ward, *The War of the Revolution,* 2 vols. (New York, 1952); George F. Scheer and Hugh F. Rankin, *Rebels and Redcoats* (New York, 1957); Willard Wallace, *Appeal to Arms* (New York, 1951); Lynn Montross, *Rag, Tag and Bobtail: The Story of the Continental Army, 1775–1783* (New York, 1951); Douglas

Southall Freeman, *George Washington,* 6 vols. (New York, 1948–1954); James T. Flexner, *George Washington in the American Revolution* (Boston, 1967); George A. Billias, ed., *George Washington's Generals* (New York, 1964); John R. Alden, *General Charles Lee* (Baton Rouge, 1951); North Callahan, *Henry Knox: George Washington's General* (New York, 1958); Samuel W. Patterson, *Horatio Gates* (New York, 1951).

31. Piers Mackesy, *The War for America, 1775–1783* (Cambridge, Mass., 1964); Eric Robson, *The American Revolution in Its Political and Military Aspects, 1763–1783* (New York, 1966). For the eighteenth century's "other war," see North Callahan, *Royal Raiders* (Indianapolis, 1963), and Paul H. Smith, *Loyalists and Redcoats: A Study in British Revolutionary Policy* (Chapel Hill, 1965).

32. John R. Alden, *The South in the Revolution, 1763–1789* (Baton Rouge, 1957); John Bakeless, *Background to Glory: The Life of George Rogers Clark* (New York, 1957); Robert D. Bass, *Gamecock: The Life and Campaigns of General Thomas Sumter* (New York, 1961); Don Higginbotham, *Daniel Morgan: Revolutionary Rifleman* (Chapel Hill, 1961); Kenneth R. Rossman, *Thomas Mifflin and the Politics of the American Revolution* (Chapel Hill., 1952); Jack M. Sosin, *The Revolutionary Frontier, 1763–1783* (New York, 1967); Mildred F. Treacy, *Prelude to Yorktown: The Southern Campaign of Nathanael Greene, 1780–1781* (Chapel Hill, 1963); Alice N. Waring, *The Fighting Elder: Andrew Pickens* (Columbia, S.C., 1962); Charles P. Whittemore, *A General of the Revolution: John Sullivan of New Hampshire* (New York, 1961). See also Don Higginbotham, "American Historians and the Military History of the American Revolution," *American Historical Review,* LXX (October 1964), 18–34.

33. Harry L. Coles, *The War of 1812* (Chicago, 1965); Irving Brant, *James Madison: Commander-in-Chief, 1812–1836* (Indianapolis, 1961); Charles B. Brooks, *The Siege of New Orleans* (Seattle, 1961); Alec R. Gilpin, *The War of 1812 in the Old Northwest* (East Lansing, Mich., 1958); Neil Swanson, *The Perilous Fight* (New York, 1945).

34. For conventional summaries, see Robert S. Henry, *The Story of the Mexican War* (Indianapolis, 1950), and Otis Singletary, *The Mexican War* (Chicago, 1960). For another regional war, see John K. Mahon, *History of the Second Seminole War* (Gainesville, Fla., 1968), and Rembert W. Patrick, *Aristocrat in Uniform: General Duncan L. Clinch* (Gainesville, Fla., 1963).

35. Don E. Fehrenbacher, "Disunion and Reunion," in John Higham, ed., *The Reconstruction of American History* (New York, 1962), pp. 98–118; Hal Bridges, *Civil War and Reconstruction,* AHA Service Center for Teachers of History Publication No. 5 (Washington, D.C., 1962); John G. Barrett, "The Confederate States of America at War on Land and Sea," and Mary Elizabeth Massey, "The Confederate States of America: The Homefront," in Arthur S. Link and Rembert W. Patrick, eds., *Writing Southern History* (Baton Rouge, 1967), pp. 249–294; David Donald, ed., *Why the North Won the Civil War* (Baton Rouge, 1960); Grady McWhiney, ed., *Grant, Lee, Lincoln and the Radicals* (Chicago, 1964).

36. Bruce Catton, *The Coming Fury* (New York, 1961), *Terrible Swift Sword* (New York, 1963), and *Never Call Retreat* (New York, 1965); Allan Nevins, *The War for the Union,* 2 vols. to date (New York, 1959, 1960).

37. Gilbert E. Govan and James W. Livingood, *A Different Valor: The Story of General Joseph E. Johnston, C.S.A.* (Indianapolis, 1956); Archer Jones, *Confederate Strategy from Shiloh to Vicksburg* (Baton Rouge, 1961); Joseph

H. Parks, *General Edmund Kirby Smith, C.S.A.* (Baton Rouge, 1954); Charles
P. Roland, *Albert Sidney Johnston: Soldier of Three Republics* (Austin, 1964);
Grady McWhiney, *Braxton Bragg and Confederate Defeat: Field Command*
(New York, 1969); Frank Vandiver, *Rebel Brass* (Baton Rouge, 1956); T.
Harry Williams, *P. G. T. Beauregard: Napoleon in Gray* (Baton Rouge, 1955);
Bell I. Wiley, *The Road to Appomattox* (Memphis, 1956). For the Union,
see Stephen E. Ambrose, *Halleck* (Baton Rouge, 1962); Bruce Catton, *Grant
Moves South* (Boston, 1960), and *Grant Takes Command* (Boston, 1968);
Warren W. Hassler, Jr., *General George B. McClellan* (Baton Rouge, 1957);
Wilbur Thomas, *General George H. Thomas* (New York, 1964); William M.
Lamers, *The Edge of Glory: A Biography of General William S. Rosecrans*
(New York, 1961); B. H. Liddell Hart, *Sherman* (New York, 1958); Kenneth
P. Williams, *Lincoln Finds a General,* 4 vols. (New York, 1949–1956); T.
Harry Williams, *Lincoln and His Generals* (New York, 1952).

38. For examples, see Thomas L. Connelly, *Army of the Heartland: The Army
of the Tennessee, 1861–1862* (Baton Rouge, 1967); Francis F. McKinney,
*Education in Violence. The Life of George H. Thomas and a History of the
Army of the Cumberland* (Detroit, 1961). On naval strategy, see R. W. Daly,
How the Merrimac Won: The Strategic Story of the C.S.S. Virginia (New
York, 1957), and John D. Milligan, *Gunboats down the Mississippi* (Annapolis,
1965). See also Edwin B. Coddington, *The Gettysburg Campaign: A Study of
Command* (New York, 1968).

39. Samuel R. Bright, Jr., "Confederate Coast Defense," Unpublished Ph.D.
Dissertation (Duke University, 1961); Thomas F. Thiele, "The Evolution of
Cavalry in the American Civil War, 1861–1863," Unpublished Ph.D. Dissertation (University of Michigan, 1951); Thomas V. Moseley, "Evolution of the
American Civil War Infantry Tactics," Unpublished Ph.D. Dissertation (University of North Carolina, 1967); Edward H. Hagerman, "The Evolution of
Trench Warfare in the American Civil War," Unpublished Ph.D. Dissertation
(Duke University, 1965); John Q. Imholte, "The First Minnesota Infantry
Regiment, 1861–1864," Unpublished Ph.D. Dissertation (University of Minnesota, 1961).

40. Richard S. Brownlee, *Gray Ghosts of the Confederacy: Guerrilla Warfare
in the West, 1861–1865* (Baton Rouge, 1958); Jay Monaghan, *Civil War on
the Western Border, 1854–1865* (Boston, 1955); Thomas A. Belser, Jr.,
"Military Operations in Missouri and Arkansas, 1861–1865," Unpublished Ph.D.
Dissertation (Vanderbilt University, 1958).

41. John A. Carpenter, *Sword and Olive Branch: Oliver Otis Howard* (Pittsburgh, 1964); George Bentley, *A History of the Freedmen's Bureau* (Philadelphia, 1955); James E. Sefton, *The United States Army and Reconstruction,
1865–1877* (Baton Rouge, 1967). See also William T. Alderson, "The Influence
of Military Rule and the Freedmen's Bureau on Reconstruction in Virginia,"
Unpublished Ph.D. Dissertation (Vanderbilt University, 1952); George Hendricks, "Union Army Occupation of the Southern Seaboard, 1861–1865," Unpublished Ph.D. Dissertation (Columbia University, 1954); John R. Kirkland,
"Military Occupation of the South Atlantic States During Reconstruction, 1865–
1876," Unpublished Ph.D. Dissertation (University of North Carolina, 1967);
William J. Ulrich, "The Northern Military Mind in Regard to Reconstruction,
1865–1872: The Attitudes of Ten Leading Union Generals," Unpublished
Ph.D. Dissertation (Ohio State University, 1959); Robert F. Futrell, "Federal
Military Government in the South, 1861–1865," *Military Affairs,* XV (Fall
1951), 181–191.

42. Benjamin P. Thomas and Harold M. Hyman, *Stanton: The Life and Times of Lincoln's Secretary of War* (New York, 1962); Russell F. Weigley, *Quartermaster General of the Army: A Biography of M. C. Meigs* (New York, 1959); Joseph T. Durkin, *Stephen R. Mallory: Confederate Navy Chief* (Chapel Hill, 1954); Charles B. Dew, *Ironmaker to the Confederacy: Joseph R. Anderson and the Tredegar Iron Works* (New Haven, 1966); Patricia Jahns, *Matthew Fontaine Maury and Joseph Henry: Scientists of the Civil War* (New York, 1961); Frank E. Vandiver, *Ploughshares into Swords: Josiah Gorgas and Confederate Ordnance* (Austin, Tex., 1952); Robert V. Bruce, *Lincoln and the Tools of War* (Indianapolis, 1956); Richard D. Goff, *Confederate Supply* (Durham, N.C., 1969); Donald A. MacDougall, "The Federal Ordnance Bureau, 1861–1865," Unpublished Ph.D. Dissertation (University of California, Berkeley, 1951); Palmer H. Boeger, "Hardtack and Coffee: The Commissary Department, 1861–1865," Unpublished Ph.D. Dissertation (University of Wisconsin, 1954); Girard L. McEntee, "The Confederate Munitions Area and Its Influence on Federal Strategy," Unpublished Ph.D. Dissertation (St. Johns University, 1950).

43. Angus J. Johnston II, *Virginia Railroads in the Civil War* (Chapel Hill, 1961); Robert C. Black III, *The Railroads of the Confederacy* (Chapel Hill, 1952); George E. Turner, *Victory Rode the Rails* (Indianapolis, 1953); Thomas Weber, *The Northern Railroads in the Civil War, 1861–1865* (New York, 1952). For a quantitative analysis of strategy and logistics, see John G. Moore, "Mobility and Strategy in the Civil War," *Military Affairs*, XXIV (Summer 1960), 68–77.

44. George W. Adams, *Doctors in Blue: The Medical History of the Union Army in the Civil War* (New York, 1952); H. H. Cunningham, *Doctors in Gray: The Confederate Medical Service* (Baton Rouge, 1958); Warren B. Armstrong, "The Organization, Function, and Contribution of the Chaplaincy in the United States Army, 1861–1865," Unpublished Ph.D. Dissertation (University of Michigan, 1964); Frank L. Hieronymus, "For Now and Forever: The Chaplains of the Confederate States Army," Unpublished Ph.D. Dissertation (University of California at Los Angeles, 1964); Harold M. Hyman, *Era of the Oath: Northern Loyalty Tests During the Civil War and Reconstruction* (Philadelphia, 1954); Frank W. Klingberg, *The Southern Claims Commission: A Study of Unionism* (Berkeley, 1955); Eugene Murdock, *Patriotism Limited, 1862–1865* (Kent, Ohio, 1967).

45. For partial, serious treatments, see West, *Admirals of American Empire;* Virginia Johnson, *The Unregimented General: A Biography of Nelson A. Miles* (Cambridge, Mass., 1962).

46. Graham Cosmas, "An Army for Empire: The United States Army in the Spanish-American War, 1898–1899," Unpublished Ph.D. Dissertation (University of Wisconsin, 1969), and "From Order to Chaos: The War Department, the National Guard, and Military Policy, 1898," *Military Affairs*, XXIX (Fall 1965), 105–121.

47. Clarence C. Clendenen, *The United States and Pancho Villa* (Ithaca, 1961); and *Blood on the Border: The United States Army and the Mexican Irregulars* (New York, 1969); Martin Goldwert, *The Constabulary and the Dominican Republic and Nicaragua* (Gainesville, Fla., 1961); David F. Healy, *The United States in Cuba, 1898–1902* (Madison, Wisc., 1963); James H. McCrocklin, *Garde d'Haiti* (Annapolis, 1956); Neill Macaulay, *The Sandino Affair* (Chicago, 1967); Allan R. Millett, *The Politics of Intervention: The Military Occupation of Cuba, 1906–1909* (Columbus, Ohio, 1968); Robert

Quirk, *An Affair of Honor: Woodrow Wilson and the Occupation of Vera Cruz* (Lexington, Ky., 1962); George Y. Coats, "The Philippine Constabulary, 1901–1917," Unpublished Ph.D. Dissertation (Ohio State University, 1968); John M. Gates, "An Experiment in Benevolent Pacification: The U.S. Army in the Philippines, 1898–1902," Unpublished Ph.D. Dissertation (Duke University, 1967); James H. Hitchman, "Leonard Wood and the Cuban Question, 1898–1902," Unpublished Ph.D. Dissertation (University of California, 1965); Robert B. Johnson, "The Punitive Expedition: A Military, Diplomatic and Political History of Pershing's Chase After Pancho Villa, 1916–1917," Unpublished Ph.D. Dissertation (University of Southern California, 1964); Richard L. Millett, "The History of the Guardia Nacional de Nicaragua, 1925–1965," Unpublished Ph.D. Dissertation (University of New Mexico, 1966).

48. Edward M. Coffman, *The War to End All Wars: The American Military Experience in World War I* (New York, 1968). See also Harvey A. DeWeerd, *President Wilson Fights His War: World War I and the American Intervention* (New York, 1968).

49. Laurence Stallings, *The Doughboys: The Story of the A.E.F., 1917–1918* (New York, 1963). See also Richard O'Connor, *Black Jack Pershing* (Garden City, 1961).

50. David F. Trask, *The United States in the Supreme War Council: American War Aims and Inter-Allied Strategy, 1917–1918* (Middletown, Conn., 1961), and *General Tasker H. Bliss and the "Sessions of the World," 1919* (Philadelphia, 1966); Daniel R. Beaver, *Newton D. Baker and the American War Effort, 1917–1918* (Lincoln, Nebr., 1966); David A. Lockmiller, *Enoch H. Crowder* (Columbia, Mo., 1955); Edward M. Coffman, *The Hilt of the Sword: The Career of Peyton C. March* (Madison, Wisc., 1966). See also Baldwin, "The American Enlisted Man in World War I," previously cited, and Keith L. Nelson, "The First American Military Occupation of Germany, 1918–1923," Unpublished Ph.D. Dissertation (University of California, Berkeley, 1965).

51. I. B. Holley, Jr., *Ideas and Weapons: Exploitation of the Aerial Weapon by the United States During World War I* (New Haven, 1953); Alfred F. Hurley, *Billy Mitchell: Crusader for Air Power* (New York, 1964); James J. Hudson, *Hostile Skies: A Combat History of the American Air Service in World War I* (Syracuse, 1968); Edwin H. Rutkowski, *The Politics of Military Aviation Procurement, 1926–1934* (Columbus, Ohio, 1966). See also Russell J. Parkinson, "Politics, Patents and Planes: Military Aeronautics in the United States, 1863–1907," Unpublished Ph.D. Dissertation (Duke University, 1963), and Raymond R. Flugel, "United States Air Power Doctrine: A Study of the Influence of William Mitchell and Giulio Douhet at the Air Corps Tactical School, 1921–1935," Unpublished Ph.D. Dissertation (University of Oklahoma, 1965).

52. For one effort on the tank, see M. H. Gillie, *Forging the Thunderbolt* (Harrisburg, Pa., 1947).

53. Dr. R. M. Johnston to the Adj. Gen. USA, April 24, 1914, and Leonard Wood to Lindley Garrison, April 24, 1914, Leonard Wood Papers, Library of Congress; Historical Section, General Staff, AEF, "The American Military Factor in the War," November 1918, George Van Horn Moseley Papers, Library of Congress.

54. Department of the Army, Office of the Chief of Military History, *United States Army in World War II,* 70 vols. to date (Washington, D.C., 1947–); Samuel Eliot Morison, *History of United States Naval Operations in World*

War II, 15 vols. (Boston, 1947–1962); Wesley Frank Craven and James Lea Cate, eds., *The Army Air Forces in World War II*, 7 vols. (Chicago, 1948–1958); Henry I. Shaw, Jr., *et al.*, *History of Marine Corps Operations in World War II*, 4 vols. to date (Washington, D.C., 1958–).

55. For example, see James A. Huston, *The Sinews of War: Army Logistics, 1775–1953* (Washington, D.C., 1967); W. R. Carter, *Beans, Bullets and Blackoil: The Story of Fleet Logistics Afloat During World War II* (Washington, D.C., 1953); Erna Risch, *Quartermaster Support for the Army: A History of the Corps, 1775–1939* (Washington, D.C., 1962); Julius A. Furer, *Administration in the Navy Department in World War II* (Washington, D.C., 1959); Roy E. Appleman, *South to the Naktong, North to the Yalu: June–November, 1950* (Washington, D.C., 1961); Walter G. Hermes, *Truce Tent and Fighting Front* (Washington, D.C., 1966); James A. Field, Jr., *History of United States Naval Operations: Korea* (Washington, D.C., 1962); Robert F. Futrell, *The United States Air Force in Korea, 1950–1953* (New York, 1961); Lynn Montross, Nicholas A. Canzona, *et al.*, *U.S. Marine Operations in Korea*, 4 vols. to date (Washington, D.C., 1954–); Robert K. Sawyer, *Military Advisors in Korea: KMAG in Peace and War* (Washington, D.C., 1962). For Vietnam, see Charles B. MacDonald, "Official History and the War in Vietnam," *Military Affairs*, XXXII (Spring 1968), 2–11.

56. Kent R. Greenfield, *The Historian and the Army* (New Brunswick, N.J., 1954), pp. 3–14; Hugh M. Cole, "Writing Contemporary Military History," *Military Affairs*, XII (Fall 1948), 162–167; Louis Morton, "Sources for the History of World War II," *World Politics*, XIII (April 1961), 435–453; Martin Blumenson, "Can Official History Be Honest History?," *Military Affairs*, XXVI (Winter 1963), 96–109; Albert F. Simpson, memo, "The USAF Historical Division and Its Program," January 1966.

57. Stetson Conn to the author, September 13, 1968; E. M. Eller to the author, September 26, 1968.

58. Philip A. Crowl, *Campaign in the Marianas* (Washington, D.C., 1960), pp. 33–262; Henry I. Shaw, Jr., Bernard C. Nalty, and Edwin T. Turnbladh, *Central Pacific Drive* (Washington, D.C., 1966), pp. 231–232; Jeter A. Isely and Philip A. Crowl, *The U.S. Marines and Amphibious War* (Princeton, 1951); Gordon B. Turner, "The Amphibious Complex: A Study of Operations at Saipan," Unpublished Ph.D. Dissertation (Princeton University, 1950).

59. Craven and Cate, eds., *Europe: TORCH to POINTBLANK*, II, *The Army Air Forces in World War II* (Chicago, 1949), 229–230, 334–337, 654–655, 679–681; Thomas H. Greer, *The Development of Air Doctrine in the Army Air Arm, 1917–1941*, USAF Historical Study No. 89 (Air University, 1955), pp. 57–60, 82–83, 116–118, 126; William R. Emerson, "Operation POINTBLANK," Harmon Memorial Lecture, USAF Academy, 1962, reprinted in Cadet Notebook, "History 204 Air Power and Twentieth Century Warfare" (USAF Academy, 1966); Bernard L. Boylan, "The Development of the American Long-Range Escort Fighter," Unpublished Ph.D. Dissertation (University of Missouri, 1955).

60. For example, Albert A. Blum, *Drafted or Deferred: Practices Past and Present* (Ann Arbor, 1967); Robert H. Connery, *The Navy and the Industrial Mobilization in World War II* (Princeton, 1951); Herbert Feis, *Churchill, Roosevelt, Stalin* (Princeton, 1957); Trumbull Higgins, *Soft Underbelly: The Anglo-American Controversy over the Italian Campaign, 1939–1945* (New York, 1968); E. E. Morison, *Turmoil and Tradition: A Study of the Life and Times of Henry L. Stimson* (Boston, 1960); Donald H. Riddle, *The*

Truman Committee (New Brunswick, N.J., 1964); Richard C. Lukas, "Air Force Aspects of American Aid to the Soviet Union: The Crucial Years, 1941–1942," Unpublished Ph.D. Dissertation (Florida State University, 1963).

61. Duncan S. Ballantine, *U.S. Naval Logistics in the Second World War* (Princeton, 1947); John M. Coleman, *The Development of Tactical Services in the Army Air Forces* (New York, 1950); Ray Leslie Anders, Jr., *The Ledo Road* (Norman, Okla., 1965); Charles H. Owens, Jr., "The Logistical Support of the Army in the Central Pacific, 1941–1944," Unpublished Ph.D. Dissertation (Georgetown University, 1954); Alfred Goldberg, "Air Logistics: Its Role in the European Theater in World War II," Unpublished Ph.D. Dissertation (Johns Hopkins University, 1950); Clark G. Reynolds, *The Fast Carriers: The Forging of an Air Navy* (New York, 1968); Walter C. Hicks, "The 97th Bombardment Group, World War II," Unpublished Ph.D. Dissertation (University of Kentucky, 1961); James M. Boyle, "The XXI Bomber Command: Primary Factor in the Defeat of Japan," Unpublished Ph.D. Dissertation (St. Louis University, 1964).

62. Walter Rundell, Jr., *Black Market Money: The Collapse of U.S. Military Currency Control* (Baton Rouge, 1964); Thomas J. Hickman, "The United States Air Force: German-American Relations, 1945–1955," Unpublished Ph.D. Dissertation (Fordham University, 1958); Franklin M. Davis, Jr., *Come as a Conqueror: The United States Occupation of Germany, 1945–1949* (New York, 1967); John J. Hunt, "The United States Occupation of Iceland, 1941–1946," Unpublished Ph.D. Dissertation (Georgetown University, 1966); E. H. F. Svensson, "The Military Occupation of Japan: The First Years. Planning, Policy Formation, and Reforms," Unpublished Ph.D. Dissertation (University of Denver, 1966).

63. David S. McLellan and John W. Reuss, "Foreign and Military Policies" in Richard S. Kirkendall, ed., *The Truman Period as a Research Field* (Columbia Mo., 1967), pp. 15–86.

64. Samuel P. Huntington, *The Common Defense* (New York, 1961); Paul Y. Hammond, *Organizing for Defense* (New York, 1961); Warner Schilling, Paul Y. Hammond, and Glenn H. Snyder, *Strategy, Politics and Defense Budgets* (New York, 1962); Demetrios Caraley, *The Politics of Military Unification* (New York, 1966); Vincent Davis, *Postwar Defense Policy and the U.S. Navy, 1943–1946* (Chapel Hill, 1966); William R. Kintner, *Forging a New Sword: A Study of the Department of Defense* (New York, 1958); Edward A. Kolodziej, *The Uncommon Defense and Congress, 1945–1963* (Columbus, Ohio, 1966); John C. Ries, *The Management of Defense* (Baltimore, 1964). See also Harold Stein, ed., *American Civil-Military Decisions* (Tuscaloosa, 1963), and Lawrence J. Legere, Jr., "Unification of the Armed Forces," Unpublished Ph.D. Dissertation (Harvard University, 1950).

65. Robert G. Albion and Robert H. Connery, *Forrestal and the Navy* (New York, 1962); Murray Green, "Stuart Symington and the B-36," Unpublished Ph.D. Dissertation (American University, 1960); Curtis W. Tarr, "Unification of America's Armed Forces: A Century and a Half of Conflict, 1789–1947," Unpublished Ph.D. Dissertation (Stanford University, 1962).

66. Huntington, *The Soldier and the State,* previously cited; John W. Spanier, *The Truman-MacArthur Controversy and the Korean War* (Cambridge, Mass., 1959); Gene M. Lyons and John W. Masland, *Education and Military Leadership: A Study of the ROTC* (Princeton, 1959); John W. Masland, *Soldiers and Scholars: Military Education and National Policy* (Princeton, 1957); Walter Millis, Harvey Mansfield, and Harold Stein, *Arms and the State* (New York,

1958); Gene M. Lyons, *Military Policy and Economic Aid: The Korean Case, 1950–1953* (Columbus, Ohio, 1961); Willard F. Barber and C. Neale Ronning, *Internal Security and Military Power: Counterinsurgency and Civic Action in Latin America* (Columbus, Ohio, 1966); Robert G. Lindsay, *This High Name: Public Relations and the U.S. Marine Corps* (Madison, Wisc., 1956); Harry Howe Ransome, *Central Intelligence and National Security* (Cambridge, Mass., 1958); Robert Gilpin, *American Scientists and Nuclear Weapons Policy* (Princeton, 1962); William F. Leventrosser, *Congress and the Citizen–Soldier* (Columbus, Ohio, 1967).

67. Paul T. Armitstead, "Retired Military Leaders in American Business," Unpublished Ph.D. Dissertation (University of Texas, 1967); Lyon Gardiner Tyler, Jr., "Civil Defense: The Impact of the Planning Years, 1945–1950," Unpublished Ph.D. Dissertation (Duke University, 1967).

On Writing the History
of American Science

CHARLES E. ROSENBERG

The historian of American science is not fully accepted as either an American historian or an historian of science. Most American historians are simply indifferent to the field; but beyond this, more than a few historians of science are openly scornful. I first became aware of this scorn some years ago when I suggested the possibility of a course on the history of American science. "Nonsense," replied a senior colleague in the history of science. Perhaps science *in* America, he condescended, but the other was an absurdity; science was an international enterprise, its ultimate essence an ever-shifting structure of ideas dependent upon a developing internal logic and not upon the peculiar circumstances in which they happened to be elaborated.

Though it is unlikely that this gentleman would have defended his distinction as absolute, the categories "internal" and "external" serve to describe contemporary research in the history of science with disheartening accuracy. No historian of science would deny that social and institutional factors are significant in themselves, or that they play a role—however indirect or difficult to evaluate—in the evolution of scientific ideas; but he simply does not study them. Social and institutional factors have, in the recent past, played a comparatively small role in this new and self-consciously professionalized discipline. A survey of the past decade's title pages of *Isis* will make this abundantly clear. Given such an undeniable emphasis upon the internal, intellectual history of science, the study of scientific ideas and institutions in any one nation must seem inevitably parochial, a confession either of atavistic nationalism or of an inability to master that higher calling, the exegesis of scientific innovation.

Social historians and sociologists of science are more familiar with the manipulation of social variables; but they are only rarely trained in the manipulation of scientific ideas and thus are unable to study interactions between the specific texture of scientific thought and the context in which it is shaped. Such narrow patterns of education are clearly undesirable. The social historian or sociologist can hardly hope to evaluate the effect of particular institutional developments upon the scientist's intellectual life without some understanding of that life.[1]

Among general historians, the study of American science is, as we have suggested, marked more by neglect than scorn. But it is not a peculiar neglect; the history of the professions or the family suffers in like manner. The New History remains largely a programmatic demand—a half-century-old embryo gestating still. Traditional public policy concerns still dominate the pages of the *Journal of American History* as they did those of its predecessor, the *Mississippi Valley Historical Review*: the basic canon of academic American history has shown itself remarkably impervious to change.

There is, as we shall see, no lack of contemporary evidences of a growing interest in the role played by science in American life. Much of this interest, however, has been evinced by journalists, scientists, and students of government policy; among academic historians the situation is still bleak. The writing of the history of science in America is troubled by chronic ills which show few signs of resolving themselves. These problems can—at least for the sake of orderly exposition—be discussed under three general rubrics: first, the existing canons of significance in the history of American science; second, the training and recruitment of historians of science; and third, a failure to use new frames of reference.

The canon of the history of American science is, on the whole, as arbitrary and intractable as that of American history generally. Perhaps the most obvious difficulty is a disproportionate concern with early America, and a dismaying lack of interest in the far more challenging and complex period between 1870 and the 1920's, the period when American science began to assume its modern form.* The existing

---

* Though clearly a contributing factor, the inability of most general historians to deal with the increasingly complex texture of scientific thought in this period does not adequately explain this neglect. For historians have ignored many opportunities for late nineteenth- and early twentieth-century studies which lie essentially in the field of institutional history.

literature tells us, for example, a great deal more about botany in the late eighteenth and early nineteenth centuries than it does about the development of cytology or biochemistry a century later—certainly an unsatisfactory if not actually whimsical state of things.

A somewhat related problem in the canon is a concern with the alleged proclivity of Americans to ignore basic science, or with attempts to locate a mature scientific community in pre–Civil War America.[2] Certainly these questions imply significant judgments upon the values and structure of American society; the fact is, however, that in the current state of the art there is no prospect of these questions finding answers. We have neither an adequate empirical knowledge of science in pre–Civil War America nor the theoretical precision with which to phrase such queries. How does one define a scientific community? What are the relationships between levels of economic development or particular class structures and the ultimate creation of such a community?

But these are perhaps minor grievances in comparison with an even more fundamental problem in the literature of American science: its lack of depth. There have simply not been enough practitioners. Too many significant subjects have never been studied. There are, of course, exceptions. A concern for the relationship between science and government has established itself, while the tradition of interest in early America has, as we have noted, motivated study of our pioneer naturalists.[3] We do have biographies in abundance, but of these only a small proportion have been written by professional historians.

Conspicuously absent from the historical literature of American science are studies of particular disciplines. Some histories of this kind do exist; but most have been written by professional scientists, underlining the obvious fact that the scientist's basic unit of orientation is his discipline or sub-discipline.[4] It is his discipline which poses questions for the investigator, which provides the intellectual and technological tools with which he attempts to solve them; it is his discipline which defines aspirations, sanctions ambitions, rewards ultimate achievement. The establishment of institutional loci for the several scientific disciplines remains perhaps the most important untold story in the history of American science.

More than this, the institutionalization of the academic disciplines was as important an event as there has been in the history of American intellectual life. When one contemplates the number of available studies of, let us say, transcendentalism, and then notes that there is no adequate history of any one of the scientific disciplines, or any one of the learned professions, the inadequacy of the existing canon becomes all too clear. What is required are not simply histories of chemistry and anthropology, much as these are necessary, but a general and meaningful acceptance by biographers, by institutional historians, by students of particular discoveries or problem areas, that the primary context for the scientist is his discipline.[5] To understand the solution of any core of scientific problems, one must look not simply at the work of those few men whose names are associated with particular discoveries but at the manner in which the discipline as a whole shaped the particular research area in which they labored.

Underlying the comparatively narrow and stylized content of historical literature on American science is the nature of the general historian's training—and perhaps his temperament as well. Historians still tend to have little scientific or mathematical background, thus disqualifying themselves from undertaking the investigation of a good many relevant problems. Few, moreover, have any knowledge of either contemporary social theory or the empirical findings of sociologists of medicine and science. This dilemma does not promise to be immediately resolved with the emergence of a new generation of historians of science more sensitive than their predecessors to social issues. Though having often left the sciences because of a concern for social problems, our younger historians of science still tend to assume that a discipline's intellectual content is its ultimate and in practice often self-sufficient reality. American history of science programs emphasize "internal" history, an approach that promises logical coherence and a comforting order to the sometime scientist. It will not be easy to integrate into contemporary models for writing the history of science those protean "soft" factors which so often alter the texture of scientific thought.

A final problem for historians of American science, and perhaps ultimately most significant, is the eclectic, almost aggressively atheoretical tradition in American history. A conspicuous example is the failure of American historians of science to use Marxist—or perhaps more accurately, Marxoid—frames of reference. (It is hardly coincidence that Dirk Struik's *Yankee Science in the Making,* a well-known exception to this generalization, was written by a Dutch mathematician and published while embers of American-Soviet friendship still faintly glowed.) [6] Yet in England alone one thinks of Bernal, of Needham and

Crowther. It is not that this particular frame of reference is peculiarly right, wrong, or even rigorously formulated; the point is that the absence among American historians of such stylized points of view leads to a bland and unquestioning eclecticism, an eclecticism unaware even that it entertains presuppositions and assumes models. The central advantage in constructing more or less elaborate and explicit models of scientific behavior or of the relationship, let us say, of science and technology to other aspects of social structure (class, for example, or attitudes toward education and change), is that such models force one to examine relationships which might otherwise be ignored. The availability of competing models only makes it the more likely that evidence marshaled by historical scholarship will be applied to significant and enduring theoretical questions.

Despite my use of the economic determinist example, it seems clear that such ideas do not promise to be of major significance in reshaping the immediate future of American historical writing. The contemporary social sciences have become the most significant source of integrating concepts for the historian and of new criteria for the ordering and evaluation of evidence. True, contemporary social theory may be contradictory, arbitrarily reductionist, or simply irrelevant in terms of creating models appropriate to the historian's implacably particular data universe and broadly synthetic temperament. Yet there are, I feel, a number of social science concerns which may well prove increasingly relevant to the interpretation of the history of American science. Let me at least briefly cite some of the conceptual areas which offer such promise. One is role theory; another the sociology of knowledge; a third, what I should like to call the higher institutionalism (including a consideration of recruitment and the formation, identification, and perpetuation of elites); and a fourth, the study of economic growth models.

Historians have failed with remarkable consistency to use contemporary role theory in explaining the behavior of scientists in the past. It would be obviously naive in the present state of the art to attempt to replicate precisely the research designs of contemporary social psychologists. Whether it is possible, let alone advisable, for historians generally to employ these methods remains to be seen. Yet it is, at the same time, impossible to ignore the way in which such sociological concepts have reshaped this generation's way of perceiving the world. I should not like to dismiss even a survey course or cocktail-party knowledge of the social sciences. On this level, at least, a good many historians are aware that there is something called role theory; and indeed, the historian, despite his traditionally eclectic and impressionistic methods, has already begun to incorporate sociological dimensions in his vision of past reality. History has always borrowed concepts and even motivating values from other disciplines—from theology, from philosophy, from physics and biological speculation, now from sociology, social psychology, and political science. Though one may object to particular examples of this tendency, one can hardly question its ultimate significance. It would be unreasonable to ask that history be as complex and tentative as reality; yet it is the historian's task to approach this goal as best he can. One can only welcome intellectual ventures that introduce new variables, widen the historian's perceived data universe, and provide new dimensions for his interpretive strategies. Historians have always worked with implicit models, and the influence of contemporary social science must be—and already has been—to make these models more complex and explicit.

To return more immediately to the scientist's role: it would seem hardly controversial to assume the existence, since at least the mid-nineteenth century, of a learned, value-dictating, and behavior-orienting social role for the scientific disciplines.[7] (It must be emphasized that a scientist's role at a particular time incorporates certain elements common to all the sciences and others peculiar to his discipline.) The delineation of such roles and an understanding of how they shaped thought and action seems a necessary prerequisite to writing the history of science; it is hardly possible to evaluate an individual's intellectual contribution without some insight into the ways in which a particular individuality succeeds in altering the social role prescribed by his discipline or profession. For the specific conceptual content of a science and the social role of the scientist are inextricable.*

* The values which sanction pure and professional science, it must be understood, sanction in practice specific configurations of intellectual assumption and instrumental procedure. Failure to accept these ideas and techniques is to provoke the charge of nonprofessionalism, a kind of intellectual malpractice. This judgment is informed by the emotional burden of those categorical and absolute values that sanction the scientist's role generally. The measure of originality in modern science must then in a sense be defined as the ability to transcend the particular set which is the intellectual content—and thus a central dimension—of the scientist's role at any particular time. The difficulty of transcending these internalized values imparts a perhaps inevitable rigidity to the system. But the absolute value granted originality and priority (thus sanctioning personal ambition and encouraging creativity) counterbalances somewhat the rigidity of "professionalism."

We need, then, studies indicating which aspects of behavior were proscribed and which encouraged by particular fields; studies illuminating the manner in which institutions shaped a discipline-specific socialization; studies outlining the precise configuration of ideas and techniques that comprised the content and thus the formal goal of this process of socialization. In the field of American science we need, for example, studies of the nineteenth-century American scientist in the German university, studies which describe not only the general values imparted—the absolutes of research, of immortality through priority, of *Lern-und-Lehrfreiheit*— but also particular Ideas and procedures.[8] We need as well similar monographs on the role played by American graduate-school departments in the early twentieth century. By way of contrast, we must try to reach a similar understanding of groups of American scientists in the late eighteenth and mid-nineteenth centuries. It would indeed be possible to argue that the elaboration and gradual clarification of precise roles was the central event in the development of science in the nineteenth century.*

The historian must not, I repeat, concern himself with the creation of research designs which conform in detail to the demands of a particular subspecies of role theory. Such attempts—in the present states of history and social psychology—must lead in many cases to a flat sterility, to a dismissal of the pragmatic strength, the interpretive flexibility, and the inclusiveness which have always been a distinguishing virtue of the best historical writing. (And this without any compensation other than a comforting assurance of having created an appropriately scientific design.) Thomas Cochran's *Railroad Leaders* provides an excellent example of an attempt to apply the general idea of social role without tying it either to particular theoretical formulations or to overly positivistic modes of handling data.[9]

The sociology of knowledge offers another kind of opportunity to the historian of American science. It is, indeed, a particularly appealing example, for the sociology of knowledge is an interest notoriously neglected within its parent discipline. Almost every discrete and consequential innovation from the mid-eighteenth century to the present represents a potential case study in the diffusion of knowledge, and thus necessarily in the social structure of the group or discipline assimilating the new idea. Though there are a number of contemporary empirical studies of American materials (most prominently the adop-

* With the understanding that this implies the parallel development of appropriate institutional mechanisms.

tion of agricultural innovations and drugs),[10] I can think of no
analogous historical studies in American science or medicine. The
opportunities are certainly abundant. In biology and medicine, my
particular field of interest, one could suggest such obvious possibilities
as the X-ray, Mendelism, Vitamin A, and the Morgan group's Dro-
sophila work. Even such landmarks in the literature as Chambers'
Vestiges and Darwin's *Origin,* surgical anaesthesia, physical diagnosis,
and Beaumont's physiological ideas have never been studied from this
point of view. The list could easily be extended.[11]

Such diffusion studies provide an indispensable means for gaining
insight into the structure of particular disciplines or professions. Since
the distribution of ideas is very much a part of the relationships among
power, prestige, and status, tracing the discussion of particular ideas or
techniques represents one of our most valuable means of access to the
inner structure of a discipline or profession. Ideas can, if the metaphor be excused, serve as discrete "tagged" elements in the system;
where and when they are recovered indicates a great deal about the
physiology and anatomy of the system into which they were originally
introduced. Certain ideas provide, moreover, a means of judging the
effect of particular scientific ideas on laymen, upon that interface where
belief and attitudinal commitment determine how scientific ideas are
to be used in the communication of social thought and values. The
social uses of Darwinism or the inevitable manipulation of currently
plausible hereditarian concepts by successive generations illustrates this
clearly.

A central problem in understanding the structure of any particular
discipline is the relationship of sub-disciplines to the larger field. In
connection with studies of citation behavior and patterns of recruitment
and education, diffusion studies will provide a sensitive indicator of
the intellectual and institutional fine structure of particular disciplines;
for the ideas of science are a necessary and integral structural element
in the total enterprise of science.* Only the historian's or sociologist's
arbitrary whim separates institutions and ideas which, common sense
tells us, ordinarily exist in an intricate and mutually dependent relationship. Good history of science is always to some degree an exercise
in the historical sociology of knowledge.

---

* The contemporary relationship between economic and general history presents a familiar example of the kinds of relationships which may subsist between
discipline and sub-discipline—and the need for understanding the intellectual
texture of each field as well as factors such as recruitment and training.

In my discussion of the roles assumed by the scientist and the potential uses of the sociology of knowledge, I have implied new dimensions for institutional history. But institutional history must in the future also become increasingly sensitive to the implications of formal and often seemingly trivial shifts in organization. Such concerns should be present as well in the research tactics of historians of science interested primarily in the development of scientific ideas; for such institutional arrangements may influence trends in scientific thought, while intellectual innovation may imply new institutional arrangements. These considerations are not radically inconsistent with traditional historical views and will, I believe, be assimilated without great difficulty by future students of the institutional history of science.

Institutional patterns are, of course, central to the study of economic growth, another social science area of potential relevance to the history of American science. Though many dimensions of scientific life are not easily, or at least successfully, reduced to econometric terms, economic historians seem increasingly willing to consider even those soft factors—such as class attitudes, attitudes toward education and the possibilities of social change, and patterns of aspiration—which largely determine the rate and extent of economic development. Since science and technology can be considered a primary factor in creating social change, one can safely predict an increasing interest in the historical relationships between science and technology, between science and relevant elements of social structure and values.[12]

Though I have described a number of instances in which the history of American science may in the future be broadened by concepts and methods from other academic disciplines, there are also important approaches well within the traditional canon of historical subject and method and still largely ignored. One kind of opportunity, for example, is case studies illustrating the relationship between basic science and technology. Another is the delineation of lay attitudes toward science and popular modes of scientific education. A related problem needing systematic discussion is the place of science as a component of social thought—science both as a source of idioms for conducting social discourse and as a value-bestowing reference area. Case studies are also needed to illustrate the manner in which social contexts have effected the initiation and even specific textures of areas of scientific research.

Although I have painted a bleak picture of the historical study of American science, I should not like to have these wails of program-

matic anguish obscure some encouraging signs. There is today a growing interest in science and the place of science in American life, though
much of it to be sure exists outside the confines of academic American
history. Many scientists have become more conscious of their role as
history-makers; in almost every major scientific discipline, national
societies are making efforts to create or enlarge archives. In this post-
Bomb, big-science era, the implications of science policy have become
a matter of concern to an increasingly sensitive and articulate minority
of scientists and policy-makers. Indeed, the news columns, editorials,
letters to the editor, and reviews in *Science* for the 1950's and 1960's
should in themselves prove a rich source for historians of future
generations.

Equally encouraging is a growing interest in the history of the behavioral sciences, an interest reflecting the values and educational
experiences of younger historians and social scientists. In its five-year
history the *Journal of the History of the Behavioral Sciences* has recorded—and presumably encouraged—an interest in the development
of the relevant disciplines in America. These disciplines have grown
to intellectual prominence during a period in which American science
generally was attaining world stature; the familiar argument that
American science before the 1920's was "too trivial" for serious attention is simply irrelevant in these areas. Psychiatry and psychology,
moreover, have come to play an increasing role in the subject matter
of intellectual history and the history of ideas; Freud, Watson, and
Boas promise to become as much staples of the intellectual history
syllabus as Emerson and Thoreau.

One may also draw encouragement from the fact that a good portion
of twentieth-century American science has taken place in the presence
of social scientists who are increasingly alert to opportunities for empirical investigation. Historians of science in the post–social survey era will
have a new abundance of data with which to work; already, for example, historians of American science benefit regularly from the
several editions of J. M. Cattell's *American Men of Science* and his
concern with the recruitment and identification of scientific elites.[13]
Even such problems as the attitudes of patients toward medical treatment will in the not too distant future be capable of analysis across
time. Research designs based on the use of such data should provide
a variety of new options for historians a half-century from now.

The history of American science is not bereft of expectations. In addition to the alternatives already suggested, there are several more general trends which promise to be of increasing significance. It seems likely that the history of science will ultimately—if clearly not immediately—concern itself more and more with the social context of science. It seems equally likely that general American history will assimilate more and more of the New History. Comparative history too gives promise—though less convincing—of becoming a reality in method and content and not simply a programmatic demand. Within each of these areas the history of a national science should play an increasingly meaningful role.

Let me conclude with a note of explanation. The aim of this essay has not been to ask that historians become instant social scientists on the pattern of any particular discipline or disciplines, but rather to predict ways in which constructive change may find its way into the canon of the history of American science. History still has a unique and in some ways higher calling in its freedom from the rigidity of scientific models and in its instinctive attempt to approach ever closer the texture and richness of a particular reality. I have sought only to suggest approaches that promise to increase this sensitivity to texture and nuance.

NOTES

1. Even if the historian is concerned with an essentially social problem—the recruitment and identification of elites, let us say—an understanding of scientific ideas might permit, for example, the textual analysis of publications as a measure of the relationship between productivity and elite membership, or as a means of identifying distinct sub-elites. It is not my intention to argue that excellent work has not been done in either the exclusively "internal" or "external" form. I do object to an existing imbalance in the history of science literature, dominated as it is by the internalist view, to the general neglect of research strategies that combine the two approaches. It is difficult to accept

the generalization made some years ago by Arthur M. Schlesinger that "the peculiar function" of the historian is "not so much to write the internal history of science as to trace the external connections of science and society." "An American Historian Looks at Science and Technology," *Isis,* XXXVI (1945–1946), 162–166.

2. See, for example, Richard Shryock, "American Indifference to Basic Science During the Nineteenth Century," *Archives Internationales d'Histoire des Sciences,* V (1948), 50–65; I. Bernard Cohen, "Some Reflections on the State of Science During the Nineteenth Century," *Proceedings of the National Academy of Science,* XLV (1959), 666–677; George H. Daniels, *American Science in the Age of Jackson* (New York and London, 1968); John C. Greene, "American Science Comes of Age," *Journal of American History,* LX (1968), 22–41.

3. For an introduction to the literature in this field, see Whitfield J. Bell, Jr., *Early American Science: Needs and Opportunities for Study* (Williamsburg, Va., 1955), and an excellent review article on botany by Jerry Stannard, "Early American Botany and Its Sources," *Bibliography and Natural History: Essays Presented at a Conference Convened in June 1964 by Thomas Buckman* (Lawrence, Kans., 1966). On the history of the relationship between science and government, the standard synthesis is that by A. Hunter Dupree, *Science in the Federal Government: A History of Policies and Activities to 1940* (Cambridge, Mass., 1957).

4. See, for example, Edgar Fahs Smith, *Chemistry in America* (New York, 1914); George P. Merrill, "Contributions to the History of American Geology," U.S. National Museum, *Report,* 1904, pt. 2, pp. 187–733; Merrill, *The First One Hundred Years of American Geology* (New Haven, 1924); David E. Smith and Jekuthiel Ginsburg. *A History of Mathematics in America Before 1900* (Chicago, 1934); Paul F. Clark, *Pioneer Microbiologists of America* (Madison, Wisc., 1961); L. O. Howard, *A History of Applied Entomology,* Smithsonian Collections, Misc. Vol. 84 (Washington, D.C., 1930), 1–198. There are some recent examples of discipline-oriented studies by historians which may indicate a trend: Edward H. Beardsley, *The Rise of the American Chemistry Profession, 1850–1900,* University of Florida Monographs, Social Sciences No. 23 (Gainesville, Fla., 1964); Frank M. Albrecht, "The New Psychology in America, 1880–1895," Unpublished Ph.D. Dissertation (Johns Hopkins University, 1960). Daniel J. Kevles is at work on a history of the physics profession in the United States from 1865 to 1945. There has been recent interest as well in the history of the engineering profession: Daniel H. Calhoun, *The American Civil Engineer: Origins and Conflicts* (Cambridge, Mass., 1960); Monte A. Calvert, *The Mechanical Engineer in America, 1830–1910: Professional Cultures in Conflict* (Baltimore, 1967).

5. Local values and particular aims or conditions may alter the goals dictated by this orientation; yet this does not impugn its intellectual and emotional primacy. It is, indeed, sometimes the conflict between the absolutist demands of a scientist's discipline and local circumstances which at once create the scientific reformer's motivation, sanction personal ambition, and provide him with a specific program. For a more elaborate discussion of the need for using the scientist's discipline as a primary focus, see Charles E. Rosenberg, "On the Study of American Biology and Medicine: Some Justifications," *Bulletin of the History of Medicine,* XXXVIII (1964), 364–376; Rosenberg, "Factors in the Development of Genetics in the United States," *Journal of the History of Medicine,* XXII (1967), 27–46.

6. Dirk J. Struik, *Yankee Science in the Making* (Boston, 1948).

7. My feeling is that the modern scientific role did not exist in essentially prototypical fashion until the nineteenth century, though elements of it have been traced to much earlier periods. For particular case studies, see Joseph Ben-David, "Scientific Productivity and Academic Organization in Nineteenth-Century Medicine," *American Sociological Review*, XXV (1960), 828–843; "Roles and Innovations in Medicine," *American Journal of Sociology*, LXV (1960), 557–568; "Social Factors in the Origins of a New Science: The Case of Psychology," *American Sociological Review*, XXXI (1966), 451–465. For a more generalized attempt to "describe" sociologically the nature of the modern scientific enterprise, see Warren O. Hagstrom, *The Scientific Community* (New York, 1965). It will be seen that my use of the role concept is not precisely the same as that of Merton, Hagstrom, or Ben-David. See also Everett Mendelson, "The Emergence of Science as a Profession in Nineteenth-Century Europe," in Karl Hill, ed., *The Management of Scientists* (Boston, 1964), pp. 3–48.

8. I have consciously avoided the words "paradigm" and "paradigmatic," for they have in recent years acquired a rather specific meaning among historians of science. It might, parenthetically, be argued that from the historian's point of view the concept of role suggested here subsumes in practice all the determinable factors implied by Thomas Kuhn's several uses of the terms "normal" or "paradigmatic" science. The structural implication of Kuhn's argument—that paradigmatic problems shape particular disciplines or sub-disciplines—seems unnecessarily arbitrary. In those cases in which this did seem to be the case, it would be subsumed logically within the role concept suggested. Thomas Kuhn, *The Structure of Scientific Revolutions* (Chicago, 1962).

9. Thomas Cochran, *Railroad Leaders, 1845–1890: The Business Mind in Action* (Cambridge, Mass., 1953).

10. On the diffusion of innovations generally, see Everett Rogers, *The Diffusion of Innovations* (New York, 1962). Rogers is particularly strong on agriculture, but includes an extraordinarily comprehensive bibliography. For the drug studies, see also the summaries in Bernard Barber, *Drugs and Society* (New York, 1967).

11. I have, in one way or another, studied the diffusion of John Snow's discovery of the water transmission of cholera, Koch's discovery of the tuberculosis bacillus, and the Sutton-Boveri suggestion of a chromosomal mechanism as basis for the Mendelian laws. For a description of the cholera work, see "The Cause of Cholera: Aspects of Etiological Thought in Nineteenth-Century America," *Bulletin of the History of Medicine*, XXXIV (1960), 331–354.

12. For examples of the influence of such factors in the synthesis of contemporary economic historians, see Simon S. Kuznets, *Modern Economic Growth: Rate, Structure, and Spread* (New Haven, 1966); Cyril Black, *The Dynamics of Modernization; A Study in Comparative History* (New York, 1966); Everett E. Hagen, *On the Theory of Social Change; How Economic Growth Begins* (Homewood, Ill., 1962). For some recent discussions by historians of some of these social factors and their relationship to science (and necessarily to economic growth), see George Basalla, "The Spread of Western Science," *Science*, CLVI (1967), 611–622; Charles E. Rosenberg, "Cholera in Nineteenth-Century Europe: A Tool for Social and Economic Analysis," *Comparative Studies in Society and History*, VIII (1966), 452–463; Donald Fleming, "Science in Australia, Canada, and the United States: Some Comparative

Remarks," *Actes du Dixième Congrès International d'Histoire des Sciences* (Paris, 1964), I, 179–196.

13. The first and second editions of Cattell's *American Men of Science: A Biographical Directory* (New York) appeared in 1906 and 1910. For Cattell's own use of the data for the directories see his work on "A Statistical Study of American Men of Science" which appears as pages 537–596 of the 1910 edition.

The Big Questions
in the History of
American Technology

GEORGE H. DANIELS

Following an approved model for "state of the field" reports, one might investigate the history of American technology by reciting the number of technologists whose biographies were unwritten, of industries that remained unstudied, of machines whose origins were still shrouded in mystery, of captains of industry whose rise was yet unchronicled. The writer would then close with a plea for historians of technology to assign their graduate students these topics, assuring his readers that a complete understanding of the subject would soon follow.

However useful this approach might be in certain fields, in the history of American technology I think it would be both depressing and superfluous—depressing because we have barely scratched the surface of any of these important areas and the lists would be very long; and superfluous because our need is not for discrete research ideas—there is an abundance of those—but for a way to organize our thoughts and separate the more important from the less.

Can one therefore conclude anything from the discrete studies that have already been published? Now that these studies have been made, the articles and books written, what do we know with a relative degree of certainty about the history of American technology? What do we have reason to suspect? In light of our present knowledge, what seem to be the most fruitful lines for further study? These lists, I find, are a great deal shorter.

In supplying these "useful questions," I realize that I am treading on dangerous ground. No one is sure what the "right" questions are, and in any case they will always vary according to the interests of the person asking them. One man's big question may be another man's irrelevancy. Yet it seems worthwhile to start somewhere.

Let me begin with some basic assumptions. First, I would reject for our purposes the definition of technology as "how things are done or made." Let us regard it rather as including this, but also including *why* they are done or made the way they are rather than in a number of other possible ways, and what difference it makes to the society in which the doing or the making is done. "How things are done or made" is not, strictly speaking, a historian's question anyway, and if we study the history of technology under this restricted definition of our subject matter, a more apt title for us would be "antiquarians of technology." For a second basic assumption is that no matter how specialized the historian, his major goal must be to contribute toward the understanding of how some society works and why it works the way it does. The big questions for us, then, will all have to do with technology as a social phenomenon. Other questions are not irrelevant, and indeed may be indispensable, but they are simply not "big."

Roger Burlingame was the first American historian who tried to deal with these big questions against the broad expanse of American history, and in the essentials, at least, most historians of technology have followed his lead. The picture of technology as a motive force in American civilization which Burlingame sketched in the two books he wrote in the late thirties [1]—that of technology as the major force leading to our unity as a nation—is a dramatic one which assigns to technology a central, one might even say a determining, role in American history.

The key methodological concept in the Burlingame analysis is that of the "social lag," a concept formalized by the sociologist W. F. Ogburn in 1923 and generally adopted by historians of technology ever since.[2] Technology, so the notion goes, changes society by changing our environment, to which we in turn adapt. Between the change and the adaptation, however, there is always a lapse of time, the social lag. Technology in this view is the primary active force; sooner or later other institutions will conform with it. The social history of technology, then, is the story of institutions trying to catch up with technological realities. Thus the failure of politics to catch up with technology was a cause of the Civil War; the individualism of the 1870's was another example of social lag; the persistence of privately owned utilities is still another.

There is probably something to the concept of a social lag, at some times and in some places, but I would like to suggest that uncritical adoption of it is one of the great difficulties besetting us in the history of American technology. For the question of whether, on the whole, technology causes social change or social change causes technological change is one of the "big" and still unresolved questions before us. Treating it as a fully resolved matter has been a cause of much confusion and misdirected effort, and it has obscured the nature of some other big questions.

My argument is not that technology has no social consequences—of course it makes a difference in the life styles of every human being in a society whether production is by machine or by hand. In American history it is perfectly true that the drift to the cities which accompanied growing industrialization altered the whole social hierarchy and political control of the nation. Nor would I be inclined to argue that the atomic bomb did not have important implications. When a new technology enters the social environment, it automatically becomes a part of that environment and plays its part in the next stage of the drama. Any new element, technological or otherwise, results in a new social configuration simply because that configuration now contains something that it did not contain before. But I think that no single technological innovation, and no group of them taken together in isolation from nontechnological elements, ever changed the direction of a society. Here, as elsewhere in history, all the variables of a system interact. Even when the innovation is imposed from without, anthropologists have demonstrated that societies display a remarkable ability to adapt it to their own life styles. Urbanization in American history, for example, was a phenomenon in which technology was involved; but the process itself was a broad social movement, beginning before the technological innovations that are often cited as its determinants, and its explanation involves immigration, population growth, finance, and other matters as well as technology. I further believe that the direction of the society determines the nature of its technological innovations; that is, it is proper to speak of a "style" of innovation peculiar to a society. Of course these are unproved assumptions, though I think that recent studies lend a certain amount of credence to them.

At any rate, the biggest question of them all has to do with the nature and the direction of causation, and at present we know very little about it. There is a pressing need for studies that will shed light on this question; but we must realize that it *is* a question.

Despite the lack of evidence, most scholars who have concerned themselves with the relations between technology and society have implicitly adopted the point of view of Ogburn and of Burlingame. To be sure, probably very few would admit to a belief in this crude form of technological determinism, but for the most part their works testify to it—and the unexamined philosophy of history is the most dangerous of them all. The research questions are characteristically formulated in such terms as: What was the effect of the automobile, or the railroad, or the typewriter, or the radio, on society? Scholars have studied the uses of such single innovations and assumed that the innovation was the direct cause of the uses. This was the "impact" of the innovation. On this approach there is agreement between those who deplore technology and those who believe that it can solve all of man's problems. Thus Ogburn and Nimkoff studied certain changes that have taken place in the American family and attributed them all to recent technology, without considering trends that antedated the technology. In the same manner Ogburn counted well over a hundred "impacts" of the airplane.[3] Modern writers are careful to make the technological background of their subject quite clear, but with rare exceptions they make no effort to explore the social conditions surrounding an innovation. There is no indication in the works of the great majority of historians of technology that they believe society ever influences technology. The assumption seems to be that technology "acts on its own"—that is, for practical purposes it can be treated as an independent variable.[4]

General American historians, on those rare occasions when they deal with technology at all, also adopt this framework. If he knows anything about technology, the general American historian is likely to have at least two facts at hand which he places somewhere in his book to demonstrate his virtuosity: (1) The cotton gin fastened slavery on the South and thereby was a major cause of the Civil War; and (2) the typewriter brought women to work in offices and thereby "liberated" them. In looking through a shelf-full of high school and college texts in the library I found that most of them contained these two "facts." Gilfillan, in commenting upon the second of these claims, made the obvious point that in Japan there were women office workers who were neither liberated nor getting much help from the type-writer.[5] More to the point than Gilfillan's objection is the fact that American women had been in the process of being "liberated" for a full generation before the appearance of the typewriter. Women had already been working in American offices and were beginning to do so in increasing numbers. They had, in fact, been working at a great variety of jobs in America previously; their moving into offices, I suspect, can be directly correlated with the increase in the total number of workers at this kind of job. One may as well credit the invention of the tin can, the contraceptive, or any of a hundred other things with the emancipation of women, a purely *social* process which took advantage of appropriate inventions when they appeared. Perhaps, in fact, the process stimulated the appearance of those inventions. That the typewriter *in America* brought more women into the offices is not altogether irrelevant. It was a machine that fit neatly into a pre-existing social process and facilitated that process, as did the tin can and the contraceptive. Would the contraceptive have been accepted in a society that firmly believed the lot of women was forever to bear children? Contemporary experience suggests that it would not. What would have happened had the typewriter been invented in a society where the very idea of women in offices was unthinkable? This is probably an unanswerable question, though a related one might be answered, namely, what happens when typewriters are introduced into societies where they have not been used before, and where women do not hold jobs outside the home? Do they bring women into offices? I doubt it, but the answer would help us to understand the role of our technology better.

The same case could be made about the other familiar example. It is perfectly true that technology contributed to the profitability of slave labor, as it did to free labor, not simply in the form of the cotton gin but with spinning machinery, power looms, and other equipment which left only the production of raw materials relatively unmechanized. But slavery was already fastened on the South; and it was on the rise before the introduction of the gin because of the opening of new lands in the West. The allegation that slavery would have disappeared and the Civil War been prevented without the cotton gin is therefore pure romanticism. The problem in the 1790's was that of *using* all the cotton that could be produced with the available labor supply; thus, invention was aimed at remedying the balance. It was a case of the same technological disequilibrium that Nathan Rosenberg found to be such a potent stimulus for innovation in the late nineteenth-century machine tool industry.[6] A high productive capacity at one level of the process stimulated invention at another. Far more significant than what the gin did to slavery is the fact that the gin was invented in a society where the labor system was based on slavery. Had there been no Eli Whitney and no cotton gin, Southerners would likely have found other uses for their slaves. Had there been a flying shuttle but no slaves, invention would likely have been aimed at the production stage of cotton manufacture.

In both these cases, and in many others that could be mentioned, the real effect of technical innovation was to help Americans do better what they had already shown a marked inclination to do. This, I suggest, and not a lack of talent or imagination on the part of historians, is the reason that after so many efforts we are still unable to specify the broad social consequences of an innovation. Historians who deal in such matters, so it seems to me, have simply been asking unanswerable questions. The use of an invention does modify the user's habits, but there is no evidence that it markedly changes the direction of the total complex of habits. Habits seem to grow out of other habits far more directly than they do out of gadgets.

Recent trends in economic history may offer a more realistic and more satisfying framework than that of the social lag, provided we make sufficient allowance for the biases of economists. For a very long time, economists and economic historians tried resolutely to ignore technology. They looked upon it as an alien force which occasionally disturbed the equilibrium of the economy. "Assuming that the state of the arts remains constant" was a phrase frequently encountered in their work, and this simplifying assumption helped them to understand other elements of the economy. When they did discover technology, their characteristic response was to try to deny its equilibrium-disturbing character. The economist concerned with the question of economic growth generally draws smooth curves showing a steady rise in productivity. His curves can account for the introduction of the telegraph, the telephone, the railroad, the automobile, or the airplane and yet show no trace of a revolution. Of course, the sheer weight and complexity of the economic structure, especially in the United States, can disguise revolutionary change. The shifting of resources and effort as some industries become obsolescent, the local effects of changing patterns, the ruining, for example, of thousands of small businessmen with the rise of the mail-order house—such things will not be revealed by gross figures such as the GNP. When dealing with economic historians we must be on guard against this possibility. Nonetheless, I think their smooth curves, even with their limitations, give us a more realistic picture of the historical process than the historian of technology with his dramatic revolutions and his discontinuous leaps.

Economic historians have taken their penchant for continuity quite far—too far, at times, one might argue. Thus Robert Fogel used statistics, logic, and argument to demonstrate that the coming of the railroad had no particular economic consequences.[7] Others have shown that even great bursts of technological activity, such as those promoted by the necessities of war, can be contained in the smooth curves that existed independently of the bursts. The Civil War has recently suffered such a downgrading as a causal factor.[8] Jacob Schmookler came close to transposing the inventor—that eccentric, unpredictable, lonely individual of legend—into an economic man rationally calculating relative advantage, assessing the market and inventing or not inventing, changing directions from railroads to electric shop motors in response to the same economic forces that the pawnbroker, the industrialist, or the merchant obeyed. Schmookler's key point was that invention was essentially an economic activity, and from this relatively simple concept a great deal followed.

Although I would not like to exchange one hackneyed stereotype for another, there is a great deal to be said for Schmookler's picture of the inventor, and in studies carried out over the ten years before his recent death he gathered a great deal of evidence to support it. He concluded that new goods and new techniques are unlikely to appear unless there is a pre-existing demand in the society. In other words, more significant than a "social lag," there exists at any time a "technological lag," a chronic tendency of technology to lag behind demand.[9] This is the same point made intuitively by Gilfillan in 1935 [10] and by Friedrich Engels much earlier, but now Schmookler has brought impressive evidence to support it. Studying a wide range of industries, he generalized that inventive effort varies directly with the output of the class of goods the inventive effort is intended to improve, with invention lagging slightly behind output. Increasing sales for one class of goods invariably produced an increase in inventions pertaining to that class; declining sales were followed by a decline in inventions. The existence of the lag implies that causation could not have been the other way around. The recent business practice of setting research budgets at a fixed percentage of sales tends to assure this relation now, but it existed long before research became institutionalized and the practice became common.

Although the points are not nearly so well substantiated, Schmookler even believed that basic inventions establishing new industries are induced by these economic forces, and that even when a scientific discovery underlies an invention, the case holds, for a discovery may contain the seeds of many potential applications, only some of which will be realized.[11] Furthermore, the technological possibilities offered by a scientific discovery do not *have* to be exploited, and in many cases they are not for decades or even centuries afterward. Here is a well-known type of "lag" which strongly suggests that supply factors (the scientific knowledge) which make technological innovation abstractly possible are not nearly so important to the historian in explaining the innovation as are the demand factors which call it into existence at a certain time. Thus Perkin's "accidental" discovery of a synthetic aniline dye led quickly to an important new industry, for it promised an end to the search for new sources of natural dyes which had been sub-sidized by governments since the sixteenth century. But on the other hand, Fresnel's 1811 discovery that sodium bicarbonate was precipi-tated from salt saturated with ammonia when carbonic acid was passed into the solution was not exploited at all before 1863, when the Solvay ammonia-soda process was patented.[12]

Recent studies suggest that the second of these cases is by far the more common. For example, a panel of research and development managers recently completed a study of ten case histories of innovation, selected especially because the panel believed they illustrated productive collaboration between scientific research and engineering. In such a biased sample, if anywhere, one would expect to find the importance of the supply factors emphasized. Yet clearly in nine of the ten cases, explicit recognition of an important need was the major stimulus in bringing about the innovation. Only rarely did basic research produce a technological opportunity that was quickly recognized and devel-oped, and just as rarely did the technological need directly generate the science used to solve the problem. In most cases, the science that led to the technological solution was already available.[13] Another survey of 567 industrial innovations likewise concluded that new scientific knowledge seldom starts the process.[14]

This view is in marked contrast to the earlier view of Ogburn, who insisted that an invention may answer no social need but may simply be a product of a scientific advance. The dispute between the two points of view is fundamental, for in the one technology is tied to society; in the other it is tied to science.

If the pattern of invention thus depends in large measure upon socio-economic change, we see once more why it is futile to attempt to trace social changes to technological innovations. Such broad social forces as urbanization, declining family size, changing status of women, increases in population and per capita income—the whole range of matters often attributed to technology—are themselves determinants of the direction of technological innovation. Technology, in a word, is used to help people do better what they have already been doing for other reasons, and what they are doing for other reasons determines the nature of their future technology.

Even the notion that economic progress depends upon technological innovation remains an unproved assumption, yielding us another of the big questions. Obviously there is some relationship between technical change and economic growth, but studies of the subject, far from delineating the precise nature of the relationship, have called into question all of the knowledge we once thought we had and left nothing solid in its place. To be sure, recent studies indicate that only about 13 per cent of the increase in output per worker in the United States between 1910 and 1950 could be statistically explained by increases in capital per worker.[15] These studies, conducted in the late 1950's, provided a valuable check on the then prevailing view of the economists which placed undue weight on capital formation, and showed that technological change has been far more important than mere growth in supplies and labor inputs—thus confirming what most historians of technology had believed despite the economists. But let us not celebrate our victory by running too far in the other direction and concluding that innovation accounted for the other 87 per cent of increased output. Greater familiarity with techniques accounts for some, organizational changes are no doubt involved, the shifting of resources and economies of scale cannot be denied their percentage, and a host of other matters will clamor for attention when we begin to analyze more carefully. What is needed are careful efforts to sort out the great number of factors involved in productivity and arrive at a measure for the amount due to technology.

Recent work involving a new approach to the study of industry shows great promise. Earlier studies of American industry were trapped in a Marshallian approach which involves the definition of an industry as a collection of firms producing a homogeneous product. It now appears that a first step in studying the importance of technological innovation must be to discard this aspect of Marshallian economics, for it is ideally designed to mask the influence of technological factors. Nathan Rosenberg has suggested that nineteenth-century developments may be understood more effectively in terms of certain functional processes which cut entirely across industrial lines. The use of machinery in the cutting of metal into precise shapes is one such functional division, which explains the convergence of firearms, sewing machines, and bicycles. Rosenberg shows that where an innovation may have only marginally affected the industry for which it was created, it often had great importance in some entirely different industry.[16] If studies of other such functional groups are made along the lines suggested by Rosenberg, we may finally be able to measure the impact of technological change in this one area.

After we have made up our minds about the impact of technology, then we can ask: what kind of technology? Major breakthroughs? Revolutionary changes? Or are minor modifications of detail more important in the long run? This is an important question, for the manner in which it is resolved will determine the most useful lines of research for the future, and it has obvious policy implications as well. I think it is fair to say that most historians of American technology have tended to emphasize the more impressive at the expense of the run-of-the-mill improvements. Schumpeter is probably responsible for elevating this cult of the heroic into scholarly respectability, for throughout his widely accepted works he showed excessive concern with the more dramatic and discontinuous aspects of innovation and he consistently neglected the cumulative effect of small innovations.

There is no evidence which establishes definitely that technical or economic progress receives greater contributions from the few large advances in knowledge than from the many smaller improvements. Economically, in fact, some scholars have concluded that for a period a community might be better off starving its scientific and major technical work and devoting its resources instead to the most thorough and systematic gathering together and exploitation of all the immediate and tiny practical improvements in ways of manufacture and design.[17] The few detailed studies that we have seem to bear out the economists on this point. Samuel Hollander, in his study of the Dupont rayon plants, concluded that such things as patents issued and expenditures for formal research and development projects (favorite indices for "inventive activity" in econometric studies) bore little relation to important changes in technique and productivity. He found that the technical changes which led to increased efficiency did not come through major innovations, but through an accretion of minor changes by the technical assistance staff at the operating level.[18] Hollander's study is, of course, subject to the same criticism made earlier of Marshallian economics, but even though his framework may have concealed the impact of major technical change, he has demonstrated that minor increments were more important than we generally recognize.

Such a finding is of obvious importance for an understanding of the role of technology, and if borne out by other studies it will have broad implications. For one thing, it may help us finally to overcome the penchant for substituting biographies of inventors for careful analysis of social processes. Of more use to the historian would be knowledge of shop practices, activities of lower-level technicians in factories, and so forth—and all of these areas are still relatively unexplored. For another thing, the importance of minor changes may help us to understand such otherwise perplexing conclusions as those of a Brookings Institution study which found no standard pattern in the relationship between highway investment (technological progress) and economic development. The addition of hard-surface roads to the environment in the ten countries studied obviously made a difference in those countries. None were the same as they had been before. But exactly *what* difference the roads made varied immensely—in fact to opposite extremes—depending upon the antecedent social and economic configurations. Sometimes it proved profitable to the country, sometimes economically neutral, and sometimes ruinous. The exact impact seemed to depend upon such things as existing economic patterns, character of the resources, and, of all things, upon the attitudes and entrepreneurial capabilities of the people.[19] An elementary principle of causation is that a genuine "cause" cannot be the motive force behind opposite results. When this appears to happen, we must look elsewhere for the cause. There is, so it is beginning to appear, no simple connection between the diffusion of technology and economic growth. That there is some kind of connection seems obvious to us, but what its nature is and how it operates appear more mysterious than ever. In fact, as two students of world history noted in 1966, the more one studies the more one wonders whether the countries that industrialized became rich because they industrialized or industrialized because they were rich.[20] Simon Kuznets had made the same point much earlier.

Such a question has obvious implications for our current drive to Westernize the world, but this is not the place to go into them. More to the present point is the fact that it immediately raises questions about our own industrialization process. What were the forces which within less than two generations—between 1800 and 1850—raised a technologically backward nation to such a level that it could begin to export to the "advanced" European nations a manufacturing technique and machine tools so different that the whole performance became known as the "American system"? Every historian of American technology has had to grapple with this really big question. A careful count would probably yield a hundred or so reasons that have been alleged. Foreign commissioners, both in the 1850's and the 1950's, emphasized such social factors as differences in the nature and diffusion of education in America; absence of rigidities and restraints of class or craft; freedom from hereditary definition of the tasks and ways to go about them; high focus on personal advancement and drives to higher material welfare; and, above all, a belief in the moral need for ever greater productivity. "Men serve God in America," concluded a visiting productivity team from England in 1953, "in all seriousness and sincerity, through striving for economic efficiency." [21] Many historians have accepted this explanation.[22] Whether or not these ideological factors explain innovation, they really did exist, and to deliberately ignore them (as Peter Temin does on the ground that "the economic importance of these characteristics is not very clear") is inexcusable.[23] For one thing, they probably *do* explain the relative lack of resistance by workmen to labor-saving machines. Workers, undoubtedly accepting the widely current belief in the continual expansion of America and the consequent need for ever greater productivity, evidently did not fear being replaced by machines. And since America's industrial revolution came during a period of rapidly increasing population as well as geographical expansion and improvements in transportation, the belief was probably well founded. To what extent this doctrine of manifest destiny expedited the transition to machine production is still one of the big unknown questions in the history of American technology.

But there are many other explanations proffered. America's comparative advantage in agriculture has been cited by some as a stimulus to industrial efficiency. It was necessary to be efficient in order to compete, so the explanation goes. To Burlingame, the lack of skilled technicians forced manufacturers to adopt labor-saving devices. More recently, Habakkuk has supported this relatively simple explanation.[24] Since men could not be found for the work, employers began an intensive search for machines. Whenever they were found, they were widely adopted. Temin, reacting to Habakkuk's work, insisted that both the high wages paid to labor in the United States and the widespread market possibilities were statistical illusions—the first because money wages were confused with real wages (which some recent students have found to be no higher than in England), and the second because the geographical was confused with the economic extent of the market. Temin found that the most important and pervasive difference between English and American technology was the use of less capital per worker, and so he concluded that the high interest rate, rather than a fictional "labor-scarcity," was the primary factor in shaping American technology.[25]

The difficulty in accounting for the rise of the American system is compounded by the fact that no one is quite sure what is being explained. Thanks to the meticulous work of Robert Woodbury,[26] no one except writers of American history textbooks believes any longer that a complete system of interchangeable-parts manufacture sprang full blown from the mind of Eli Whitney. But there is still doubt about the nature and extent of use of the major principles of the system—quantity production, interchangeable parts, specialized machinery. Paul Uselding, after an exhaustive study of the records and equipment of the major arms makers, now doubts that any American arms manufacturer had a system of interchangeable parts in the 1840's. He has demonstrated clearly that the method of rolling gun barrel scalps, patented in England in 1811, was not brought to America until 1856, when it was observed at the Enfield Armory after Enfield had begun using American machines. When one realizes that approximately 15 per cent of the labor involved in producing a musket went into making the barrel, he may reflect that the American system may not have been so highly developed by mid-century as has been assumed.[27]

Outside of gunmaking—to whatever degree it was actually used—and clockmaking, the fully developed American system was for the most part confined to woodworking. The United States in general was backward in the production and fabrication of iron. Seizing on this point, two economic historians have recently noted that the woodworking machines popular in America and neglected in England were not only labor-saving but also wasteful of wood. Their adoption in America but not in England might, they thought, be attributable primarily to the cheapness of wood in the United States and its high price in England, not to differences in the capital-labor ratio. To back up their point they have abundant evidence that American practices were relatively well known in England long before the New York Exposition, the traditional date for the "discovery" by Europe of American technology, but were deliberately rejected as unsuitable for English conditions.[28] This discovery in itself certainly casts doubt on our traditional explanations.

While I do not believe that American technology can be explained in terms of factor endowment at all—either labor or capital scarcity— I think Temin has pointed out fatal weaknesses in what is currently the most popular explanation. It is certainly true that the main features of the American system were highly developed before any of the grand explanations became operative, and at a time when comparative advantage might have argued for other lines of growth. Until after mid-century, the total internal American market was much smaller than Britain's and it was still further constricted by geographical spread and inadequate transportation. It is remarkable that historians of technology can in the same breath speak of "primitive transportation systems" and a "domestic market of continental proportions." As a matter of fact, the very lack of "a domestic market of continental proportions" may have stimulated the diffusion of technology and contributed to the build-up of technical skills. For one thing, the small market encouraged the kind of openness that many historians have observed as characteristic of American technology. As Eugene Ferguson noted, information was exchanged readily between American manufacturers, in marked contrast to the way industrial secrets were closely guarded by the government and by individuals in England.[29] It is easier to exchange information if the other party is not considered a rival. Sanford has collected evidence which indicates that early manufacturers, sincerely believing that they were setting a national example of manufacturing morality and skill, were often generous in encouraging the establishment of other factories. As Abbot Lawrence wrote to the Southerner William C. Reves, "We have not jealousy, whatever, concerning the establishment of manufactories in all parts of the country." George

Cabot expected New England operatives to "diffuse their knowledge and skill through all the states in the union where manufactories can be carried on." Cabot Lowell fostered the growth of manufacturing establishments elsewhere by letting out his patents for the power loom on easy terms.[30] This openness was prompted in part by the manufacturers' attempt to gain the acceptance of an anti-industrial people, partly because such an outlook could do them no serious harm, and partly no doubt because of a genuine sense of mission. Despite the counter example of people like Oliver Evans, our present knowledge suggests that openness and even generosity were characteristic of American manufacturers during the first half-century of industrialization. Independent of manufacturers' wishes, of course, the extraordinary mobility of American labor meant that industrial secrets could not be kept. Might not this openness be an important part of our explanation for the rise of American technological dominance? If so, it is a reflection of the American pattern of life—which can in part be traced indirectly to technology—during that period.

A closer look at the American scene at the time of industrialization reveals further weaknesses in the standard explanations. It appears, for example, in the light of recent studies, that the lack of skill has been overemphasized. While I would not argue for a return to the "Yankee ingenuity" explanation, I believe that historians have paid too much attention to statements by men like Whitney and Colt, which were surely motivated by a desire for self-aggrandizement, and have not reflected sufficiently upon the fact that there were a great many Whitneys and Colts in the population. Too often historians, upon being shown the inadequacy of a given explanation, tend to reject all of it—including those elements which are sound. This has been the case with "Yankee ingenuity," an explanation that is not so much erroneous as it is tautological. That ingenious devices are created by people of at least relative ingenuity should occasion no controversy. A priori there are a great many reasons for believing that technical skills were rather abundant in the population. Between 1760 and 1820 there were concerted efforts in every area, both by states and private organizations, to stimulate household manufactures, many of them notably successful. Extensive household manufacturing would clearly produce a vast number of people who were at least familiar with machinery. Furthermore the movement, due to the English embargo, reached its height just before the emergence of the American system. The embargo, one might argue, not only forced Americans to industrialize but forced a certain amount of originality as well. One careful student of New England textile machinery concluded that "the Industrial Revolution in its infancy produced surprisingly few basic skills not already familiar the American mechanics." [31]

In short, I think that the presence of skills and not their absence will be an important part of the explanation. If this is so, we are led immediately to another big question. Where did those skills come from? Many of them, it is becoming increasingly clear, were imported as the need arose, and some came in from the outside quite by chance. Our preoccupation with our later inventiveness and eminence as the world's leading industrial nation has made us, until recently, overlook this source of much of our technology, and consequently to misunderstand its nature. It is generally understood that by the end of the Colonial period most of the trades known in Europe were practiced in America, primarily because of the importation of skilled labor. Ferguson points out that in the nineteenth century itinerant craftsmen may have brought essential skills and instructed American mechanics.[32] The continuous influx of population during that period, even if it were random, must have provided many such as the one well-documented case Ferguson found. Norman Wilkinson, in a study of the Brandywine industries from 1791 to 1816, demonstrated that in such key industries as textiles, tanning, powder mills, and papermaking, the essential techniques, equipment, and workers came from England and France. Studies of the half-dozen or more river valleys where the first factories appeared should give us a better idea of the extent of such borrowings.[33]

We will probably never know the real extent of the importation of skilled workers and techniques during the first few decades after the Revolution. Finding out is especially difficult in the case of the United States, because the historian gets no real clue from "foreign names" as he does in studying industrialization in, say, Russia or Germany. At any rate, case studies have shown that it was much greater than anyone ever dreamed. Much of this importation, we know, was encouraged by Americans, who acted as quasi-official representatives of the government in direct violation of British law. This was, in fact, no less than *de facto* American political policy. The pace was so rapid that one student concluded that the smuggling of machinery and the seduction of mechanics was turned into a "fine art" immediately after the Revolution.[34] We have long known of the importance of Samuel Slater, whose success has turned him into a legend; we are now beginning to realize that he was only one among many. The process continued for a long time and brought skills essential to our developing technology—tinsmiths from Wales in the late nineteenth century, chemical technology from Germany after the First World War, German rocket experts after the Second. In general, the contributions of the later technologists are better known than those of the earlier; yet it is clear that the earlier group was of great importance in shaping our technology. How many there were, when they came and why, and what skills they brought to American technology are big questions for some future historian.

Another fact to be dealt with is American interest in British discoveries throughout the early nineteenth century. It was far greater than the British concern with American developments. The resulting asymmetry in the flow of information became a positive advantage for Americans. Perhaps this was due to that "higher degree of education" which is often alleged of American workmen, perhaps only to the feeling of inferiority which Americans continued to have toward Europeans beneath the surface of their blustery nationalism during that period; or perhaps the fault lies simply in a peculiar British reluctance to learn from former colonials. At any rate, Americans eagerly assimilated British improvements while the British ignored American improvements *of which they had full knowledge.* This important point has been too often ignored.

We also know, thanks to the work of recent scholars, that American mechanicians went abroad in large but still unknown numbers in search of know-how. The practice of going to Europe for information, or even for machines, continued throughout the nineteenth century. Before the Erie Canal was begun, an agent was sent to England. The Pennsylvania Society for the Promotion of Internal Improvements sent an agent to Europe to report on technological developments in 1826.[35] The City of New York in 1844 sent an engineer abroad to study European municipal transit systems immediately after authorizing its own rapid-transit system. Precisely what information these and other agents like them brought back, and to what use it was put, are unknown. Ferguson tells of the Maudsley lathe slide rest that was smuggled out of England and brought to the Philadelphia shop of William Mason and Rufus Taylor in 1822. Mason and Taylor, making only minor (albeit essential) changes, produced a sturdy and widely accepted

American version.[36] One has only to try to use a lathe without a slide rest to comprehend the transcendent importance of this introduction to the American system.

Although these examples have only scratched the surface of the transatlantic movement of technology, they make it clear that a great deal of our technology involved in the American system came from Europe, principally England. Every new study turns up further evidences. For example, the study by Paul Uselding, referred to earlier, shows an essential part of the machine production of muskets being brought to America in the late 1850's. It also demonstrates that Americans did not have a monopoly on labor-saving inventions.

We now need to determine the full extent of the borrowing, to assess its importance, and to study characteristic changes (if any) that Americans made in the equipment and techniques they brought from Europe. The fragmentary evidence we now have suggests that American changes to imported technology increased its marketability by making it cheaper or adapting it for broader uses. Native inventions generally had these same features. The metallic woodworking plane described by Peter Welsh is a good example of such an invention.[37] The "consumer orientation" of American technologists and inventors may turn out to be an important distinguishing feature. One gets the idea that when Americans invented, they tended to concentrate on devices with immediate widespread sales possibilities. This was true even of industrial inventions like the milling machine and the grinding machine, both of which had widespread sales possibilities because of technological convergence. The market orientation which Burlingame thought began with Edison now seems to have been a characteristic of American inventors before the beginning of the century. Europeans often invent at a stage removed from sales. They have concentrated on such things as heavy machine tools, steam boiler improvements, construction equipment, and huge industrial equipment. This may have been because American inventors were also entrepreneurs; they therefore always looked at the potential market. By contrast, British inventors esteemed their position in scientific societies and society in general; they therefore gave greater weight to machines that were "complex" and impressive from a technical point of view.[38] This, I emphasize, is an impression only. Detailed comparative study must test it. Only through further investigation of such questions as these can we begin to understand what is unique in American technology and what have been its driving forces.

One other contrast between European and American technology has curiously been passed over with only an occasional mention. This has to do with the organization of work. If the little I know about the matter is accurate, American practice produced a broader diffusion of skills and proved to be precisely right for stimulating the kind of inventive activity involved in creating the American system. Ferguson, in his study of the origin of American know-how, tells of George Escoll Sellers visiting England in 1832 and being told by a mechanician that he could not understand how machine works could be successfully run without a strict division of labor, as in England where each workman mastered only a single operation, such as turning, filing, or wielding a cold chisel.[39] The English practice, however efficient it might have been, militated in two ways against the possibility of developing an "American system" and, I think, might go a long way toward explaining why no such system developed in England. First of all, the workman, confined to his cold chisel, his file, or his lathe, had no way to develop a sense of the job as a whole; he corresponded in this respect to the modern American assembly-line worker. Those who planned the manufacture thought in terms of breaking down a job into human actions—as we know, the great obstacle that nineteenth-century inventors had to overcome. The machine sequence is usually not similar to the sequence of human actions in performing a job. The Blanchard lathe, for example, which is really a sequence of sixteen different machines first used in processing gunstocks, was a characteristic American invention. The essential point about the Blanchard lathe is that while each replaced standard carpenter's tools as well as the labor of skilled carpenters, the sequence of operations performed by Blanchard lathes does not correspond to the sequence of manual operations, and one cannot associate particular lathes with particular carpenters or tools. Only someone thoroughly familiar with the job of making a gunstock, as opposed to cutting a blank, filing, or fitting a gunstock, could have conceived of the Blanchard lathe. And this, during that period, implies an American mechanician. Too early division of labor may be a positive disadvantage. Had historians taken Peter Drucker up on his suggestion that the organization of work be used as a unifying concept in the history of technology, I might be able to report many other interesting comparisons.[40] Thus far, however, his suggestion seems to have fallen on deaf ears.

As mass production seems to be the chief distinguishing feature of our technology, it is only natural that so much effort has been devoted to describing its origin. But what of its effects? Considerable effort has been devoted to these as well. A frequently encountered allegation is that mass production produced standardization, and this standardization has led to a standardization of thought and opinion. Burlingame emphasized this point and at times took a rather dim view of the technology which he had invested with such active force. Once again there is an element of truth in the allegation, but it is not directly traceable to machinery. Indeed, the fact that American conditions and American thought were amenable to standardization may have had a great deal to do with the success of mass production. Long before the Machine Age, long before the first glimmerings of interchangeable parts and mass production—even if one be as charitable as possible and trace it to the time of Whitney—standardized people had been an article of American faith. Crèvecoeur in the pre-Revolutionary period made quite a point of the fact that there were no extremes in America; it was a land of "middling competence." Simplicity and the lack of useless ornamentation had been an American ideal from Puritan times; it was made an article of patriotism by the pre-Revolutionary crisis and further intensified by the post-Revolutionary effort to achieve independence in manufactures. Americans, in short, had become accustomed to dressing alike and using the simplest implements available for a whole complex of reasons, including the necessities of frontier life, the political situation, a Puritan heritage, and an expanding population. When the age of mass production came, it merely confirmed long-existing tendencies. The power loom, for example, was widely accepted in America simply because there was a demand for the coarse, completely unaesthetic cloth which it could produce. As an 1832 report of the Franklin Institute advised, American manufacturers should produce "simple and neat" commodities because these were more popular. In short, Burlingame and others recognized a real tendency in American life, but it is no longer clear that they were correct in attributing it to our system of production. Rather, our system of production seems to have derived from long-standing attitudes of the population. To put it another way, the development of interchangeable parts and all the other characteristics of the American system may be due not so much to American ingenuity as to American preference.

And one can, I think, generalize on this point. If there is anything that seems clear from the knowledge we now have, it is that people's preferences have a lot to do with the development of their technology. If this recognition forces historians of technology to consider intangible factors and assign a somewhat lesser role to technology than they have in the past; if it forces them even to learn a little history, it will at least make it unnecessary for them to play the futile game of trying to find direct, mechanically operating connections between technological innovation and social change. If we stop misdirecting our work, we may one day find out how to direct it.

NOTES

1. *March of the Iron Men* (New York, 1938); *Engines of Democracy* (New York, 1940).

2. *Social Change with Respect to Culture and Original Nature* (New York, 1923). The concept of differential social change had, of course, existed long before in the writings of historians, anthropologists, economists, and others. Ogburn was merely the first modern sociologist to give it a name.

3. William F. Ogburn and N. F. Nimkoff, *Technology and the Changing Family* (Boston, 1955); W. F. Ogburn, *The Social Effects of Aviation* (Boston, 1946).

4. Edwin Layton, "Comments" delivered at the meeting of the Organization of American Historians, Philadelphia, April 17, 1969.

5. S. C. Gilfillan, "Social Implications of Technological Advance," *Current Sociology*, I (1953), 191.

6. Nathan Rosenberg, "Technological Change in the Machine Tool Industry, 1840–1910," *Journal of Economic History*, XXIII (December 1963), 414–443.

7. Robert W. Fogel, *Railroads and American Economic Growth: Essays in Econometric History* (Baltimore, 1964).

8. Stanley L. Engerman, "The Economic Impact of the Civil War," *Explorations in Entrepreneurial History*, III (1966), 176–199.

9. Jacob Schmookler, "Economic Sources of Inventive Activity," *Journal of Economic History*, XXI (1962), 1–20. See also his *Invention and Economic Growth* (Cambridge, Mass., 1966) for a more complete statement.

10. S. C. Gilfillan, *The Sociology of Invention* (Chicago, 1935), chap. 1.

11. Schmookler, *Invention and Economic Growth*, pp. 2, 17, 18.

12. John Jewkes, David Sawers, and Richard Stillerman, *The Sources of Invention* (London, 1958), p. 51.

13. Morris Tanenbaum, *et al.*, "Report of the Ad Hoc Committee on Principles of Research Engineering Interaction," *National Academy of Science—National Research Council Materials Advisory Board Publication*, MAB 222-M (1966).

14. Sumner Myers, "Technology Transfer and Industrial Innovation," *R&D*

Utilization Project, National Planning Association Publication, M8961 (1967).

15. Robert M. Solow, "Technical Change and the Aggregate Production Function," *Review of Economics and Statistics,* XXXIX (1957), 312–320; Moses Abramovitz, "Resource and Output Trends in the United States Since 1870," *American Economic Review,* XLVI (1956), 5–23.

16. Rosenberg, "Technological Change," p. 423.

17. Jewkes, Sawers, and Stillerman, *Sources of Invention;* Edwin Mansfield, *The Economics of Technological Change* (New York, 1968).

18. Samuel Hollander, *The Sources of Increased Efficiency: A Study of Dupont Rayon Plants* (Cambridge, Mass., 1965).

19. George W. Wilson, *et al., The Impact of Highway Investment on Development* (Washington, D.C., 1966). The history of technology abounds in such examples of contrary effects; e.g., the addition of radios to the American environment resulted in a broadening of the political consciousness of Americans and, for good or ill, there followed an increasing subjection of politics to public opinion. In other countries the radio was the instrument for a hardening of totalitarian control and a *decrease* in the relevance of public opinion.

20. William and Helga Woodruff, "Economic Growth: Myth and Reality: The Interrelatedness of Continents and the Diffusion of Technology, 1860–1960," *Technology and Culture,* VII (1966), 453–474.

21. Graham Hutton, as cited in C. L. Sandford, "The Intellectual Origins and New Worldliness of American Industry," *Journal of Economic History,* XVIII (March 1958), 1.

22. See, for example, J. E. Sawyer, "The Social Basis of the American System of Manufacturing," *Journal of Economic History,* XIV (Fall 1964), 361–379.

23. Peter Temin, "Labor Scarcity and the Problem of American Industrial Efficiency in the 1850's," *Journal of Economic History,* XXVI (September 1966), 295.

24. H. J. Habakkuk, *American and British Technology in the Nineteenth Century* (Cambridge, Mass., 1962).

25. Temin, "Labor Scarcity," p. 294.

26. Robert S. Woodbury, "The Legend of Eli Whitney and Interchangeable Parts," *Technology and Culture,* I (1960), 235.

27. Paul Uselding, "Henry Burden, the 'Magnificent Scotchman,' " mimeograph, 1969. John Hall at the Harpers Ferry Rifle Factory apparently used a system of interchangeable parts for a brief period after 1824, but it was a small operation and not influential.

28. Edward Ames and Nathan Rosenberg, "The Relationship Between Factor Endowments and Technological Change: The Habakkuk-Temin Controversy," paper presented to the Workshop in Economic History, Purdue University, January 1967, pp. 34–35.

29. Eugene S. Ferguson, "On the Origin and Development of American Mechanical 'Know-How,' " *Midcontinent American Studies Journal,* III (1962), 3–16.

30. Sandford, "Intellectual Origins," pp. 1–16.

31. George S. Gibb, *Saco-Lowell Shops: Textile Machinery in New England, 1813–1949* (Boston, 1950), p. 10.

32. Ferguson, "Origin and Development," p. 12.

33. Norman B. Wilkinson, "Brandywine Borrowings from European Technology," *Technology and Culture,* IV (1963), 1.

34. Carroll W. Pursell, Jr., "Thomas Digges and William Pearce: An Ex-

ample of the Transit of Technology," *William and Mary Quarterly*, 3rd ser., XXI (1964), 551.

35. Robert E. Carlson, "British Railroads and Engineers and the Beginnings of American Railroad Development," *Business History Review*, XXXIV (1960), 139–140.

36. Ferguson, "Origin and Development," p. 10.

37. Peter Welsh, "The Metallic Woodworking Plane: An American Contribution to Hand-Tool Design," *Technology and Culture*, VII (1966), 38.

38. I owe the origin of this idea to a conversation with Paul Uselding.

39. Ferguson, "Origin and Development," 13.

40. Peter F. Drucker, "Work and Tools," *Technology and Culture*, I (1959), 28.

The State of
Agricultural History

HAROLD D. WOODMAN

If the analogue to the "State of Agricultural History" is the President's address on the State of the Union, my task in this essay is threefold: I should discuss past accomplishments, current problems, and, finally, future tasks. This assumes that we agree on the subject to be discussed; that is, that we already have a more or less precise purview of the scope of agricultural history. But such an assumption, to my mind, is unwarranted. Our conception of agricultural history is so amorphous and unstructured that much of the work in the field lacks breadth and coherence. My criticism is not meant as denigration: much that has been done is significant and lasting. Yet we need to to break new ground, and to do so we must first be clear in our own minds about what agricultural history really is.

The organization of the Agricultural History Society in 1919 reflected a growing professional interest in the United States [1] in agricultural history as a specialized field. The sources of such interest had been varied. From its beginning in 1862, the Department of Agriculture had staff members with an interest in history who often provided historical background in their reports on special agricultural problems. Although the amount of such work gradually increased, it remained peripheral to other projects in the Department. The appointment of O. C. Stine to the staff of the Office of Farm Management in 1916 marked the beginnings of full-time attention to agricultural history in the Department. Henry C. Taylor, who had recommended Stine's appointment, gave added support to historical research in the Department when he became chief of the Office of Farm Management in 1919. When, three years later, Taylor became the head of the new Bureau of Agricultural Economics, Stine joined his staff as head of the Division of Statistical and Historical Research, which included a group of research workers who devoted full time to agricultural history.

The introduction of historical research in the Department of Agriculture by such men as Stine and Taylor evidenced a growing interest in agricultural history in academic circles. Both were educated at the University of Wisconsin where they had been influenced by such scholars as Frederick Jackson Turner, whose writings about the frontier had emphasized the importance of agricultural history, and Richard T. Ely, a leading advocate of historical economics. Here was the "new history," at once practical and broad. It was a history that could be useful in the formulation of policy and democratic enough to include the common man. Equally important, it was a history that broke the artificial boundaries that separated it from such social sciences as economics and rural sociology; in the Department of Agriculture even biological and physical scientists such as plant pathologists and soil chemists found the historical approach to their research valuable.[2]

A further step in the development of agricultural history as a special field was taken in 1914 when Louis Bernard Schmidt introduced the first formal course in the field at Iowa State College.[3] A year later he announced to the American Historical Association that the new history would end the neglect of agricultural history in America. This he found "encouraging" because it would deepen our understanding of the past and provide background and insights that would be invaluable in dealing with farmers' problems.[4]

In February 1919 this varied group of historians and social, physical, and biological scientists organized the Agricultural History Society "to promote interest, study, and research in the history of agriculture." Initial research under the aegis of the Society was published in the annual reports of the American Historical Association, but in 1927 the Society began publication of its own journal, *Agricultural History*. After the initial year during which two issues were published, the journal became a quarterly. Its stated aims reflect the varied interests of the Society's founders and have not changed over the years:

Agricultural History is designed as a medium for the publication of research and documents pertaining to the history of agriculture and as a clearing house for information of interest and value to workers in this field. The words, "agricultural history," are interpreted broadly. Materials on the history of agriculture not only in the United States but in all countries and in all periods of history are included, and also materials on institutions, organizations, and sciences which have been factors in changes in agriculture.[5]

The interest and the enthusiasm of the founders of the Agricultural History Society proved contagious. The Society grew, the journal received its share of articles, and scholars throughout the country turned out an increasing number of articles and monographs dealing with various aspects of agricultural history. An inkling of the staggering amount of work in what may be called agricultural history can be gained by glancing at the bibliographies assembled by Everett Eugene Edwards, who served as editor of *Agricultural History* for twenty years.[6] The literally thousands of items in these bibliographies may be supplemented by the bibliographical index Edwards assembled in his office in the Department of Agriculture. According to Herbert A. Kellar, by 1952 Edwards had collected a card file of references numbering about a million items.[7]

Despite this prodigious output, agricultural historians were strangely dissatisfied. Louis Bernard Schmidt, who in 1915 had welcomed the new history in the expectation that agricultural history would no longer be ignored, found it necessary to repeat his welcome at regular intervals over the following quarter of a century. He was certainly not unaware of the new work; he had published several important articles himself, assembled a bibliography on the subject, and, with Earle D. Ross, published a book of readings designed to "provide adequate discussion material for courses in the economic history of American agriculture which are being developed in our state colleges and technical schools." [8] Nevertheless, as late as 1940, Schmidt apparently still felt it necessary to direct attention to the need to study agricultural history. In virtually the same words he had used in 1915, he declared in 1940 that "this phase of our history had not hitherto received the attention at the hands of historians which its importance merits." [9]

Other historians echoed these sentiments. When on the occasion of the twenty-fifth anniversary of the Agricultural History Society, Everett E. Edwards was asked to outline objectives for the next quarter-century, he listed a series of tasks that would leave the uninitiated observer with the impression that virtually nothing had been done in the field.[10] Similarly, on the Society's fortieth birthday, Wayne D. Rasmussen reviewed the "current state of agricultural history" and concluded that "there have been tremendous achievements in the past forty years, but there are still unlimited rich and mellow fields to till." [11] Less sanguine was Gilbert C. Fite, who in his presidential address to the Society lamented the lack of interest in agricultural history. He surveyed leading professional journals devoted to history and found they gave relatively little space to agricultural history; popular college textbooks were similarly deficient. The public, the publishers, indeed, the profession itself paid scant attention to a tiny and embattled group of agricultural historians: "Few in number and weak in financial resources, we [agricultural historians] have been ignored, slighted, and pushed aside until we feel like second-class citizens." [12]

Why this half-century-long lament about the weakness of scholarship in agricultural history in the face of a tremendous outpouring of scholarly work in the field during the same period? The answer, quite simply, is that there is a concern, and properly so, about the quality and focus of much of this work. What has been most lacking in a good deal of previous work and what is now needed in agricultural history is a synthesis, a conceptual framework. I am not arguing for what C. Wright Mills attacked in sociology as a "grand theory," a single generalizing principle or universal explanation.[13] Rather, what I am urging is what H. Stuart Hughes has called a "tentative synthesis," a "middle ground" between "airy generalities" and the "compulsive heed to the minute details." [14]

Agricultural history seems to have been trapped longer than most other fields of study by the Rankean notions of scientific history. This is true despite my earlier assertion that interest in the field derived from the new history; for, as John Higham has noted, the radical rhetoric of the dissenters often hid the fact that they accepted much of the orthodoxy they attacked.[15] If, as they argued, history was now to be relevant, if it was to be more than merely past politics, this did not mean that history could no longer be an objective ordering of the facts; indeed, the new history could be an invaluable aid to show the past as it really was.

This perspective, apparent in all fields of study in American history, was especially strengthened and perpetuated in agricultural history because of the special and disparate interests of its early practitioners. As I have already indicated, prominent among the founders of the Agricultural History Society were men in the Department of Agriculture, many of whom were not historians. Such men—natural and social

scientists—provided the breadth of interests as well as the relevancy
demanded by the new historians, but at the same time the scientists
along with the historians adopted the orthodoxy of scientific history.
Furthermore, many of these people remained insular and unaffected by
changes in the historical profession, in part because so many of them
were not professional historians, but primarily because their work was so
problem-oriented, tied as it was to the policy problems being considered
by the particular bureau or office which employed them. Their history
was, after all, to provide background and perspective for intelligent
policies and planning. It is not my intent to denigrate the contributions
to agricultural history made by such people as Lyman Carrier, an agrono-
mist, or Rodney H. True, a botanist, or Henry C. Taylor, an agricultural economist, or Alfred Charles True, a Department administrator;
their work was and often remains useful.[16] My point is simply that
the policy orientation of their research and writing tended to promote
and perpetuate a rather narrow perspective for the study of American
agricultural history. Historians within the Department of Agriculture
were under similar pressures, as were many academic historians who
clung to the new history with all of its conservative implications.

The resulting tendency in the writing of American agricultural history may be illustrated in the words of Everett E. Edwards. A Wis-
consin-trained historian, a staff member in the Department, and editor
of *Agricultural History,* Edwards became president of the Agricultural
History Society in 1940. In his presidential address to the Society
he outlined the tasks before agricultural historians. His words clearly
convey the amalgam of scientific history, new history, and policy-
oriented studies that then prevailed among agricultural historians:

Specifically, the objective of research in American agricultural history is the careful delineation of the historical background of each
and every community, subregion, and region in rural United States.
Just as the soil scientists have provided data basic to a comprehensive soil map of the entire country, so the agricultural historians
must develop a many-dimensional social and economic map of rural
America. To achieve something approximating a map of this kind,
they must collect sources of historical information, analyze the pertinent data embodied therein, and present their findings in written
form for use in relation to current problems. If the historians provide these analyses of the economic and social factors which have
operated in any given community or region to produce the present

situation, the economists and other scientists who are charged with drafting and executing plans for more rational utilization of the natural and human resources of the area can proceed with more comprehension and therefore with more likelihood of success.[17]

Here was a dominant tendency in agricultural history expressed by one of its most able exponents. And yet, there was another tradition in agricultural history. Its roots were the same as those of the dominant group, but it was watered from different sources and grew in a different direction. Behind the complaints of those who decried the paucity of work in agricultural history was the promise of this second tradition. Edwards himself seemed to recognize it. In his statement on the "objective of research" quoted above, he added: "Finally, but not least in importance, the agricultural historians must give cognizance to the overall patterns of culture and action into which their subjects fall." This rather vague suggestion was made more specific by another veteran agricultural historian. "Investigators in agricultural history," said Earle D. Ross in his 1947 presidential address to the Society, ". . . have concentrated too narrowly and self-containedly upon their area, or it may be even upon some subdivision of it, with little or no recognition of interrelations with other areas and consequently with the national economy as a whole." [18]

The desire to see agricultural history in the context of the nation's history in general is part of the legacy of Frederick Jackson Turner. If Turner's contribution as a new historian legitimized the study of agricultural history, his work on the frontier did even more. It made agricultural history—or a part of it at least—the central theme in American history. When he turned his attention to sectionalism, agriculture continued to receive major emphasis in an analysis that attempted to integrate and interpret the broad sweep of American history. But Turner did more than relate agricultural history to the whole of American history; his synthesis was an exciting attempt to explain the dynamics of social change in America.[19]

That this aspect of Turner's work had a profound influence on the the writing of American history needs no documentation here. Nor is it necessary to survey in detail the writings of his critics. It is enough to note that in the furor of criticism and defense, Turner's basic contribution was often obscured. Mechanical application of his ideas often proved sterile; discussion shifted very early to a consideration of the theory itself and to the man who had presented it. Often opportunities for the creative use of his insights were neglected in favor of arguments over what Turner really meant by this or that phrase, or in lengthy discussions of his ideological derivations. But not all opportunities remained unrealized. When used as generalizing concepts, as insights rather than mechanisms to understand the American past, Turner's ideas provided the basis for outstanding work.[20]

Obviously, the two tendencies in agricultural history were never as distinct as I have implied. No one, whatever his intentions, can write strictly factual history and let the facts speak for themselves; and synthesis and interpretation are meaningless unless supported by empirical data. Nevertheless, the genealogist tracing the pedigree of agricultural history in the United States will find two different families emerging from a common ancestor. Occasional intermarriage complicates the two family trees but does not merge them. Both families could live in peace in the same house. The Society and its journal, *Agricultural History,* conceived of their discipline as broadly inclusive. As Edwards argued, agricultural history was not a discipline at all; it was simply an area of study, and the Society was wise when it declined "to set it apart as a separate and distinct discipline." [21]

When the field was largely virginal this was without doubt the wise course to follow. The efforts of Edwards and others to encourage research, collect documents, assemble bibliographies, and suggest new fields for inquiry have been indispensable. Nor is such work finished; there are important areas of agricultural history where significant, even initial work is yet to be done. To add new studies in these areas is obviously to increase our knowledge. But it does not follow that it will increase our understanding. The regular call by agricultural historians that we undertake research on this or that problem is not wrong so much as it is incomplete. Most historians now reject the Rankean notion that we can somehow build the edifice of the past with the building blocks of monographs. But, if most agree that the builder needs plans as well as building blocks, too few scholars in agricultural history have undertaken to supply the plans. A decade ago, Wayne Rasmussen noted that "agricultural history as a clearly defined and fully accepted field of study and research is still in the process of formulation." He gave credit to Edwards for defining the field and outlining its purposes, but concluded wisely that "such concepts need periodic review and redefinition." [22]

What we need now is a conceptual framework—or perhaps several—in which to place the valuable work already done as well as the new studies that should be done. A number of factors make the present particularly ripe for this kind of development. Gilbert Fite has noted that as the importance of farming declines in our economy, study of agriculture will increase because it will no longer be dealing with "familiar and commonplace affairs." [23] This does not say enough. What is especially important is not the decline of agriculture in the United States—this has been going on for generations—but the realization, especially since World War II, that agriculture is a central problem in economic development. Scholars dealing with the problems of modernization in underdeveloped countries have had to give major emphasis to agriculture; their analytical tools can be useful to the historian investigating the history of American agriculture. Used creatively —and with caution —the work of the developmentalists (political scientists, sociologists, and economists) can breathe new vigor into a somewhat submerged but still viable tradition in agricultural history

Recently Thomas C. Cochran called for a new synthesis in American history that would emphasize the key place of business in our society, a synthesis that would see "business history not as merely a part of economic history but as a major element in general social history." [24] I shall not counter with a suggestion that agricultural history also be considered a "major element," although I do quarrel with Cochran's placing agriculture under the general rubric of business. What I find of particular value for agricultural history is his suggestion that we develop a synthesis on the level of our social history. To describe and explain the role of agriculture in social change will help to create a conceptual framework that will integrate past work and direct new studies. The experiences and the hypotheses of social scientists, particularly those who study economic development, will help historians ask the right questions and even suggest tentative answers. In the remainder of this essay, I shall explore a few key areas in agricultural history to illustrate the advantages (as well as the dangers) of this approach.

An oft-repeated truism about American history is that many of the old European ways could not be transplanted to American soil and, rightly, historians have attempted to explain why this was so. Yet the more important point may be not that European institutions failed to thrive in America, but that Americans, unlike Europeans, had a choice: in America, Englishmen had to create their institutions as they built the communities in which they lived. This is not to say that the choice was completely free. Obviously it was not. Previous experience, the general physical environment, and the resources available were all limiting factors. But even within such limitations, choice was relatively wide. Indeed, even if there was little or no choice—which was *not* the case—the very fact that communities had to be built would prove significant.

English and European society, however much it was changing in the seventeenth and eighteenth centuries, was stable as compared with society in America, at least when observed from the bottom rungs of the social ladder. Even in the midst of political and economic revolution, the day-to-day life of most Europeans was relatively stable. This was especially true of the agricultural population, dominated by the requirements of sowing and harvesting crops and guided in their community relationships by customs and laws of long standing.[25]

How different it was in America where, as Oscar Handlin has perceptively noted, disorder rather than stability was characteristic. The shock of immigration, the difficulties encountered in a strange and often hostile environment, and the disruption of constant mobility and the intrusion of new people into communities were all important in creating and sustaining this disorder.[26]

But this is only half the story. If life was disorderly because it was hard and unpredictable, it was disorderly (in another sense) because people were constantly faced with the problem of creating order. The customs and institutions which in Europe had served to create a measure of order and stability were absent in America; suitable surrogates had to be created. The point is not that many old customs could not be transported intact; what is important here is that *custom*s were left in Europe. Even if European ways of thought and action could be brought to America unchanged, the very manner in which they would be instituted had to be new. Americans had to legislate customs. In so doing, of course, customs were not customs at all; they were fiats. Sumner Chilton Powell provides an excellent example in his admirable study of Sudbury, Massachusetts. In 1643 the citizens of Sudbury were notified that should the number of cattle increase, limitations would have to be imposed on the number each citizen would be allowed to graze on the commons. Powell then notes the significance of this seemingly minor act: "The great difference between this bylaw and a traditional 'sizing of the commons' in England lay in the fact that this order of 1643 was a legislative decree, subject to the vote of the citizens, not a custom which had existed 'time out of mind.' " [27]

Thus in America, day-to-day activities could not be taken for granted as they were in Europe. What in Europe were customary practices of the most elementary kind, in America had to be legislated into being. A society in which nothing could be taken for granted, or, perhaps more precisely, in which virtually anything might be legislated into custom, necessarily had a certain basic instability. Yet this instability might have been minimized or at least its effect diminished if there could be agreement on what should be legislated into being. Had American communities been simply microcosms of European societies in an alien environment, many customs could have continued to be taken for granted. Old World class relations, the traditional hierarchy of social and economic power arrangements, might have served as the base for the re-creation of traditional patterns of life in the New World. But as Sigmund Diamond and Bernard Bailyn have shown, conditions in the New World blocked such easy adjustment.[28] Equally important is the fact that the migration of customs in toto did not occur simply because the society in which these customs developed and existed did not migrate in toto. As Louis Hartz has noted, American societies were only a "fragment" torn loose from traditional European society. Although the net result of this, according to Hartz, was to be a basic conservatism, an underlying homogeneity of thought arising from the absence of contending classes and ideologies,[29] for our purposes here its significance lies in the fact that the fragment did not contain the elements necessary to re-create Old World society in the New World. Not only was the environment alien, the society itself was alien because it was only a part of the whole. A substitution for the whole had to be created.[30]

Complicating matters further was the fact that settlers even in a single town did not all have a common set of customs and traditions in their backgrounds, even when they all came from England. As Powell has noted, "The settlers of Sudbury came from many different areas, each with a different set of bylaws, thus making impossible a commonly understood pattern of social behavior." [31] What was true of the most homogeneous part of the New World, New England in the seventeenth century, was true also in other colonies and in the United States during the nineteenth century. Every new area was peopled by settlers from a number of different states as well as several European countries.[32] As a result, the mixing of people of diverse backgrounds required constant accommodation. The description of this process in the Old Northwest by Richard Lyle Power is a contribution which could well be repeated for other regions.[33]

The result of this process was a basic instability or disorder in American society, an instability compounded and increased by the very process of creating order. The effect of this instability was to be far-reaching, but for my purposes here its importance lies in the ways it influenced the development of American agriculture within the broader context of general economic and social change.

A decade ago Allan Bogue proposed that historians "develop the implications" of Turner's contention that the West was "a form of society, rather than an area." [34] Basing his analysis on the work of historians and social scientists, particularly sociologists, and on his own extensive research in the development of prairie agriculture, Bogue suggested that "social behavior of a continuing sort" might arise in part from the instabilities associated with the building of new social structures in the West. "Such social structures," he wrote, "no doubt might take as long as a generation to acquire the relative stability found in older communities while leaders jockeyed for position and followers wavered in their allegiances, while the disillusioned were replaced and the newcomers fitted into the locality and interest groups of the community." Bogue concluded his analysis with a set of generalizations (in the form of hypotheses) about frontier communities. A heterogeneous population lacking clear-cut norms of behavior in an alien environment found itself in conflict as it sought to create a community and achieve a measure of cooperation. These conditions, Bogue maintained, helped to explain a great deal about frontier life: "high crime rates, resort to emotional religion, heavy incidence of mental disease, and continued mobility" along with widespread participation in politics as frontiersmen sought to use politics to gain status, to achieve unity and stability, and to reap economic rewards.

Bogue's analysis could be extended beyond the frontier. The features he described were generally characteristic of the whole of American society. If behavioral norms were absent on the frontier, they were never fully established in the settled areas from which the frontiersmen came. Not only were the older areas not really old and established in the European sense, but most were faced with new sources of disruption and instability such as immigration, urbanization, and industrialization.[35] In short, the usefulness of Bogue's insights might be increased if applied in a less limited manner. George W. Pierson has suggested that the key to American history might be what he calls the "M-Factor"—mobility.[36] He emphasizes not simply the experience of moving, which Bogue rightly notes is a short-term experience, possibly without long-term effects on personality and social structure, but instead stresses the effects that constant movement has had and continues to have on our society. Mobility, Pierson argues, provides new opportunities in new places and allows the dissatisfied to move. This is an important insight, but it stops short of illuminating a more generic phenomenon. Mobility, I would argue, engenders and perpetuates social instability which in turn requires constant adjustment and accommodation.

It just this instability which social scientists argue is lacking in underdeveloped countries today. Sociologist Wilbert E. Moore has put it this way:

> If one were to attempt a one-word summary of the institutional re-
> quirements of economic development, that word would be *mobility*.
> Property rights, consumer goods, and laborers must be freed from
> traditional bonds and restraints, from aristocratic traditions, quasi-
> feudal arrangements, paternalistic and other multi-bonded relations.[37]

Note, similarly, the conclusion of Bert F. Hoselitz, an economist and sociologist:

> A society on a low level of economic development is . . . one in
> which productivity is low because division of labor is little devel-
> oped, in which the objectives of economic activity are more com-
> monly the maintenance or strengthening of status relations, in which
> social and geographical mobility is low, and in which the hard cake
> of custom determines the manner, and often the effects, of economic
> performance.[38]

The conditions these scholars describe as missing in underdeveloped nations are precisely the ones that obtained in the New World. I would suggest that American society was so mobile, so lacking in day-to-day stability, that traditional ways of doing things had no opportunity to develop. Or, to put the matter somewhat differently, Americans so often had to accommodate themselves to new social situations that in-novation became an imperative. Not unexpectedly, this found its re-flection in political institutions and social structure; it also had its effect on individual and group psychology.[39]

An investigation of American agricultural history in this context should deepen our understanding of the process of development in agriculture and at the same time provide insights into the role of agriculture in our general economic and social development. Closer in-vestigation of a number of key areas in agricultural history may serve to illustrate my point.

The precise role of agriculture in economic development may be arguable,[40] but certain general features seem beyond debate. If there is to be a division of labor between agriculture and other economic activities, then agriculture must produce a surplus to support people who no longer till the land. The form this surplus takes will vary, and this variation in turn will affect the resulting pattern of economic development. The surplus may be produced by a very small part of the agricultural sector. Thus the income from the export of a staple commodity—agricultural or extractive—might serve to support non-food producers involved in the production and export of the staple. If this income is used primarily to pay for imports of food and manufactured items, its greatest effects will be on a foreign economy. In what may be termed the typical colonial situation, growth in the domestic economy will be confined to the production and export of the staple. If, however, the income creates a demand for domestic production which the domestic economy is able to satisfy, then its effects will be primarily on the domestic economy.

When the problem is put in this way, the emphasis is on the market, domestic or foreign. Restated in Adam Smith's familiar dictum that "the division of labor is limited by the extent of the market," this concept has for at least half a century been used to explain American economic development. Guy S. Callender argued that the initial prosperity of the Colonies—indeed any colony—depended upon available markets for their staple products. A sparse population and limited transportation facilities precluded an internal market of any size. Economic progress by necessity depended upon foreign markets. Fortunately, American staples found ready markets in Europe, and the colonies prospered. But until internal markets were also developed, this prosperity was limited to those areas that produced the staples. With these new markets, internal commerce became "the means by which the economic advantage arising from an increasing foreign demand for our extractive products was diffused over the entire country and made to stimulate nearly all of its industries." [41] A more recent presentation of this point of view is that by Douglass C. North. North, like Callender, emphasizes the key role of market growth and, again like Callender, he places major emphasis on the foreign demand for cotton. Cotton, he writes, was the "independent variable" initiating growth, the stimulus that induced expansion of other economic activities. Cotton producers, as they concentrated on meeting foreign demand, became a market for Western food producers; markets in the

South and the West stimulated the development of improved commercial and transportation facilities and finally the growth of manufacturing in the East.[42]

When put in terms of a thesis summary, North's book is simply a restatement of Callender's analysis of fifty years earlier. But North goes much further, for he uses an impressive array of empirical evidence to support the thesis. He relates population movements to the West to increasing commodity prices and declining transportation costs. As demand for cotton and foodstuffs increased, prices tended to increase; this in turn induced a westward population surge. The resulting new sources of supply then outstripped demand, forcing prices down, and migration to the West slackened until demand again stimulated a new population surge.

North makes a significant contribution to the agricultural and economic history of the United States. Like all good syntheses, North's book should open the doors to new research and not stand as the final word on the subject.[43] It is especially important that agricultural historians give North's work the attention it deserves, for he has provided an analysis that makes agriculture pivotal in economic and social change; at the same time we must understand that North's analysis is sharply economic, an approach he shares with the other so-called "new economic historians." His narrow economic approach weakens his synthesis but in so doing lights the path to new research.

When Stuart Bruchey reviewed North's book he noted that North gave inadequate attention to the question of incentive. "In the final analysis," he wrote, "economic growth depends on people, on community contagion, on sharpened motivations permeating an enlarging segment of management, work-force, and market. North clearly regards motivation, values, and traditions as important factors in growth. But they are for him among the 'givens'; they are constants. I would emphasize *change* in the intensity of motivation as an important causal agent in the process of growth." [44]

In his reply, North indicated his basic agreement with Bruchey on this point, arguing that it "would certainly be consistent with the whole theoretical framework of the book; namely that the widening of the market and the increased opportunities for people to improve their material welfare when they moved from self-sufficiency to the market economy were the basic factors in increasing motivation." He added, however, that "there is no operational way known by which to measure changing intensity of motivation in America," and that Bruchey's evidence on the matter was inadequate: "his argument rests upon the miscellany of quotations from memoirs by assorted literary figures, which make interesting comments but not anything that can be used to further our knowledge." [45]

There are two points of significance here. The first is the question of how much emphasis we are to place on motivation. Bruchey simply argued that the matter should be considered, even if other factors were more fundamental; North responded by making motivation a variable dependent upon market changes. This difference becomes clear when we raise a second question: Is our inability to measure such matters as motivation reason enough to consign this factor to a secondary status? For North, the question need not be asked. He finds the "market mechanism" to be crucial: "I think the pervasiveness of the price system in the allocation of resources in the western world of the last three or four centuries is central to any study in economic history, and that the use of price theory is an essential theoretical tool of the economic historian." If this is so, then the question of motivation assumes a secondary role, not unimportant but nevertheless a dependent variable.

Yet it is just this that North must take on faith. We may grant him his contention that there is no way to measure motivation, at least no way we can quantify it in terms comparable to the way in which we can measure income or production. But it does not follow from this that changing motivation—or, more broadly, social and psychological factors in general—is secondary to the market mechanism in inducing economic growth. It is one thing to isolate a factor and then measure it; it is quite another matter to claim that the factor so isolated and measured is fundamental, especially when other possibly more important factors cannot be measured in the same way. It would be most convenient if all the important matters were those that could be precisely measured, but, alas, to make this assumption is to leap into metaphysics. If the leap is to be made, we should be aware we are making it and avoid calling the result scientific.

This is not the place to open a full critique of the general problem of the use of quantitative methods in history, or of the work of the new economic historians.[46] My point here is simply to note that North's basic *assumption* is a proposition that agricultural historians might properly take as a starting point for further research. In short, what determines if and how an economy will respond to external changes in demand? In more familiar terms, the problem is the nature of the transition from self-sufficient to commercial agriculture. At the moment we know very little about the transition except that it took place.

From the start it should be made clear that complete or pure self-sufficiency never existed. Like Locke's state of nature, it is an ideal or hypothetical construct. Even in its most primitive form, agriculture in the United States was never completely self-sufficient, as Rodney C. Loehr has noted. In a brief study in 1952, Loehr surveyed travelers' accounts and concluded that self-sufficiency was at most a very temporary phenomenon "on the frontier for the first year or two, when access to market was difficult." He urged that historians consider self-sufficiency "as a relative matter and cease dealing in absolutes." [47]

Loehr's argument is well taken, though it should be noted that he is defeating a straw man. The existence of country stores, gristmills, and artisan shops in rural villages along with the periodic visits of peddlers are evidence of the lack of complete self-sufficiency in the most primitive agricultural communities. Even Loehr's caveat concerning temporary self-sufficiency is not well taken; frontiersmen who brought tools, clothing, and seed with them could hardly be termed self-sufficient. Nevertheless, if pure self-sufficiency is a historical fiction, it does not follow that we should discard it as a tool for the analysis of social change in the United States. In the most general terms, the problem of the transition from self-sufficiency to commercialism is the problem of explaining why people change. More specifically, we must know why farmers tended to emphasize the marketing of their surpluses, why they introduced new crops, new methods, and new machinery, and finally we must know what effects the changes had on them. The matter cannot be dealt with adequately in purely economic terms, that is, as simply a response to the market. A market will be no more than a potential unless the population is able and willing to respond to it.

Perhaps part of the difficulty we face in dealing with this problem is that we know how the story ended. It seems obvious to us that higher prices, better lands, greater opportunities, and improved transportation would pull people west and induce specialization and commercial agriculture. Yet social scientists dealing with underdeveloped countries find development to be much more complex. Ragnar Nurske, for example, notes that "agriculture in most underdeveloped areas is a conservative, sometimes feudal, always tradition-bound, passive and non-capitalist sector of economic activity. Innovation in this sector cannot be relied upon to happen in response to market incentives alone." [48] This suggests that cultural and social behavioral patterns are important in stimulating or retarding development, especially in agriculture. Wilbert E. Moore, in his outline of a "social framework" in which to view economic development, identifies four areas—ideological, institutional, organizational, and motivational—which must be considered as factors in economic change.[49] Somewhat different is the approach of Theodore W. Schultz. He does not deny that cultural factors are important, but argues that they can be treated as economic variables. He finds traditional agriculture to be efficient within the confines of the productive factors available. If increased efficiency is therefore impossible within traditional methods, so too is expansion, because traditional factors of production are expensive, that is, their marginal return is low. Expansion therefore depends upon the introduction and acceptance of a new set of factors with a higher marginal return.[50]

I do not introduce the work of Nurske, Moore, and Schultz to suggest that they have *the* answers for American agricultural historians. I mean only to suggest that scholars dealing with economies that did not grow, or grew slowly, or grew differently from the American economy may offer useful insights into the history of American agriculture. They may help us to identify problems which, because they were overcome, may not appear to have been problems at all; they may also help us to identify conditions which did not exist in America and in so doing deepen our understanding of the process of change.

Thus, to return to the problem of the transition from self-sufficient to commercial agriculture, we might ask at the outset whether self-sufficient agriculture in the United States was "traditional" in the sense used today. The answer will depend on time and place. Self-sufficiency predominated in large areas for a long time during the Colonial period; it was short-lived, indeed sometimes nonexistent in the Midwest; but at the same time it lasted a long time in parts of the South. The transformation of New England agriculture may serve as an example for further analysis. Percy W. Bidwell has argued that local markets brought commercialization to New England farmers after 1810. Commercial farmers with money incomes could then buy manufactured goods, and there followed a decline of household manufacture. As a result, a whole new set of attitudes arose. Self-sufficiency "emphasized the virtues of self-reliance and independence, of frugality and thrift"; but with commercial agriculture these attitudes were no longer sufficient: "Shrewdness in buying and selling must now be added to the simpler qualities of hard work and saving." [51]

These are familiar points, but they do not say enough. When prices (and hence income) depend upon the impersonal market, success indeed depends upon more than hard work. But shrewdness in buying and selling alone is hardly the quality required for success. The ability to drive a hard bargain might at any given moment allow a farmer to get slightly more for his crop, but price bargaining would always be within the very narrow limits of the market at any given moment. Moreover, a shrewd farmer would presumably be faced with an equally shrewd buyer or seller, and this would also serve to limit any advantages he could gain. Farmers even in the most primitive economies haul goods to market and attempt to get favorable prices. But the structure of the market and the process of bargaining are confined by a traditional institutional framework. Haggling in this context takes on the attributes of traditional ways of doing things and does not create the attitudes arising out of the modern market.[52]

More important than his shrewdness at the bargaining table would be the farmer's ability to know market prices and forecast possible changes. This, of course, would depend upon the information available to him and upon his ability to use it to his advantage. The former depends upon adequate communication; the latter requires both an understanding of economic principles and facilities adequate to utilize this understanding. This opens up a crucial area in our investigation of the transition from self sufficiency to commercial agriculture which has received little attention.

To deal with this question requires that the transition be treated as a process, and that the investigation center on the process itself rather than upon the beginning and the end the before and after. We must know something about the growth of information as the farmer moved from self-sufficiency to commercialism. Such information as well as the speed with which it was assimilated are significant; but we cannot stop there. For information means little if the farmer is unable to use it. When a farmer hauls his goods to market and sells them off the wagon, his ability to bargain depends upon the range of prices during a part of a single day. To play the market—that is, to use his shrewdness over the space of more than a few hours—a farmer must have storage and credit facilities available to him in the market. Thus market organization is an essential aspect of the transition from self-sufficiency to commercial agriculture. With storage facilities at hand, a farmer could choose to sell immediately off the wagon or to store his crop awaiting a possible rise. But storage facilities alone would be inadequate; because the farmer often needed cash immediately to supply his needs until his crop was sold, he required credit, either on the basis of his stored crop or upon some other security.

The success or failure of a farmer in the transition period, his relative well-being, indeed his decisions concerning his move to commercialism depended, in part at least, on the development of marketing facilities. It is not a matter of cause and effect here, but a problem of the interaction of town and country. To describe and analyze this interaction is an important problem in agricultural history. But adjustment to the dictates of the market through specialization is but one of many changes which took place during the transition. Farmers tended to put more of their land into the commercial crops, but they also attempted to increase their yields of the commercial crop both through capital investment in machinery and other tools and through more efficient organization. Therefore we need to know more about sources of capital investment as well as the ways in which new methods were developed and spread. New machines and new methods not only had to be available; they also had to be available at a cost that the farmer was willing to pay. This in turn required that the farmer be aware of the new methods and of their cost and be willing to adopt them. Obstacles to change—for example, inadequate transportation, poor marketing mechanisms, general conservatism and fear of the unknown, faulty information, high interest rates, and the like—had to be overcome.

Obviously, a great deal has already been done on the very questions I raise. Just to mention the well-known work of such people as Joseph Schafer, Paul Gates, Fred A. Shannon, and Allan Bogue is enough to make this point clear. And the list could easily be extended. Nevertheless, there are large areas where little work has been done. Despite the contributions of scholars such as Leo Rogin, Reynold M. Wik, Lewis Atherton, Thomas D. Clark, and Morton Rothstein,[53] mechanization and marketing are neglected subjects. Marvin W. Towne and Wayne D. Rasmussen have provided invaluable figures on agricultural productivity,[54] and Robert E. Gallman and Richard A. Easterlin have assembled figures on commodity output and income useful to the agricultural historian,[55] but their aggregated figures must be broken down if they are to be the basis for detailed analyses of social and economic change. Clarence H. Danhof's significant study of farm-making costs in the 1850's has stood as virtually the first and last word on this important subject,[56] though similar studies for other periods are needed. Still another area in which additional work must be done is an analysis of farm laborers and tenants; the fine contributions of LaWanda F. Cox and others should be only a beginning if we are to increase our understanding of the social structure of rural America.[57]

The goal of additional work should not be merely to fill gaps in our knowledge, to provide a few more details on one or another subject. These studies should be aimed at deepening our understanding of economic and social change. We must know more about rural society, its class relations, its internal power structure, and the relation of the various classes in rural society to each other and to the outside world. We must know the sources of change and how various groups responded to change.

As I have tried to indicate, the work of social scientists dealing with traditional societies offers American agricultural historians useful insights. This comparative approach can be equally useful when applied to different regions in the United States. A brief look at the South will illustrate my point.

The South is a most intriguing field for the agricultural historian. Certainly the notion that somehow the South was different has been an element in attracting scholarly attention, if only to deny that the South was indeed different from the rest of the nation. Because agriculture has been the economic base of the South throughout most of its history, and because the peculiar institutions of slavery and the plantation system are so intimately connected to Southern agriculture, the agricultural history of the South has received a great deal of attention, as the perceptive studies by James C. Bonner and Bennett H. Wall have shown.[58]

One of the most important problems for the Southern agricultural historian is simply the persistence of agriculture. Where historians dealing with agriculture in the North must explain the transition from self-sufficiency to commercial agriculture and then deal with the gradual decline of agriculture in relation to manufacturing, the historian of the South must explain a much more static agricultural development. Comparison with the North is an obvious tool for such analysis; equally important is the tool of international comparison. As James C. Bonner has noted, "A complete understanding of the plantation as an institution and of the societies based upon it must . . . await expansion of research into other areas than the American South and other periods than the eighteenth and nineteenth centuries." [59] What follows is one possible approach along the lines suggested by Bonner.

Eugene Genovese's contention that the Southern market was too

shallow to support indigenous manufacturing [60] has recently been attacked by Stanley Engerman. Taking Genovese's estimates of cash
expenditures in the South, Engerman concludes that "the region could
have supported over 50 cotton textile plants and more than 200 boot
and shoe establishments of Massachusetts size." [61] For Engerman, the
South's failure to establish such plants may be explained by the doctrine of comparative advantage. But this really explains nothing because
it amounts to nothing more than circular reasoning: the South specialized in the production of staple crops using slave labor because it
was to its comparative advantage. How do we know that such production was to the South's comparative advantage? Because it continued
in such production and did not open textile and shoe factories.

Everett E. Hagen's contention that behavior patterns in a traditional
society might limit investment in manufacturing even when a market
was available [62] provides a potentially useful explanation that avoids
the self-fulfilling prophecy of the doctrine of comparative advantage.
Moreover, Genovese and Fabian Linden have provided some empirical
evidence to support Hagen's generalizations when applied to the South.
Both trace the sources of traditional behavior to the slave labor system.[63]

But other scholars have disputed the claim that the Southern planter
was as tradition-bound as Genovese's and Linden's explanations would
imply. Thomas Govan has argued that the Southern planters were simply
businessmen of a particular kind. Like businessmen elsewhere in the
country, they were motivated by the desire to invest for a profit, and
production of staple crops with slave labor was just such a profitable
investment. When other opportunities presented themselves, Southerners were not reluctant to invest in them; Govan lists Southern investments in mercantile houses, banking, railroads, mines, and iron
foundries to support this generalization. That Southern investment in
manufacturing did not reach Eastern proportions is not attributed to
peculiar social attitudes but rather to "geological formations, climatic
conditions, facilities for transportation, and other factors." He notes
that Southern mineral deposits, unlike those in the North, were usually
far removed from transportation facilities, and that Southern rivers
could not be tapped for their water power as easily and efficiently as
those in New England.[64]

Govan's argument is unconvincing; he states more than he proves. If
indeed the water power on the Southern fall line was more difficult to
tap than that in the North, this difficulty does not explain the slow investment in steam power; if railroads did not penetrate mineral-rich

regions in the South, this does not explain why investment in railroads to such areas was not forthcoming. In the final analysis, Govan is forced to fall back on his argument that slave production was profitable. This is merely the doctrine of comparative advantage in disguise, and as a result Govan ends by assuming that which he set out to prove.

More sophisticated is the approach of Morton Rothstein, who investigated the economic activities of a group of wealthy planters in the Natchez region. He found these men to be very typical businessmen who were acutely aware of shifting business conditions, and who made their varied business investments south, north, and abroad only after a careful evaluation of economic opportunities. Rothstein's aim in presenting this material was quite different from Govan's. He did not seek to prove that the South was no different economically from the North; on the contrary, his effort was to show that the economy in the South was really a "dual economy," and that the very wealthy planters might be compared with "the elite groups in the modern plantation economies" while the rest of the population might be classed as "the 'tradition-bound' sector" in such economies.[65]

The concept of the dual economy as outlined by Rothstein provides added insight into Southern economic and social development. It must be used with caution, as Rothstein notes, and perhaps for this reason he does not press his insights to extreme interpretations. In applying the concept to the South, Rothstein divides the economy between the "traditional" or largely self-sufficient farmers and poor whites, and the "modern" or planter aristocracy. He notes that the planter aristocracy, especially the Natchez nabobs he investigates, were very "modern" in their attitudes toward investment opportunities, in their economic and social outlook, and in their general style of life. The conclusion implicit in this analysis is that Southern economic problems stemmed from the fact that only a small group—the "nabobs"—was modern. But in making this point, Rothstein departs from the dual economy analysis and therefore misses, I think, the most significant value of his conceptual framework.

A member of the modern sector of a dual economy in a present-day colonial country has, it is true, a modern attitude toward the outside world, but his attitude toward the system in which he participates is very traditional. This is the essential problem dual societies face. The leaders of the modern sector, in order to promote their well-being and their social and economic status, must maintain the status quo. Existing systems of land tenure, of property relations, of social ordering, of ideological outlook are to their advantage. Moreover, their economic activities are not directed toward the home market; they are local representatives of an outside interest, usually an imperial country, but at least an outside investor. Their high incomes go to support a luxurious standard of living (often in the traditional manner) and to investments in foreign enterprises.[66]

If we look at the nineteenth-century South from this perspective we get new insights into the society based on Southern agriculture. For example, it might help us to understand the relative lack of industrialization in the South both before and after the Civil War. A large class of nonslaveholding whites before the war and the millions of blacks and whites who approached peonage after the war should have provided a cheap supply of labor to support industrial development. But, as Nurske has argued, "Even in densely populated areas labor may not be really cheap for the purposes of industrialization, when it is illiterate, unskilled, and undisciplined." [67] Perhaps this is the most important legacy of slavery and the plantation system. In a way much different from what Ulrich B. Phillips had in mind, slavery and the plantation system and the society it supported and perpetuated might have been a school which inculcated traditions that blocked the path to economic and social change.

It may be argued that I have pushed the concept too far, that to compare the nineteenth-century South with, say, present-day India does violence to both logic and empirical evidence. But this is not my purpose. The historian does not aim to create universal propositions which may apply to all societies; investigation of these similarities and the formulation of "laws" about them can be left to sociologists and political scientists. We seek not laws but insights. The concept of the dual economy can direct our attention to matters which we have ignored or seen in a much different light. If the concept allows us to deal more effectively with questions of the nature of the Southern economy, class relations in Southern agriculture, urban-rural conflicts (or the absence of them), or the nature of Southern agricultural methods, then it should be used.

What, then, is the state of agricultural history in the United States today? The field is healthy, the prognosis positive. I have here tried to identify two trends in the writing of agricultural history and have argued that what may be called the "integrating" trend is what now needs emphasis. I do not mean to limit the field to a single approach or point of view, nor to suggest that I have outlined all of the important areas in which new work must be done. What I do urge is a synthesis in agricultural history which will allow for explanations on the level of social change. This requires, on the one hand, that we develop a conceptual framework from which to view and understand change; in this area I have noted the significance of the basic instability of American society. On the other hand, the American experience or, specifically, the effects of instability can best be understood in comparative terms; in this area I have noted the relevance of current work in underdeveloped economies.

To understand social change, the historian must make use of the insights provided by social scientists, but in the last analysis he will make his greatest contribution by using his most important tool—his historical imagination. This was the genius of Frederick Jackson Turner, who fathered an approach to agricultural history which has the greatest promise for extending our understanding.

NOTES

1. My main concern in this essay is the agricultural history of the United States. Although I shall have occasion to touch on the work of historians and social scientists dealing with other countries, I do so only as their work relates to American agricultural history.

2. Everett E. Edwards, "Agricultural History and the Department of Agriculture," *Agricultural History*, XVI (July 1942), 129–136; Wayne D. Rasmussen, "Forty Years of Agricultural History," *ibid.*, XXXIII (October 1959), 177; Rasmussen, "The Growth of Agricultural History," in William B. Hesseltine and Donald R. McNeil, eds., *In Support of Clio: Essays in Memory of Herbert A. Kellar* (Madison, Wisc., 1958), pp. 153–156. A perceptive analysis of the "new history" and the contributions of the Wisconsin "school" may be found in John Higham, *et al., History* (Englewood Cliffs, N.J., 1965), pp. 110–116, 174–179, 183.

3. Rasmussen, "Growth of Agricultural History," p. 162.

4. Louis Bernard Schmidt, "The Economic History of American Agriculture as a Field of Study," *Mississippi Valley Historical Review*, III (June 1916), 39–40.

5. The quoted words are from the inside front cover of *Agricultural History*, II (October 1928). Recent issues of the journal carry essentially the same statement, the minor changes being stylistic rather than substantive.

6. For these bibliographies, see Herbert A. Kellar, "Everett Eugene Edwards," *Agricultural History*, XXVII (January 1963), 10–13; Wayne D. Rasmussen and Helen H. Edwards, "A Bibliography of the Writings of Everett Eugene Edwards," *ibid.*, pp. 26–37. During his term as editor, 1931–1952, Edwards collected lists of current works in agricultural history and published them in each volume of *Agricultural History*.

7. Kellar, "Everett Eugene Edwards," p. 12.

8. Schmidt published a number of significant articles on agriculture in the Midwest in the *Iowa Journal of History and Politics* during the early twenties. Several of these are reprinted in Schmidt and Ross, *Readings in the Economic History of American Agriculture* (New York, 1925). For Schmidt's writings on the agricultural revolution in the United States, see "Some Significant· Aspects of the Agrarian Revolution in the United States," *Iowa Journal of History and Politics*, XVIII (July 1920), 371–395, reprinted in revised form in Schmidt and Ross, *Readings*, pp. 331–338; "The Agricultural Revolution in the United States, 1860–1930," *Science*, LXXII (December 12, 1930), 585–594. See also his influential article on ante-bellum intersectional trade: "Internal Commerce and the Development of National Economy Before 1860," *Journal of Political Economy*, XLVII (December 1939), 798–822. Schmidt's bibliography is *Topical Studies and References on the Economic History of American Agriculture* (Philadelphia, 1919). A revised edition was published in 1923.

9. "The History of American Agriculture as a Field of Research," *Agricultural History*, XIV (July 1940), 117–126. The quoted words are on p. 118. Schmidt published the essence of this article at least seven times between 1916 and 1940. For a history of this publication, see the editor's note, *ibid.*, p. 117.

10. Everett E. Edwards, "Objectives for the Agricultural History Society During Its Second Twenty-Five Years," *Agricultural History*, XVIII (October 1944), 187–192.

11. Rasmussen, "Forty Years of Agricultural History," pp. 117–184.

12. Gilbert C. Fite, "Expanded Frontiers in Agricultural History," *Agricultural History*, XXXV (October 1961), 175–181.

13. C. Wright Mills, *The Sociological Imagination*, paperback ed. (New York, 1967), pp. 25–49.

14. H. Stuart Hughes, "The Historian and the Social Scientist," *American Historical Review*, LXVI (October 1960), 23.

15. Higham, *History*, pp. 104–105, 114–116.

16. See Lyman Carrier, *The Beginnings of Agriculture in America* (New York, 1923); Carrier, "The United States Agricultural Society, 1852–1860," *Agricultural History*, XI (October 1937), 278–288; Carrier and Katherine S. Bort, "The History of Kentucky Bluegrass and White Clover in the United States," American Society of Agronomy, *Journal*, VII (July–August 1916), 256–266; Rodney H. True, "Early Days of the Albemarle Agricultural Society," American Historical Association, *Annual Report, 1918,* I (Washington, D.C., 1921), 241–259; R. H. True, ed., "Minute Book of the Albemarle (Virginia) Agricultural Society," *ibid.*, pp. 261–349; R. H. True, "The Early Development of Agricultural Societies in the United States," *ibid.*, 1920 (Washington, D.C., 1925), pp. 293–306; R. H. True, "Thomas Jefferson in Relation to Botany," *Scientific Monthly*, III (October 1916), 345–360; R. H. True, "John Binns of Loudoun," *William and Mary Quarterly*, 2nd ser., II (January 1922), 20–39; R. H. True, "Jared Eliot, Minister, Physician, and Farmer," *Agricultural History*, II (October 1928), 185–212; Henry C. Taylor, "Early History of Agri-

cultural Economics," *Journal of Farm Economics*, XXII (February 1940), 84–97; Taylor and Anne Dewees Taylor, *The Story of Agricultural Economics in the United States, 1840–1932* (Ames, Iowa, 1952); Alfred Charles True, *A History of Agricultural Extension Work in the United States, 1785–1923*, U.S. Department of Agriculture, Miscellaneous Publication No. 15 (Washington, D.C., 1928); A. C. True, *A History of Agricultural Education in the United States, 1785–1925*, U.S. Department of Agriculture, Miscellaneous Publication No. 36 (Washington, D.C., 1929); A. C. True, *A History of Agricultural Experimentation and Research in the United States, 1607–1925*, U.S. Department of Agriculture, Miscellaneous Publication No. 251 (Washington, D.C., 1937). For a discussion of these and other scientists with an interest in history in the Department of Agriculture, see Edwards, "Agricultural History and the Department of Agriculture," pp. 130–132.

17. Edwards, "Agricultural History and the Department of Agriculture," p. 134.

18. Earle D. Ross, "Agriculture in Our Economic History," *Agricultural History*, XXII (April 1948), 65–69. The quoted words are on p. 65.

19. Frederick Jackson Turner, *The Frontier in American History* (New York, 1920); Turner, *The Significance of Sections in American History* (New York, 1932); Turner, *Rise of the New West, 1819–1829* (New York, 1906); Turner, *The United States, 1830–1860* (New York, 1935).

20. For a convenient sampling of some of the best, see Richard Hofstadter and Seymour Martin Lipset, eds., *Turner and the Sociology of the Frontier* (New York, 1968).

21. Edwards, "Objectives for the Agricultural History Society During Its Second Twenty-Five Years," p. 187.

22. Rasmussen, "Forty Years of Agricultural History," p. 183.

23. Fite, "Expanded Frontiers in Agricultural History," p. 179.

24. Thomas C. Cochran, "The History of a Business Society," *Journal of American History*, LIV (June 1967), 5–18. The quoted words are on p. 8.

25. See E. L. Jones, *Agriculture and Economic Growth in England, 1650–1815* (London, 1967), pp. 15, 17.

26. Oscar Handlin, "The Significance of the Seventeenth Century," in James Morton Smith, ed., *Seventeenth-Century America: Essays in Colonial History* (Chapel Hill, 1959), pp. 3–12.

27. Sumner Chilton Powell, *Puritan Village* (Garden City, 1965), pp. 120–121.

28. Sigmund Diamond, "From Organization to Society: Virginia in the Seventeenth Century," *American Journal of Sociology*, LXIII (March 1958), 457–475; Bernard Bailyn, "Politics and Social Structure in Virginia," in Smith, ed., *Seventeenth-Century America*, pp. 90–115.

29. Louis Hartz, *The Founding of New Societies* (New York, 1964). This thoughtful study in comparative history has not received the attention it deserves from historians.

30. See again Bailyn, "Politics and Social Structure in Virginia."

31. Powell, *Puritan Village*, p. 15.

32. See, for example, Neil Adams McNall, *An Agricultural History of the Genesee Valley, 1790–1860* (Philadelphia, 1952), pp. 66–77; Allan G. Bogue, *From Prairie to Corn Belt* (Chicago, 1963), pp. 8–28.

33. Richard Lyle Power, *Planting Corn Belt Culture* (Indianapolis, 1953).

34. Allan G. Bogue, "Social Theory and the Pioneer," *Agricultural History*, XXXIV (January 1960), 21–34. This article has been reprinted with minor

corrections in Hofstadter and Lipset, eds., *Turner and the Sociology of the Frontier,* pp. 73–99. The article has greatly influenced my thinking.

35. See Stephan Thernstrom, *Poverty and Progress* (Cambridge, Mass., 1964).

36. George W. Pierson, "The Moving American," *Yale Review,* XLIV (Autumn 1954), 99–112; Pierson, "The M-Factor in American History," *American Quarterly,* XIV (Summer 1962), 275–289; Pierson, "Mobility," in C. Vann Woodward, ed., *The Comparative Approach to American History* (New York, 1968), 106–120; Pierson, "A Restless Temper," *American Historical Review,* LXIX (July 1964), 969–989.

37. Wilbert E. Moore, "The Social Framework of Economic Development," in Ralph Braibanti and Joseph J. Spengler, eds., *Tradition, Values, and Socio-Economic Development* (Durham, N.C., 1961), p. 71.

38. Bert F. Hoselitz, *Sociological Aspects of Economic Growth* (Glencoe, Ill., 1960), p. 60. See also pp. 72–73.

39. Extremely relevant in this connection is David Potter's discussion of "The Behavioral Scientists and National Character," a neglected part of his brilliant *People of Plenty* (Chicago, 1954). See also the suggestive discussion by Michael Argyle, "The Social Psychology of Social Change," in Tom Burns and S. B. Saul, eds., *Social Theory and Economic Change* (London, 1967), pp. 87–101. Interesting also is Everett E. Hagen, *On the Theory of Social Change: How Economic Growth Begins* (Homewood, Ill., 1962).

40. Theoretical and empirical literature on this question is extensive—and controversial. Much of it is by agricultural economists and other social scientists involved in contemporary problems of economic development. Although little is directly aimed at the history and development of American agriculture, much of it contains suggestive insights which may with profit be used in analyzing the history of American agriculture. Convenient collections of recent work with extensive bibliographies are Carl K. Eicher and Lawrence W. Witt, eds., *Agriculture in Economic Development* (New York, 1964), and Herman M. Southworth and Bruce F. Jonstron, eds., *Agricultural Development and Economic Growth* (Ithaca, 1967).

41. Guy Stevens Callender, *Selections from the Economic History of the United States, 1765–1860* (Boston, 1909), pp. 6–9, 271–275.

42. Douglass C. North, *The Economic Growth of the United States, 1790–1860* (Englewood Cliffs, N.J., 1961).

43. See the review of North's book by Richard A. Easterlin, *Journal of Economic History,* XXII (March 1962), 122–126.

44. Stuart Bruchey, "Douglass C. North on American Economic Growth," *Explorations in Entrepreneurial History,* 2nd ser., I (Winter 1964), 145–158. The quoted words are on p. 153. For Bruchey's own approach, see his *The Roots of American Economic Growth, 1607–1861: An Essay in Social Causation* (New York, 1965).

45. Douglass C. North, "Comments on Stuart Bruchey's Paper," *Explorations in Entrepreneurial History,* 2nd ser., I (Winter 1964), 159–163.

46. For a sampling of the discussion on these important matters, see Robert William Fogel, "The Reunification of Economic History with Economic Theory," *American Economic Review,* LV (May 1965), 92–98; Fogel, "The New Economic History," *Economic History Review,* XIX (December 1966), 642–656; Douglass C. North, "The State of Economic History," *American Economic Review,* LV (May 1965), 86–91; North, "Quantitative Research in American Economic History," *ibid.,* LIII (March 1963), 128–130; Lance E. Davis, " 'And It Will Never Be Literature': The New Economic History: A Critique," *Explora-*

tions in Entrepreneurial History, 2nd ser., VI (February 1968), 75–92; Alfred H. Conrad and John R. Meyer, "Economic Theory, Statistical Inference and Economic History," *Journal of Economic History,* XVII (December 1957), 524–544; Fritz Redlich, "New and Traditional Approaches to Economic History and Their Interdependence," *Journal of Economic History,* XXV (December 1965), 480–495; Stephan Thernstrom, "Quantitative Methods in History: Some Notes," in Seymour Martin Lipset and Richard Hofstadter, eds., *Sociology and History: Methods* (New York, 1968), pp. 59–78; William O. Aydelotte, "Quantification in History," *American Historical Review,* LXXI (April 1966), 803–825.

47. Rodney C. Loehr, "Self-Sufficiency on the Farm," *Agricultural History,* XXVI (April 1952), 37–41.

48. Ragnar Nurske, *Problems of Capital Formation in Underdeveloped Countries and Patterns of Trade and Development* (New York, 1967), p. 204.

49. Moore, "Social Framework of Economic Development," pp. 57–82.

50. Theodore W. Schultz, *Transforming Traditional Agriculture* (New Haven, 1964).

51. Percy W. Bidwell, "The Agricultural Revolution in New England," *American Historical Review,* XXVI (July 1921), 683–702.

52. See Victor C. Uchendu, "Some Principles of Haggling in Peasant Markets," *Economic Development and Cultural Change,* XVI (October 1967), 37–50.

53. Leo Rogin, *The Introduction of Farm Machinery in Its Relation to the Productivity in Labor in the Agriculture of the United States During the Nineteenth Century* (Berkeley, 1931); Reynold M. Wik, *Steam Power on the American Farm* (Philadelphia, 1953); Lewis Atherton, *The Pioneer Merchant in Mid-America* (Columbia, Mo., 1939); Atherton, *The Southern Country Store, 1800–1860* (Baton Rouge, La., 1949); Atherton, *Main Street on the Middle Border* (Bloomington, Ind., 1954); Thomas D. Clark, *Pills, Petticoats and Plows: The Southern Country Store* (Indianapolis, 1944); Morton Rothstein, "Antebellum Wheat and Cotton Exports: A Contrast in Marketing Organization and Economic Development," *Agricultural History,* XL (April 1966), 91–100.

54. Marvin W. Towne and Wayne D. Rasmussen, "Farm Gross Product and Gross Investment in the Nineteenth Century," in National Bureau of Economic Research, *Trends in the American Economy in the Nineteenth Century,* Vol. XXIV of *Studies in Income and Wealth* (Princeton, 1960), 255–312.

55. Robert E. Gallman, "Commodity Output, 1839–1899," *ibid.,* pp. 13–71; Richard A. Easterlin, "Interregional Differences in Per Capita Income, Population, and Total Income, 1840–1950," *ibid.,* pp. 73–140.

56. Clarence H. Danhof, "Farm-Making Costs and the 'Safety Valve': 1850–1860," *Journal of Political Economy,* XLIX (June 1941), 317–359.

57. LaWanda F. Cox, "The American Agricultural Wage Earner, 1865–1900: The Emergence of a Modern Labor Problem," *Agricultural History,* XXII (April 1948), 95–114; Cox, "Tenancy in the United States, 1865–1900; A Consideration of the Agricultural Ladder Hypothesis," *ibid.,* XVIII (July 1944), 97–105. See also Paul W. Gates, "Frontier Estate Builders and Farm Laborers," in Walker D. Wyman and Clifton B. Kroeber, eds., *The Frontier in Perspective* (Madison, Wisc., 1957), pp. 144–163; Gates, *Frontier Landlords and Pioneer Tenants* (Ithaca, 1945). Stanley Lebergott, *Manpower in Economic Growth: The American Record Since 1800* (New York, 1964), pp. 257–267, 539–541, provides estimates of wage trends in agriculture.

58. James C. Bonner, "Plantation and Farm: The Agricultural South," in Arthur S. Link and Rembert W. Patrick, eds., *Writing Southern History: Essays in Historiography in Honor of Fletcher M. Green* (Baton Rouge, La., 1965) pp. 147–174; Bennett H. Wall, "African Slavery," *ibid.*, pp. 175–197.

59. Bonner, "Plantation and Farm," p. 152.

60. Eugene D. Genovese, *The Political Economy of Slavery* (New York, 1965), pp. 157–179.

61. Stanley L. Engerman, "The Effects of Slavery upon the Southern Economy: A Review of the Recent Debate," *Explorations in Entrepreneurial History*, 2nd ser., IV (Winter 1967), 71–97.

62. Hagen, *On the Theory of Social Change*, pp. 42–44.

63. Genovese, *Political Economy of Slavery*, pp. 180–259 and *passim*; Fabian Linden, "Repercussions of Manufacturing in the Ante-Bellum South," *North Carolina Historical Review*, XVII (October 1940), 313–331.

64. Thomas G. Govan, "Americans Below the Potomac," in Charles Grier Sellers, Jr., ed., *The Southerner as American* (New York, 1966), pp. 19–39 (originally published as "Was the Old South Different?," *Journal of Southern History*, XXI [November 1955], 447–455).

65. Morton Rothstein, "The Antebellum South As a Dual Economy: A Tentative Hypothesis," *Agricultural History*, XLI (October 1967), 373–382.

66. On the dual economy, see Dale W. Jorgenson, "The Development of a Dual Economy," *Economic Journal*, LXXI (June 1961), 309–344 and the references therein.

67. Nurske, *Problems of Capital Formation . . . and Patterns of Trade and Development*, p. 198.

The State of Environmental History

RODERICK NASH

> *To the rapid traveler the number of elms in a town*
> *is the measure of its civility.*
> —Henry David Thoreau

Until recently I responded to the student's perennial question—"Can you recommend something to read over the vacation?"—by ticking off the usual list of books and articles. I even had a list mimeographed for the eager beavers. About a year ago, however, I altered the pattern. I was walking to my car after delivering the final lecture in the first half of a course in American cultural and intellectual history, when a student came roaring up on a motorbike. "Thanks for the course," he said. "And what could I read to prepare for next quarter?" I started to answer in the accustomed way when I noticed the boy had a sleeping bag and some light camping gear strapped to the bike. I changed my mind. "Forget the books," I said. "Get on that thing, travel as far as you can in the vacation, and 'read' the landscape." He looked startled, so I explained how the environment can be a historical document. The condition of the land, I pointed out, reflects the thought and culture of a people just as clearly as orthodox written evidence. I suggested that he make the environment his text for the next couple of weeks. He did, too, but he returned with a recommendation for a change in the assignment: there was so much to "read" he wished he had left the motorcycle traveled on foot!

On other occasions I have asked an audience to look out the nearest window and consider the face of the land. If there isn't a window, I point out, that is also very revealing about our attitude toward the natural part of the environment. But supposing there is, the scene is a human creation. The tree or shrub or patch of grass is there, in other words, either because men put it there or because they allowed it to remain. Is the vegetation beyond the window carefully manicured, farmed, or growing wild? If the last, is it from choice or neglect? Are birds and other wildlife present? Such questions lead quickly to a consideration of public taste and value. Perhaps the view from the window reveals only concrete and asphalt; this complete exclusion of nature tells something else about social attitudes, preferences, and goals. And what of the buildings, utility installations, and highways? What considerations determined their appearance?

Such questions should not be strange. We ask them frequently, practicing environmental history unconsciously in buying a home or even choosing accommodations while traveling. Certainly any woman can discriminate between houses or motels just by looking at them. The location (in reference to hills, for instance), lot size, presence or absence of trees, lawn and plantings, style of architecture, and level of upkeep tell a great deal about the owner. His taste is on public display. Environmental history simply extends these criteria to the nation as a whole. It assumes that one can learn about American character and culture by examining what Americans have done to their land.

The environment today is in large part an artifact—an object made by man. The landscape is synthetic. Technology has placed tools in man's hands that allow him to sculpt the physical world. In one hour a bulldozer or chain saw performs the equivalent of ten thousand years of erosion. As geographers have long told us, man is the primary agent of environmental change. This is obvious in the case of cities and other settled areas. In most parts of the world, moreover, nature itself is also synthetic. That is to say, the choice *not* to change natural conditions—to leave them undeveloped as a park or preserve—also involves a conscious exercise of human will. In this sense even wilderness is man-made. As a consequence, *any* landscape, rightly seen, reveals social values.

This ability to "read" the environment, combined with more orthodox ways of understanding what men have done to and thought about the physical world, forms the basis of environmental history.* It is a

---

* "Conservation history" or "the history of land and resources" are older terms but limited in their application. "Environmental history" refers to the total contact of man with his habitat and includes everything from urban design to wilderness preservation. I regard it as a variety of intellectual history, an approach to understanding the history of thought.

new field, a recent addition to the century-long revolution in historical purpose and method that produced the "new history," the "new criticism," intellectual, social, and cultural history, and American Studies. Like these approaches to the past, environmental history demands redefinition of what constitutes an historical document. Interdisciplinary techniques are required. Under its banner, geographers, psychologists, sociologists, anthropologists, and ecologists should combine with historians and with students of literature, speech, art, and music to investigate the many facets of man's relationship to nature. Only through such a pooling of skills is it possible to begin to understand how and why people react to environment.

Present explorers of American environmental history have a sizable backlog of secondary writing on which to draw. Most of the early studies, to be sure, were traditional in that they focused on "what?" rather than "why?" For example, we have considerable data on the history of lumbering and federal land policy in the United States. But the level of analysis is comparatively shallow. The value of these works lies in demonstrating that the history of the environment could be written in the first place, and in doing the groundwork necessary for deeper understanding.*

One of the first Americans to regard the environment as a document was George Perkins Marsh, whose multifaceted career is carefully described in David Lowenthal's *George Perkins Marsh: Versatile Vermonter* (1958). Marsh's own book, *Man and Nature; or, Physical Geography as Modified by Human Action,* appeared in 1864 and argued that the present condition of the earth must be regarded as largely the result of several thousand years of man's occupation. Deserts replace forests, sources of water vanish, even climate changes, Marsh contended, as man transforms the physical environment. Professional geographers and, more recently, human ecologists, have continued the examination of these and related elements of environmental history. The fruits of their labors may be found in collections such as William L. Thomas, Jr., ed., *Man's Role in Changing the Face of the Earth*

---

* It will be apparent from what follows that I am not attempting a comprehensive bibliography. Those works mentioned seem to me to be either seminal or most representative of their type. For more complete bibliographies in conservation and environmental history, see Gordon B. Dodds, "The Historiography of American Conservation," *Pacific Northwest Quarterly* (April 1965), 75–81; Richard Lillard's review essay in *American Quarterly,* XX (Fall 1968), 650–657; and Roderick Nash, "A Selected Bibliography" in his edited collection *The American Environment: Readings in the History of Conservation* (Reading, Mass., 1969), pp. 223–236.

(1956), which was dedicated to Marsh, and in F. Fraser Darling and John P. Milton, eds., *Future Environments of North America* (1966). Such investigations, however, study man's modification of the earth from the point of view of the earth; they stop short of asking what the modification of the environment tells about man and his ideas.

Two specializations within the broad field of geography hold more promise for environmental history. One is historical geography, which undertakes to explain how natural features influenced man's life in the past. W. Gordon East even includes a chapter entitled "Geography as an Historical Document" in his *The Geography Behind History* (rev. ed., 1965). Like most works of its kind, East's book concentrates on the distant and non-American past. Only a few books such as Ellen Churchill Semple's *American History and Its Geographic Conditions* (1903) and Ralph H. Brown's *Historical Geography of the United States* (1948) begin to fill the gap.

The other specialized pursuit within the field of geography takes man rather than land as its focus. It goes beyond the traditional limits of the discipline to consider man's perception of and response to environmental features. It studies attitudes toward the landscape and the assumptions and values that underlie those attitudes. These concerns take what might be called "perceptual geography" into the realms of behavioral psychology, social anthropology, metaphysics, and the history of ideas. David Lowenthal has written a short manifesto for the perceptual geographer as the introduction to *Environmental Perception and Behavior* (1967) which he edited. "What we see," says Lowenthal, ". . . and the way we shape and build in the landscape is selected and structured for each of us by custom, culture, desire, and faith. . . . Underlying all our expressed attitudes toward the milieu is a core of assumptions and values about the nature of man and of nature."

Perceptual geography is still inchoate. Its practitioners are in the stage of working out method, concept, and even vocabulary to express their findings. Many of them cling to what they can actually see, photograph, and ask opinions about in the manner of a pollster. One thinks of Kevin Lynch's *The Image of the City* (1960) and the book on which he collaborated with Donald Appleyard and John R. Myer, *The View from the Road* (1964). Also essentially nonhistorical is Ian Nairn's *The American Landscape: A Critical View* (1965). As the perceptual geographers gain skill and confidence, they will no doubt increasingly turn to past attitudes toward the environment as a subject for investigation. Already there are some pioneering works, notably Clarence J. Glacken's massive *Traces on the Rhodian Shore* (1967), which examines man's conception of the environment from ancient times to the end of the eighteenth century. Glacken, who is a geographer, has drawn on the visual arts as well as literature to write splendid intellectual history. Yi-Fu Tuan's "Attitudes Toward Environment: Themes and Approaches," in *Environmental Perception and Behavior,* and Lowenthal's "Geography, Experience, and Imagination: Towards a Geographical Epistemology," in the *Annals of the Association of American Geographers,* LI (1961), 241–260, provide further definition and direction. As for the American story, Lowenthal's "Is Wilderness 'Paradise Enow'?: Images of Nature in America," *Columbia University Forum,* VII (Spring 1964), 34–40; "The American Scene," *Geographical Review,* LVIII (January 1968), 61–88; and "The American Image of Nature as Virtue," *Landscape,* IX (1959–1960), 16–26, whet the appetite for his promised book-length study of the American and nature.

American land and resource policy, the mainstay of the old conservation history, is well documented. Most American historians are familiar with the work of Roy M. Robbins, E. Louise Peffer, and Marion Clawson. William R. Van Dersal's *The American Land, Its History and Its Uses* (1943) is an environmental history, albeit simplified. David Cushman Coyle, *Conservation: An American Story of Conflict and Accomplishment* (1957), and Stewart Udall, *The Quiet Crisis* (1963) are among the attempts to describe the American conservation movement under one cover. Henry Clepper's edited *Origins of American Conservation* (1966) has the same purpose but uses a different method—short, historical sketches by leaders in various fields of resource management. More limited chronologically, hence more detailed, are Samuel P. Hays, *Conservation and the Gospel of Efficiency: The Progressive Conservation Movement, 1890–1920* (1959); Elmo R. Richardson, *The Politics of Conservation: Crusades and Controversies, 1897–1913* (1962); and Donald C. Swain, *Federal Conservation Policy, 1921–1933* (1963). With Swain's promised continuation of the history of national conservation to the present time, we will have a detailed account of the entire movement. But such books, with their concentration on policy and legislation, will disappoint those in search of information about how Americans *felt* toward the environment. They will also gain little from otherwise distinguished studies of limited scope, such as Samuel T. Dana's *Forest and Range Policy: Its*

Development in the United States (1956), or Preston Hubbard's *Origins of the TVA* (1961). Chronological narratives, to be sure, are needed, but it seems particularly unfortunate when books like John Ise's *Our National Park Policy* (1961) penetrate no deeper than an act-by-act survey. Richard G. Lillard, *The Great Forest* (1947), and Rutherford Platt, *The Great American Forest* (1965), are more sensitive to the impact of environment on emotion and feeling.

Regional historians have made an impressive record in treating the impact of man upon the land and vice versa. Hallmarks of this kind of book are its preference for natural boundaries over artificial ones like state lines, and its use of environmental features to define its limits. Walter P. Webb's *The Great Plains* (1931) broke the path for scholars like James C. Malin, whose *The Grassland of North America* (1947) borrowed the techniques of biologists, agronomists, ecologists, and even meteorologists. Malin literally wrote a history of the land as well as its settlers. "The sciences," he declared in his preface, "bring to the aid of the historian new tools and new methods whose possibilities have been little explored." They still are. Few individuals have mastered such diverse skills, and interdisciplinary collaborations are unfortunately rare. Nevertheless, significant studies of particular regions have appeared. Francis P. Farquhar, *History of the Sierra Nevada* (1965); Michael Frome, *Strangers in High Places: The Story of the Great Smoky Mountains* (1966); Donald W. Meinig, *The Great Columbia Plain: A Historical Geography, 1805–1910* (1968); and T. H. Watkins, ed., *The Grand Colorado* (1969), suggest the need for comparable work on other parts of the country. *The Destruction of California* (1965) by Raymond F. Dasmann deserves special commendation for its sensitivity to the impact of rapid settlement on all aspects of the Californian environment. Richard G. Lillard's *Eden in Jeopardy* (1966) concerns an even more limited area—the Los Angeles basin. Mention should also be made of the more than fifty volumes in the generally undervalued "Rivers of America" series, which together constitute the closest approximation extant to a comprehensive American environmental history.

Rather than concentrate on a particular region, some scholars have built their books around a particular kind of environment. The American city, for instance, has had several talented historians, most recently John W. Reps with *The Making of Urban America* (1965). Specialized studies such as George F. Chadwick's *The Park and the Town:*

Public Landscape in the 19th and 20th Centuries (1966) have great value for environmental history .So does the writing of internationalists like Lewis Mumford, whose *The Culture of Cities* (1938) and *The City in History* (1961) put the American experience in world perspective. Morton and Lucia White have specialized both in terms of environment and of society in *The Intellectual versus the City* (1962). The suburb and the village have also received consideration in the work of Page Smith and Robert C. Wood, among others, and in *Wilderness and the American Mind* (1967) I endeavored to describe and explain changing American attitudes toward still another kind of environment.

Implicit in this variety of history is the idea that a relationship exists between where men live and what they think. Frederick Jackson Turner led the way in discerning this link. His investigation of the meaning of the frontier really launched American environmental history. The New World, Turner contended, shaped American ideals and institutions. Considering when he wrote, we can hardly blame him for failing to see that these same ideals also shaped the New World. In fact, the ax produced as valuable a document as the pen. As civilization rolled westward it wrote a record of its beliefs upon the face of the land.

Historians of American thought and culture have occasionally addressed themselves to understanding the significance of the environment. Hans Huth's *Nature and the American: Three Centuries of Changing Attitudes* (1957) is a rewarding introduction to the general field. Also comprehensive are Arthur A. Ekirch, Jr., *Man and Nature in America* (1963), and Russel B. Nye's "The American View of Nature" in his *This Almost Chosen People* (1966). Some of the field's finest talents have seen the possibilities of exploring American thought about the environment. Perry Miller's "Nature and the National Ego" in his *Errand into the Wilderness* (1956), Miller's posthumous collection *Nature's Nation* (1967), and Howard Mumford Jones's *O Strange New World* (1964) contain ideas of striking originality, as does Charles L. Sanford's *The Quest for Paradise* (1961). In 1950 a milestone in intellectual as well as environmental history was reached with the publication of Henry Nash Smith's *Virgin Land: The American West as Symbol and Myth*. Recognizing that what people *believed* was often as important as the actuality, Smith analyzed the lenses through which Americans up to Turner saw the West. Peter J.

Schmitt's *Back to Nature: The Arcadian Myth in Urban America*
(1969) explores the meaning of nature in the early twentieth century,
using new documents from the realm of popular culture. Paul Shepard,
Man in the Landscape (1967) is not limited to America but is remarkable for its imaginative combination of disciplines as diverse as
physiology (the structure of the eye as it bears on perception and the
meaning of smell, for instance) and folklore.

The final major category of scholars of concern here are the historians of literature, art, and architecture. Among the early studies
of American writing as it concerned the environment, Norman Foerster,
Nature in American Literature (1927), and Lucy Lockwood Hazard,
The Frontier in American Literature (1927) are still important. But
the questions and answers of literary historians were considerably refined in the interval between these books and recent ones by Leo Marx,
Wilson O. Clough, and Edwin Fussell. In *The Machine in the Garden*
(1964) Marx has shown us the potential that careful examination
of attitude toward environment has for understanding American culture. Reading his book, one quickly senses that the tension he posits
between natural and technological values in eighteenth- and nineteenth-
century literature can be used to explain other aspects of American
thought right into our own time. Landscape painting is also a fruitful
document. James Thomas Flexner, *That Wilder Image: The Painting
of America's Native School from Thomas Cole to Winslow Homer*
(1962), and Neil Harris, *The Artist in American Society* (1966),
suggest new uses for visual evidence. Architecture is both a form of
expression and a feature of the landscape. Its historians, such as
Christopher Tunnard, Wayne Andrews, and Albert Busch-Brown, have
made important contributions toward understanding the environment.

The potential of environment history is great because of the many
new approaches it offers for the student of the American experience.
Attitude toward the physical world was and is intertwined with key
ideas. The national character and sense of identity are related at a basic
level to the land, the setting, the place. Like plants, we are in our
beliefs more the products of the environment than we realize. It is
possible to leave books unread and to avoid museums and concert halls
and colleges; but one cannot ignore the landscape. Granted that Turner
may have overstated the case when he referred to democracy stalking
out of the tall uncut, still his instinct for associating environment and
character was correct. The land shaped American ethics, aesthetics,

and religion. It impelled us toward individualism, optimism, pragmatism, and wastefulness. It helped build the concept of mission. We intuit these properties of the land; scholarship must now catch up to the feeling in our bones.

The ways in which Americans shaped their land also needs further study. Almost uniquely among modern peoples, those who settled the New World had the opportunity and the responsibility to *make* their own environment. Indian civilization had made few marks on the pre-Columbian landscape. It was largely wilderness—a clean slate. Asians or Europeans of the same era, by way of contrast, had no alternative but to live in a physical setting shaped by thousands of years of occupancy. Except in a limited way, the landscape could not express their preferences. Americans, however, had and to some extent still have the chance to make fundamental choices about the character of their environment. Attitudes toward the past, contemporary tastes, and ideals for the future combine to influence such decisions. The historian who examines them mines a rich vein.

Consider, as an example, the way environmental history illuminates the chronic controversy between utilitarian and aesthetic interests. A particular natural object, such as a tree, can be claimed by both sides —as lumber or as scenery. The same is true of a canyon that could be dammed for use as a reservoir or preserved as wilderness. The fact that neither tree nor canyon can satisfy both demands simultaneously has given rise to violent altercations. Thus in the course of allocating resources Americans have been confronted with basic questions of value and ultimately with choices about the nature of their civilization. Frequently the issue reduces to the question of whether the nation, with its well-known material abilities and appetites, also possesses an aesthetic and spiritual sense. Additional opportunities arise from asking what kinds of people prefer wilderness and what kinds prefer dams and amusement parks.

On another front, environmental history is an excellent vantage point from which to examine the tension in American life between individual freedom and social purpose. Enlightened use of the land demands a limitation on the freedom of the landowner because the easiest, most lucrative method of exploiting a resource is seldom in the best long-term interest of the nation as a whole. But in a society that covets individualism and free enterprise, especially as they concern the land, conservation principles are often unpopular. The professional

land manager has time and again been checked by public unwillingness. In environmental history the tension in a democracy between
the expert and the people is brought front stage and center.

The history of movements to preserve both the natural and historic
parts of the environment is replete with data on the structure of
American thought. In the case of national parks and similar preserves,
we have not sufficiently understood them as reflecting basic assumptions about nature on the one hand and people on the other. Nor are
we fully aware of the national park idea as a unique American contribution to world civilization. Comparative studies of the preservation of nature and wildlife in various nations seem certain to reveal
significant information about the cultures involved. As for historic
preservation, there is no finer gauge of a country's attitude toward
its past than its custodianship of tangible documents. The restoration
and display of a Colonial home, for example, tells as much about
those who undertook the project as it does about the original builders.

Pursuing environmental history will not be a simple matter. Untangling the meaning of concepts such as garden or wilderness,
determining the significance of the color green, or investigating the
vogue of camping plunge the scholar into complex and deeply rooted
layers of custom, symbol, prejudice, and myth. It is increasingly apparent that the most basic explanations of our attitude and behavior
toward the environment lie not in the four-thousand-year veneer we
smugly call "history" but in the mind-boggling millennia that went
before. As an example, after putting the final draft of *Wilderness and
the American Mind* in press, I was nagged by a feeling that the
hostility toward wild country I described ran further back in time
and in the human psyche than I had assumed. Man's relationship to
wilderness, I now think, is a product of human evolution in a natural
environment. Consider that for millions of years our ancestors dwelt
in trees. They were at home in the forest or jungle—the wilderness.
Consequently there was no dichotomy between these prehumans and
wild country. The creatures that later evolved into men were part
of the wilderness. But approximately fifteen million years ago, anthropologists and geologists tell us, climatic changes began to reduce the
area of forest-jungle in central Africa and other seedbeds of man.
Some apes responded by leaving the arboreal environment for the
open grassland. In the new setting, vision assumed an importance
it lacked in the dense, dark forest. To survive on the plains the

man-apes needed and developed remarkable visual ability. In part this compensated for the superior smell, hearing, speed, and strength of other animals.

It followed that early man preferred an open environment, where he could employ his vision and his brain, to the shadowy wilderness. In the forest keen sight was of little advantage; there the race usually went to the smellers, the hearers, and the physically powerful. Thus once man had forsaken the wilderness he was loath to return to an environment that stripped him of his ability to see. For the same reason he feared the night. Conversely, he preferred openness—a room with a view. At night he sought the security of a cave and, in time, of fire which I do not think has been sufficiently understood as an aid to vision as well as a means of warming and cooking.

Millions of years of life in open places stamped a bias against wilderness on the mind of early man and man himself. This attitude ran so deep that it proved difficult to erase even after the advent of civilization. The instinctive fear of forest and night persisted. It is evident, for instance, in the experience of man in North America. In the thick forest of the Atlantic coast he felt uneasy. The wilderness hemmed him in, frustrating his vision and seeming to conceal a host of dangers both real and imaginary. The pioneers spoke of this environment as "dark" and "gloomy"; they rejoiced when the oppressive trees were removed and light flooded the clearing, giving them the security of sight. This bringing of light into darkness by transforming wilderness into pastoral land was inevitably used as a metaphor to express the advance of Christianity on a pagan continent. Everywhere in early North American letters one finds this Manichean orientation, with wilderness on the side of devils, demons, and darkness.

It is interesting to note that many accounts of westward migration in North America contain expressions of relief upon emerging from the Eastern greenwood wilderness to the openness of the Great Plains. All at once the pioneer could *see*, and his spirits brightened immediately. In rhapsodic language, accounts such as James Hall's *Notes on the Western States* (1838) described the waving grass, the profusion of flowers, the brilliant sunshine. The plains, to be sure, were just as devoid of civilization as the Eastern forest, but from the pioneers' perspective they were a different kind of environment. The term "wilderness" was seldom applied to the grassland of the Midwest; "garden," on the other hand, was frequently used. In a way, the emergence from forest to plains in North America repeated the process of fifteen million years before, that resulted in tree-dwelling apes becoming both plains-dwellers and the ancestors of man.

If the suggestion is valid that man instinctively fears wilderness, it should explain present attitudes. I mean that in spite of a growing appreciation of wild country, some remnants of the old bias should persist. And I think they do, even if unconsciously, in our environmental preferences. Why, for example, do sites with views bring higher prices on the real estate market? One could say it is simply a matter of aesthetics or happiness or prestige, but, probing deeper, perhaps the *reason* for these feelings is related to the ancient association of security with seeing, and consequently with views. The same predilection for openness influences our choice of camping sites. Isn't it true that we prefer meadows and lake shores and riverbanks and ridge tops? Don't we avoid camping in the dark, dense forest, the old wilderness, when we can? I may be more primitive than most, but I have always felt vaguely oppressed and discomfited when obliged to camp in deep woods. I noticed, before I understood, how vision and security are linked. Untangling this attitude is one of the challenges of environmental history.

There was a time, not long ago, when literature, folklore, and art were generally unrecognized as valuable tools for the study of history. Gradually scholars learned how to use these rich sources of evidence. In time the sophisticated analysis of novels and legend, as well as art criticism, found an important place in the revolution of historical documentation. Environmental criticism will be one of the next frontiers.

The Economic History of the United States in the Twentieth Century

DOUGLAS F. DOWD

"The generation since 1945 has . . . been brought up amid institutional and international problems. If this is the case, perhaps economic history must broaden its traditional scope." Thus Thomas C. Cochran, when ten years ago he was asked to speak to the present topic for the Economic History Association.[1] The "institutional and international problems" that became evident between 1945 and 1959 have of course broadened and deepened, both at home and abroad, and there is nothing about which we care—the economy, the university, the polity, the family, religion and morality, the young, our cities, the relationships between the races, peace—that is not now imbedded in crisis, lurching along paths that lead we know not where. Is it irrelevant to our condition that the social sciences, and among them economic history, have since 1945, and even more since Professor Cochran issued his muted warning, narrowed, not broadened, their scope? It is with these matters and questions in mind that I would like to evaluate the economic historiography of our country in this century.

Let me acknowledge, or rather assert, at the outset that of course this is not the only legitimate focus for an essay on the economic history of the United States in the twentieth century. A substantial amount of valuable work has been done in this century by economic historians of the United States, work whose value is measured only in part by the fact that the larger and undone tasks cannot be accomplished without leaning on it. Especially since the mid-1930's, economists with a historical approach have provided us with numerous studies of particular firms, industries, sectors, and regions, and of particular unions, labor markets, financial institutions, and patterns of foreign trade and finance. Those who wish an efficient compendium of such works up to 1959 will find them noted by Professor Cochran in the essay cited above, and they may be assured that the quantity of such works has greatly increased in the past decade, without any diminution in quality.

But one may also be assured that such works do not speak to our condition. What is that condition? And, if economic historians have failed to speak to it adequately, is this because such an accomplishment is not within their abilities, not part of their mandate, or something else? Let me turn to the latter questions first, before examining what I have called our condition, and before making suggestions as to what kinds of work are thus urgently required. What will emerge will be much more in the nature of a polemic than a review essay; but it is a polemic we require if there is to be much of anything worth reviewing in the future.

As a way of beginning, it may be noted that the very category "economic historian" points to one corner of the problem. In an essay as delightful as it is incisive, J. H. Hexter has written of the proclivity of historians to "split the past into a series of tunnels, each continuous from the remote past to the present, but practically self-contained at every point and sealed off from contact with or contamination by anything that was going on in any of the other tunnels."[2] He went on in the same vein to decry the use of "factors" as tools of historical explanation, and saw the factor approach as having its main source in the various tunnels. If all this conjures up visions of moles tunneling blindly (and happily?) in directions that bear little or no promise of ever intersecting, and using as their instruments the sharp teeth that the varieties of moles—economic, social, political, military, and so forth—have, then that is the appropriate vision to contemplate. It is also appropriate to remember that when moles do surface they are helpless; they have the defects of their virtues.

What Hexter has to say about historians in general may be said *a fortiori* of those economic historians who have been trained as economists. This species of tunnel historians is by its training inclined to partial equilibrium analysis, which means not only that its habitat is a tunnel but that its inclination is to burrow in tiny branches and sub-branches of the main. Thus, an economic historian will commonly be found confining his attention to the specifically "economic" processes and relationships in a given time period, and within that to one particular market, industry, firm, or relationship (which satisfies his partial equilibrium itch); and even more, he will usually emphasize the importance of one factor of production—e.g., labor, capital, resources—in the "determination" of the process. The full implications of this sort of investigative process unhappily need not be left to speculation; they are available for study in the work of the so-called Cliometricians. These "new economic historians" emerged from their tunnels through apertures that might be thought of as underground silos, and they have lifted off, bright and shiny, into outer space. There they orbit and would do no harm were it not that much of the training of oncoming economic historians is in their hands.

As yet, in my own reading, the social astronauts have done no work on the twentieth century, despite the fact that the paucity of data is severely limiting for the earlier periods they have chosen to study. This gives a daring quality to what they do, which may or may not be fortuitous here, as with real astronauts. Soon, however, they and their students may be expected to take heed of the obvious: or, to put it more usefully, econometricians who deal with questions of this century are likely to find Cliometrics an engaging way to extend their studies into what they will see as a historical perspective.

I dwell this long on the Cliometricians not because they are villains, which, as honorable men, they are not; but because they represent in extreme and extended form the manner in which the training of economists shapes the methodology of economic historians. The latter tend quite naturally to ask the kinds of questions that economists ask and to ask them in the economist's way. If we are looking for methodological shortcomings, we must therefore look to the disciplines, and to the compartmentalization and departmentalization of disciplines, from which such qualities have sprung—a point that was central to Hexter in the essay noted above. In short, if we are to make critical comments on the training, the methodology, and the output of economic historians, we shall soon find ourselves peering mostly not into the corner where economic historians dwell, but into the entire structure and functioning of the higher learning in the social sciences.

That structure is one aptly characterized as a network of specializations with, as time goes on, ever finer threads being added to the network. Given our world, and its desperate need for social understanding, it may be imagined that at some time—and some would guess that the time is already upon us—the network will sunder and disintegrate. If that is so, it will be because our network of specializations, functional though it may or may not have been in the past, has now become disfunctional. To say that, and to support it, requires that we ask not only what trained minds have done and how they have done it, but what they have not done and why they have not. In turn, this requires that we ask questions about the institutional stimuli that impinge upon the universities, the social functions they perform, and the prime beneficiaries of what ensues.

It is a commonplace that the universities, from their medieval beginnings to the present, have substantially reflected, and in subtle or obvious ways served, the society within which they have subsisted. How subtle or obvious that relationship has been is clearly a matter not so much of the importance of the relationship but of the degree to which it is or is not called into question; and that is a matter of whether or not and to what degree the general performance of the society is called into question. It is also a commonplace, or should be if it is not, that the universities have been at once a prime source of subversion and an important bastion of conservatism in society. The subversion has issued from developments in science and technology, most especially in the more recent past; the conserving function has been performed by the social sciences and the humanities. Would that more had been conserved; but would, also, that more had been subverted. To put it more clearly, would that the social sciences had found ways of understanding which would have allowed technological change, institutional change, and the quality of life all to move along together in balance with each other and with an acceptable notion of the *summum bonum*. A bit of everything happens, of course; but one cannot help being impressed with how what has been conserved has created problems by its persistence, and being frightened by how little we really know of how to cope with either the problems or the possibilities posed by rapidly changing technologies.

The social scientists (I shall not comment one way or another on the humanists) have neglected their proper function, and we shall have no chance to find out what difference it might have made if they had not. In any case, we now have a society which is being called into question from all sides—but least of all, it should be noted, by social scientists, who go about finding ways of making the existing system work better. There is an alternative, and it begins by asking a different set of questions in a different mood: How does the society work, where "work" means who gains and who loses? What is gained and lost? What are the dynamics at work, and how and why? Science is critical, or it is not science. To be scientific a social scientist must be a social critic, if for no other reason than that a scientific approach to society should take no institutions as given, nothing as beyond critical examination. Values should define our ends; not the preservation of particular institutions.

None of this is meant to be *ad hominem*. We are concerned with a *social* phenomenon, which is to say that the behavior of social scientists must be approached institutionally, for the social sciences are themselves an institution. Veblen traveled this road long ago when he began to wonder what was wrong in the universities, and to explain the at best tame and at worst misleading and dangerous contributions of the social sciences.

> Distempered critics have even alleged that the academic leaders in the social sciences are held under some constraint, as being, in some sort, in the pay of the well-to-do conservative element. . . . Now it may be conceded without violence to notorious facts, that these official leaders of science do commonly reach conclusions innocuous to the existing law and order, particularly with respect to religion, ownership, and the distribution of wealth. But this need imply no constraint, nor even any peculiar degree of tact, much less a moral obliquity . . . [for they] are free to give the fullest expression to any conclusions or convictions to which their inquiries may carry them. That they are able to do so is a fortunate circumstance, due to the fact that their intellectual horizon is bounded by the same limits of commonplace insight and preconceptions as are the prevailing opinions of the conservative middle class.[3]

When Veblen's approach is trained on economics, we find that both before and since his time economists have come to conclusions that are not only innocuous to the status quo but frequently useful—to the status quo, as distinct from social understanding. Some apparent exceptions to this generalization will be noted shortly, but we may say here that they strengthen rather than weaken the rule, and for the moment set them aside.

The nature and the focus of contemporary economics finds its principal origins in late nineteenth-century Britain, as it finds its principal questions for analysis the questions whose answers were most needed by the businesslike society of Great Britain. Naturally, what we can learn is limited by the questions we ask; of those things we place outside our framework, those things we take as given, we can learn nothing. What was set aside by the British theorists were all those matters that have to do with institutional and technological change— the very matters, you will note, that make up the heart of social change —and what was examined were those matters that, viewed most abstractly, made for efficiency. The resulting body of analysis came to be preoccupied with *partial* equilibrium models, to the point that when *whole* economies found themselves in dire straits—e.g., Great Britain throughout the 1920's, and all the industrial capitalist economies in the 1930's—economics not only found itself unable to explain what was happening but was led for an excruciatingly long moment to deny the reality of what was happening: was it not theoretically impossible? Thus it was that Keynes, in the preface to his pathbreaking *General Theory* (1936), was led to say that his was an "attempt by an economist to bring to an issue the deep divergences of opinion between fellow economists which have for the time being almost destroyed the practical influence of economic theory, and will, until they are resolved, continue to do so." And later, "the difficulty lies, not in the new ideas, but in escaping from the old ones, which ramify, for those brought up as most of us have been, into every corner of our minds." [4]

What was remarkable about Keynesian theory was not that it was a source of considerable controversy within the profession and as between the profession and the business community, but that the larger implications and possibilities of the new theoretical departure were so soon placed once more back into the methodological cocoon that insulates economics from the fundamental thrusts of institutional and technological change. As for the early controversy, not only economists but politicians and businessmen today assert: "We are all Keynesians now." The New Economics, in short, has been housebroken.

However, just as pre-Keynesian economics was irrelevant to the economic crisis of the interwar years, so too is contemporary economics largely irrelevant or even misleading for the social crisis of today— in our own country, and as regards our country in the world. If there are substantial differences between economics and the other social sciences, one would have to say that our irrelevancy is more elegant, more sophisticated than that in the other social sciences. All this is nicely reflected in economic history, and best of all in the new economic history.

Earlier, some exceptions to these melancholy observations were mentioned as requiring discussion. The discussion need only be brief. Departures from the focus and the method of neo-classical economics have taken place, some of them seeking to speak out to our present condition. But to the degree that they have been undertaken by conventionally trained economists, using the tools they have learned to use, they have added considerably more in the way of incoherence to economics than an understanding of the place and meaning of economic affairs in our society. The *theory* that economics has developed—micro- and macroeconomics—possesses whatever relevance it has only for advanced economies,[5] and only for those aspects of the performance of advanced economies that have to do with achieving short-run efficiency and stability.

Some economists think they are providing meaningful analyses of growth; but that must be questioned. They are providing models of growth, assuming that neither institutional nor technological change takes place. When one moves from such assumptions, he is in the complex and widely misunderstood area of economic development—a veritable jungle of concepts, "theories," assumptions, and methods—whose results tempt one to believe that the people of the world would be better off if economists would stay in bed. As for the problem areas cited earlier—race, poverty, the economy (yes, the economy), our cities—that are clearly close to the concerns of economists, not to mention those other areas (the polity, the university, the young, peace) that seem distant but cannot be said to be so in the absence of a systematic understanding of how society moves and changes—as for all these, what has the economist told us that can be trusted, and be the basis for intelligent decisions?

Such churlish questions take me back to economic history. I am not one who believes that social scientists and historians should look at the day's headlines and plunge into examination of the connected matters in their own disciplines. Indeed, I complained above because that is just what many have been doing, and doing so badly. What is essential, as was earlier suggested, is an ever-richer understanding of how society moves and changes. If we possessed, having developed, even a modest part of such understanding, we might not be so surprised at the headlines, nor would we find so much occasion for shock. Social understanding is not necessary for some one group or faction; it is necessary for all who wish to behave responsibly in their society, whatever the star that guides them.

It is asking too much, but also just enough, to suggest that social

scientists consider explicitly whom they are serving. Economists of
the neoclassical persuasion were serving the needs of the business
society in which they lived, whatever they may have thought they were
(and are) doing. And in doing that, they contributed to making the
effective dominance of business in society greater than it might otherwise have been. They helped to make the status quo work better. There
is nothing wrong with that, if there is nothing basically wrong with
the status quo. But how are we to know the degree to and the ways
in which there is something wrong with the status quo, except from
(1) the understanding provided by objective (which is not to say
neutral) scholars, or (2) the turbulence caused by those who seek
change as they interact with those who try to stop it? The condition
of our own day is that our knowledge that there is something basically
wrong has come almost exclusively from the turbulence, not from the
accumulated understanding, of our times. Nor is it incautious to believe
that when our sources of information are the cries of the wounded, and
of those who are wounding them, it may well be too late to hope for
processes of change that are both needed and constructive.

When Hegel said that the Owl of Minerva takes wing at twilight,
he was saying that twilight is too late for wisdom and understanding
to hold off the night. There is a hopeful (if also ironic) reservation
we may make about that probability, however. We know so little about
the process of social change that we are genuinely unable to predict
where we are going, and that is to say we really don't know where
we are. Our ignorance may be making us gloomier than the objective
situation—if only we knew what that is—warrants. Where there's life
there's hope. So it may not be too late for social scientists to begin to
provide what society so badly needs: understanding. How might we go
about gaining the kinds of understanding we need, and how different
are they from what we now gain?

My first proposal may be rude enough to deter anyone from paying
attention to anything that follows it. It is that we should seek, in the
words of a British economist, "to be vaguely right rather than precisely
wrong." In different words, our desperate needs are for gross understanding rather than for precise formulation of matters that, whether
we understand them or not, leave us in a sinking boat—in which, to
quote another Britisher, we cannot afford "lectures on navigation while
the ship is going down." Gross understanding of what? And how to
go about gaining it?

I find it promising and intellectually exciting to have as an analytical goal a part in the effort to understand "the place of economic affairs in society," the mundane phrase used earlier. For the economic historian, to understand that place is to understand how economic affairs relate dynamically to what are called noneconomic affairs, over time. This is not as mundane a view as the noneconomist might think. The most recent definition of economics I have seen is the

> . . . study of a society's use of its resources with reference to (1) the extent to which they are used, (2) how efficiently they are used, (3) the choice between competing alternative uses, and (4) the nature and [economic] consequences of changes in productive power over time.[6]

Scarcity, choice, and efficiency, over time. How economic matters relate to society in any systematic or analytic way is excluded, by definition.

The economic historian cannot of course study everything, and he will do well indeed if he is able to study anything well. In turn, that requires that he have a firm notion of what it is he is trying to do, and why, and what part his own work plays in a larger inquiry. Science is cooperative and purposive. Whatever else is needed these days, it is methodological clarity, which requires self-consciousness as to one's purposes. As will be argued later, however, clarity by itself is not enough; we need a guiding analytical framework.

Is it not possible that the methodological confusion so much characterizing the social sciences today is due to an implicit unwillingness to face the question: What am I doing, and why? That necessarily returns one to the question of who and what are being served by the inquiry. Is it not clear that the largest part by far of social science today serves those most who can best afford to pay, and serves those (or that) least that most need help? Those who are served—in business, in government, in the military—are those who have power and who derive it from what exists; they are not much interested in finding a critical analysis of the system, current or historical.

All this does not come down to prostitution, for a prostitute is seldom unclear about the client-servant relationship. Perhaps, just perhaps, this is to say something optimistic; that is, self-consciousness by social scientists could lead many to seek ways of becoming scientific in procedure a well as in name. What might that mean?

What might it mean, specifically, as regards the economic history of the twentieth-century United States? That question takes me back to one posed earlier: What is our present condition? It is a condition we understand only dimly, at best; a condition we would understand considerably better if economic history (and its earlier disciplines) had done their job properly. Let me now be specific on this score, and do so by recalling the "areas" of crisis noted earlier—the economy, the university, the polity, the family, religion and morality, the young, our cities, the relationships between the races, peace.

One need not adhere to a particular political position—be it conservative, liberal, or radical—to read down that list with a deep sense of uneasiness and apprehension concerning the future. Let us assume that at no time in our history has any of these areas been trouble-free. There has been no Golden Age. The compelling characteristic of our day is not that trouble has suddenly arisen here and there, but that the imperfections in each of these areas have become painfully and often turbulently evident, and that in the very recent past all have shown the same signs of crisis. More than that, it is quite clear that crisis in one area meshes with and is intensified by crisis in the others. We are, in short, a society in crisis, living in a world in crisis. Troubles there have always been, to be sure; but it is not historical innocence to argue that there has never been anything quite like this.

Nor is it a new species of economic determinism to argue that both the general dimensions of our crisis, and the means by which it may be resolved, are economic at their center. More specifically, the priority that has been given to economic criteria in our own society, and the manner in which political, sociological, psychological, and ethical considerations have thus been allowed (or been led) to become secondary, have produced the kind of warping in society that might be reasonably expected from such processes.

Fundamental to the ability to bring off such an achievement has been the astounding productivity of modern technology, especially in the last century. The result has been a society that finds it natural and desirable to carry specialization of all functions to undreamed-of heights, and to find its rewards for doing so in material—i.e., quantitatively defined—satisfactions. There is no aspect of social existence that has been left untouched—my own inclination is to say undamaged—by the resulting dominance of quantitative criteria.

Not only, to paraphrase Oscar Wilde, do we know the quantities of everything and the qualities of nothing; we both analyze and attempt to resolve what problems we perceive in quantitative terms. (There was a time when it appeared that, with the help of the Kinsey Report, we were about to make our judgments even on sexual morality by the statistical frequencies of various sexual patterns.) "Science is measurement," we are told by those who believe it; and they are numerous. But even if that were all there is to science—which is not so—it is important (1) to discover what it is that is measured and what left unmeasured, and (2) to inquire as to what motivates the measuring process.

For example, it was not until very recently that economists attempted seriously to measure, even to define, the numbers of poor. When they began, it swiftly became evident that our measuring techniques were (as they are still) inadequate to that task, as it also became evident that the definition of poverty was at the same time narrowly quantitative and largely politic. The economists identify and count the poor, and try to relate their condition to their economic function. They ask who, and how many, and believe they are asking why. But to ask *why* is to ask a question that is simultaneously historical, sociological, political, psychological, economic, and ethical. And it is to do so not with a politic definition, handed down by a government agency, but by human concern. The latter is of course more difficult to frame, cannot help being controversial, and requires explicitness regarding the values of the inquirer. An adequate process of inquiry into poverty would have as its simplest problem that of measurement, and its results would probably include considerably more in the way of qualitative than of quantitative conclusions. It is my own view that the conclusions would also stand as an indictment of our society. And that takes me away from this example and back to an earlier assertion, namely, that both the general dimensions of our crisis and the means of its resolution are economic. (As it is equally clear that for those means to be utilized effectively will require much in the way of political transformation and effort.)

What is meant is both simpler and more complicated than the statement itself suggests. Economic achievement has swept through all corners of society and has been able to do so because it had the brooms of modern technology to clear the way. One consequence is that the social sciences have become varieties of political arithmetic. Another is that older values have been vitiated in practice by redefinition into quantitative terms. Still another consequence has been the widespread recognition that "for the first time in human history enough metabolic and mechanical energy is available to provide high standards of living for everyone in North America almost immediately and everyone in the world within forty years, even considering the population explosion." [7]

A philosopher, not an economist, wrote those words. If he is right, and many of us think he is, a larger question emerges. If modern technology has made these things possible, why is it that none of us really believes that what is possible will take place? Indeed, why do so many of us sit convinced that, far from things moving in desirable directions, they are likely to accelerate in their already fearsome ways? If the answers to such questions are to come forth, they will come forth systematically and convincingly only from trained social scientists, and not least among those making a contribution must be economic historians.

What they will all have to comprehend is the unprecedentedly rapid rate of structural change in this century—structural change within the economy, between the economy and other aspects of life, within those other aspects of life (the "areas" cited above), and as between the United States and the rest of the world. What finally has to be comprehended is the relationship of all those changes to what seems to be our central problem: what is desirable and possible economically is also highly improbable.

Let me cite a few questions that therefore need answering, all of them requiring that the economic historian relate economic to non-economic matters. In this century there has been a vast and rapid rural to urban migration, a decline of agriculture in relative terms in our economy, a rapid growth of cities, and an evident process of deep racial oppression and unrest in, along with the strangulation of, those cities. Students attack the universities for their deadness as academic centers and their liveliness as participants in the military-industrial complex. Students drop out, drug themselves, and turn against their elders and the system as a whole; the family disintegrates. Blacks reject not only white advice but white politics, culture, and standards. The churches are torn from within over questions of authority and ethics, and the referent of the latter comes down to those other matters cited, and what stance the religious should have regarding them.

None of these developments can be explained by examining only economic affairs. But can any of them be explained without taking heavy account of our economic development? And can our economic development be understood without taking due account of changing structures and relationships between the economy and politics, education, demography, ethical transformation, and so forth? How, for example, did the term "military-industrial complex" become transformed from a startling expression, less than a decade ago, into an accepted and basic characteristic of American society? And what are the historical roots of that development, its relationships with racial, university, and other problems?

Such questions cannot be pursued effectively without guiding hypotheses, an analytical framework, and theory. Must we begin from scratch in those regards, or can we, by taking our purposes firmly in hand, find substantial assistance in what has already been thought and done? I believe the more optimistic assessment is the correct one, if we understand its implications.

The first among these is neither the most difficult nor the simplest. It is that we become conscious of our purposes, and that those purposes be the understanding of society as a means of allowing us to find ways to realize fundamental values. Are those values impossible to state, in such a way as to achieve widespread agreement? Perhaps; but among social scientists we might at worst find contending groups, a resolution healthier and more promising than the current state of indifference or superficial agreement. The group in which I would find myself would seek a working combination of the following: democracy, freedom, equality, material well-being, peace, and a society encouraging individual creativity and diversity, with a wide dispersion of power. To make the position clear, I do not believe that any of these, let alone their combination, may be found in the United States today, except superficially and restrictively. Just as I am sure that many social scientists would honestly disagree with my position on such matters, I am equally sure that many would not. I should like to work with the latter, but the present state of the social sciences, far from encouraging such cooperation, denies the need for it.

Second among the implications of doing important, essential, and effective work is the need to take what social theory we have that suits our purposes and test it, elaborate it, understand it, and modify its assumptions for current conditions. For some this might mean Marxian, for others Veblenian, for others Freudian, and for still others Parsonian and Weberian theories—to mention no others, of which there are doubtless many. We cannot expect a social genius to appear, that being something modern society is least likely to produce; we can expect that extant theories can be examined critically, combined, even abandoned, with serious testing.

Third, what is meant by testing? The trite observation that the laboratory of the social scientist is the past is no less true for being trite. But that notion does not exclude the "present" any more than it sets aside any particular time or place in the past as the location of the laboratory. What does determine the time and the location of historical inquiry for these purposes is just that: our purposes. Thus I do not believe that twentieth-century America can be understood without studying that time and place; but neither is it plausible to expect adequate understanding of twentieth-century America by study-ing only that time and place. Whatever else the uses of history may be, they are the laboratory of the social scientist in a very special sense: History does not of course repeat itself; but a study of different times and places asking the same kinds of questions does allow us to know what kinds of key relationships to explore in other times and places (including our own), assuming we know what we are trying to understand.

If I may be forgiven a personal example to illustrate the foregoing, I have found it illuminating to study fourteenth-century Lombardy, thirteenth-century Bologna, and parts of nineteenth-century Europe in terms of one large, but still particular, relationship; and I have been motivated to do so by a tentative hypothesis. The relationship is that between the sources, structure, and uses of power on the one hand, and the interacting process of economic development on the other. I have been led to study such relationships under the guidance of social theory (Marx and Veblen, mostly) and with the stimulus of what I take to be a central problem of our own time—namely, the growing struggle in all quarters between the powerful and the powerless, and the manner in which that relates to economic affairs. If I have come to any conclusions they are mostly that the relationships I study have yet to be understood by anyone, let alone myself, that their under-standing is vital to *any* understanding of society, that such understand-ing requires the cooperative work of people trained in the other social sciences, and, finally, that such an inquiry is very promising—as part of a still larger inquiry into the processes of social change.

I begged your forgiveness for relating this personal history for the usual reasons of modesty, but also for a more important reason. I do not believe that my way is the only way, let alone the best way, for others. I do believe, however, that it is the best way for me, and an instance of the kind of thing others might find suitable, if any or all of us are to get a solid grip on the process of understanding how society moves and changes, with what problems and possibilities—given our values.

For social scientists, and among them economic historians, to move along the suggested lines would constitute and require a reconstruction of a large part of the field. But if, as seems clear, our society is in need of reconstruction, what more is being said than that now—as always—the university reflects and serves the society?

NOTES

1. "Recent Contributions to Economic History: The United States, The Twentieth Century," *Journal of Economic History*, XIX (March 1959), 64–75.

2. J. H. Hexter, *Reappraisals in History* (New York, 1961), p. 194

3. Thorstein Veblen, *The Higher Learning in America* (New York, 1957), pp. 135–136. Originally published in 1918, the book is understood to have been completed by 1908.

4. John Maynard Keynes, *The General Theory of Employment, Interest, and Money* (New York, 1965), pp. vi and viii.

5. Or for a variety of corporations, trade unions, or government agencies. As the scope of business activities has broadened, e.g., and specialization has narrowed the focus of the economist, the purposes of the former and the methodology of the latter have made for a happy wedding, with society the only loser.

6. Richard G. Lipsey and Peter O. Steiner, *Economics*, 2nd ed. (New York, 1969), p. 9. This is a highly regarded and increasingly popular textbook.

7. Huston Smith, "Like It Is: The University Today," *Key Reporter*, Winter 1968–1969, p. 3.

On Psychohistory

ROBERT JAY LIFTON

Granted there is such a thing as a "psychohistorical approach," can we then speak of a "new psychohistory"? If so we had best be tentative. Historians know well—and psychologists should know—that anything now new will soon be old, and that we often label as new (or New) that which does not yet quite exist. As for psychohistory, it is in one sense already old, and in another hardly born.

None can deny the logic of a marriage between psychology and history. Many writers from both traditions have emphasized their common concern with narrative sequence and with the nature of man's experience in the midst of that sequence. But a certain amount of skepticism about logical marriages (and their offspring) is always in order. And the greater one's commitment to this marriage, the more convinced one becomes of the impossibility—and undesirability—of an easy union.

I

Skepticism, in fact, is as good a principle as any for approaching psychohistory. Most of us involved in the project are not only critical of traditional psychoanalytic views of history but skeptical of the kind of pristine cause and effect—and therefore of the kind of knowledge—claimed by *any* monocausal and hyper-reductive approach to history. Our simple commitment to develop a psychological framework that takes historical currents seriously is itself an act of skepticism toward what I shall soon identify as the ahistorical position of most psychological thought. But this kind of skepticism must be distinguished from the automatic dismissal of all psychological approaches to history—and even from the more subtle dismissal of psychological efforts by insisting that one cannot "really know" anything significant about the minds of men (great or ordinary) of the past, or about the ways in which current individual and collective ideas and emotions connect with wider historical currents.

We are dealing, then, with three levels of skepticism: immediate and total rejection (the assumption that the knowledge sought is unobtainable and the whole enterprise futile); anticipated rejection (the attitude, "You have to show me"; implicitly, "I don't expect or wish to be shown"); and a sense (which I share with a number of colleagues in the enterprise) that the kind of knowledge we seek is extremely refractory, and our methods of seeking it highly vulnerable. This third stance turns out to be in many ways the most skeptical of all.

It is tempting, especially for those with clinical experience, to speak of those forms of skepticism that dismiss out-of-hand, or nearly so, as "resistance." For the term suggests the kind of psychological force and need that can accompany the rejection. But I think the temptation itself should be "resisted," because the word also implies—whether used by classical psychoanalysts or Protestant evangelists or Chinese thought-reformers—that there is a true direction or intention that is ultimately to be accepted, even embraced, once the "resistance" has been overcome. This last assumption, dubious enough when applied to the individual, could be disastrous when applied to history. Moreover, by invoking the term "resistance" one could all too readily fall into the psychologistic fallacy of explaining away criticism by examining critics' involvements and needs, thereby avoiding any consideration of the weaknesses of that which is being criticized.

Yet the psychological approach to history does cause discomfort, because it entails formidable problems in method, and because, for many working in both traditions and in other branches of social thought, it threatens to undermine explicit concepts and implicit images about how men behave, why societies change, and what constitutes an acceptable professional discipline or "field." We are all, in other words, formatively bound by our own psychohistorical "place," and by our activity in that place. And so we should be, at least to a point, if our skepticism is to be rooted as well as fertile.

But what are the impediments? Why is it so difficult for psychology and history to get together? Generally speaking, I would say that not only do the two traditions often work at cross-purposes; worse, each has something of an impulse to eliminate the other. And this is so even if we limit our observations to depth psychology and to man-centered history.

For instance, there is in classical psychoanalysis an implicit assumption that the larger historical universe is *nothing but* a manifestation of the projections or emanations of the individual psyche. Or if not that, history is seen as a kind of featureless background for those projections and emanations—something "out there" which is "given," but which does not significantly influence what is "in here." The emergence, over the past few decades, of a more developed "ego psychology" has somewhat altered the situation by directing our attention to the influence of the environment on the development of the self. But, as Erikson has pointed out, the grudging and impoverished terms used in the psychoanalytic approach to the environment reveal the approach itself to have remained grudging and impoverished. Ego psychology, moreover, has had very little to say about shifts in social ethos central to historical change, especially those related to the new technological environment and its destructive capacities.

Neo-Freudian psychoanalysis has been ahistorical in other ways. More open to the influence of environment, it has for the most part failed to evolve compelling general principles in the social sphere. And where it has actively sought such principles, as in the work of Abram Kardiner, it has tended to view a culture or a society as a more or less cross-sectional entity within which one can study the relationship of social institutions and "basic personality," but not as evolving phenomena whose relationship is importantly defined by change.[1] Neo-Freudian psychoanalysis thus still finds itself, as much as or at times even more than the Freudian tradition it rebelled against, bound by certain limitations of the rationalistic and mechanistic imagery of the nineteenth-century world view. And when psychoanalysis has moved in a phenomenological or existential direction, its intrapsychic insights, however valuable, have tended to be insulated from historical issues.

Historical writing, about which I can speak with considerably less authority, seems (perhaps somewhat analogously) to replace a psychological perspective with commonsense assumptions about human motivation, or else to drown psychological man—that is, the inner life of individual man—in a sea of collectivity.

And yet there is much evidence of a longing from both sides for some kind of union—of widely shared recognition that psychological man lives in a history extending beyond himself, and that history is bound up with conflicts and struggles within the minds of men. Indeed, these two simple principles form the basis for a contemporary psychohistory.

II

I have suggested that the general idea of a psychological approach to history is by no means new. But rather than attempt to document comprehensively the various efforts that have been made in the name of that idea, I would like to focus upon four models (really paradigms) of psychohistory, all of which have emerged in some relationship to the psychoanalytic tradition. Two of them are Freudian, and the other two both draw upon Freud and move away from his historical assumptions.

Freud's most fundamental historical model is not really historical at all, but is rather a *pre*historical paradigm: the primeval encounter between father and sons, in which the sons rebel against the father's authority and kill him, with the entire encounter psychologically centered on the Oedipus complex. This model was first put forward in *Totem and Taboo* (1912–1913) as an explanation for the origins of society itself; and then again in modified form toward the end of Freud's life in *Moses and Monotheism* (1934–1938), to account for the origins of Jewish religion and Jewish identity—for how, as Freud put it, the "one man, the man Moses . . . created the Jews." Freud saw Moses as a kind of foster-father, an Egyptian who "chose" the Jews as his people and gave to them the gift of monotheism, only to be eventually rejected and murdered by his "chosen people," his symbolic sons.

As Philip Rieff has pointed out, the model here is that of "a certain event, or events, necessarily in remote rather than near history—indeed, at the beginning—become[ing] determinative of all that must follow." Rieff suggests that Freud was influenced by certain facets of Judeo-Christian millennial thought and of German historicism, according to which one crucial Event determines and explains all subsequent, and even previous, history. The principle is that of *Kairos,* of the "decisive moment," as opposed to that of *Chronos,* the more orderly sequence of qualitatively identical units of "mathematical time." Freud's historical Event can be said to be a mythical one—the primeval murder of the father, as allegedly reenacted in the Jews' murder of Moses. But it is also individual-psychological, in the sense of being a product of the Oedipus complex, which is seen as the ultimate source of these decisive occurrences. Indeed, one could view Freud's overall historical method as a kind of apologia for the Oedipal Event.[2]

Now there are powerful insights in the two books expressed around this prehistorical encounter, insights that center upon the psychological significance of the perceived historical past for both present and future, and for the movement of history itself. And I shall soon suggest ways in which this model has nourished more recent psycho-historical approaches. But since since the model is a mythic one which transcends history as such, it can be profoundly misleading when used to explain specific historical events. (I have in mind particularly a current vogue among psychoanalytic and psychoanalytically minded observers of viewing recent student rebellions as little more than a repetition of the primeval rebellion of enraged sons against their fathers, as a rebellion explained by—and reducible to—the Oedipus complex. The explanation happens to be congenial to those in author-ity, the symbolic [or as I prefer, formative] fathers involved. But it totally neglects the larger historical currents that so forcibly intrude upon the psyches of young and old alike, and therefore misrepresents both the individual-psychological and the group processes at play.) For within Freud's prehistoric paradigm there is bequeathed to us an iron mold of psychological repetition (or "repetition-compulsion"), enveloping indiscriminately the individual and the undifferentiated collectivity. When this principle of repetition is seen as the essence of historical experience, there can be nothing new in history; indeed, if (in Rieff's paraphrase of Freud) "history is predestination," then there is no history.

The second Freudian paradigm is perhaps the more obvious one, the one most likely to come to mind when people think of a psychoana-lytic approach to history: that of individual psychopathology. The best known example here is the Freud-Bullitt biography of Woodrow Wilson,[3] a work which Bullitt almost certainly wrote but which ex-emplifies the Freudian approach to history more than many present-day followers of Freud would care to admit. In language and quality of thought, the Wilson biography is a vulgarization of the Freudian para-digm—Freud himself never wrote without elegance. But the idea of interpreting the outcomes of major historical events as expressions of the individual psychopathology of a particular national leader—in this case Wilson's struggles with masculinity and his need to fail—was prefigured in Freud's own work. I have in mind not only his treatment of men like Leonardo and Dostoevsky (as great artists rather than political leaders), but also Freud's general focus upon individual psychopathology as existing more or less apart from history. When this second paradigm dominates, psychopathology becomes a substitute for the psychohistorical interface. The psychopathological idiom for individual development (so prominent in the literature of psychoanalysis) becomes extended to the point where it serves as the idiom for history, or psychohistory. When this happens there is, once more, no history.

These two Freudian paradigms—the prehistorical confrontation and the leader's individual psychopathology—come together in their assumption that, in one way or another, history represents the intrapsychic struggles of the individual writ large: the same intrapsychic struggles that can be observed by the psychoanalyst in his therapeutic work. For instance, the scenario of *Totem and Taboo* includes not only the murderous rebellion against the father and the consuming of the father in the totem feast, but the subsequent remorse and residual guilt of the sons, and of their sons and daughters ad infinitum, which then reasserts itself periodically in the phenomenon of the "return of the repressed." * The entire argument derives from an individual-psychological model; and precisely the "return of the repressed" becomes the basis for Freud's view of history as psychological recurrence. And in the individual-psychopathological model, it is the *aberration* of a specific person that is writ large as historical explanation.

No wonder, then, that Freudian models are frustrating to the historian: they interpret but avoid history. They are equally problematic for the historically minded psychologist. On the one hand Freud's clinical method, as many have pointed out, is entirely historical: it works on the assumption that a man automatically reveals his personal history if he merely lets his mind wander freely, that is, if he engages in free association. And Freud's fundamental discoveries—of the significance of man's individual and collective past—provide the basis for psychohistory. Yet on the other hand these same Freudian principles, when applied with closed-system finality, tend to reduce history

---

* I shall not discuss the question of *how* this guilt is transmitted through the generations, or the problems surrounding the Lamarckian position on inheritance of acquired characteristics which Freud held to throughout his work.

to *nothing but recurrence* (or "repetition-compulsion") and thereby to eliminate virtually all that is innovative, or even accumulative, in the story of man.

The Faustian intellectual temptation is to dismiss the paradox and make things simple—either by direct and uncritical application of classical Freudian terms to all manner of historical events, or else by pretending that neither Freud nor the emotional turmoil he described (and himself stimulated) has ever existed. We do better, I am certain, to embrace the paradox. For it can be energizing.

III

Erik Erikson has done just that. He has retained a focus upon the individual—the great man—and upon the kinds of inner conflicts illuminated by the Freudian tradition. But he has placed the great man within a specific historical context: hence the model of *the great man in history*. With Erikson's elaboration of this paradigm something approaching a new psychohistory began to take shape.

Erikson's *Young Man Luther*,[4] a pivotal work for the psychohistorical enterprise, has a direct historical relationship to Freud's *Moses and Monotheism*. Apart from Erikson's connection as a young man with the Freudian circle in Vienna, and his continuing identification of himself as a Freudian, his title is meant to echo Freud's phrase (mentioned earlier) "the man Moses." Freud used that same phrase as his original title for the book he later called *Moses and Monotheism*. I might add that Freud's original subtitle was, "A Historical Novel," which suggests an interesting element of self-irony in relationship to a historical method we must now view as highly dubious (I refer to the kind of evidence Freud used to develop his thesis that Moses was an Egyptian, and that Moses was killed by the Jews). That subtitle has also found another recent echo, probably less intentional—"History as a Novel, The Novel as History"—the subtitle chosen by a promising young existentialist psychohistorian named Norman Mailer for his much-awarded book *Armies of the Night*. The self-irony in juxtaposing history and fiction does not necessarily suggest that either Freud or Mailer lacked belief in his own views, but rather that each felt he was dealing with a kind of truth that took him beyond conventional historical description. Rather than truth stranger than fiction, each was suggesting a form of fictionalized truth, or perhaps fiction truer than truth.

Returning to Erikson, there are other ways in which his concept of the great man parallels Freud's. At the end of *Moses,* Freud said, "The great man influences his contemporaries in two ways: through his personality and through the idea for which he stands"—an "idea" which may "lay stress on an old group of wishes in the masses, or point to a new aim for their wishes." Freud saw Moses as having taken the Jews to a "higher level of spirituality," largely by means of the "dematerializing" of God and the prohibiting of the worship of a visible form of God. Similarly, Erikson saw as Luther's fundamental achievement his "new emphasis on man in *inner* conflict and his salvaton through introspective perfection"—an achievement and an emphasis Erikson compared with Kierkegaard's existentialism and Freud's psychoanalysis. Freud and Erikson both depicted the great man as a spiritual hero, as a man who achieves an intrapsychic breakthrough.

But Erikson also took several crucial steps away from Freud. Instead of an instinctual idiom—Freud's view of the great man as appealing to instinctual wishes (particularly aggressive ones) and possessing the ability to bring about in the masses a form of "instinctual renunciation" (control of aggression and "subordina[tion of] sense perception to abstract ideas")—Erikson has sought out more specifically *historical* ground, the intersection of individual and collective histories. Luther's achievement, then, depends not so much upon instinctual renunciation as upon a quality Erikson sees Luther, Gandhi, and Freud to have all shared: "a grim willingness to do the dirty work of their ages."

That "dirty work," though clearly involved with psychological universals, is historically specific. "We cannot lift a case history out of history," Erikson also tells us. And he feels constrained to ask of himself and of his readers the kind of immersion he imagines Luther to have had in such early sixteenth-century matters confronting the young German aspirant to the priesthood as the contradictions between ideal Catholic spirituality and the "high spiritual finance" of monetary purchase of immortality through the practice of indulgences, the influence of Occamism in Catholic theology, the prevailing child-rearing practices and standards of family (especially father-son) relationships, the discipline of monastic training, and the complexities of the Catholic response to the Renaissance. In all this we leave behind Freud's concept of the traumatic historical event, followed by repression, and then by the "return of the repressed" in the form of guilt and conflict. We concern ourselves instead with the great man's monumental struggles at the border of religion and politics, with his simultaneous effort to remake himself and his world. For Luther to emerge from his own identity crisis, he had to bring about a shift in the historical identity of his epoch. He had to engage in a desperate effort "to lift his individual patienthood to the level of the universal one, and to try to solve for all what he could not solve for himself alone."

By "patienthood" Erikson (here following Kierkegaard) means exemplar of ultimate alternatives. And one of the extraordinary qualities of Erikson's rendition of the young Luther is the book's painstaking exploration of the very tenuous psychic boundaries between identity crisis, psychosis, theological innovation, and individual and historical revitalization. What Erikson has demonstrated—in this study of Luther as in his more recent book on Gandhi—is a combination of psychoanalytic sensitivity and historical imagination. The combination has been long in coming.

IV

But the great man tends to be inaccessible, at least to direct interview, or if accessible not yet great. One must usually approach him through records, or, if he belongs to recent history, through interviews with surviving friends and followers. This does not mean that the psychohistorian cannot say useful things on the basis of careful observations from a distance. But when he is centuries removed from the individual he wishes to study in depth, problems of historical reconstruction are inevitable.

Freud faced these problems with the cavalier grandiosity of a genius —as one particularly memorable footnote in _Moses and Monotheism_ makes clear.

I am very well aware that in dealing so autocratically and arbitrarily with Biblical tradition—bringing it up to confirm my views when it suits me and unhesitatingly rejecting it when it contradicts me—I am exposing myself to serious methodological criticism and weakening the convincing force of my arguments. But this is the only way in which one can treat material of which one knows definitely that its trustworthiness has been severely impaired by the distorting influence of tendentious purposes. It is to be hoped that I shall find some degree of justification later on, when I come upon the track of these secret motives. Certainty is in any case unattainable and moreover it may be said that every other writer on the subject has adopted the same procedure.[5]

While one cannot but admire Freud's honesty and boldness, the method seems a somewhat dubious one for the aspiring psychohistorian.

Erikson is much more careful with his historical data, but he too runs into difficulties. For instance, he is forced to re-create certain psychological themes of Luther's early family life on the basis of very limited evidence. Problems have also been raised about events in Luther's adult life, notably his celebrated "fit in the choir" during which he made his dramatic statement of negation of identity: "I am *not!*" Erikson himself points out that it is not known whether "Martin roared in Latin or in German," and others have questioned whether he roared at all—that is, whether the episode actually took place.

Apart from specific problems of reconstruction, there is the larger question of the extent to which any individual, great or otherwise, can exemplify an entire historical epoch—or even (as in Erikson's treatment of Luther) its major collective psychological struggles. The question takes on special force during our unprecedentedly diverse and fickle century, no less so if raised in connection with the past.

Hence the emergence of another recent approach: that of *shared psychohistorical themes,* as observed in men and women exposed to particular kinds of individual and collective experience. Examples here are Kenneth Keniston's studies of alienated, and then activist, American students; and Robert Coles's work with children and adults in the midst of racial antagonism and social change.[6] I have been much concerned with the development of this method and ask indulgence for discussing it in relationship to my own work.

I have conducted interview studies of three specific groups of people whose historical exposures seemed to me to have bearing on important characteristics of our era: Chinese and Westerners who underwent Chinese thought reform (or "brainwashing"); Japanese university students during the early sixties; and Hiroshima survivors of the atomic bomb.[7] My focus has been upon themes, forms, and images that are in significant ways shared, rather than upon the life of a single person as such.

The shared-themes approach is based upon a psychoanalytically derived stress upon what goes on inside of people. But, as compared with Erikson's great-man paradigm, it moves still further from classical analytic tradition. That is, it moves outward from the individual in the direction of collective historical experience. It explicitly rejects the nineteenth-century scientific model of man as a mechanism propelled by quantities of energy—energy internally generated by means of instinctual drives, partially held in check by certain defense mechanisms (notably repression), but eventually erupting in the form of various actions of the individual directed at his outer environment. This instinctual idiom (and, one may say, world view) gives way to a symbolic and formative one.

The shared-themes approach also requires considerable innovation in interview method. For more than fifteen years I have found myself struggling with modifications of the psychiatric and psychoanalytic interview, in order to approach and understand various kinds of people who have not sought therapeutic help but, on the contrary, have been sought out by me. And sought out not because of any form of psychological disturbance as such, but because of particular experiences they have undergone—experiences which may indeed be (and usually have been) disturbing, but which both they and I see as having wider significance than any individual incapacities, psychological or otherwise. I found myself developing a much freer interview style than that I was taught in my professional training. It remains probing, encouraging the widest range of associations, and includes detailed life histories and explorations of dreams. But it focuses upon the specific situation responsible for bringing the two of us (most of the interviews have been individual ones) together, and takes the form of something close to an open dialogue emerging from that situation.

The relationship we develop is neither that of doctor and patient nor of ordinary friends, though at moments it can seem to resemble either. It is more one of shared exploration—mostly of the world of the person sought out * but including a great deal of give-and-take,

*We have no good term for the person in this situation. The traditional one, "research subject," seems increasingly unsatisfactory to me because it suggests someone merely "studied" or "investigated" in a more or less passive way. "Patient" is entirely inappropriate, and "client" is not much better. "Historical actor" and "pivotal person" come closer, but they have their own ambiguities. I believe there will be a number of new terms developed, and also new methods of investigation and interview (we already depend, to a much greater extent than my discussion indicates, upon group interviews and a host of other informal approaches) which capture, in *active ways,* lived history. I would go so far as to say that progress in psychohistory depends upon these innovations in method. Once developed in the study of contemporary matters, such innovations could also be applied to the study of the past, though mainly in relationship to the search for and interpretation of various kinds of records and documents.

and more than a little discussion of my own attitudes and interests. It requires, in other words, a combination of humane spontaneity and professional discipline. Needless to say, one's way of combining the two is always idiosyncratic, and always less than ideal.

The method I am describing is partly empirical (in its stress upon specific data from interviews); partly phenomenological, or, as I prefer, formative (in its stress upon forms and images that are simultaneously individual and collective); and partly speculative (in its use of interview data, together with many other observations, to posit relationships between man and his history, and to suggest concepts that eliminate the artificial separation of the two). In this speculation the investigator has the advantage of beginning from concrete information that is a product of his own direct perceptions. Recognizing that subjective distortion can render the advantage a mixed one, so can it be said that exaggerated concerns with detached objectivity have too often caused us to undervalue what can be learned of history from our direct perceptions.

Within this perspective, all shared behavior is seen as simultaneously involved in a trinity of universality (that which is related to the psychobiological quests of all men in all historical epochs), specific cultural emphasis and style (as evolved by a particular people over centuries), and recent and contemporary historical influences (the part of the trinity most likely to be neglected in psychological work). My point is that any shared event is all of these. The weighting of the components may vary, but nothing is *purely* universal, or cultural-historical, or contemporary-historical; everything is all three. The over-all approach, or at least my sense of it, is most fundamentally influenced by Freud and Erikson, but also by Susanne Langer and Ernst Cassirer, Otto Rank, Albert Camus, Lancelot Law Whyte, David Riesman, and R. G. Collingwood; and by Leslie Farber, Kenneth Keniston, Benjamin Schwartz, and Philip Rieff.

V

Let me describe my use of the shared-themes approach in six months of research in Hiroshima (in 1962) on the psychological effects of the atomic bomb, and in subsequent writings on that subject. The work centered mainly on intensive interviews with seventy-five atomic-bomb survivors, about half of them chosen at random from an official list, the other half specially selected because of their active involvement

over the years in atomic-bomb problems. Most of the interviews were
tape-recorded, and the book I wrote about the work took shape mainly
from those interviews and made extensive use of direct quotations to
illustrate the death-haunted responses I encountered. But in both the
research and the later book I moved outward from interviews with
individual survivors to groups they formed, leaders emerging from
among them, and social currents in Hiroshima which they both
created and were affected by. This in turn required close attention to
the post-atomic-bomb history of the city, and to the relationship of
that special history to the rest of Japan and to the world at large, as
well as to the city's own earlier heritage. A significant part of that
history consisted of creative struggles—of writers, painters, and film-
makers from both within and without the city—to come to terms with
Hiroshima. And these historical and creative struggles were deeply
bound up with issues of memorialization and commemoration, with
efforts to move beyond the bomb while remaining true to its dead.

Finally, through a detailed elaboration of the ethos of the survivor,
I was in some degree able to unite the individual-psychological and
historical currents I had observed. I compared survival of the atomic
bomb to survival of other massive death immersions—of Nazi perse-
cutions in our time, and of the plagues in the Middle Ages (as the
latter reveal themselves through records), as well as to survival of
natural disasters, and of the "ordinary" deaths of close friends and
family members. I could then (in this and subsequent studies) raise
questions about the general importance of the survivor ethos of our age,
of the degree to which we have become historically prone to the survivor's retained death imprint, to his death guilt and his psychic
numbing (or desensitization to death-dominated images), and to his
struggle for significance (or what I call, after Langer, his *formulation*).
These questions now intrude into virtually all of my work, and I do
not think it is too much to say that they haunt the contemporary
imagination.

Thus, in my more recent book, *Revolutionary Immortality,* I discuss
Mao Tse-tung's relationship to the Chinese Cultural Revolution in
terms of his many experiences of individual and revolutionary survival.
I relate his creative use of the survivor state to his extraordinary accomplishments as a leader, and consider the general relevance of death
symbolism, in broadest historical perspective, to the present Chinese
Cultural Revolution. By connecting certain psychological characteristics

of Mao's personal and revolutionary style with the predominant themes of the Cultural Revolution, I attempt to combine the great-man and shared-themes approaches.

The central thesis of the book revolves around Mao's anticipation of his own impending death as well as his and his followers' fear of the "death of the revolution." What I see as the overwhelming threat Mao faces is not so much death itself as the suggestion that his "revolutionary works" will not endure. By revolutionary immortality, then, I mean a shared sense of participating in permanent revolutionary ferment, and of transcending individual death by "living on" indefinitely within this continuing revolution. I point out that some such vision has been present in all revolutions, and was directly expressed in Trotsky's principle of "permanent revolution"; but that it has taken on unprecedented intensity in present-day Chinese Communist experience. This quest for revolutionary immortality provides a general framework within which the political and economic struggles and anti-bureaucratic and anti-revisionist assaults of the Cultural Revolution can be examined, without being reduced to anyone's particular psychological or psychopathological trait.

Also related to that quest is a pattern which reflects the excruciating Maoist struggles with technology. I call that pattern "psychism," by which I mean an exaggerated reliance upon psychic power as a means of controlling the external environment, an attempt to replace the requirements of technology with pure revolutionary will. Technology is desperately sought, but feelings are cultivated. In this pattern of psychism there is once more a coming together of Mao's personal-revolutionary style—including what Chinese Communist commentators themselves refer to as his "revolutionary romanticism"—and a number of larger currents surrounding the Cultural Revolution. The concept of psychism, like that of revolutionary immortality, is an attempt to say something about precisely that psychohistorical interface.

The book was not based upon the kind of detailed interview approach I described in relationship to my Hiroshima work. Rather, it is a brief, interpretive essay, which draws heavily upon documents and observations by others of the Cultural Revolution as well as upon the writings of Mao; and only upon a very limited number of interviews with participants and observers of the events described. Compared to the Hiroshima study, it is more tenuous and more vulnerable. But I wrote it because I was convinced that the themes and concepts I develop in it could shed light on a mysteriously explosive social upheaval, and because I thought it a useful experiment in the pursuit of psychohistory.

VI

Yet the post-Freudian paradigms, like the Freudian ones, do not make clear exactly what they "explain," and fall far short of providing coherent theories of historical causation. The Freudian paradigms, we recall, lean heavily upon instinctual energies and struggles, which inevitably reduce themselves to the Oedipal Event, whether in connection with a prehistorical generational conflict or with the psychopathology of a leading historical actor. Now if broadened, this principle of the Oedipal Event could be made to connect with more inclusive versions of generational impasse, in keeping with Ortega y Gasset's belief that "the concept of the generation is the most important one in the whole of history." But Ortega had in mind the "three different and vital times" (or twenty-, forty-, and sixty–year–olds) "lodged together in a single external and chronological fragment of time," which in turn provide an "internal lack of equilibrium," because of which "history moves, changes, wheels, and flows." [8] Implicit in Ortega's view, then, is an examination of the precise nature of these "three different and vital times," of precisely the historical dimension which Freudian models have tended to ignore.

Erikson's great-man paradigm looks for historical causation in the leader's singular capacity, and absolute need, so to speak, to carry history with him as he breaks out from, and transcends, his own demonic intrapsychic conflicts. Since these conflicts are rooted in the leader's historical period, and his solution affects a great collectivity of his contemporaries, as well as subsequent generations, the great-man approach is relatively more specific than the other paradigms in its causal explanations. But we still sense a theoretical gap between the individual and the collectivity which none of the paradigms has fully bridged.

The shared-themes approach is the most diffuse of the four paradigms, though in many ways the most attuned to historical complexity. Within it, effect can become virtually indistinguishable from cause. A group understood to be *created by* a particular historical event (the Hiroshima survivors) or by an evolving set of historical vicissitudes (dissident Japanese or American youth) is also seen simultaneously to *act upon* and affect history—by epitomizing, exacerbating, and suggesting something beyond the immediate conflicts and visions of large numbers of contemporaries. If this kind of explanation, strictly speaking, deals more with historical flow than cause, it at least leaves open many possibilities for more subtle theoretical explorations which relate cause and effect to evolving patterns and directions. Among these future possibilities are additional combinations of the shared-themes and great-man approach; and new ways of conceptualizing radical historical shifts—the breakdown and re-creation of the forms of human culture (biological, experiential, institutional, technological, aesthetic, and interpretive)—or what I call a New History.[9]

In both of the post-Freudian paradigms, the social theory necessary to bridge the gap between individual and collectivity remains fragmented, implicit, unclear, or nonexistent. One solution would be to graft onto either of the two paradigms such relatively established and comprehensive social theory as the neo-Marxist concepts of alienation and overspecialization. Useful as that might be, my own view is that much of the necessary theory will have to be constructed anew. When approaching intellectual traditions of all kinds, we may do better to draw upon them partially and critically—sometimes even fragmentally—as we construct new combinations of ideas from our continuing investigation of shared psychohistorical themes. Most of all, we should avoid that form of professional territoriality which insists that psychological, sociological, and historical realms remain categorically discrete, with each holding fast to an explanatory principle claimed to subsume, or exist independently of, all else.

VII

The concept of revolutionary immortality is part of a more general theory of symbolic immortality I have been attempting to develop,[10] which concerns man's need, in the face of inevitable biological death, to maintain an inner sense of continuity with what has gone on before, and what will go on after, his own individual existence. From this standpoint the *sense* of immortality is much more than mere denial of death (though it can certainly be bound up with denial). Rather, it is part of compelling, life-enhancing imagery binding each individual to significant groups and events removed from him in place and time. The sense of immortality may be expressed biologically, by living on through (or in) one's sons and daughters and their sons and daughters; theologically, in the idea of a life after death, or in other forms of spiritual conquest of death; creatively, or through "works" and influences perceived as persisting beyond biological death; through identification with nature and its infinite extension into time and space (the idea of "eternal nature"); or experientially, through a feeling-state—one I speak of as experiential transcendence—so intense that, at least temporarily, time and death are eliminated (the mode classically employed by mystics).

What I wish to suggest is that this sense of immortality serves as the individual's connection with man's general past and future, as the individual's inner perception of his involvement in what we call the historical process. Much of human history consists of the struggle to achieve, maintain, and reaffirm a shared or collective sense of immortality under constantly changing psychic and material conditions.

Generally speaking, imagery of immortality has shifted, over the course of history, from the magical, to the supernatural, to the natural and man-centered—from *literal* promise of eternal life to more *symbolic* expressions of human continuity. One must add, however, that the emerging discussion and practice of "cryonics," the freezing of bodies from the time of death in the hope of later restoring life, returns us to the most literal kind of quest for direct bodily immortality. In any case, the shifting and re-combining of modes of immortality mark great turning points in human history. The Darwinian Revolution, for instance, epitomized the shift from the theological to the biological mode, and did so in relationship both to man's origins and his destiny. A shift of this kind, of course, can be neither total nor unopposed, and we are still in the midst of its reverberations.

Hiroshima and the subsequent development of nuclear weapons can be viewed as another major shift, perhaps more in the undermining of existing modes of immortality than in any clear suggestion of new combinations. Indeed, one way of viewing our present world-wide crisis, in terms other than political, is as a form of radical psycho-historical dislocation associated with the breakdown of viable modes of symbolic immortality. What has broken down is the sense of connection men have long felt with the vital and nourishing symbols of their cultural traditions, the sense of connection with their own history. Our sense of historical continuity (or of symbolic immortality) is now being profoundly threatened: by simple historical velocity, which subverts the imagery—notably the theological imagery—in which it has been traditionally maintained; and by nuclear and other ultimate weap-

ons which, by their very existence, call into question all modes of immortality. When we consider (more often unconsciously or precon-
sciously than with clear awareness) the possibility of nuclear or bacterio-
logical warfare, we can hardly be certain of living on in our children
or grandchildren, in our works or influences upon others, in some
form of theological conquest of death, or even in nature, which we
now know to be itself vulnerable to our weapons. The striking contemporary reliance upon the fifth mode of symbolic immortality mentioned earlier, that of experiential transcendence—whether through
drugs or other forms of "turned-on" psychic states—may well be a
reflection of precisely this decline in our belief in the other four
modes. We hunger for both connection and transcendence, and we
have need to experiment with the historical and anti-historical boundaries of both.

In America we feel this kind of dislocation profoundly, so much
so that we may well be in the vanguard of two specific responses to it.
The first, which can have highly malignant consequences, entails an
embrace—even deification—of technology as a new mode of immortality through which we seek to perpetuate ourselves. This embrace of
technology can be associated with great adventure and with other forms
of imaginative transcendence, as in the case of the space program. But
it takes on grotesque contours when the technology involved is that of
weaponry. We then witness the development, not only in America
but throughout the world, of what I call the religion of nuclearism,
an attitude of worship toward weapons of destruction, and a dependence
upon them to solve otherwise baffling human problems—ultimately
the investment in them of the sense of immortality that has been lost.

A second response to historical dislocation is the emergence of what
I call Protean man [11]—by which I mean a relatively new life style,
characterized by interminable exploration and flux, by a self-process
capable of relatively easy shifts in belief and identification—a life
style that is postmodern and in some ways post-Freudian. Protean man
has been created not only by the dislocations I have mentioned but by
the revolution in mass media as well. I have in mind the flooding of
imagery produced by the extraordinary flow of postmodern cultural
influences over mass communications networks, so that each individual
can be touched, and at times significantly affected, by virtually everything, and presented with endless partial alternatives in every sphere
of life, whether superficial messages, undigested cultural elements, or
moving evocations.

These two concepts—symbolic immortality and Protean man—provide a way of returning to where we began, to psychologists and historians in the midst of a difficult struggle to create a new psychohistory.

To be sure, the theory of symbolic immortality can hardly resolve the many-sided dilemmas of historical causation. But it does seem to me a potentially useful way of looking at man in history, most specifically as a framework for the study of revolutions and a variety of related problems of historical continuity and discontinuity. The general point of view seems also to be given force by the death-dominated times in which it emerges; history does much to create the ways in which we, at any particular moment, decide to study it.

Concerning the Protean style, I bring it up not only as a way of epitomizing contemporary experience but for another reason as well. Since I believe this style in some degree inhabits us all, I assume further that it affects our relationship to ideas—the ways in which we respond to them, believe them, and attach them to our sense of self. Protean man is continuously open to new ideas and can move among them rather freely. His difficulty lies in giving lasting allegiance to any particular idea or idea system. I do not believe that scholars are immune from precisely this pattern. Hence the intellectual restlessness within most disciplines—the dissatisfaction with established concepts, together with the failure of newer concepts of equal authority to appear.

Those working in the area of psychohistory, where established concepts hardly exist, are especially likely to encounter such restlessness in both their readers and themselves. It will not be easy to discover, and then collectively maintain, the kind of authoritative conceptual principles we have come to expect and depend upon within an intellectual tradition. Moreover, there is a sense in which psychohistory adds to the burdens of a historical discipline already immersed in difficult struggles to replace no longer acceptable nineteenth-century versions of history as clear narrative or epic or inevitable destiny, struggles to come to grips with the convoluted, opaque, and deadly actualities of the twentieth century. Psychohistory, at least in the version I have been describing, tends to complexify rather than simplify, which I think is as it should be. And Protean tendencies among scholars can render them receptive to the new principles of psychohistory and yet cautious in granting them intellectual authority, which is also as it should be.

Within these uncertainties lie extraordinary possibilities. These too are Protean, and I think one can observe in contemporary man an increasing capacity for coming to what would have previously been viewed as impossible intellectual combinations and innovations. Compared with his predecessors he is not only less bound by tradition but much more fluid in his potential integration of very diverse conceptual elements. And the new psychohistory—having stated my reservations and qualifications, I think I can begin to call it that— emerges as itself a radical investigative response to a radically dislocated historical epoch.

Despite what I speak of as Protean possibilities, and what some perceive as an exotic aura surrounding the idea of psychohistory, all that I have said here and experienced in my investigations militates strongly against facile intellectual efforts or the creation of "instant psychohistorians." To the contrary, the approach seems to require not only a central commitment to one of the disciplines (or a related one) and a considerable knowledge of the other, but something more: a considerable ethical concern wtih the problems being investigated. Erik Erikson has hardly been neutral in his feelings about Luther's achievements or about what Gandhi's legacy may still mean for the world. Nor has Keniston been neutral about student radicals, Coles about minority-group aspirations, nor I about Hiroshima and its legacy. Rather, all of us have been struggling toward ways of acknowledging our involvements and exploring their relationship to our findings, toward making conceptual use of these very involvements.[12]

The developments I have discussed have for the most part come from the psychological direction. This is not because historians have been totally aloof from psychohistory: they have in fact produced a number of important studies within it. But at this phase, beginning with Erikson, the focus seems to be upon concepts emerging from the psychoanalytic heritage, even if in great tension with that heritage. No one knows what will happen in the future, but one can be sure that things will change. Psychohistory could be an avenue toward the revitalization of psychoanalysis itself, through which the latter might rediscover its own history and thereby transform itself. Or psychohistory could develop more autonomously and, despite (partly because of) its profound debt to psychoanalysis, separate itself decisively from the ahistorical bias of that tradition.

In the end, psychohistory may turn out to be nothing more than a minor intellectual curiosity. Or, as I confess to be my belief, it could develop into a significant body of thought whose evolving ideas will be as compelling as they are difficult to establish. However things turn out, psychohistory will benefit from the disciplined free spirits who, whatever their origin, bring their critical imaginations to bear upon it.

NOTES

1. Kardiner was aware of the problem, but precisely the historical complexities of advanced Western (specifically American) society proved refractory to the approach he had evolved in the study of primitive societies. Primitive societies too, of course, could have revealed very different insights had they been approached from the perspective of historical change. See especially Kardiner, *The Individual and His Society* (New York, 1939), and Kardiner and associates, *The Psychological Frontiers of Society* (New York, 1945).

2. See Philip Rieff, "The Meaning of History and Religion in Freud's Thought," in Bruce Mazlish, ed., *Psychoanalysis and History* (Englewood Cliffs, N.J., 1963). Discussions suggesting the significance of the Moses Event for Freud can be found in the Jones biography, *The Life and Work of Sigmund Freud* (New York, 1953, 1955, 1957); in James Strachey's Introduction to *Moses and Monotheism* in vol. XXIII of the *Standard Edition of the Complete Psychological Works of Sigmund Freud* (London, 1964) and in Freud's own elaborate series of introductory and prefatory notes and summaries interspersed throughout the study; and in Maryse Choisy, *Sigmund Freud: A New Appraisal* (New York, 1963). Rieff, Erik Erikson, and Kenneth Keniston contributed directly to my understanding of these matters in their comments following my presentation of much of this paper at our small working group in psychohistory.

3. William C. Bullitt and Sigmund Freud, *Thomas Woodrow Wilson, Twenty-Eighth President of the United States: A Psychological Study* (Boston, 1967). Erik Erikson's review of the book in *International Journal of Psycho-Analysis*, XLVIII (1967), 462–468, is itself an important statement on psychohistorical method.

4. New York, 1958. See also Erikson's *Gandhi's Truth* (New York, 1969), his early study, *Childhood and Society* (New York, 1950), and his two more recent collections of essays, *Insight and Responsibility* (New York, 1964), and *Identity: Youth and Crisis* (New York, 1968).

5. Freud, *Standard Edition*, XXIII, 27.

6. See Keniston's two books, *The Uncommitted* (New York, 1965) and *Young Radicals* (New York, 1968); and Coles's *Children of Crisis* (Boston, 1967).

7. These studies are reported respectively in *Thought Reform and the Psychology of Totalism* (New York, 1961), *History and Human Survival* (forthcoming), and *Death in Life: Survivors of Hiroshima* (New York, 1968).

8. José Ortega y Gasset, *What Is Philosophy?* (New York, 1960), pp. 32–39.

9. "The Young and the Old—Notes on a New History," *Atlantic Monthly* (September and October 1969), and in *History and Human Survival.*

10. I introduce the concept of symbolic immortality in my essay "On Death and Symbolism: The Hiroshima Disaster," *Psychiatry*, XXVII (August 1964), 191–210, refer to it in a number of subsequent writings, and discuss in detail its general (and especially historical) ramifications in a forthcoming volume, *The Broken Connection.*

11. "Protean Man," *Partisan Review*, XXXV (Winter 1968), 13–27, reprinted with further commentary on the concept in *History and Human Survival.*

12. See Erik H. Erikson, "On the Nature of Psycho-Historical Evidence: In Search of Gandhi," *Daedalus* (Summer 1968).

Quantification and American History: An Assessment

MORTON ROTHSTEIN
SAMUEL T. McSEVENEY
PHILIP J. GREVEN, JR.
ROBERT ZEMSKY
and JOEL SILBEY

A little more than ten years ago Lee Benson first pleaded for more precision in the study of American political history through the systematic use of electoral statistics. The next year Alfred Conrad and John Meyer published the first of their pathbreaking quantitative analyses of the profitability of slavery. Within a few years Benson himself published a far-reaching quantitative examination of the politics of Jacksonian America, and the pioneering population and mobility studies of Sam B. Warner and Stephan Thernstrom dramatized the way extensive quantitative commitment could deepen and revise social history.[1] Of course, others had already been advocating similar approaches, and in other disciplines scholars had used statistics in a variety of ways for some time. But these publications were important points of departure for the current interest in and use of quantification in American history.

Although the work of Benson, Conrad, Meyer, Thernstrom, *et al.* has appeared to some as the opening wedge for a new type of the ongoing treason of the intellectuals, and although, perhaps, there has

This paper is a joint effort of all five authors, though Rothstein is largely responsible for the section on economic history, McSeveny for the section on political history, Greven for the section on social history, and Zemsky for the section on the problems and implications of the use of statistics by historians. Silbey wrote the introduction and conclusion, and edited and combined the work of the others with their consent and editorial criticism. We wish to thank Michael Kammen for his aid and advice.

not been as much commitment to the use of quantification as the pioneers would like, other historians have picked up their challenge and example in the last decade and found quantification to be a useful, often necessary, tool for the fuller understanding of the American past. Allan Bogue remarked a few years ago that "political historians today number an overwhelming majority of standpatters, a small group of dedicated switchers [to quantification], and a growing number of their new votaries." He concluded that "it will be some time before there is a sizable cadre of historians confidently aware of the promises and pitfalls inherent in quantification." [2] Nevertheless, Bogue did list more than fifty articles and books that used quantification at some level of sophistication. And in the two years since his article appeared there have been significant additions to his list. One must also add the much more extensive quantitative work in economic history as well as the growing body of quantitative social history. And we are witnessing the increasing importance of historical statistics in the data banks of the originally presentist-oriented Inter-University Consortium for Political Research; the mushrooming use of such computer-related data; the growth of well-attended conferences of economic, political, and social historians interested in using statistics; the appearance of anthologies involving the "new" economic and political history; the training of more historians in research design and quantitative methodology by the Consortium and by a number of graduate departments; the appearance of the *Historical Methods Newsletter,* facilitating communication among scholars; the writing of the first text on quantitative methods by historians for historians; and the appearance of panels on quantification at professional meetings. All these phenomena are symptomatic of the growing interest in and use of quantification by American historians.[3]

After these years of effort and the amount of work we now have, some assessment of the enterprise is in order. In the following comments we have not dealt with every published work, nor with all aspects of the various fields of American history in which quantification has been utilized. We have tried rather to discuss the main concerns of recent quantitative research so as to demonstrate what has occurred over the whole range of American economic, political, and social history. Our emphasis is on an evaluation of contributions already made: the possibilities in, as well as the limits and failures of, the current body of work.

I

The application of quantitative techniques was a major characteristic of economic history long before it became fashionable in other branches of the discipline. Over the course of the nineteenth century the development of a central body of economic theory enhanced and strengthened inherent pressures for more and better numbers, as well as for the more rigorous use of data. The basic theoretical constructs lay within the grasp of the uninitiated historian, the problems under attack were still loosely defined and open to useful thrusts from both economists and historians, and the methods for gathering and manipulating data were still crude enough so that investigators in either discipline could make significant contributions and raise vital new issues. Within living memory, feelings of mutual respect, open communication, and tolerant understanding generally prevailed in the gatherings of scholars from both disciplines who were interested in economic change over time.

Much of this spirit seems to have changed. Economic history is currently undergoing the same kind of revolutionary and divisive challenge by champions of new techniques and methods of analysis as in those areas of history where quantification is relatively new. Differences of opinion over the merits of the "traditional" and the "new" may be sharper and more bitter in economic history than in other fields, in part because of the more elegant and refined nature of the theory employed, in part because the more pervasive tradition of quantification provided a springboard for higher leaps with the adoption of new mathematical tools and concepts. Economic historians now find themselves embroiled in controversies that may not differ in degree from those of the past, but do differ in kind. Many economic historians are in fact suffering from something akin to an identity crisis.

The seeds of this change were planted in the late 1930's with the innovation of mathematical economics, and began sprouting in the aftermath of World War II when economists discovered that the problems of growth and development, which had become matters of overriding concern, were intimately related to economic history. The "new economic history" did not burst into full bloom, however, until fairly recently, with the Conrad and Meyer article on the profitability of slavery in 1958, the appearance of Douglass North's book on antebellum economic growth in 1961, and with that heady exotic flower, Robert Fogel's book on railroads, published in 1964.[4] Other offshoots

of this new approach, which employs sophisticated econometric techniques and rigorous theoretical models, have appeared with great profusion during the last decade.[5] If nothing else, this work has proven
enormously provocative. Historians' reactions have run the gamut
from adoration to rage, from uncritical acceptance to amused scorn.
Yet one suspects that the dominant response among those who have
little or no training in the methods of quantification and model building is neither to embrace nor to attack but to remain vitally interested
—but also skeptical. They are occasionally puzzled and excited at the
same time.

The new economic historians are engaged in two different but
overlapping enterprises. The first is the gathering and processing of
data, and the measurement of the entire gamut of economic activity
in the past. Essentially this is a sophisticated continuation of the
tradition that received a new thrust in the 1920's from the work of
such men as Frederick Mills, Simon Kuznets, and Wesley Clair
Mitchell, and flourished under the aegis of the National Bureau of
Economic Research, the Brookings Institution, and other organizations.[6]
Measurement of this kind involves far more than merely collecting
numbers; the construction of meaningful time series requires extraordinary diligence, care, and sensitivity to the questions implicit in the
data themselves. No one is more aware than the scholars involved in
this work of the frail, tentative nature of the numbers. The best evidence for this lies in the perceptive introductions by William N. Parker
and Dorothy Brady to the two outstanding books on the nineteenth
century American economy published by the National Bureau.[7]

Beyond question, this kind of work has given us a vastly improved
empirical base. It may very well have a more lasting impact than any
other form of quantification. One has only to think of the brilliant
investigations by Robert Lipsey and Ilse Mintz on foreign trade, Alvin
Tostlebe on capital in agriculture, Clarence Long on wages, Richard
Easterlin on regional differentials in income, Robert Gallman on value-
added in the major sectors, M. J. Ulmer on transportation, the monumental books of Kuznets on capital formation and financial intermediaries, and many other noteworthy achievements to realize how far we
have come in a single generation.[8]

There are occasional weaknesses in these books, of course, in particular where the authors have breached the boundary between gathering data and using it to resolve major issues in economic history. At
times such breaches have produced quite thoughtful analysis, but on

other occasions the boundary has been crossed without profit to historical understanding—as, for example, when the brilliant economist Milton Friedman resorted to the great-man theory to explain aspects of the monetary history of the 1920's, or seemed to use evidence more to support current policy proposals than to understand the past.[9]

The feature of the new economic history that has generated the most excitement, however, is not advances in measurement but the new techniques of manipulating and analyzing. Econometric methods and models applied to the reexamination of the conventional wisdom of economic history have proved themselves to be powerful critical tools. An essential characteristic of this technique lies in its precisely articulating assumptions and identified key variables. The supporting characteristics are equally impressive: the "predictive testing" of the models to insure their adequacy; the careful substitution of one form of available data as a surrogate for another that is not available; the use of both upper and lower extremes in estimating variables for which surrogate data cannot be obtained. No one who carefully reads Fogel, Fishlow, Temin, Williamson, and others can fail to be impressed with the rigor and ingenuity that pervade their work. Even when they disagree, as they do with apparently increasing frequency, their arguments are about fundamental concepts—such as the appropriateness of the basic models, their explanatory power, and the measurable relationships between causal variables—rather than whether one piece of discrete data is superior to another. Fogel, Fishlow, Lebergott, and McClelland may argue with each other in a language we do not fully understand, but they have at least succeeded in making clear many of the limitations of our current knowledge about the contribution of railroads to American economic development.[10]

Can these new techniques do more than reveal, with great precision, deficiencies in our writing of history? We should retain a healthy skepticism about their results as long as we know that econometrics itself still is plagued by two basic deficiencies: (1) the mathematical models are still inadequate, especially for a dynamic conceptual universe (or, in the immortal words of Lance Davis, "our growth models stink"); (2) the new methods can only work on the basis of assumptions which are not necessarily true. These deficiencies seem all the more glaring when the method is used to attack old shibboleths or changes that extend over broad time periods. Admittedly, many prevailing notions in the traditional literature are extraordinarily vulnerable, but they are often collapsing under the weight of accumulating conventional evidence anyway. Nor is it wise to engage in any kind of historical analysis without an exceptional sensitivity to that basic factor, time.[11]

Two brief examples can illustrate this last point. Part of Fogel's analysis of the railroads rests upon the assumption that the costs of interruptions to the flow of goods can be subsumed under inventory costs for the system as a whole. Yet we know that one of the key elements in the growth of large-scale manufacturing was the entrepreneur's ability to rely on a continuous flow of raw materials into his plant and of finished goods out of it. There is also much evidence to suggest that manufacturers in the mid-nineteenth century were chronically short of working capital. Can we really assume that they, or other groups within the market economy, could carry inventory costs without imposing a serious constraint on growth? In other words, is the element of time open to such casual manipulation? [12] Again, Paul David, who has made some brilliant contributions, fell afoul of this problem when he attempted to explain the impact of wage rates on the adoption of the reaper in the ante-bellum Midwest.[13] Several of his assumptions seem questionable; his negative one on the sharing of machines has already received attention, and the implication that Illinois farmers had already shifted from oxen to horses for draught animals needs further testing. But the basic flaw, in our judgment, is David's failure to recognize the full implications of the pressure on the farmer to bring in the harvest as quickly as possible. The man who gambled much of his year's capital and labor on small grain production did not really have the ten days that David assumes for him. One bad rain- or hailstorm at the beginning of the harvest period simply ended it, and there was therefore a premium on reducing uncertainty. This element of risk could probably be plugged into David's model without doing it violence conceptually, but it is hard to imagine that it would not change the result.

Each of us could just as readily vent his own doubts and suspicions about another scholar's findings, but this was always the case and is the hallmark of free inquiry. We must not allow our misgivings to deflect us from appreciating the exciting new work that a decade of effort has given us. The more durable findings, in our opinion, will come from those new economic historians whose interest in quantification goes beyond the possibilities it presents for proving how inadequate the work of their predecessors may have been, and who instead address themselves to issues that are better defined and have greater relevance. The painstaking work currently underway in the Parker-Gallman project will probably contribute more to our firm understanding of nineteenth-century Southern agriculture than anything in sight.[14] The work of Jeffrey Williamson of the University of Wisconsin on the long swings in the balance of payments, the determinants of railroad investment, and urbanization in the ante-bellum Northeast are fundamental contributions. The same can be said for econometricians working on a variety of problems: Gary Walton and James Shepherd on colonial shipping and trade; Rasmussen, Parker, David, and others on growth rates before 1840; Temin on the iron and steel industry; Solmon, Bowman, and Engerman on education; and Stanley Lebergott on employment.[15] The list grows longer, and the work gets not only more interesting but indispensable. Certainly economic history benefits enormously as the level of quantification grows more sophisticated, as our analytical tools become more complex, and as we become better equipped to achieve that elusive and frail thing, historical understanding.

II

After economic history, the quantitative revolution has probably most affected the study of American political history.[16] The past decade's research in that field falls into one of two categories. Some historians and political scientists have made macroanalytical studies of time series of national, state, county, and (in some cases) local election data to measure shifts in support for the major political parties and the strength of "the two-party norm" itself; to identify voting cycles in nineteenth-century New York State and "secular realignment" and "critical elections" in New England; and to test in Illinois and California V. O. Key's hypothesis regarding critical elections in New England.[17] The Illinois and California articles are important not only in their findings but in the way they demonstrate an important use to which county-level election data, now available for most of the nation's history in machine-readable form at the Inter-University Consortium for Political Research, may be put—analyses of extended time series of county returns from states, regions, and the nation, to identify more precisely continuities and discontinuities in voting behavior on this level. These identifications in turn suggest subjects for more detailed analysis. Such macroanalyses, involving masses of data and several statistical measuring devices, will necessarily employ computers.[18]

Meanwhile, a larger number of scholars has studied more narrowly defined subjects—popular and legislative voting, and the composition of leadership groups in various settings and periods—the better to comprehend political behavior on all levels. These case studies rest on quantitative sources (e.g., local election and population data, legislative roll calls, collective biographies) as well as manuscript, newspaper, and archival sources. One cannot deal individually with the many microanalytical studies of American political history, but we can categorize them, and, by analyzing a significant part of the whole— that dealing with popular voting from the 1850's to the 1930's—highlight their contributions to our understanding of political behavior and identify some problems before us.

American politics has been characterized by long periods during which popular support for the major parties has remained stable, and shorter crises—during the 1850's, 1890's, and 1920's and 1930's—during which major and enduring popular shifts have occurred. Quantitative researchers have so far followed the lead of other historians, dealing primarily with the unstable periods. Thus for the nineteenth century, attention has focused on the 1850's and 1890's. Recent analyses of voting during the 1850's stress cultural rather than economic conflicts; prohibition, Sabbatarianism, and Catholic-Protestant tension now share the limelight with anti-slavery in case studies of the emergence of the Republican coalition. Paul Kleppner and Michael Holt contribute most to our understanding of this development. Kleppner ingeniously reconstructs the religious composition of Pittsburgh's German and Irish populations; he concludes that religion, not ethnicity, was crucial to their voting behavior. Holt's recent book further illumines complex political patterns in Pittsburgh.[19] Quantitative analyses of referenda on Negro suffrage during the Civil War era contribute to our understanding of similarities and dissimilarities among Caucasian groups on one racial issue; they also reveal a growing research interest in referenda —in which the electorate directly indicates its position on economic and cultural questions.[20]

An economic depression (1893) was central to the political realignment of the 1890's, unlike that of the 1850's, but recent studies of the later period also establish the importance of cultural factors in the short-lived Democratic upswing at the beginning of the decade, in differences between voting shifts in 1894 and 1896, and in the roles played by the People's, Prohibition, and Socialist Labor parties. We now need state legislative analyses to determine whether the victorious

Republicans sought to achieve the long-standing objectives of various cultural sub-groups within their party or, having broken the political stalemate by exploiting depression discontent, they sought rather to dampen the cultural conflicts that had weakened them before 1893.[21] One regrets that quantitative studies of Congress still outnumber by far those of state legislatures, for legislatures dealt with many important issues, particularly the cultural ones that separated parties and groups on the local level.

The only stable period for which we now have a cross-section of case studies (i.e., popular and legislative voting, leadership) is that preceding the 1850's. Lee Benson triggered current interest in popular voting behavior during this era; indeed, his approach to political history and emphasis on cultural factors in the shaping of party identification influenced researchers in other periods. Similarly, Richard McCormick's analysis of popular voting behavior revised many notions about voter turnout and class voting in the Jacksonian period. Joel Silbey's Guttman scaling of roll calls demonstrated that partisan lines were generally firm in Congress, as well as among voters, during the 1840's. Meanwhile, the results of quantitative analyses of party and abolitionist leaders entered the literature even as they provoked methodological and substantive debates.[22]

Quantitative analyses of legislative voting behavior carry at least through the Civil War and Reconstruction, but we lack studies of popular voting behavior during the next period of political equilibrium, that between 1860 and 1892.[23] One trusts that potential researchers have not been put off by traditional charges that the politics of the period was meaningless, for—as Walter Burnham indicates—"the late nineteenth century voting universe was marked by a more complete and intensely party-oriented voting participation among the . . . electorate than ever before or since." [24] Even as national political leaders talked tariff, currency, and civil service reform, other issues defined grass-roots politics: recurring cultural conflicts, the emergence of protest parties (Prohibition, in particular), the changing composition of the electorate itself—all contributed to the dynamics of equilibrium. Frederick Luebke's analysis of the response to the issues of the period among sub-groups within Nebraska's German population suggests the value of approaching political history through the study of particular groups over time.[25] As with other approaches, comparisons are in order. In the Northeast, as in the West, German Lutherans reacted against Republican pietism, but they sometimes moved the other way in reaction to the rise of Irish Catholics within the Democracy. Cross-pressures such as these merit attention: they contributed to support for and opposition to the administration of Grover Cleveland and various municipal reform campaigns.[26]

Analyses of popular voting during the Progressive Era are also scarce, though studies of legislative behavior and political leadership abound. Significantly, the more recent collective biographies shed light on various levels of Progressive leadership and compare factional leaders.[27] Unfortunately, analysts of early twentieth-century popular voting may face thorny research problems, for lower turnout, heavy immigration, and population shifts increased the likelihood of discrepancies between the characteristics of total population and the characteristics of voting populations within affected districts, a situation made worse by the unavailability of manuscript federal censuses and the decline of state censuses. The paucity of voting studies obscures important developments during the period— e.g., the Democratic resurgence beginning in 1906, and the forging and disintegration of the Democratic coalition of 1916—and contributed to the questionable research design of early studies that measured elections of the 1920's, particularly the "critical" one of 1928, against the Republican landslide of 1920.[28] Recent studies make clear that not all cities, and more importantly not all ethnic groups, responded in the same way to the cultural conflicts of the 1920's or to Al Smith's candidacy. Most of our literature deals essentially with those urban groups among whom both cultural issues and economic issues arising out of the depression worked to the advantage of the Democrats. We need additional studies of those urban and rural groups for whom the depression and early Roosevelt years were pivotal in this regard. More research on relations between rural and urban groups on the state level would also be welcome, for to this point only the grass-roots responses of Midwestern ruralites to urbanization have been analyzed.[29] Such studies should permit us to draw a more complete picture of the political coalition that emerged during the realignment of 1928–1936 to influence American politics until the present.

Turning from recent research to the immediate future, the time has come for quantitatively oriented political historians to discuss among themselves and with like-minded economic and social historians a number of matters of mutual concern. Many of the quantitative works alluded to here contain methodological sections. The sources of data and the techniques used in analyzing them are easy enough to determine; but comparing the findings of two or more quantitative analyses is a more difficult task, for the works are not generally methodologically comparable. Obviously, such analyses sometimes cannot be so: data vary widely; differences in research techniques often reflect these variations. Still, there exist divergences—in the units or data selected for analysis, or in the statistical tools chosen to analyze the data—that cannot be accounted for in this way. We mean neither to criticize the pioneering studies nor to propose that all quantitative analyses be cast in one methodological mold; but do suggest that we consider ways in which to make methods more similar so that we may more confidently compare findings.

Given the general reliability of election data on every political level, we should, in detailed studies, analyze the smallest (e.g., most homogeneous) political units for which reliable population data exist, though this will sometimes necessitate reaggregating data, and use the techniques most appropriate to this data. Wherever practicable, we should also seek to systematize our cultural and economic classifications of political units. In developing cultural classification guidelines, we will probably face fewer problems regarding race and nativity, on which "hard" data generally exist, than religion, on which "soft" data are frequently more abundant. In practice, classifications will usually be based on the systematic analysis of both types of data.

Given the limitations of economic data available to us for the nineteenth century, the developing of economic classification guidelines will probably prove more difficult than the devising of cultural ones; certainly one finds in the current quantitative literature greater disagreement over the standards by which rural and urban localities should be economically categorized.[30] The evidence presently at hand supports the hypothesis that cultural, rather than economic, differences underlay rival partisan identifications during the nineteenth century.[31] Still, as Allan Bogue has warned us, our "emphasis" on "ethno-cultural groups may in part reflect the fact that the ethno-cultural reference group is the easiest to identify in historical data." [32] Appreciating the stultifying effects of dependence on traditional (i.e., nonquantitative) sources on the study of political behavior, we must also be alert to the danger of following paths of least resistance in analyzing quantitative data compiled during earlier periods for purposes unrelated to our own.

On another front, political and social historians may be able to cooperate in dealing with questions relating to mobility, which deserve more study. Politics is often viewed as providing social mobility, though

Stephan Thernstrom's negative finding in regard to the Irish of New-buryport, Massachusetts, during 1850–1880, suggests that we must test the generalization in various settings and periods.[33] Quantitative studies of this subject should deal with change and continuity in ethnic, religious, racial, and socio-economic patterns of recruitment and advancement in party hierarchies and public offices on various levels. We have pioneering and illuminating case studies of this type, but our reluctance to deal systematically with the problem frequently leaves us standing on uncertain ground.[34]

Social and economic historians have also recognized the significance of geographic mobility, analyzing population turnover in various rural and urban settings.[35] To the extent that these studies rest on federal and state censuses they provide views of their subjects at five- or ten-year intervals. Meanwhile, political historians have begun to dip for their own purposes into registration and voting lists that survive in various political units. In effect, these provide annual information, including address and sometimes place of birth, for a high percentage of those eligible to vote in such units. Study of these lists in conjunction with censuses may permit, for at least a sampling of individuals or districts, year-by-year analyses of population turnover, which would strengthen the generalizations of social and economic historians regarding the effect of changing economic conditions and other factors on such turnover. These analyses should also prove valuable to political historians; they would shed light on the effects of population turnover on the political identification of political units, whose stability we usually discuss without regard to the instability of population, or whose instability we generally discuss in terms of voting shifts rather than population shifts. Whether we pursue these leads or others of greater potential, the quantitative political history research of the past decade is a solid foundation on which to base future explorations.

III

Any assessment of the role of quantification in American social history is inhibited by the relative dearth of works involving an extensive and systematic use of numbers. During the past decade, however, a number of studies have appeared which have sought to use quantifiable data as a basis for the analysis of particular aspects of American social history. Almost without exception, these studies have broken new ground, provided much new information, and transformed our under-

standing of many critically important aspects of experience and behavior in the past. It is not accidental that they have been among the
most exciting and challenging works to appear in recent years.

Much of this excitement stems from their pioneering efforts to explore sources and acquire and analyze data in ways which differ fundamentally from the studies of earlier generations of social historians.
Even the limited work which has been done so far has raised many basic
questions about the validity of some deeply rooted assumptions. Equally
important, though, these new studies in American social history have
helped to reveal to us the appalling extent of our ignorance about the
nature and the history of American society. What has been missing
from our accounts of society in the past, most of which have been
impressionistic and based upon literary sources alone, has been much
of the data that is essential to a convincing analysis of any social
system. This is why many social historians have begun to discover the
need for quantification.

Because the nature of the population is basic to the history of society,
such matters as birth rates, sizes of families, mortality rates, and typical
age at marriage are critically important. But populations themselves
have histories: they are subject to changes through time, and these
changes, and the demographic characteristics of a society, can best be
studied quantitatively. Most social historians have used literary evidence
and folklore as the basis for their assumptions about such matters. Until
very recently, almost no one bothered to find out such facts as the ages
at which men and women actually married, or the actual sizes of families. The brief studies of families and population in Plymouth Colony
by John Demos; in Dedham, Massachusetts, by Kenneth Lockridge; in
seventeenth-century Barbados by Richard Dunn; in Andover, Massachusetts, by Philip Greven; as well as James Potter's study of a later
period (American population trends in general in the eighteenth and
nineteenth centuries) are among the few which have attempted to
provide some reliable, or at least reasonably reliable, data on the
nature of selected populations.[36] For the most part, we are still in the
dark about the demographic history of America, particularly in the
post-Colonial period.

Equally important, and equally neglected, is the question of mobility
in America. The literature is full of commentaries on mobility and its
implications for patterns of social structure and social experience in the
Colonial and national periods. Yet we actually know almost nothing
about social and geographic mobility. How extensive was the move-

ment of people from place to place and from time to time? What was the extent of economic and social opportunity in the seventeenth, eighteenth, or nineteenth centuries, and how did they differ? Of course, the lack of evidence has rarely inhibited historians from discussing these issues. But a few recent studies have tried to provide some firm quantitative data as a basis for an analysis of mobility. One of the most important of these is Stephan Thernstrom's examination of laborers in nineteenth-century Newburyport, which provides a limited but well-substantiated analysis of social and geographic mobility based largely upon the use of quantifiable data.[37] Similarly, the demographic studies by Demos, Lockridge, and Greven also provide data on mobility, particularly geographic mobility in the Colonial period—and the data are sufficiently contradictory that these studies probably raise more questions than they answer. But at least they offer some evidence and a satisfactory point of departure. The question of social mobility has also begun to be examined, but Lockridge's study of "Land, Population, and the Evolution of New England Society," James Henretta's study of economic development and social structure in colonial Boston, and the study of eighteenth-century Virginia by Robert and Katherine Brown have each provided a considerable body of data, as well as many fresh and challenging—and often quite contradictory—perspectives on the issue. For the nineteenth century, Merle Curti's pioneering study of Trempeleau County, Wisconsin, based upon the analysis of quantitative data, still stands in uncomfortable isolation.[38]

The larger question of the changing structure of American society invites the use of quantitative methods and an analysis of the abundant sources that exist for studies of the distribution of wealth, social class, and other such matters. Yet relatively little has been done. The extraordinarily detailed and extensive study of *The Social Structure of Revolutionary America* by Jackson Turner Main is unique for the Colonial period, and there is, as yet, nothing comparable to it for the nineteenth century.[39]

In seeking answers to these and other questions about the nature of American society, historians using quantitative analysis will be able to secure information about the lives and actions of countless thousands of people who have never been studied adequately. More often than not, social historians have limited their studies to small elite groups. Literary sources generally reflect the thoughts of the elite and the nature of their lives adequately. They usually do not reveal much about the thoughts and lives of the far more numerous nonelite groups in the

American past.[40] Thernstrom's study of laborers, Curti's study of pioneers, and Greven's study of Andover farmers share a common concern with the histories of men whose social experiences have been neglected by historians. More often than not, we are limited by our sources to studying outward behavior, but even this often proves to be informative and important for a reconstruction of the society in which these common men lived.

Another important gain to be realized from more extensive quantification in social history is a reliable basis for comparisons between different societies and different periods. Demographic studies, mobility studies, and studies of social structure all can be used to establish precise distinctions between patterns of experience in varying places and periods. Until we have made such comparisons, we will never know the extent to which the history of American society has been distinctive.

Another immensely important gain from quantitative social history, it appears, will be new perspectives on the process of social change through time. Our present conceptions of the rates and character of social change are primitive, at best. Statistical and graphic data can be of tremendous value in determining cycles and patterns of change. The work which Michael Harris is doing, based upon a computer study of Harvard graduates and people in the *Dictionary of American Biography,* should transform many of our conceptions of social change through time.[41] It will also be one of the most sophisticated studies of American society we have. When Harris' work finally appears, one suspects that a new stage in the study of American social history will have been reached.

Nearly all of the studies which have been published so far have been relatively unsophisticated in terms of their methodology and use of data. Very few have used complex forms of statistical analysis, and only one has employed a computer. Yet it is obvious that even with the simplest of methods and minimal statistics, the quantitative studies have provided some extraordinarily important gains in knowledge and understanding. The use of the computer will no doubt continue to spread as more historians discover its utility. It clearly offers undeniable advantages for the social historian over the crude techniques which many of us have hitherto used. One of the most important, perhaps, is the tremendous increase in our control over variables which affected the process of social development in the past, and far greater flexibility in our analyses of social behavior.

As the earlier parts of this assessment have noted, history of society, too, is not limited to those things which can be measured and turned into statistics. The statistics themselves very often rest on very shaky foundations. What we can expect, therefore, is a tremendous increase in data—and an equally impressive increase in the problems of analysis and understanding of the data which we retrieve. To determine the meaning of much of the data still requires an historian with imagination, intuition, and considerable tenacity and patience—virtues which have always characterized the profession.

IV

The discussion thus far has stressed the accomplishments and promise of quantitative analysis in American history. Several areas of the discussion have pointed to particular problems and pitfalls, particularly of execution or neglect, problems of data and the like. But there is a more general and more important issue as well. Those groups interested in statistical analysis are already displaying that same emphasis on evangelical conversion, that same concern with legitimacy, that same penchant for conferences instead of research, and that same insistence on establishing data banks before we know what to do with data, that once characterized the work of the behavioral sciences. If American history follows this same path, the net result will be a similar air of confusion and helplessness, an aimless wandering amidst mountains of computer print-out which do nothing more than confirm our original hunches.

An illustration of this problem can be found in the reaction to Frederick Mosteller and David Wallace's *Inference and Disputed Authorship,* a highly complex and sophisticated study which used statistical inference to help decide whether Madison or Hamilton wrote the disputed portions of *The Federalist Papers.*[42]

The book received rather short shrift from the historical journals. The *New England Quarterly* simply ignored it; the *Journal of American History* relegated it to the "Book Notes" section; and the *American Historical Review* dismissed Mosteller's work as being "by mathematicians and for mathematicians."[43] Only in the *William and Mary Quarterly* did the study receive an extended review, and even here there was a misreading of the significance of what Mosteller had accomplished. The reviewer rightly celebrated the work as a major breakthrough in the melding of two seemingly disparate disciplines, history and statistics. Yet the implication was that virtue ultimately rested on the side of the historian. "Even the most defiantly humanistic historian," the review proclaimed, "will find much to convince him of the relevance of mechanized statistical methods for history in Mosteller and Wallace's urbane and candid work. In their translation of a nonmathematical problem into mathematical terms, the authors perform a splendid service. They bring to bear on an historical question vast amounts of non-intellectual, wholly impersonal, and utterly objective evidence." [44]

The impression left, then, is that statistics is essentially a mechanical skill, and that because the statistician works with numbers he can be utterly objective, wholly impersonal, and to some extent nonintellectual. Yet this is precisely what Mosteller's work *disproves*. The study is a brilliant tour de force, a highly creative, highly subjective evaluation of both *The Federalist Papers* and a two-centuries-old proposition, known as Bayes' Theorem, which provides a means of introducing prior probabilities into statistical models.[45] And Mosteller's study is mechanical only in the sense that he used computers—a facet of the study all but ignored in the presentation.

Why should historians ignore or misunderstand Mosteller's work? The answer lies in the very assumptions on which the study is built, assumptions which many historians interested in quantification have either ignored or downgraded in their attempts to build a new kind of history.

The first and foremost of these assumptions is that human behavior is constant and thus predictable. Mosteller counted words because he believed a man like Madison was constant even in his eccentricities—for example, Madison, unlike Hamilton, was fond of the word "consequently" and used it regularly. All statistical analysis of human activity is based on this assumption—that even when individuals deviate from norms they do so in predictable ways. In large part the task of the statistician is to develop mathematical models to identify such patterns of constant activity.[46]

To be sure, most quantifiers give lip service to this assumption. But to believe in it fully is to dissent from the views of most of our brethren. Several years ago C. Vann Woodward drew the line between the historian and the social scientist on precisely this issue: "The sciences seek out the general, the abstract, the repetitive, while history rejoices in the particular, the concrete, the unique." [47] Statistical analyses seldom isolate particular or unique phenomena. Even Mosteller's work, though concerned with only two actors, Madison and Hamilton, fits this dictum. The technical subjects of the analysis were not *The Federalist*

Papers but the words in those essays. Each paper was a unique collage of ideas, but the word patterns were general and hence susceptible to statistical analysis.

Indeed, the primary task of any statistical analyses of historical data is to gauge the amount of basic continuity in things, to submerge the individual in a mass of other like-thinking, like-behaving human beings. Hence we cannot have our cake and eat it too. When we say we want to use statistical techniques we are confessing that we want to ask new kinds of questions about the past—questions which have only a tangential relationship to the historian's traditional calling. Or, to put the matter more bluntly, statistical analysis should hold little appeal for those interested in narrative history. There is little prospect, for example, of developing a statistical model to explain the American Revolution or the acceptance of the Constitution. On the other hand, such models can be used to ask what factors encourage geographic mobility or patriarchal families or political development. To repeat, statistical models assume we wish to analyze repeated behavior, not single or unique events.

Mosteller's second assumption is that the mathematical manipulation of symbols can lead to conclusions that are not intuitively obvious. Reducing a human relationship to mathematical notation is itself an act of faith—for example, expressing the relationship between wealth and status in colonial Massachusetts in terms of the regression equation, $Y = a + bX$. But once we have come this far there is no reason not to take full advantage of our recklessness. Specifically, we can now apply the full range of mathematical insight to the relationship $Y = a + bX$—that is, we can manipulate the equation without losing our faith in its initial appropriateness. This willingness to manipulate his original symbols provides the guts of Mosteller's analysis. Specifically he suggests that there are a number of mathematical systems that can be used in this case of disputed authorship, and then proceeds to do so. Hence the real importance of Mosteller's work lies not in his answer to the question, Who wrote the disputed words in a given Federalist essay?—but in his demonstration of the relative strength and weakness of four different approaches to the same mathematical problem.

Unfortunately, many quantifiers have abandoned this dimension of their work largely because few historians interested in quantification have sufficient mathematical expertise either to build their own or to understand someone else's statistical models. Perhaps such expertise is not really needed as long as statisticians like Mosteller are willing to work on historical problems. But this is more hope than reality. In the first place, Mosteller is singular in his interest in historical problems. More important, we can never really use such discoveries unless we can, in a very real sense, understand them, that is, unless we can explain the mathematics of the models we employ.

Yet many quantifiers have sought to do just that when they employ canned computer programs developed by the behavioral sciences. One unfortunate by-product of our statistical naiveté is the popularity of highly complex but largely automated computer programs, such as factor analysis and Guttman scaling. After all, no more than a basic understanding of job procedures and the ability to write a format statement are required to make the program work. The mechanical simplicity of this process, however, is grossly misleading. A canned program is easy to use because it allows the nonexpert to use the particular form of the model most often employed by whoever converted it to machine-readable language. Yet a variety of forms of the model are always available. To choose among them is not unlike choosing among competing theories of personality. Certainly few of us will accept a Freudian interpretation of Lincoln's war policy from a biographer whose appreciation of Freudian psychology is limited to cocktail-party expertise. Unfortunately this is what some historians have asked of us when they employ complex statistical models, like factor analysis, without understanding how, in the mathematical sense, the model works.

What we are suggesting is that whenever a historian embarks on a statistical analysis he crosses a kind of personal Rubicon. He enters a world where there are very definite rules for reaching conclusions. His first task is to understand such rules so as not to misapply the statistical model. His second obligation is to make these rules work to his advantage, in short to get the maximum advantage from his initial assumption that human activity is susceptible to statistical analysis. To quantify historical evidence historians simply must become credible statisticians.

The third assumption implicit in Mosteller's study is the notion that historical problems are best attacked in terms of probabilities. In the course of his analysis Mosteller never decides who wrote a particular *Federalist* essay. Rather, he calculates the odds as to whether Madison or Hamilton was most likely the author of the disputed essay. Moreover, Mosteller argues that there are a number of different ways to calculate such odds depending on the kinds of mathematical assumptions one wishes to make.

It is here that Mosteller most directly challenges the historical tradition. If there is a method to the historical craft it is that of the detective—the careful collection of clues, the matching of one piece of evidence with another, and ultimately the formation of an answer as to what really happened. For all their radical use of new methods, most historians interested in quantification have remained within this tradition. Indeed, most quantifiers claim that they simply possess a superior way of gathering objective clues.

Such an argument is ultimately self-defeating. Counting is neither more nor less objective than any other way of gathering information. What a statistical model can provide, however, is an estimate, given the assumptions we make, of the worth of a particular conclusion. In fact, this is precisely the reasoning underlying Mosteller's study, which historians might profitably embrace. From this perspective quantification is not a way of gathering facts designed to solve a particular puzzle, but rather a method for estimating probabilities. Or, if one prefers a negative formulation of the problem, a statistical model can help measure just how uncertain one is of what really happened in the past.

For example, one of the principal questions before Colonial historians is the extent of the franchise in eighteenth-century America. The most persuasive study of this issue is still Robert Brown's work on Massachusetts before the Revolution.[48] Brown will probably continue to have the best of most arguments on this question largely because he has proved an excellent detective and has thus marshaled considerable evidence to support his contention that more than 80 per cent of Massachusetts' adult males could qualify as electors. Yet Brown's evidence also suggests that the franchise question is essentially a problem involving estimates for two basic probabilities. The first involves the proportion of Massachusetts total population which was both male and over twenty-one. From fragmentary demographic evidence Brown concluded that roughly 25 per cent of the population was comprised of adult males. Approaching this question in terms of probabilities allows a more robust treatment of the data. Instead of making a single rough estimate, as Brown did, we might talk about a range of possible answers and attach to each a probability of its being the right one. In short, approaching the problem in terms of probabilities allows us to preserve mathematically the uncertainty which Brown acknowledges is inherent in his work.

The second major estimate required in studying the franchise is the distribution of land holdings. Here we must guess both the mean of this distribution and the amount of dispersion about that mean. Instead of making a single estimate of the mean and accompanying dispersion, again we might more profitably make a number of guesses, each time varying both the mean and degree of dispersion. To each projected answer we could also attach a probability of its representing the true distribution. Finally, we would answer the question, Who could vote in Massachusetts?, by combining these two ranges of possible answers, one for the proportion of the total population which was adult and male, and one for the distribution of land holdings. In turn, whenever the size of the electorate was needed in some further analysis, we could simply plug in these probabilities and thus in some sense preserve our initial uncertainty. Once again, however, such reasoning is neither easy nor objective. A variety of methods for calculating such probabilities exists, and choosing among them requires first an understanding of the mathematics involved, and second a good deal of subjective faith. Thus we have come full circle.

Three major lessons emerge from initial attempts at melding history and numbers:

First, we must acknowledge that the introduction of statistical techniques explicitly changes the nature of our craft.

Second, we must, if we are to remain credible, become better statisticians.

Third, we should seek out and develop a statistical methodology which preserves the uncertainties inherent in every attempt to make sense out of fragments of information. Probability theories like those employed by Mosteller and Wallace seem to offer the best avenue for such fruitful investigation.

V

At the outset of this essay we remarked upon the relative newness of the quantification enterprise in American history. Twelve years, the period of renewed interest and increased sophistication in the use of quantification, is not a long time in the life of a discipline. There are still occasional strident debates over the appropriateness of quantification in the historical enterprise at all, but these appear to be lessening in number—if not in tone—as the findings of the accumulated work of the past decade or so have increasingly become part of the conventional wisdom of American historiography. There are, to paraphrase Lee Benson, more than faint breezes of change in the readiness of historians to adopt quantitative techniques for their own purposes. And more and more of them have done so. Problems nevertheless remain, for not all of the work published has been properly conceived or executed. One is struck, too, in reviewing the literature, by how many different levels of methodological sophistication there are to be found. In economic history, elaborate model-building based on great quantities of available data and highly developed statistical abilities are the rule; in political history, relatively simple levels of correlation analysis and attitude scaling have dominated our work, while social history has thus far been the least developed methodologically—although the use of computers in social mobility and urban development studies is extensive and increasingly sophisticated.[49] But the problems of data, the conceptions and aims of the research worker, the size of the unit of analysis, as well as the low level of statistical knowledge have all limited the level of applications there. Clearly, when we assess quantification in American history we are assessing many different types of things under one rubric.

Nevertheless, there have been some significant changes in our traditional view of certain problems and events in our past due to the existing quantitative work. The macroanalytic analyses of political and economic development have helped to place events in more exact context for subsequent understanding. Our conception of when certain periods of political, social, or economic change began or ended, and the reasons underlying political outcome or economic situation, have been more precisely determined. We certainly know more than we ever did about both political behavior and the social and economic complexities of the American past. Furthermore, as the amount of work and the number of people involved have increased, we have learned more about methods and pitfalls so that the problems connected with such analyses appear to be less perilous in the future than heretofore. The forthcoming quantitative methods textbook by Richard Jensen and Charles Dollar, which is conceived with a specific historic bent by historians for historians, is one indication of the useful breakthroughs occurring in our acquisition of methodological knowledge and the necessary tools for further quantitative investigations.[50] We can, therefore, conclude on a positive and optimistic note. Any assessment of quantification in American history has to concern itself with the pitfalls, failures, and the many areas still short of desired achievement. It must also note the accomplishments and real advances we have made thanks to the quantitative research of the past decade.

NOTES

1. Lee Benson, "Research Problems in American Political Historiography," in Mirra Komarovsky, ed., *Common Frontiers of the Social Sciences* (Glencoe, Ill., 1957), pp. 113–183; Alfred H. Conrad and John R. Meyer, "The Economics of Slavery in the Ante-Bellum South," *Journal of Political Economy,* LXVI (April 1958), 95–122. See also their "Economic Theory, Statistical Inference and Economic History," *Journal of Economic History,* XVII (December 1957), 524–544, and *The Economics of Slavery, and Other Studies in Econometric History* (Chicago, 1964). Lee Benson, *The Concept of Jacksonian Democracy: New York as a Test Case* (Princeton, 1961); Sam B. Warner, Jr., *Street Car Suburbs: The Process of Growth in Boston, 1870–1900* (Cambridge, Mass., 1962); Stephan Thernstrom, *Poverty and Progress: Social Mobility in a Nineteenth-Century City* (Cambridge, Mass., 1964).
2. Allan G. Bogue, "United States: The 'New' Political History," in Walter Laqueur and George Mosse, eds., *The New History: Trends in Historical Research Since World War II* (New York, 1967), p. 190.
3. The best place to follow the various activities of quantitative historical scholarship is in *Historical Methods Newsletter: Quantitative Analyses of Social, Economic and Political Development* (December 1967–), published at the Department of History, University of Pittsburgh, and edited by Professor Jonathan Levine.
4. Conrad and Meyer, "Economics of Slavery"; Douglass C. North, *The Economic Growth of the United States, 1790–1860* (Englewood Cliffs, N.J., 1961); Robert W. Fogel, *Railroads and American Growth: Essays in Econometric History* (Baltimore, 1964).
5. Among the best of the recent works are Albert Fishlow, *American Railroads and the Transformation of the Ante-Bellum Economy* (Cambridge, Mass., 1965); Peter Temin, *The Jacksonian Economy* (New York, 1969); Robert P. Swierenga, *Pioneers and Profits: Land Speculation on the Iowa Frontier* (Ames, Ia., 1968). See also the works cited in Douglass C. North, *Growth and Welfare in the American Past* (Englewood Cliffs, N.J., 1966), and two fine collections, Seymour Harris, *American Economic History* (New York, 1961) and Ralph L. Andreano, *New Views on American Economic Development* (Cambridge, Mass., 1965).

6. See William N. Parker's introduction to *Trends in the American Economy in the Nineteenth Century,* National Bureau of Economic Research, Studies in Income and Wealth, vol. 24 (Princeton, 1960), for a perceptive discussion of the earlier scholarly achievements.

7. *Ibid.; Output, Employment, and Productivity in the United States After 1800,* National Bureau of Economic Research, Studies in Income and Wealth, vol. 30 (New York, 1966).

8. Robert E. Lipsey, *Price and Quantity Trends in the Foreign Trade of the United States* (Princeton, 1963); Ilse Mintz, *Trade Balances During Business Cycles: U.S. and Britain Since 1880,* National Bureau of Economic Research, Occasional Paper 67 (New York, 1959); Alvin S. Tostlebe, *Capital in Agriculture: Its Formation and Financing Since 1870* (Princeton, 1957); Clarence D. Long, *Wages and Earnings in the United States, 1860–1890* (Princeton, 1960); Richard Easterlin, "Regional Income Trends, 1840–1950," in Harris, *American Economic History,* pp. 525–548; Robert E. Gallman, "Gross National Product in the United States, 1834–1909," in *Output, Employment, and Productivity;* M. J. Ulmer, *Capital Formation in Transportation, Communications, and Public Utilities: Its Formation and Financing* (Princeton, 1960); Simon Kuznets, *Capital in the American Economy: Its Formation and Financing* (Princeton, 1961). Much of the best work is still in the form of articles or occasional papers, but a fine example of the kind of work inspired by Kuznets and others can be seen in Essays in the Quantitative Study of Economic Growth," in *Economic Development and Cultural Change,* IX (April 1961).

9. Milton Friedman and Anna J. Schwartz, *A Monetary History of the United States, 1867–1960* (Princeton, 1963).

10. For the critiques of Fogel's study of railroads, see Stanley Lebergott, "United States Transport Advance and Externalities," *Journal of Economic History,* XXVI (December 1966), 437–461; Marc Nerlove, "Railroads and American Economic Growth," *Journal of Economic History,* XXVI (March 1966), 107–115; Peter D. McClelland, "Railroads, American Growth, and the New Economic History: A Critique," *Journal of Economic History,* XXVIII (March 1968), 102–123. For an excellent exposition of the case for the new approaches, see Robert W. Fogel and Lance Davis, "The New Economic History," *Economic History Review,* XIX (December 1966), 642–663.

11. On the limitations of economic theory and measurement, see Oskar Morgenstern, *On the Accuracy of Economic Observations* (Princeton, 1965); Gunnar Myrdal, "The Beam in Our Eyes," his prologue to *Asian Dream,* 3 vols. (New York, 1968); R. J. Bassman, "The Role of the Economic Historian in Predictive Testing of Proffered 'Economic Laws,'" *Explorations in Entrepreneurial History,* II, 2nd series (Spring/Summer 1965), 159–186; J. R. T. Hughes, "Fact and Theory in Economic History," *Explorations in Entrepreneurial History,* III (Winter 1966), 75–100. For the differences between the use of economic theory and concepts, as compared with those of other disciplines, in historical analysis, see Robert F. Berkhofer, Jr., *A Behavioral Approach to Historical Analysis* (New York, 1969).

12. Alfred D. Chandler, "The Organization of Manufacturing and Transportation," in D. T. Gilchrist and W. D. Lewis, eds., *Economic Change in the Civil War Era* (Greenville, Del., 1965). We are grateful to Harold Livesay, now working on a dissertation under Chandler, for sharing his knowledge and insights on the commission merchant as a source of working capital in the mid-nineteenth century.

13. Paul David, "The Mechanization of Reaping in the Ante-Bellum Mid-

west," in Henry Rosovsky, ed., *Industrialization in Two Systems: Essays in Honor of Alexander Gerschenkron* (New York, 1966), pp. 3–39.

14. In addition to results already published at this writing, Parker and Gallman will have a paper each in the forthcoming extra-length issue of *Agricultural History,* devoted largely to the fruits of their project, in January 1970.

15. See Wayne D. Rasmussen, "Farm Gross Product and Gross Investment in the Nineteenth Century" (co-authored with Marvin W. Towne) and William N. Parker's introduction and article, in *Trends in the American Economy in the 19th Century;* Paul David, "The Growth of Real Product in the United States Before 1840: New Evidence, Controlled Conjectures," *Journal of Economic History,* XXVII (June 1967), 151–197; George R. Taylor, "American Economic Growth Before 1840: An Exploratory Essay," *ibid.,* XXIV (September 1964), 427–444; Peter Temin, *Iron and Steel in Nineteenth-Century America: An Economic Inquiry* (Cambridge, Mass., 1964); Gary Walton, "Obstacles to Technical Diffusion in Ocean Shipping," *Explorations in Economic History* (forthcoming); Walton, "New Evidence on Colonial Commerce," *Journal of Economic History,* XXVIII (September 1968), 363–389; Walton, "A Measure of Productivity Change in American Colonial Shipping," *Economic History Review,* XXI (August 1968), 268–282; Walton and James Shepherd, "Estimates of 'Invisible' Earnings in the Balance of Payments of the British North American Colonies," *Journal of Economic History,* XXIX (June 1969), 230–263; James Shepherd, "Commodity Exports from the British North American Colonies," *Explorations in Economic History* (forthcoming); Mary Jean Bowman, "The Land-Grant Colleges and Universities in Human-Resource Development," *Journal of Economic History,* XXII (December 1962), 523–546; Lewis Solmon, "Estimates of the Cost of Schooling in 1880 and 1890," *Explorations in Economic History* (forthcoming special supplement); Stanley L. Engerman, "Human Capital, Education, and Economic Growth" (mimeographed); Stanley Lebergott, *Manpower in Economic Growth: The American Record Since 1800* (New York, 1964).

16. For a useful introduction to some of this work, see, besides the Bogue article referred to in note 2, William O. Aydelotte, "Notes on the Problem of Historical Generalization," in Louis Gottschalk, ed., *Generalization in the Writing of History: A Report of the Committee on Historical Analysis of the Social Science Research Council* (Chicago, 1963), pp. 145–177; Aydelotte, "Quantification in History," *American Historical Review,* LXXI (April 1966), 803–825; Lee Benson, "Causation and the American Civil War," *History and Theory,* I (1961), 163–175; Benson, "An Approach to the Scientific Study of Past Public Opinion," *Public Opinion Quarterly,* XXXI (Winter 1967–1968), 522–567; Samuel P. Hays, "History as Human Behavior," *Iowa Journal of History,* LVIII (July 1960), 193–206; Hays, "The Politics of Reform in Municipal Government in the Progressive Era," *Pacific Northwest Quarterly,* LV (October 1964), 157–169; Hays, "Archival Sources for American Political History," *American Archivist,* XXVIII (January 1965), 17–30; Hays, "New Possibilities for American Political Hstory: The Social Analysis of Political Life" (Ann Arbor: The Inter-University Consortium for Political Research, 1964); Hays, "The Social Analysis of American Political History, 1880–1920," *Political Science Quarterly,* LXXX (September 1965), 373–394; Hays, "Political Parties and the Community-Society Continuum," in William Nisbet Chambers and Walter Dean Burnham, eds., *The American Party Systems: Stages of Political Development* (New York, 1967), pp. 152–181.

Also Lee Benson and Thomas J. Pressly, "Can Differences in Interpretations of the Causes of the American Civil War Be Resolved Objectively?" (New York: Columbia University, Bureau of Applied Social Research, 1956); comments of William O. Aydelotte and Lee Benson, panel discussion: "Computers in Historical Research," *Conference on the Use of Computers in Humanistic Research* (sponsored by Rutgers, The State University, and the International Business Machines Corporation, December 4, 1964), pp. 8–13; Samuel P. Hays, "Quantification in History: The Implications and Challenges for Graduate Training," and Lee Benson, "Quantification, Scientific History, and Scholarly Innovation," both in *AHA Newsletter,* IV (June 1966), 8–11 and 11–16.

17. Charles Sellers, "The Equilibrium Cycle in Two-Party Politics," *Public Opinion Quarterly,* XXIX (Spring 1965) 16–38; Gerald Pomper, "Classification of Presidential Elections," *Journal of Politics,* XXIX (August 1967), 535–566; William Nisbet Chambers, "The Two-Party Norm in American Politics: Will It Survive?" (paper presented before the American Historical Association, December 28, 1968); Benson, *Concept of Jacksonian Democracy,* pp. 125–131; V. O. Key, Jr., "Secular Realignment and the Party System," *Journal of Politics,* XXI (May 1959), 198–210; Key, "A Theory of Critical Elections," *Journal of Politics,* XVII (February 1955), 3–18; Duncan Macrae, Jr., and James A. Meldrum, "Critical Elections in Illinois: 1888–1958," *American Political Science Review,* LIV (September 1960), 669–683; John L. Shover, "Was 1928 a Critical Election in California?," *Pacific Northwest Quarterly,* LVIII (October 1967), 196–204.

18. On computers, see Jerome M. Clubb and Howard Allen, "Computers and Historical Studies," *Journal of American History,* LIV (December 1967), 599–607; Samuel P. Hays, "Computers and Historical Research," and Stephan Thernstrom, "The Historian and the Computer," both in Edmund A. Bowles, ed., *Computers in Humanistic Research* (Englewood Cliffs, N.J., 1967), pp. 62–72 and 73–81; Charles Dollar, "Innovation in Historical Research: A Computer Approach," *Computers and the Humanities,* III (January 1969), 139–151; also *Annual Reports,* Inter-University Consortium for Political Research (Ann Arbor, Mich.), 1962–1963—; and regular issues of *Computers and the Humanities* (Queens College, Queens, N.Y.), 1966—. Paul Kleppner, "The Politics of Change in the Midwest: The 1890's in Historical and Behavioral Perspective," Unpublished Ph.D. Dissertation, University of Pittsburgh, 1967, pp. 9–26, makes excellent use of county-level data in dealing with 1860–1892 in the Midwest.

19. See George H. Daniels, "Immigrant Vote in the 1860 Election: The Case of Iowa," *Mid-America,* XLIV (July 1962), 146–162; Robert P. Swierenga, "The Ethnic Voter and the First Lincoln Election," *Civil War History,* XI (March 1965), 27–43; and especially Paul Kleppner, "Lincoln and the Immigrant Vote: A Case of Religious Polarization," *Mid-America,* XLVIII (July 1966), 176–195; Michael Holt, *Forging a Majority: The Formation of the Republican Party in Pittsburgh, 1848–1860* (New Haven, 1969). Also, Aida Di Pace Donald, "The Decline of Whiggery and the Formation of the Republican Party in Rochester, 1848–1856," *Rochester History,* XX (July 1958), 1–19; Joel H. Silbey, "The Civil War Synthesis in American Political History," *Civil War History,* X (June 1964), 130–140.

20. Robert R. Dykstra and Harlan Hahn, "Northern Voters and Negro Suffrage: The Case of Iowa, 1868," *Public Opinion Quarterly,* XXXII (Summer 1968), 202–215; John L. Stanley, "Majority Tyranny in Tocqueville's America: The Failure of Negro Suffrage in New York State in 1846," *Political Science Quarterly,* LXXXIV (September 1969), 412–435; Benson, *Concept of*

Jacksonian Democracy, pp. 303–304, 315–316, 318–320. Other works cited here make various uses of returns from referenda.

21. In addition to the dissertation by Kleppner, see also Richard Jensen, "The Winning of the Midwest: A Social History of Midwestern Elections, 1888–1896," Unpublished Ph.D. Dissertation, Yale University, 1967; Samuel T. McSeveney, "The Politics of Depression: Voting Behavior in Connecticut, New York, and New Jersey, 1893–1896," Unpublished Ph.D. Dissertation, University of Iowa, 1965; Roger E. Wyman, "Wisconsin Ethnic Groups and the Election of 1890," *Wisconsin Magazine of History,* LI (Summer 1968), 269–294; Benson, "Research Problems," pp. 155–171; Elmer E. Cornwell, Jr., "A Note on Providence Politics in the Age of Bryan," *Rhode Island History,* XIX (April 1960), 33–40; Key, "Critical Elections"; Macrae and Meldrum, "Critical Elections in Illinois"; Stanley B. Parsons, Jr., "The Populist Context: Nebraska Farmers and Their Antagonists, 1882–1895," Unpublished Ph.D. Dissertation, University of Iowa, 1964; Parsons, "Who Were the Nebraska Populists?," *Nebraska History,* XLIV (June 1963), 83–99; Walter T. K. Nugent, "Some Parameters of Populism," *Agricultural History,* XL (October 1966), 255–270.

22. Benson, *Concept of Jacksonian Democracy;* Ronald Formisano, "The Social Bases of American Voting Behavior, Wayne County, Michigan, 1837–1852, as a Test Case," Unpublished Ph.D. Dissertation, Wayne State University, 1966; Richard P. McCormick, "New Perspectives on Jacksonian Politics," *American Historical Review,* LXV (January 1960), 253–301; McCormick, "Suffrage Classes and Party Alignments: A Study in Voter Behavior," *Mississippi Valley Historical Review,* XLVI (December 1959), 397–410; McCormick, *The Second American Party System* (Chapel Hill, 1966); Joel H. Silbey, *The Shrine of Party: Congressional Voting Behavior, 1841–1852* (Pittsburgh, 1967); also Rodney O. Davis, "Illinois Legislators and Jacksonian Democracy, 1834–1841," Unpublished Ph.D. Dissertation, University of Iowa, 1966; Erling A. Erickson, "Banks and Politics Before the Civil War: The Case of Iowa, 1836–1865," Unpublished Ph.D. Dissertation, University of Iowa, 1967.

On leaderships, compare Benson, *Concept of Jacksonian Democracy,* chap. 4, and Alexandra McCoy, "Political Affiliations of American Economic Elites: Wayne County, Michigan, 1844, 1860, as a Test Case," Unpublished Ph.D. Dissertation, Wayne State University, 1965, with Frank Otto Gatell, "Money and Party in Jacksonian America: A Quantitative Look at New York City's Men of Quality," *Political Science Quarterly,* LXXXII (June 1967) 235–252, and Holt, *Forging A Majority.* Also David Donald, "Toward a Reconsideration of Abolitionists," in *Lincoln Reconsidered: Essays on the Civil War Era,* 2nd ed., enlarged (New York, 1961), chap. 2, with Robert A. Skotheim, "A Note on Historical Method: David Donald's 'Toward a Reconsideration of Abolitionists,'" *Journal of Southern History,* XXV (August 1959), 356–365, and Gerald Sorin's forthcoming study of anti-slavery leaders in New York State.

On the South, see Grady McWhiney, "Were the Whigs a Class Party in Alabama?," *Journal of Southern History,* XXIII (November 1957), 510–522; Thomas B. Alexander, *et al.,* "Who Were the Alabama Whigs?," *Alabama Review,* XVI (January 1963), 5–19; Thomas B. Alexander and Peggy J. Duckworth, "Alabama Black Belt Whigs During Secession; A New Viewpoint," *Alabama Review,* XVII (July 1964), 181–197; Thomas B. Alexander, *et al.,* "The Basis of Alabama's Ante-Bellum Two-Party System," *Alabama Review,* XIX (October 1966), 243–276; and David N. Young, "The Mississippi Whigs," Unpublished Ph.D. Dissertation, University of Alabama, 1968.

23. On legislative behavior, Silbey, *Shrine of Party;* Thomas B. Alexander, *Sectional Stress and Party Strength: A Study of Roll-Call Voting Patterns in the United States House of Representatives, 1836–1860* (Nashville, 1967); Gerald Wolff, "The Slavocracy and the Homestead Problem of 1854," *Agricultural History,* XL (April 1966), 101–112; Glenn M. Linden, "Congressmen, 'Radicalism' and Economic Issues, 1861 to 1873," Unpublished Ph.D. Dissertation, University of Washington, 1963; Linden, " 'Radicals' and Economic Policies: The Senate, 1861–1873," *Journal of Southern History,* XXXII (May 1966), 189–199; Linden, " 'Radicals' and Economic Policies: The House of Representatives, 1861–1873," *Civil War History,* XIII (March 1967), 51–65; Linden, " 'Radical' Political and Economic Policies: The Senate, 1873–1877," *Civil War History,* XIV (September 1968), 240–249; Allan G. Bogue, "Bloc and Party in the United States Senate, 1861–1863," *Civil War History,* XIII (September 1967), 221–241; Edward L. Gambill, "Who Were the Senate Radicals?," *Civil War History,* XI (September 1965), 237–244; John K. Folmar, "The Erosion of Republican Support for Congressional Reconstruction in the House of Representatives, 1871–1877: A Roll-Call Analysis," Unpublished Ph.D. Dissertation, University of Alabama, 1968; Richard Eugene Beringer, "Political Factionalism in the Confederate Congress," Unpublished Ph.D. Dissertation, Northwestern University, 1966; David Donald, *The Politics of Reconstruction, 1863–1867* (Baton Rouge, 1965).

On leadership groups, see Ralph A. Wooster, *The Secession Conventions of the South* (Princeton, 1962); Richard E. Beringer, "A Profile of Members of the Confederate Congress," *Journal of Southern History,* XXXIII (November 1967), 518–541.

24. Walter Dean Burnham, "The Changing Shape of the American Political Universe," *American Political Science Review,* LIX (March 1965), 7–28. Those interested in voting behavior during the pre-1893 period should turn to the introductory chapters of works on the realignment of 1893–1896. See Kleppner, "The Politics of Change in the Midwest"; Jensen, "The Winning of the Midwest"; and McSeveney, "Politics of Depression."

25. Frederick C. Luebke, "The Political Behavior of an Immigrant Group: The Germans of Nebraska, 1880–1900," Unpublished Ph.D. Dissertation, University of Nebraska, 1966. Also Howard W. Allen, "Studies of Political Loyalties of Two Nationality Groups: Isolationism and German-Americans," *Journal of the Illinois State Historical Society,* LVII (Summer 1964), 143–149.

26. Gerald W. McFarland, "The New York Mugwumps of 1884: A Profile," *Political Science Quarterly,* LXXVIII (March 1963), 40–58, analyzes Mugwump leaders but does not compare them with other political leaders (e.g., Republicans who did not bolt Blaine) or deal with Mugwumpery's effects on voting patterns in 1884. See also Ari A. Hoogenboom, "An Analysis of Civil Service Reformers," *The Historian,* XXIII (November 1960), 54–78. On 1884, see Benson, "Research Problems," pp. 123–146.

27. Jerome M. Clubb, "Congressional Opponents of Reform, 1901–1913," Unpublished Ph.D. Dissertation, University of Washington, 1963; Clubb and Howard W. Allen, "Party Loyalty in the Progressive Years: The Senate, 1909–1915," *Journal of Politics,* XXIX (August 1967), 567–584; Howard W. Allen, "Geography and Politics: Voting on Reform Issues in the United States Senate, 1911–1916," *Journal of Southern History,* XXVII (May 1961), 216–228; Edward M. Silbert, "Support for Reform Among Congressional Democrats, 1897–1913," Unpublished Ph.D. Dissertation, University of Florida, 1966; Kenneth C. Acrea, Jr., "Wisconsin Progressivism: Legislative Response to

Social Change, 1891 to 1909," Unpublished Ph.D. Dissertation, University of Wisconsin, 1968.

Compare George E. Mowry, "The California Progressive and His Rationale: A Study in Middle Class Politics," *Mississippi Valley Historical Review,* XXXVI (September 1949), 239–250, and Alfred D. Chandler, Jr., "The Origins of Progressive Leadership," in Elting Morison, *et al.,* eds., *The Letters of Theodore Roosevelt* (Cambridge, Mass., 1951–1954), VIII, 1462–1465, with William T. Kerr, Jr., "The Progressives of Washington, 1910–12," *Pacific Northwest Quarterly,* LV (January 1964), 16–27; E. Daniel Potts, "The Progressive Profile in Iowa," *Mid-America,* XLVII (October 1965), 257–268; Richard B. Sherman, "The Status Revolution and Massachusetts Progressive Leadership," *Political Science Quarterly,* LXXVIII (March 1963),· 59–65; Norman M. Wilensky, *Conservatives in the Progressive Era: The Taft Republicans of 1912,* University of Florida Monographs, Social Sciences, No. 25, Winter 1965 (Gainesville, 1965), chap. 3; Hays, "Political Parties and the Community-Society Continuum," pp. 163–165; Hays, "The Politics of Reform in Municipal Government"; and Bonnie R. Fox, "The Philadelphia Progressives: A Test of the Hofstadter-Hays Thesis," *Pennsylvania History,* XXXIV (October 1967), 372–394.

Among voting analyses of the early twentieth century, see Arthur Gorenstein, "A Portrait of Ethnic Politics: The Socialists and the 1908 and 1910 Congressional Elections on the East Side," *Publications of the American Jewish Historical Society,* L (March 1961), 202–238; and Melvyn Dubofsky, "Success and Failure of Socialism in New York City, 1900–1918: A Case Study," *Labor History,* IX (Fall 1968), 361–375. For various reasons, William M. Leary, Jr., "Woodrow Wilson, Irish American, and the Elections of 1916," *Journal of American History,* LIV (June 1967), 57–72, and Michael Rogin, "Progressivism and the California Electorate," *Journal of American History,* LV (September 1968), 297–314, are less convincing.

28. Samuel J. Eldersveld, "The Influence of Metropolitan Party Pluralities in Presidential Elections Since 1920: A Study of Twelve Key Cities," *American Political Science Review,* XLIII (December 1949), 1189–1206; Samuel Lubell, *The Future of American Politics,* 3rd ed., rev. (New York, 1965), pp. 43–55; Carl N. Degler, "American Political Parties and the Rise of the Ciites: An Interpretation," *Journal of American History,* LI (June 1964), 41–59, esp. 50–57. Eldersveld exaggerated the problem when he stated that "projection of the analysis into the pre-1920 era is difficult, due to the unavailability or unreliability of urban election statistics." Lubell based much of his analysis on Eldersveld's data, while Degler based his on Eldersveld and Lubell, among others. (Degler neglected to cover 1900–1916; his treatment of 1880–1896 was spotty.)

Shover, "Was 1928 a Critical Election in California?"; Key, "Secular Realignment" and "Critical Elections"; Macrae and Meldrum, "Critical Elections in Illinois"; David Burner, *The Politics of Provincialism: The Democratic Party in Transition, 1918–1932* (New York, 1968); and Jerome M. Clubb and Howard W. Allen, "The Cities and the Election of 1928: Partisan Realignment?" *American Historical Review,* LXXV (April 1969), 1205–1220, deal with longer time spans and place the election of 1928 in perspective. Charles M. Dollar, "The Senate Progressive Movement, 1921–1933. A Roll Call Analysis," Unpublished Ph.D. Dissertation, University of Kentucky, 1966, is important on behavior in the United States Senate.

29. On various aspects of the 1920's and early 1930's, see John M. Allswang,

"The Political Behavior of Chicago's Ethnic Groups, 1918–1932," Unpublished Ph.D. Dissertation, University of Pittsburgh, 1967; Allswang, "The Chicago Negro Voter and the Democratic Consensus: A Case Study, 1918–1936," *Journal of the Illinois State Historical Society,* LX (Summer 1967), 145–175; Bruce M. Stave, "The New Deal and the Building of an Urban Political Machine: Pittsburgh, A Case Study," Unpublished Ph.D. Dissertation, University of Pittsburgh, 1966; Stave, "The 'LaFollette Revolution' and the Pittsburgh Vote, 1932," *Mid-America,* XLIX (October 1967), 244–251; Burner, *Politics of Provincialism;* J. Joseph Huthmacher, *Massachusetts People and Politics, 1919–1933* (Cambridge, Mass., 1959); Arthur Mann, *La Guardia Comes to Power: 1933* (Philadelphia and New York, 1965); Don S. Kirschner, "Conflict in the Corn Belt: Rural Responses to Urbanization, 1919–1929," Unpublished Ph.D. Dissertation, University of Iowa, 1964; John Shover, "Populism in the Nineteen-Thirties: The Battle for the AAA," *Agricultural History,* XXXIX (January 1965), 17–24.

30. See the points raised by Carl Degler, Joseph G. Rayback, and Ronald Formisano, as reported in Formisano, "The Social Bases of American Voting Behavior," pp. 18–20, 31, 33, 37–40, 466–467. Also Michael A. Lebowitz, "The Jacksonians: Paradox Lost?," in Barton J. Bernstein, ed., *Towards a New Past: Dissenting Essays in American History* (New York, 1968), pp. 73–74. For the best brief discussion of the questions covered in this section, see Ronald Formisano, "Analyzing American Voting, 1830–1860: Methods," *Historical Methods Newsletter,* II (March 1969), 1–12.

31. In addition to Benson, *Concept of Jacksonian Democracy,* and the dissertations by Formisano, Jensen, Kleppner, and McSeveney, see McCormick, "Suffrage Classes and Party Alignments"; and Cornwell, "A Note on Providence Politics."

32. Bogue, "The 'New' Political History," p. 204.

33. Thernstrom, *Poverty and Progress,* pp. 103, 111, 182–185, and 271 (footnotes 39–47, esp. footnote 47).

34. Elmer E. Cornwell, Jr., "Party Absorption of Ethnic Groups: The Case of Providence, Rhode Island," *Social Forces,* XXXVIII (March 1960), 205–210; Norman Dain, "The Social Composition of the Leadership of Tammany Hall in New York City: 1855–1865," Unpublished M.A. Thesis, Columbia University, 1957; James R. Green, "A Study of the Political and Social Consequences of a Critical Election: The Case of New Haven, Connecticut, 1894–1920," Seminar Paper, Yale University, 1967; Bruce M. Stave, "The New Deal and the Building of an Urban Political Machine: Pittsburgh, A Case Study," Unpublished Ph.D. Dissertation, University of Pittsburgh, 1967; Stave, "The New Deal, The Last Hurrah, and the Building of an Urban Political Machine: Pittsburgh Committeemen, A Case Study," *Pennsylvania History,* XXXIII (October 1966), 460–483; Hays, "The Politics of Reform in Municipal Government." On those who climbed to the Senate, see David J. Rothman, *Politics and Power: The United States Senate, 1869–1901* (Cambridge, Mass., 1966), chap. 4, Notes (pp. 313–315), Appendixes A and B.

Note the uncertainty expressed by Charles Garrett: "Agreement *seems* to be lacking on when the Irish took control of Tammany . . . Peel states . . . the late 1890s. But this date *seems* too late. McGoldrick's view . . . *appears* to set the date too early, though *it does seem that the average New York City politician* in the 1860s, and *perhaps* for a while before, was an Irishman. Our *feeling* is that the triumph of the Irish—or any group—in Tammany cannot easily be pinpointed; it depends upon your criteria." Charles Garrett, *The*

LaGuardia Years, Machine and Reform Politics in New York City (New Brunswick, N.J., 1961), p. 338 (footnote 23), emphasis added.

35. James C. Malin, "The Turnover of Farm Population in Kansas," *Kansas Historical Quarterly,* IV (November 1935), 339–372; Allan G. Bogue, *From Prairie to Cornbelt: Farming on the Illinois and Iowa Prairies in the Nineteenth Century* (Chicago, 1963), pp. 25–28; Merle Curti, *The Making of an American Community: A Case Study of Democracy in a Frontier County* (Stanford, 1959), pp. 65–77, 140–143, 163, 169, 178ff, 218, 224, 361ff, 404, 421, 443, 446–447; Thernstrom, *Poverty and Progress,* pp. 31, 84–90, 167–168, 195–199, and 273 (footnotes 8–10, esp. works cited in footnotes 9 and 10).

36. John Demos, "Notes on Life in Plymouth Colony," *William and Mary Quarterly,* 3rd ser., XXII (April 1965), 264–286; Kenneth A. Lockridge, "The Population of Dedham, Massachusetts, 1636–1676," *Economic History Review,* XIX (August 1966), 318–344; and his forthcoming *A New England Town: The First Hundred Years, Dedham, Massachusetts, 1636–1736;* Richard Dunn, "The Barbados Census of 1680: Profile of the Richest Colony in English America," *William and Mary Quarterly,* 3rd ser., XXVI (January 1969), 3–30; Philip J. Greven, Jr., "Family Structure in Seventeenth-Century Andover, Massachusetts," *William and Mary Quarterly,* 3rd ser., XXIII (April 1966), 234–256; Greven, "Historical Demography and Colonial America, A Review Article," *William and Mary Quarterly,* 3rd ser., XXII (July 1967), 438–454; Greven, "Old Patterns in the New World: The Distribution of Land in 17th-Century Andover," *Essex Institute Historical Collections,* CI (April 1965), 133–148; and his forthcoming *Four Generations: Population, Land and Family in Colonial Andover, Massachusetts;* James Potter, "The Growth of Population in America, 1700–1860," in D V. Glass and D. E. C. Eversley, eds., *Population in History* (Chicago, 1965), pp. 631–688.

37. Thernstrom, *Poverty and Progress.* There are at the dissertation stage several studies of population and mobility in selected cities in the nineteenth century. In particular, Peter Knights is studying Boston, 1830–1860; Lawrence Glasco, Erie County, New York (Buffalo), in the mid- and late nineteenth century; Stuart Blumin, Philadelphia, 1820–1860; and Richard Sennett, Chicago at the end of the century. See, for example, Stuart Blumin, "Mobility in a Nineteenth-Century American City: Philadelphia, 1820–1860," Unpublished Ph.D. Dissertation, University of Pennsylvania, 1968, and "The Historical Study of Vertical Mobility," *Historical Methods Newsletter,* I (September 1968), 1–13; Stephan Thernstrom and Richard Sennett, eds., *Nineteenth-Century Cities: Essays in the New Urban History* (New Haven, 1969). For a discussion of some of the research problems connected with such studies, see Peter R. Knights, "City Directories as Aids to Ante-Bellum Urban Studies: A Research Note," *Historical Methods Newsletter,* II (September 1969), 1–10.

38. Kenneth A. Lockridge, "Land, Population, and the Evolution of New England Society, 1630–1790," *Past and Present,* XXXIX (April 1968), 62–80; James Henretta, "Economic Development and Social Structure in Colonial Boston," *William and Mary Quarterly,* 3rd ser., XXII (January 1965), 75–92; Robert S. and B. Katherine Brown, *Virginia, 1705–1786: Democracy or Aristocracy?* (East Lansing, 1964); Curti, *Making of an American Community.*

39. Jackson Turner Main, *The Social Structure of Revolutionary America* (Princeton, 1965).

40. Even some of the pioneering quantitative studies of social background have focused on the elite level. See, for example, William Miller, ed., *Men in*

Business (Cambridge, Mass., 1952); and Thomas Cochran, *Railroad Leaders, 1845–1890* (Cambridge, Mass., 1953).

41. The fruits of Harris' study will appear in *Perspectives in American History,* III, 1969, published by the Charles Warren Center at Harvard University. For a small-scale study focusing on changes over time in the nature of political elites, see Ari Hoogenboom, "Industrialism and Political Leadership: A Case Study of the United States Senate," in Frederic Jaher, ed., *The Age of Industrialism in America: Essays in Social Structure and Cultural Values* (New York, 1968).

42. Frederick Mosteller and David L. Wallace, *Inference and Disputed Authorship: The Federalist Papers* (Reading, Mass., 1964).

43. *American Historical Review,* LXX (July 1965), 1233.

44. *William and Mary Quarterly,* 3rd ser., XXIII (April 1966), 354.

45. Mosteller and Wallace used frequency theory to determine their prior probabilities It is equally possible to introduce subjective probabilities, initial guesses based on experience, intuition, or the collective wisdom of historical scholarship. On the uses and applications of subjective probabilities, see Richard Jeffrey, *The Logic of Decision* (New York, 1965), and Henry Kyburg and Howard Smokler, eds., *Studies in Subjective Probability* (New York, 1964).

46. The most readable discussion of this and related problems is Hayward R. Alker, Jr., *Mathematics and Politics* (New York, 1965).

47. *New York Times,* January 24, 1965, sec. 7, p. 44. Professor Woodward went on to remark: "Fundamentally the historian feels that he is past-minded, time conscious. humanistic in spirit; skeptical in outlook. . . . He doubts that the most important problems are amenable to quantitative analysis and suspects that the social scientists pick problems their methods will solve and neglect others."

48. Robert E. Brown, *Middle-Class Democracy and the Revolution in Massachusetts, 1691–1780* (Ithaca, 1955).

49. See, for example, Sam Bass Warner, Jr., *The Private City: Philadelphia in Three Periods of Its Growth* (Philadelphia, 1968).

50. The Dollar-Jensen text will be published by Holt, Rinehart and Winston. V. O. Key, Jr., *A Primer of Statistics for Political Scientists* (New York, 1954), and Hubert M. Blalock, Jr., *Social Statistics* (New York, 1960), have been basic to quantitative research.

Understanding the Puritans

DAVID D. HALL

"How does one define Puritanism?" This question, the first sentence of Alan Simpson's *Puritanism in Old and New England*, is one to which the answers in recent years have grown increasingly complex and contradictory.[1] Thirty years ago there was no doubt about the answer; the scholarship of Morison and Haller, and, towering over both, the massive symmetry of Perry Miller's *The New England Mind*, gave compelling definition to the subject.[2] But climates of opinion change, and with them the historian's angle of perception. What Perry Miller had to say now has the ring of the 1930's, for the period in which he wrote saw the old myth that the Puritan hated life still strong upon us. If Miller's great achievement was to free us from that myth, the question remains as to the proper understanding of Puritanism. To describe the differences of opinion between Miller and his critics is one purpose of this essay.[3] But its deeper task is to identify the problems that every student of the Puritans must inevitably confront, the problems of interpretation and methodology that always seem to turn up in dealing with this subject.[4]

Abraham Lincoln once said that slavery was "somehow" the cause of the Civil War. Historians of Puritanism know likewise that the history of the movement was somehow related to the contemporary culture and social structure. Puritanism had social sources and social consequences; were historians to define precisely which groups supported (and dissented from) the Puritan program, as well as the movement's consequences for the broader culture, they would move closer to an understanding of its nature. One of their tasks, then, is to determine how Puritanism was socially functional.

A second problem arises out of the close relationship between Puritanism and two other religious movements, the Reformed tradition and Pietism. Heir of the first and parent of the second, Puritanism at the onset of its history depended for ideas on Reformed Protestantism, and at the close faded into Pietism. John Eusden has suggested that Puritanism may be understood as an "evangelical Calvinism," a term that links it both to the sixteenth-century world of Calvin and to the eighteenth-century world of the Pietists.[5] If Eusden's suggestion is correct, historians must also be able to distinguish between Puritanism and these other movements. At the same time their task is to fix the time span within which Puritanism played out its course; to give dates to a movement is, perforce, to make a statement about its origins and legacy. A periodization of Puritanism and an inventory of its distinctive (or shared) religious ideas are two sides of the same problem: to mark off the historical and intellectual boundaries of the movement.

A third problem is to construct a definition that includes the range of Puritan types. Here I agree with Alan Simpson, who insists on viewing the broad spectrum from Presbyterians to Quakers as one continuous whole. He is right in criticizing historians who legitimize too narrow a slice of this spectrum, and he is right also in asking if there is not something fundamental in the nature of Puritanism that made it dynamic and expansive.[6] The history of the movement offers innumerable examples of the Puritan as a man in motion, a man possessed by a peculiar restlessness, a man who may attack the idea of a gathered church while still a minister in England, yet form such a group within his English parish and, publicly defend the practice once he reached America. These inconsistencies, and more besides, mark the career of John Cotton, and the life histories of countless other Puritans were fashioned in the same erratic manner.

We need a definition of Puritanism which takes account of this restlessness, and if dissatisfaction with the scholarship of the 1930's is on the rise, the reason is largely its failure to meet such a test. It fails this test in one obvious way. Together with the denominational historians, Perry Miller assumed that denominational categories could be imposed upon Puritan conceptions of the church.[7] But can we call the New England Puritans "congregationalists" with a capital C when the actual working-out of their church order was so confused and contradictory? Or can we call Thomas Cartwright a "presbyterian" with a capital P when his conception of the church involved recognizably "congregational" elements? More recent studies, in recognition of these ambiguities, have moved away from the categories of denominational history, substituting in their place an emphasis upon the "continuity of experience" which united all Puritans.[8] The result may be a certain loss of clarity, but the new scholarship at least has the virtue of restoring the dynamic quality of Puritanism to the center of any definition.

The scholarship of the 1930's minimized the restlessness within Puritanism because of another assumption. In Perry Miller's view, "Puritanism was not only a religious creed, it was a philosophy and a metaphysic; it was an organization of man's whole life, emotional and intellectual." The structure of *The New England Mind* imposed a coherence upon Puritanism which Miller described as the reconciliation of "piety" and "intellect." To define the movement in these terms was explicitly to rule out any spiritualists as un-Puritan; it was to cut off the spectrum short of the Quakers and Antinomians. Here again, recent scholarship points toward a more inclusive definition. In place of the intellectual commitments Miller saw as crucial, Alan Simpson would put the terms "experience" and "thrust," intending by them a particular type of religious experience which unleashed the zeal of the Puritan saint.[9] The value of these terms must not obscure their weaknesses; though they permit the Quakers to reenter the fold as authentic Puritans, their meaning seems inherently subjective,[10] and they may act to exclude the array of distinctions that Miller so successfully identified as woven into the texture of Puritanism.

An adequate definition of the Puritan movement must therefore seek to unite the experiential dimension with the formal structure of the Puritan intellect. It must locate the movement within a particular time period, and with reference to the Reformed tradition and Pietism. It must identify the bond between the social sources of the movement and its history, between its rhetoric and its social consequences.

How close do we stand to such a definition? The literature that deals with the relationship between John Calvin and the Puritans is both extensive and contradictory, and for these reasons affords an opportunity to begin the task of evaluation. All historians agree that Puritanism belongs within the family of Reformed churches.[11] Yet the family resemblance has not prevented many historians from detecting differences between the two—differences, broadly speaking, of two kinds, philosophical and theological. The philosophical loom especially large in Perry Miller's account. "In defining the intellectual character of the

New England Puritans," he declared in 1938, "we must always exercise caution about calling them Calvinists. John Calvin's metaphysics were still Aristotelian and scholastic; New Englanders had thrown aside much of the philosophy which is implied at every point in Calvin's theology, and had taken up a system of which the implications were quite different." These differences were due largely to the Puritans' acceptance of Peter Ramus, a French educator and logician; because the New Englanders were Ramists, Miller argued, they had emancipated themselves from Aristotle and scholasticism. More profoundly, Calvin was a nominalist who asserted the doctrine of an "arbitrary" God wholly unconditioned and deterministic in His actions; Puritans (at least those in New England) imposed limitations on the will of God and order upon the universe.[12]

More recent scholarship suggests, on the other hand, that the philosophical differences between Calvin and the Puritans were not very great. The essential continuity between the two was partly a matter of their common reliance upon the nominalistic distinction between *potentia absoluta* and *potentia ordinata*. Sharing the same confidence in the order of the world, they shared also the scholastic definition of man as a rational animal. Both agreed that God respected the nature of man in the process of redemption. Both agreed that in the "order of nature" (another concept taken over from scholasticism) man's will was free in such a way that he voluntarily obeyed the laws of God. And if the comparison stand between the Puritans and the continental theologians commonly known as Reformed scholastics, the continuities in philosophy and metaphysics are still more striking.[13]

But what of Peter Ramus? The road to an understanding of his significance for the Puritans is littered with obstacles, some of them placed there by Perry Miller. *The New England Mind* contains the suggestion that Ramus, a victim of the St. Bartholomew's Day massacre, "died equally for the cause of logic" and for the cause of Protestantism. In a manner characteristic of his approach to intellectual history, Miller framed the difference between Ramus and Aristotle as one between mortal enemies: those who murdered Ramus must have been disciples of Aristotle. For the New England Puritans to read Ramist texts thus amounted to a declaration of war; it was a decision, declared Miller, that entailed enormous consequences.[14] But no war between Aristotelians and Ramists was ever fought in New England, or even on the continent. The curriculum at Harvard College depended on textbooks written by a group of continental Reformed scholastics—Alsted, Keckermann, Heereboord, Burgersdicius—who blended Ramist and scholastic elements into an eclectic whole.[15] The second president of Harvard, Charles Chauncy, was hostile to Ramus, but he was never martyred on this account. To drain the ferocity from the mortal combat between Aristotelian and Ramist is, admittedly, to lessen the drama of the Puritan mind. But the truth seems to be that Ramist method, though practiced in New England, did not serve in any major way to divide the Puritans from the Reformed tradition. Nor did their reading in Ramus provide the New England Puritans with a metaphysic, the congregational church order, and a "plain style" of preaching, as Miller argued; all of these have other sources that far outweigh Ramus in importance.[16]

As for the second category of difference, there is general agreement among many historians that Puritanism has a different theological outlook from Calvinism. Comparison of the Puritans with John Calvin easily turns up some divergences: Calvin retained a sense of the real presence in his understanding of the Lord's Supper, while most Puritans followed Zwingli in adopting a memorialist view; Calvin's doctrine of assurance excluded the evidence of "works," evidence which many Puritans thought legitimate.[17] In broader terms, Thomas Torrance has contrasted Calvin's Christocentric focus to the anthropocentric orientation of the Puritans. And Perry Miller declared that the New England Puritans fashioned the covenant theology in order to escape from the rigors of "strict Calvinism." [18]

No idea of Miller's has gained greater currency, or been more widely attacked. Counter-interpretations of the covenant theology have generally succeeded in establishing two points. One is that the covenantal idiom figured in the Reformed tradition long before it appeared among the Puritans whom Miller cited. Certain of these studies suggest, in other words, that the Puritans in resorting to the idiom were not particularly novel or illegitimate by Reformed standards. The second point is that the idea of a covenant, though apparently implying a voluntary, contractual relationship between God and man, was not intended by the Puritans as a means of bringing God more within man's reach, but rather to accomplish other ends—to provide a rationale for the sacraments, or a basis for their doctrine of assurance.[19]

In spite of all this scholarship we still lack a clear understanding of the covenant theology, and on the larger question of the theological differences between Calvin and the Puritans the confusion is just as great. The time has come, I believe, to reconsider the terms of the question, for we seem to be dealing with a question *mal posée,* so posed as to lead to answers which are never satisfactory. The essential error has been to postulate a "strict" orthodoxy, a "pure" Calvinism, defined in terms of John Calvin and the *Institutes of the Christian Religion.* Once the name of Calvin becomes synonymous with "orthodoxy," certain deadly consequences ensue: the concept presumes a static system of ideas, so that change of any kind—any variation, no matter how slight—is taken as evidence of declining rigor and faith. Perry Miller fell into this trap, and so have many others.[20] But we have been warned against it by the post-Millerian scholarship on the covenant theology: on the one hand this scholarship suggests that the strict orthodoxy of the pure Calvin must not be interpreted so narrowly as to exclude the idiom of the covenant, and on the other, that the Puritans who invoked the idiom did not thereby fall from the heights of orthodoxy. These warnings must be extended. In particular, the differences between Puritans and continental Reformed theology must not be measured solely in terms of Calvin. Reformed theology [21] was a system of thought elaborated and defended in varying ways by many persons in the sixteenth century. Several of these Reformed theologians—Beza, Piscator, Zanchy, Bullinger, Pareus—figure more often than Calvin in the religious thought of seventeenth-century New England.[22] To overlook these intermediary figures, in any case, is to risk overlooking the complexities of the Reformed tradition, and consequently the materials for proving the continuity between this tradition and the Puritans. In fact, once these Calvinists, and not Calvin, are brought into the comparison, the continuities far outweigh the differences.

Let me cite some recent scholarship in support of this assertion. One of the more notable contributions of the past decade to our understanding of Puritanism is Norman Pettit's *The Heart Prepared,* a history of the doctrine of "preparation for salvation" as invoked (or rejected) by Reformed theologians from Calvin to Stoddard. Pettit's approach is significantly different from that of Miller, who argued that the Puritans in New England developed the idea as a means of extending social control over the entire population. Miller set the doctrine within a functional context, Pettit within a scriptural one, for he begins by showing how Scripture itself establishes the problem of reconciling man's initiative with God's. Thereafter the focus is upon a continuity of speculation which begins with Calvin and moves on through English to American Puritanism. In this fashion Pettit locates the New England appropriation of the doctrine firmly within the broad context of Reformed theology.[23]

Recent scholarship on William Perkins provides further evidence of continuity between Puritanism and the Reformed tradition on the continent. Perkins was a key link between Reformed scholasticism and English Puritanism. He drew freely on the writings of continental theologians for ideas and even actual texts; included in his collected works were translations (or adaptations) of treatises by Beza and Zanchy. At the same time his own writings were widely reprinted on the continent, where his reputation was nearly as considerable as in England. It is not surprising, therefore, that Jacobus Arminius should have challenged Perkins on the doctrine of predestination, thereby precipitating the debate that led eventually to the synod of Dort.[24] Such evidence of connections between Puritanism and Reformed theology could be multipled many times over, and all of it goes to suggest that the two were essentially congruent, if not identical.[25]

Yet we need not rely on external evidence to demonstrate the congruence. Calvin, his successors on the continent, and the Puritans all shared a theological outlook founded on a common understanding of God. The God they defined was the sovereign creator of the world, a creator who stood aloof from His handiwork. Calvinist and Puritan alike asserted the radical separation of grace and nature, declaring that an ever-free and independent God stood over and above "the created world of man and nature." Both went on to describe God in terms of His will, and for both the action of the Holy Spirit in restoring fallen man to the state of grace was the focus of "divinity." Both Calvinist and Puritan saw God as ceaselessly at work bending the course of human history toward the goal of the kingdom.[26]

It was this eschatological understanding of God which gave the Reformed tradition (including Puritanism) its special cast. To put the matter broadly, all Calvinists were imbued with a certain kind of historical consciousness. All of them understood reality as dynamic, not static. All of them looked forward to the coming of the new order, and the urge to hasten on the kingdom was what lay behind their programs of communal discipline. The same historical consciousness may account for the prominence of the decree of election in their thought. As they interpreted the doctrine of predestination, it was a statement of God's promise to enter into and renew a fallen world. The doctrine offered men the assurance that "God has willed and is acting in his power to restore and justify them through his love." Restated in this fashion, the doctrine took on an eschatological significance, for it linked the election of the saints with the coming of the kingdom.[27]

Elsewhere the activist, historical orientation of Reformed divinity was reflected in the great interest Calvin and the Puritans expressed in the Holy Spirit and in the Atonement, rather than the Incarnation; in their use of the covenant theology,[28] and in their fascination with "method." William Perkins provided readers of his works with a fold-out chart marking off the stages of salvation. This chart was actually a form of history, for when the Puritan wrote his spiritual autobiography, he ordered his life according to the spatial and dynamic plan that Perkins had outlined. The methodizing of the *ordo salutis,* the elaboration of the "morphology of conversion," the development of a "plain style" of preaching that was deliberately "practical"—these aspects of seventeenth-century Puritanism emerged from an eschatological consciousness which the Puritans shared with the Reformed tradition.[29]

If it is important in understanding the Puritans to recognize their alliance with the international Reformed tradition, certain differences between the two must also be noted. Like members of a family, the national churches within the Reformed tradition resembled one another but also varied in detail, for each adapted a common idiom to particular circumstances. The special character of Puritanism arose from the refusal of Elizabeth I to allow certain changes in the structure and worship of the Church of England, changes favored by many English Protestants but especially by a group which gained the name of "Puritans." Denied a hearing by the Queen, these Puritans turned to Parliament and to the population at large for support, at the same time sharpening their indictment of the Church beyond what Calvin would have said. By the 1570's they were declaring that the bishops of the Church—the persons charged with suppressing them —were unlawful, which was to say that their office had no warrant in the word of God. Calvin had never been so explicit, nor did he make the validity of the Church depend on the exercise of discipline, as many Puritans maintained. It was Calvin, to be sure, who taught the Puritans their legalism, but the political situation in which they found themselves encouraged the development of this legalism beyond the point where he had stopped. Similarly, the Puritans inherited a bias against Catholic sacerdotalism, a bias intensified in England in

the heat of struggle against the "popish remnants" in the Church.
And because the Puritans could not rely on bishops or civil magis-
trates to enforce the moral code they taught, the preachers in the
movement directed their attention increasingly to the individual conscience, encouraging the practice of pietistic self-scrutiny.[30]

This final tendency is one to which many historians have pointed
as the crucial difference between the Reformed tradition (or Calvin)
and the Puritans. When more is known of the Reformed scholastics
from whom the Puritans borrowed so deeply, this "piety" may not
seem so original.[31] Nor was it taught in the same way by every
preacher.[32] Throughout the history of the movement, Puritans debated
a wide range of religious issues, many of them arising out of the
tension between this pietistic bias and Reformed sacramentalism, others
out of the complexities of methodizing the *ordo salutis*. What was
the normative experience of conversion, an awakening by degrees or
some compressed reaction? [33] How was man's striving for grace and
his cleansing under the Law to be accommodated with the gospel
promise of grace without conditions? What was the role and nature
of the means of grace—the ministry and the sacraments—in a system
in which the elect were predestinated to salvation? These questions
arose in part because most Puritans, as heirs of the Reformed tradition, held on to the sacraments and an objective understanding of the
ministry. To be sure, they held on to both in an attenuated form; their
heightened interest in the workings of the Holy Spirit left little room
for a high doctrine of the sacraments or a sacerdotal view of the
ministry. The logic of their spiritism was such, moreover, that
amidst the turmoil of the seventeenth century some Puritans would
overthrow the sacraments and ministry altogether.[34] Perhaps it could
be said that Puritans finally divided on these issues according to their
view of history and the world. Millennarian Puritans saw the world
as in process of renewal, and discounted all existing structures; others
saw it in legalistic and static terms as composed of ordained institutions
and fixed forms, and spoke of the millennium as far off.

The political situation of the Puritans had one further consequence.
Resentful of the Church's imperfection, yet believing that schism was
a sin, Puritans found themselves caught in a dilemma from which
flowed much of their restlessness.[35] The same dilemma was a cause
of the fragmentation of the movement into sects, a process that began
in the late sixteenth century with the emergence of the separatists. By
one set of Reformed standards the separatists were perfectly legitimate

in demanding freedom for the church to cleanse itself; by another they were schismatics who carried their legalism too far. The emergence of the separatists is thus a perfect measure of how the English situation acted to confuse the meaning and application of Reformed ideas.[36]

It is in this context, moreover, that denominational categories become inadequate; too abstract and rigid, they sever the Puritan sects from their dynamic and fluid relationship with the Reformed tradition. Denominational categories conceal the fact that all Puritans, whether "presbyterian" or "congregationalist" or some other group, held four propositions in common: the revitalization of the laymen's role, including greater privileges in the government of the church; the purification of church membership; the assignment of the power of the keys to each parish or congregation; and the separation of church and state so as to give the church effective responsibility for discipline. Many historians would add a fifth proposition to this list: the assertion that the nature of the church must conform to the will of God.[37] But the Biblicism of the Puritans is less important in explaining their ecclesiology than the emphasis they placed upon the Holy Spirit. The essential impulse within the movement was to relate the church to the intervention of the Spirit, to understand the community of the saints as a type of the kingdom. In this they were not unique. Calvin himself looked upon the church in two ways, as an institution ordained by God to exist upon earth, and as the realm of the Spirit, a realm in which "the original order of creation" had been restored.[38] Inheriting both views, the Puritans were driven to identify the first with the Church of England, and so to emphasize the second. But the issue of keeping the two in balance was inherent within the Reformed tradition.

There is another reason for discarding denominational categories. Puritanism began as a movement within the Church of England at the time of the Elizabethan religious settlement of 1559. From that time until the accession of William III, most Puritans thought of themselves as members of the Church, not as founders of new churches. It was only when the religious settlement under William denied the legitimacy of this claim that the connections between English Puritans and the Church were finally severed. On this side of the Atlantic, the new charter of 1691 and the events associated with it mark a similar end to the affiliation. Thereafter, any colonist who claimed membership or ministerial orders within the Church would have to renounce his current status and formally rejoin the mother body.[39]

The historic association of Puritanism with the Church of England is a means of giving dates to the movement, a periodization which other evidence sustains. The decade of the 1690's saw Reformed scholasticism giving way under the impact of the Enlightenment, leaving eighteenth-century Reformed theologians to work out a new alliance between philosophy and religion.[40] On the whole, however, Pietists were content to abandon philosophy and science, just as they abandoned the theocratic vision of a holy commonwealth which inspired Calvin and the Puritans. What passed from Puritanism to Pietism was the assertion that religion fundamentally involved the affective self, the heart, rather than the reason.[41]

An adequate definition of Puritanism must incorporate this periodization of the movement, and go on from there to recognize the essential continuity between Calvinists and Puritans. An adequate definition must allow for the adaptation of Reformed ideas to England, a process that eventually resulted in the splintering of the movement into many sects. Despite this splintering, an adequate definition must recognize the wholeness to Puritan history. What gave substance to the movement was a certain inventory of ideas—the separation of grace and nature, an understanding of God and man as active forces, an eschatology. And what linked the Puritan program for reform of the church to Puritan descriptions of the spiritual life was the common motif of renewal. Edmund S. Morgan has seen the Puritan as caught in the dilemma of remaining pure while living in the world. Such a posture was forced upon the Puritan by the dynamic relationship between this world and the next. He knew himself to be a mid-point between these worlds, and his striving for self-discipline, his endless self-scrutiny were directed toward the end of winning freedom from the world and entrance to the kingdom.[42]

There still remains to be answered, finally, the problem of the relationship between Puritanism and culture. What we know for sure is very little. The extensive scholarship of Christopher Hill has shown that class, status, and occupation have something to do with Puritanism, but Hill himself would surely agree that they are not sufficient as analytical categories.[43] It seems likely that the social sources of Puritanism will eventually be described in terms of personality structure (and thus of family structure), life style, generations, and negative reference groups, but exact information is wanting on all of these for both England and America. It is possible to declare with more certainty that the dynamics of Puritanism in England bear a direct relationship to its status as an outgroup remote from the center of power; the greater this distance, the more intense became the urge to free the church from the world and hasten on the coming kingdom.[44]

The millennarian fervor which runs through Puritanism may provide the best clue to the social function of the movement. Puritanism, it seems, furnished certain Englishmen with a new identity as members of a special group. All English Protestants believed that the history of the Christian church revealed God's favoring providence toward England. And Christian history also taught that God's people must fight a cruel and bloody war against Anti-Christ and all his minions.[45] The Puritans were able to appropriate this rhetoric and apply it to their cause for two reasons: they were most outspoken in attacking Catholicism, and their outgroup status lent itself to a sense of persecution. The identity of the Puritan as saint in covenant with God was reinforced by the idea that history was moving rapidly toward the coming of the kingdom. The prophetic stance of the Puritan teachers grew out of an historical perspective which saw the task of reformation as increasingly urgent, lest the final day prove a day of judgment. Those who responded to this preaching, those Englishmen who in life style withdrew from the "world" and set their hearts upon the kingdom, established a new identity for themselves as the Lord's free people.

From this identity flowed the Puritan understanding of the church as a voluntary, gathered congregation. From it came also the Puritan theory of community, the vision of a social order (to quote John Winthrop) "knit together" in a "bond of love." The immigration to New England can equally be counted as a consequence of this millennarianism. In the late 1620's events in England and abroad convinced many Puritans that the final day was close at hand. New England loomed before them both as refuge and as paradise, the wilderness which they could make into the kingdom. Not only did the chiliastic zeal of certain Puritans precipitate their immigration; it also inspired the congregationalism that emerged in New England in the 1630's— the strict limits on church membership, the more democratic church structure.[46]

Whether the colonists were exceptional in their chiliasm is not clear. In their general vision of the kingdom, and in their activist drive, they stood as one with the entire Puritan movement, sharing in a historical consciousness that originated with Calvin and Bucer. Any understanding of Puritanism in America must ignore artificial boundaries and distinctions and build instead upon the continuities that linked England and America. On this matter of continuities, American scholarship has far to go in working out the relationships between institutional forms, and even ideas.[47]

Does this mean there is nothing distinctive about American Puritanism, nothing American historians can study without going back to Perkins or Calvin? There is not as much as many would assert, but there is something. We can speak of the Americanizing of Puritan ideas just as historians of the Revolutionary period speak of the Americanizing of Whig ideas. The analogy is nearly exact; the colonists imported the radical Whig ideology from abroad, and we can only understand what they are saying by reference to the English sources. Yet there is a difference, for although the ideas seem the same on both sides of the Atlantic, the pattern of culture in America had departed from the English model in ways that affected the meaning and consequences of these ideas.[48] So also in the seventeenth century, the Reformed tradition took on a new significance in the "free air of a new world." Here Puritanism became the majority point of view, and preachers who had whetted their fiery preaching on targets that the Church of England had to offer underwent an agonizing adjustment to a new life style. Here the ideal of a gathered church had strange consequences, and here the alliance between church and state gave the "New England Way" its notoriety.[49] The future of Puritan studies in America, a future that seems without limit, lies in articulating these differences, as well as the continuities, between Old World and New.

NOTES

1. I am indebted to John Eusden of Williams College and Sacvan Bercovitch of the University of California, San Diego, for comments that enlarged my view of the subject.

2. Samuel Eliot Morison, *The Puritan Pronaos* (New York, 1936); William

Haller, *The Rise of Puritanism* (New York, 1938); Perry Miller, *The New England Mind: The Seventeenth Century* (Cambridge, Mass., 1939). Miller's contributions in the 1930's also included many of the essays in *Errand into the Wilderness* (Cambridge, Mass., 1956), as well as the anthology *The Puritans* (New York, 1938), co-edited with Thomas Johnson.

3. It falls beyond the limits of this essay to describe the intersection of Puritan scholarship in America with the search for a "usable past" in which Americans have engaged in the twentieth century. A good beginning on the history of this search, including information on changing views of the Puritans, is Richard Ruland, *The Reinterpretation of American Literature* (Cambridge, Mass., 1967).

4. There have been several other published essays of a similar nature: Edmund S. Morgan, "The Historians of Early New England," in Ray Billington, ed., *The Reinterpretation of Early American History* (San Marino, Calif., 1966); Richard Schlatter, "The Puritan Strain," in John Higham, ed., *The Reconstruction of American History* (New York, 1962); Sidney James, introduction, *The New England Puritans* (New York, 1968). Since this essay is based on the assumption that American Puritanism is broadly continuous with Puritanism in England, it may be pertinent to note the differences of approach between British and American scholarship. When American historians investigate the period of Puritan history before 1630, on the whole they are seeking the origins of ideas and institutions found in New England. This purpose entails several consequences, one of them the postulating of ideal types (like "non-separating congregationalism") which presumably the colonists imported, another an emphasis on intellectual history, and a third a principle of selection in reading pre-1630 material, namely those writers who were most cited in New England. Much of British scholarship—and this includes Americans writing on English history—is concerned with the social and political consequences of Puritanism, especially the relationship between the movement and the English Revolution, or else with its local and institutional history. In this scholarship the variety and fluidity of opinion is often allowed to obscure the fundamental stance of the Puritan.

5. William Ames, *The Marrow of Theology*, translated and edited by John Eusden (Boston, 1968), p. 19.

6. Alan Simpson, *Puritanism in Old and New England*, paperback ed. (Chicago, 1961), pp. 1–2.

7. Though Miller distinguished between "separating" and "nonseparating" Congregationalists, thereby departing from earlier explanations of the genesis of Massachusetts Congregationalism, he left unchallenged the premise of denominational scholarship (as represented by Williston Walker and Henry Martyn Dexter) that the thread of Congregationalism could be unraveled from the tapestry of Puritanism. The most important critique of Miller, careful to distinguish true Congregationalism from its "prehistory," is Geoffrey Nuttall, *Visible Saints, The Congregational Way, 1640–1660* (Oxford, 1957), though I would press Nuttall's critique of denominational history further than he does. See also Robert Paul, ed., *An Apologeticall Narration* (Philadelphia, 1963), pp. 57–66, and the scholarship cited therein.

8. Simpson, *Puritanism in Old and New England*, p. 2. In a footnote, Simpson cites A. S. P. Woodhouse, *Puritanism and Liberty* (London, 1938), p. xxxvii: "It is unnecessary to posit a unity in all Puritan thought; it is sufficient to recognize a continuity."

9. Simpson, *Puritanism in Old and New England,* chap. 1. Earlier, William Haller had criticized denominational historians for their "historical piety," and called for an inclusive definition of Puritanism structured around the figure of the preacher: "The disagreements that rendered Puritans into presbyterians, independents, separatists, and baptists were in the long run not so significant as the qualities of character, of mind and imagination, which kept them all alike Puritans." *The Rise of Puritanism,* paperback ed. (New York, 1957), p. 17. Earlier still, William York Tindall had insisted upon "the essential identity of the radical sects in both nature and purpose." *John Bunyan, Mechanick Preacher* (New York, 1934), p. 5. See also James F. Maclear, " 'The Heart of New England Rent': The Mystical Element in Early Puritan History," *Mississippi Valley Historical Review,* XLII (1956), 621–656.

10. Cf. the remark by Richard T. Vann—"This 'thrust'—whatever that means"—in his review essay of Michael Walzer, *Revolution of the Saints,* in *History and Theory,* VII (1968), 108.

11. Much can be learned about Puritanism from general histories of the Reformed tradition, among which are John T. McNeill, *The History and Character of Calvinism* (New York, 1954); James L. Ainslie, *The Doctrine of Ministerial Order in the Reformed Churches of the Sixteenth and Seventeenth Centuries* (Edinburgh, 1940); Geddes MacGregor, *Corpus Christi: The Nature of the Church According to the Reformed Tradition* (London, 1959).

12. Miller, *The Puritans,* pp. 24, 32–33; Miller, *The New England Mind,* pp. 92–97, 157, 194–195. One of the problems with his argument is to agree on a meaning of "scholasticism." The Puritans frequently denounced the "School-men," as Miller pointed out; but he also warned against taking their denunciations at "face value." On the one hand he thus asserted that the Puritans "revolted" against scholasticism, while on the other he perceived that they accepted "scholastic premises in physics and astronomy, the scholastic theory of the four elements or the four causes," and much else besides. Miller, *The Puritans,* pp. 25–26; *The New England Mind,* pp. 100–102.

13. Francois Wendel, *Calvin: The Origins and Development of His Religious Thought* (New York, 1963), pp. 127ff, 179; Eusden, ed., *The Marrow of Theology,* pp. 51–52; Heinrich Heppe, *Reformed Dogmatics* (London, 1950), pp. 144, 155, 159, 167; David D. Hall, ed., *The Antinomian Controversy, 1636–1638: A Documentary History* (Middletown, Conn., 1968), see "Cause" and "Order" under index. More precise study is needed of the place such scholastic terms had in the Puritan mind.

14. Miller, *The New England Mind,* pp. 117–120.

15. Samuel Eliot Morison, *Harvard College in the Seventeenth Century* (Cambridge, Mass., 1936), I, 157–159, 191–192. Miller drew heavily upon these same writers in reconstructing the Puritan mind—the statements and extended quotation on page 264 are from Zanchy and Ursinus, and the quotation bridging pages 287–288 is from Zanchy—to an extent that the text does not reveal, though he also was explicit in recognizing the importance of these Protestant scholastics. *The New England Mind,* pp. 102–105; the citations above are drawn from the annotated copy in the Harvard Library. The fullest study of Keckermann, Heereboord, and Burgersdicius in the educational setting of the late sixteenth and early seventeenth centuries is Paul Dibon, *L'Enseignement Philosophique dans les Universités Néerlandaises à l'Epoque Pré-Cartésienne (1575–1650)* (Paris, 1954). Dibon argues (pp. 10, 133, and throughout) against reading the philosophical instruction of the period as a battle between Aristotelianism and Ramism; instead he perceives "une tendence

conciliatrice" in the logic teaching: "Il ne s'agit pas tant d'opposer Ramus à Aristote que de compléter celui-ci par celui-là" (p. 133).

16. Miller, *The New England Mind*, chaps. 5, 6, 11, and 12. On the rhetoric of the Puritans, cf. J. W. Blench, *Preaching in England in the Late Fifteenth and Sixteenth Centuries* (New York, 1964), and Wilbur S. Howell, *Logic and Rhetoric in England, 1500–1700* (Princeton, 1961).

17. Wilhelm Niesel, *The Theology of Calvin* (London, 1956), pp. 170–171, cites Calvin's disapproval of the "practical syllogism" and his carefully hedged exegesis of 2 Peter 1.10, a text William Perkins placed on the title page of a treatise dealing with assurance, and which the "legal" preachers in New England invoked repeatedly during the Antinomian controversy, together with the "practical syllogism." Perkins, *Works* (London, 1608–1631), I, 419; Hall, *The Antinomian Controversy*, pp. 58, 237.

18. Thomas Torrance, *The School of Faith* (New York, 1959); Torrance, "Justification: Its Radical Nature and Place in Reformed Doctrine and Life," *Scottish Journal of Theology*, XIII (1960), 225–246; Miller, *Errand into the Wilderness*, pp. 51–53, an argument repeated in *The New England Mind*.

19. Leonard J. Trinterud, "The Origins of Puritanism," *Church History*, XX (1951), 37–57; Jens G. Moller, "The Beginnings of Puritan Covenant Theology," *Journal of Ecclesiastical History*, XIV (1963), 46–67; Everett H. Emerson, "Calvin and the Covenant Theology," *Church History*, XXV (1956), 136–144; Emerson, "Thomas Hooker: The Puritan as Theologian," *Anglican Theological Review*, XLIX (1967), 190–203; John von Rohr, "Covenant and Assurance in Early English Puritanism," *Church History*, XXXIV (1965), 195–203; C. J. Sommerville, "Conversion *versus* the Early Puritan Covenant of Grace," *Journal of Presbyterian History*, XLIV (1966), 178–197; J. A. Ross MacKenzie, "The Covenant Theology—A Review Article," *Journal of Presbyterian History*, XLIV (1966), 198–204. Also of importance are E. R. Daniel, "Reconciliation, Covenant and Election: A Study in the Theology of John Donne," *Anglican Theological Review*, XLVIII (1966), 14–30; Richard L. Greaves, "John Bunyan and Covenant Theology in the Seventeenth Century," *Church History*, XXXVI (1967), 151–169, which clarifies three different uses of the covenantal idiom; and Norman Pettit, *The Heart Prepared* (New Haven, 1966), pp. 217–221.

20. In describing Calvin's theology, Miller relied as much upon tone as upon specific doctrines. Both the tone and content of his "Calvin" are suggested by the following citations: Calvinism was "the relatively simple dogmatism of its founder"; "pure Calvinism"; "the absolute dogmatism of original Calvinism"; "primitive Calvinism"; "the doctrine of divine determinism"; "the inexorable logic of Calvin"; "Calvinism pictured man as lifeless clay in the potter's hand." Miller, *Errand into the Wilderness* (Cambridge, Mass., 1956), pp. 53, 69, 84; Miller, *Nature's Nation* (Cambridge, Mass., 1967), pp. 50, 53–54. The point is not only that Miller relied upon a stage-figure Calvin (the same Calvin, ironically, which V. L. Parrington depicted in *Main Currents of American Thought*) but that he played off the ideas of the New England Puritans against this false stereotype, thereby producing a divergence of views. Had Miller's understanding of Calvin been closer to the truth, the divergence would not have seemed so important. For other critiques of Miller's view of Calvin, see Pettit, *The Heart Prepared*, p. 40n, and Conrad Cherry, *The Theology of Jonathan Edwards*, paperback ed. (New York, 1966), pp. 2–6 and *passim*.

21. "Reformed" is a better term than "Calvinist," precisely for the reason that it avoids the unnecessary connotations of direct discipleship. "Calvinist"

is, in any event, an overused and much abused term. Cf. Basil Hall, "Calvin Against the Calvinists," *Proceedings* of the Huguenot Society of London, XX (1958–1964), 284–301.

22. Miller himself called attention to these theologians: *The New England Mind,* pp. 92–93. John Norton's annotations in *The Orthodox Evangelist* (London, 1657), and John Cotton's references in the debates during the Antinomian controversy (cf. Hall, *The Antinomian Controversy, 1636–1638*) provide other leads to the colonists' indebtedness to Reformed scholasticism.

23. Norman Pettit, *The Heart Prepared;* Miller, " 'Preparation for Salvation' in Seventeenth-Century New England," in *Nature's Nation.*

24. I. Breward, "The Significance of William Perkins," *Journal of Religious History,* IV (1966–1967), 113–128.

25. The career of William Ames is a case in point: cf. Eusden, introduction to Ames, *Marrow of Theology,* and Karl Reuter, *William Ames: The Leading Theologian in the Awakening of Reformed Pietism,* trans. D. Horton (Cambridge, Mass., 1965).

26. David Little, "Max Weber Revisited: The 'Protestant Ethic' and the Puritan Experience of Order," *Harvard Theological Review,* LIX (1966), 422; Eusden, ed., Ames, *Marrow of Theology,* pp. 21–23, 77–78.

27. A major work spelling out in detail the "relation of eschatology to the life of the Church" in the theology of Calvin and Bucer is Thomas Torrance, *Kingdom and Church* (Edinburgh, 1956). There is a growing literature on millennarian thought among the Puritans, much of it originating in studies of typology and aesthetics. Cf. Bercovitch, "Typology in Puritan New England: The Williams-Cotton Controversy Reassessed," *American Quarterly,* XIX (1967), 166–190; Jesper Rosenmeier, "Veritas: The Sealing of the Promise," *Harvard Library Bulletin,* XVI (1968), 26–37; Joy B. Gilsdorf, "The Puritan Apocalypse: New England Eschatology in the Seventeenth Century," Unpublished Ph.D. Dissertation (Yale University, 1964); Le Roy Edwin Froom, *The Prophetic Faith of Our Fathers* (Washington, D.C., 1946), III.

28. Charles S. McCoy, "Johannes Cocceius: Federal Theologian," *Scottish Journal of Theology,* XVI (1963), 352–370; and Eusden, introduction, Ames, *Marrow of Theology.*

29. The chart precedes page 11 in Perkins, *Works,* I. The fullest study of how Puritans methodized the spiritual life remains Haller, *The Rise of Puritanism;* the phrase "morphology of conversion" is taken from Edmund S. Morgan, *Visible Saints: The History of a Puritan Idea* (New York, 1963). On Puritan rhetoric as eschatological, see Larzer Ziff, *The Career of John Cotton* (Princeton, 1962), chap. 5.

30. George Yule, "Theological Developments in Elizabethan Puritanism," *Journal of Ecclesiastical History,* I (1960–1961), 21–23; Patrick Collinson, *The Elizabethan Puritan Movement* (London, 1967).

31. Pettit, *The Heart Prepared,* p. 6. In his comments on this paper John Eusden sketched a number of sub-traditions within Reformed theology, one of which included William Ames and the Puritans in New England. These "covenant of grace" theologians, as Eusden calls them, are the subject of an extended study he is making.

32. Charles H. and Katherine George, *The Protestant Mind of the English Reformation* (Princeton, 1961), argue that Puritan and Anglican shared the same faith. Although this is disputed by John New, *Anglican and Puritan* (Stanford, 1964), the argument reminds us that the meaning of the terms Puritan and Anglican was relative and changing. Just as the line between the

two in England was a fluid one, so the relationship of the Puritans to Calvin varied from one period to another, from William Perkins, say, to John Bunyan. Methodologically the problem is to abstract an ideal type while doing justice to variety.

33. The tendency among modern historians has been to single out the most tormented accounts of the conversion experience and make of them the normative pattern. Alan Simpson, who bases his interpretation upon such accounts, also noted that "Puritans acknowledged the possibility that the saint might have grown into his condition without any recollection of a violent rebirth. But it was sufficiently unusual for it to be a matter of anxiety to some of the godly that they could not date their conversion." *Puritanism in Old and New England,* p. 115. The problem loomed larger for the Puritans than Simpson allows; there was a continuous debate among Puritans and their descendants, stretching from Richard Greenham and Perkins down to Horace Bushnell and Harriet Beecher Stowe, over the normative pattern of the spiritual life.

34. The logic of spiritism is explained in Maclear, "'The Heart of New England Rent': The Mystical Element in Early Puritan History," and in Geoffrey Nuttall, *The Holy Spirit in Puritan Faith and Experience* (Oxford, 1946). The contradictions within Puritanism have been variously described by Nuttall, Maclear, Morgan, Miller, Sommerville, Pettit, and others, but agreement would be general on the proposition that Puritan sacramentalism, together with a "preparationist" approach to the spiritual life, clashed with Puritan spiritism, together with a "conversionist" mentality. Pettit has noted the connections between the doctrine of preparation and sacramental views, *The Heart Prepared,* pp. 117–124, 134–136. The problem is a legacy from the Reformed tradition, as John Baillie indicates in *Baptism and Conversion* (London, 1964).

35. Collinson, *The Elizabethan Puritan Movement,* p. 132.

36. Morgan, *Visible Saints,* cites the separatist Henry Barrow's explicit denunciation of Calvin, an action forced upon Barrow by the contradictions in which he was enmeshed.

37. Paul, *An Apologeticall Narration,* pp. 123–125; Miller, *The Puritans,* pp. 41–55. Sacvan Bercovitch writes, ". . . the connection between eschatology and historiography—one which relies heavily on scriptural exegesis and prediction—should make us hesitate to render tribute to the things of the Spirit *at the expense* of giving due emphasis to the settlers' profound 'Biblicism.'"

38. Benjamin C. Milner, Jr., "Calvin's Doctrine of the Church," *Harvard Theological Review,* LVIII (1965), 458; Little, "Max Weber Revisited: The 'Protestant Ethic' and the Puritan Experience of Order," p. 423. The problem that Calvin passed on to the Puritans was described by Ernst Troeltsch in these terms: ". . . how could a 'holy community' composed of sterling Christians, whose faith was a matter of profound personal conviction, and whose lives were controlled by an exalted and austere ideal, be at the same time a Church which would provide a spiritual home for the masses of the population?" *The Social Teaching of the Christian Churches* (Glencoe, Ill., 1949), II, 659. See also Geoffrey Nuttall, "The Early Congregational Conception of the Church," *Transactions of the Congregational Historical Society,* XIV, 197–204, and George H. Williams, *The Radical Reformation* (Philadelphia, 1962), pp. 581n, 787–788.

39. It could, of course, be argued that the significant break came in 1640 or 1662, the date of the act excluding nonconformists from the Church and declaring their orders illegitimate. The most important studies that seek to transcend denominational categories are Collinson, *The Elizabethan Puritan Move-*

ment, and Morgan, *Visible Saints,* a carefully measured reply to Perry Miller, *Orthodoxy in Massachusetts* (Cambridge, Mass., 1933).

40. Perry Miller, *Jonathan Edwards* (New York, 1949), describes Edwards' labors in this regard. The collapse of scholasticism occurred more rapidly in England than in America; rational theology was making inroads among English presbyterians in the 1690's, and the dissenting academies were ahead of their time in teaching the new logic and the new sciences. The situation in New England with respect to the academic curriculum is described in Edmund S. Morgan, *The Gentle Puritan* (New Haven, 1962), chap. 3, and in Perry Miller, *The New England Mind: From Colony to Province* (Cambridge, Mass., 1953). On the English side, Olive M. Griffiths, *Religion and Learning: A Study in English Presbyterian Thought from the Bartholomew Ejections (1662) to the Foundation of the Unitarian Movement* (Cambridge, 1935) is valuable.

41. The emergence of Pietism is described in Reuter, *William Ames,* and in F. Ernest Stoeffler, *The Rise of Evangelical Pietism* (Leyden, 1965).

42. Morgan, *The Puritan Dilemma* (Boston, 1958).

43. Perhaps the best of Hill's many surveys is *Society and Puritanism in Pre-Revolutionary England* (New York, 1964).

44. "The fertilized ground [for the word as preached by Puritans] was the ground which for one reason or another was out of sympathy with official policy." A list of outgroups, together with a brief critique of Hill's position, is in Simpson, *Puritanism in Old and New England,* pp. 11–12. In the 1930's there were attempts to link left-wing Puritanism (measured theologically) with lower social and economic groups; cf. Tindall, *John Bunyan, Mechanick Preacher.*

As for the social consequences of Puritanism, recent studies suggest that the movement worked to create a new kind of personality—Michael Walzer's radical saint, or, more correctly, David Little's self-disciplining activist. Walzer, *Revolution of the Saints: A Study in the Origins of Radical Politics* (Cambridge, Mass., 1965); Little, *Religion, Order and Law,* paperback ed. (New York, 1970). Walzer's study should be read in the light of two extended reviews, both indicating difficulties with his interpretation: Little, "Max Weber Revisited," and Richard T. Vann, *History and Theory,* VII (1968), 102–114.

45. William Haller, *Foxe's Book of Martyrs and the Elect Nation* (London, 1967).

46. Cf. Gilsdorf, "The Puritan Apocalypse."

47. Harvard College, which Morison located within the broad context of Western humanism, needs to be studied in the context of Reformed educational practices; one of the major characteristics of Reformed Protestantism in the sixteenth century was the founding of schools for training ministers. New England political history needs to be studied in light of the "holy commonwealth" literature, both continental and English.

48. Oscar and Mary Handlin, "James Burgh and American Revolutionary Theory." *Proceedings* of the Massachusetts Historical Society, LXXIII, 38–57; Bernard Bailyn, *The Ideological Origins of the American Revolution* (Cambridge, Mass., 1967).

49. The bibliography of relevant studies is too immense to be listed here. An interesting overview is Darrett B. Rutman, "The Mirror of Puritan Authority," in G. A. Billias, ed., *Law and Authority in Colonial America* (Barre, Mass., 1965). The accommodation of Puritanism to the "wilderness" is the theme of *From Colony to Province,* the second volume of Miller's *The New England Mind.* The first describes a static system of ideas (hedging on whether

they were held only in New England or also abroad), the second the meaning and consequence of these ideas in America. *From Colony to Province* is open to many criticisms. Still, it offers an amazing number of insights into the nature of New England history. A fair estimate of Miller is not easy to achieve, and although I have joined in the "ritual patricidal totem feast" (to borrow Bercovitch's phrase), I share his feeling that *The New England Mind* continues to supply "the best overview we have of American Puritanism."

Beyond Jacksonian Consensus

FRANK OTTO GATELL

The Jacksonian period once ruled American historiography, and much of our past seemingly could be explained through its study. It received high grades from historians, while many younger scholars gravitated toward the field as naturally as they move into others today. Early in the century Progressive historians relied greatly on Jacksonianism to construct their combative yet optimistic overview, and its Golden Age ended triumphantly in 1945 when Arthur Schlesinger, Jr., urbanized the Jacksonians.[1]

Since no historiographical school holds the field permanently, Schlesinger's urban-Progressive view had to fall in time. The initial success of *The Age of Jackson* did not impede the rapid rise of a counter-interpretation which became in many respects a negative gloss on Schlesinger's work. The work of the consensus school of the 1950's soon became well enough established to warrant attention in numerous essays and even a monograph or two.[2] Jacksonian consensus historiography has largely, though not exclusively, been entrepreneurial historiography, smoothing down where it did not pass over the rough edges of class conflict. The representative Jacksonian became the middle-class entrepreneur, rising, ever-rising; Americans shared a liberal, capitalist outlook. In handling party politics, the consensus historians stressed the absence of ideological differences between Democrat and Whig, and the presence of all sorts of viewpoints within the amorphous coalitions that then passed for national parties. Jacksonians might be ex-Federalists, Whigs might be ex-Jeffersonians; and whatever they had been or were, however boisterously or sincerely they fought party battles, they agreed on fundamentals.

Consensus history has not so much triumphed as it has persisted. In Jacksonian historiography it remains the last comprehensive interpretation or school to be identified, and subsequent work in the period, although increasingly chary of the consensus-enterpreneurial beliefs, has not been unified to form an overview. Complaints and qualifications about consensus have nevertheless been voiced frequently. In 1962, John Higham reacted with apprehension: "A certain tameness and amiability have crept into our view of things. . . . The conservative frame of reference is giving us a bland history, in which conflict is muted. . . . Now that the progressive impulse is subsiding, scholarship is threatened with a moral vacuum." And directly bearing on the theme of this essay, J. R. Pole recently asked us to remember that "the history we have to record is that of the United States under Jackson and Van Buren, not under Clay; yet it is permissible to think that the history of that period would have been significantly different if Clay had been elected in 1832, and that such differences would have been due to genuine differences of purpose." [3]

Similar observations by other historians are not hard to find. They add up to a growing reluctance to abandon altogether traditional interpretative roads to Jacksonianism. They increasingly reject Charles Sydnor's characterization of the party battles of that era as the clank of tin swords. Some think they hear the sound of clashing steel.

One of the recurring items of the entrepreneurial consensus brief has been an emphasis upon ex-Federalist support for Jackson in 1828. In assessing the residual effects of the breakup of the first party system upon the second, the consensus historians maintained that Jacksonism may have drawn as much strength, particularly as much leadership, from ex-Federalists as from ex-Jeffersonians; that a politician, whatever his former partisan loyalties, including Federalism, was as likely to support Jackson as Adams in 1828, in short that President Jefferson's remark about Federalists and Republicans in his first inaugural was not merely tactical but prophetic.

Such propositions strike me as untenable for 1828, and out of the question for 1840. By the latter date, a two-party system had been reestablished, a system in which the major parties displayed what was for that time remarkably well-distributed strength throughout the Union. The prime stimulant to North-South sectionalism, slavery, remained in a relatively quiescent state. Men could and did argue about national economic issues, if not always intelligently then certainly passionately. And these issues, the inevitable outgrowths of a maturing, nationalizing economy, influenced and in some cases determined political realignments which made the 1830's an exceptional decade in early national history.

Wherever the ex-Federalists of 1828 may have lined up, those still alive and still in politics in 1840 were decidedly in the anti-Jacksonian camp. It is unfortunate, in view of the fact that the issue of Federalist Jacksonians has been raised so often for homogenizing purposes, that the few existing studies of ex-Federalists do not extend into the Jackson and Van Buren administrations. It is now twenty-five years since Schlesinger argued that "no amount of inference based on what Jackson was like before 1828 can be a substitute for the facts after 1828." [4] I agree, but would amend the stricture to add the election year of 1828 to the excluded period. Jackson took office in 1829, and who did or did not support him a year earlier is an important but hardly controlling element in the subsequent development of Jacksonian politics.

The cleaning-out process, voluntary and involuntary, began early. Understandably, the first disputes exploded over patronage. A center of Federalist-Jacksonism frequently cited is Boston, where many Federalist leaders declared for Jackson in 1828.[5] But the Republican machine politicians—in Massachusetts the Henshaw group—had relatively little trouble quickly besting the ex-Federalists, and partly because they *were* ex-Federalists. I neither defend nor condemn the proscription, but merely note the prejudices that still circulated among the Republican political pros. Thurlow Weed recalled that an ex-Federalist, a New York Democrat who "had been a Federal member of a former [state] House [of Representatives], and did not always work easy in his Democratic harness," asked Weed to criticize him in print in order to allay Albany Regency suspicions.[6] But although some ex-Federalists who prospered in Jacksonian politics can be named—Roger B. Taney and James Buchanan come immediately to mind—the exceptions do not establish the rule. Finally, it should be noted that ex-Federalists did not generally show a Jackson preference in 1828, nor did they even split evenly between Adams and Jackson. And the corps of ex-Federalists who took refuge in the Jacksonian camp produced many defectors in the following decade.

A significant aspect of the Federalism issue, seldom noted, concerns support at the polls. Active politicians, former members of a decayed party, can be expected to shop around. But what about the voters? Answers must for the moment be tentative, until studies of voter continuity are made. But on the basis of available information we can hypothesize a Federalist-to-anti-Jackson voting pattern. For example, in an article on the rise of the Jacksonians in Maryland, Mark Haller stressed the inchoate condition of the state's parties, Federalist Jacksonianism among the leadership, and the absence of issues. Yet Haller also noted that in the 1820's the old Federalist strongholds in southern Maryland and the Eastern Shore voted for Adams, while Jackson carried traditional Republican territory, the western counties and Baltimore. Similarly, in a study of New Hampshire, Donald B. Cole noted that townships voting heavily National Republican were those where Federalism had been strongest. In Pennsylvania, the urban centers, including Philadelphia, Lancaster, and Pittsburgh, were first Federalist then anti-Jacksonian.[7] And finally, Shaw Livermore has made an important point: Federalist Jacksonians did not take their party beliefs along with them. Like repentant sinners they had to purge themselves of political sin.[8]

After this discussion of vestigial Federalism in the Jacksonian era, it might be well to comment on Louis Hartz's handling of the "Whig Dilemma" in his *The Liberal Tradition in America,* perhaps the single most influential book in the consensus school, since it has a Federalist reference point.[9]

There can be little quarrel with the importance of Hartz's thesis: that the absence of feudalism in American history, the absence of rigidly stratified classes, fundamentally affected American development. Our relative classlessness simply cannot be understood without reference to the omission of a feudal stage. The decline and rapid disappearance of deferential behavior in American society in the late eighteenth and early nineteenth centuries cannot be attributed to mobility and economic abundance alone, for economic growth, industrialism, and urbanization have all come to other nations which did not thereupon transform themselves into egalitarian societies.

Granting this, a problem remains. The dilemma Hartz explores, and the Whiggish point of view he develops at length, do not fit the facts of American life during the Jacksonian Era. First, what is meant by "Whig"? In many places Hartz uses the term "Federalist-Whig," and he quotes amply from Hamilton and such backward-looking worthies as Fisher Ames. Hartz's Whiggery is essentially of the post-Revolutionary variety; he is talking about the Federalist party of the 1790's.

It is not useful to extend their concepts far into the nineteenth century. In fact, as David H. Fischer has shown, even the Federalist party after 1800 must not be equated with the Federalism of the preceding decade.[10] It certainly should not be equated with the Whig party of the 1830's and -40's. Hartz's Jacksonian world is one in which William Leggett, the Locofoco editor, battles Harrison Gray Otis, the unreconstructed New England Federalist. And Hartz claims, ruefully, they battle needlessly.

The Whigs, of course, did respond to realities. They did not regard the democratic mass as a rabble to be kept down by conservative institutions and force if necessary. As William Seward put it in 1831: "The tendency of all our principles of government is to democracy." [11] Operationally, the parties differed little, though the Democrats were on the whole more successful. Whigs courted the voters. Their relative failure may be attributed to several factors, among them: first, the Democrats led in professionalizing and nationalizing the political process; and second, the American voter may have been too shrewd and cynical (attributes usually reserved by historians for party managers) to accept the bland images of a classless society offered them by Whig orators. "All that I have been able to see in the United States," mused Francis J. Grund, "convinced me that the wealthy classes are in no other country as much opposed to the existing government; and that, consequently, no other government can be considered as less permanently established. . . . And this state of danger the soft speeches of the Whigs try to conceal from the people by directing their attention almost exclusively to the financial concerns of the country." [12]

Perhaps many of the Jacksonians were nascent capitalists, as Hartz claims. *Perhaps* no basic ideological quarrels raged between the parties. But the Whig party had an aura of economic elitism around it, and the voters knew it. It was no secret, however many individual exceptions can be produced, that the leading entrepreneurs were Whigs, especially by the late 1830's. Men like Thurlow Weed knew that elections could not be won by defending banks. The Whig appeal had to be masked behind a strained camaraderie of supposedly complementary interests. American politics was much more than a simple tale of rich against poor; but with the rich then preferring one party, and with the poor going to the polls, it is no surprise that Whigs experienced so much trouble.

The entrepreneurial school is basically about entrepreneurs. In this regard no historian surpasses the late Bray Hammond. In him, Nicho-

las Biddle found at last his most effective and persuasive apologist—
and I *do* use the word admiringly.[13] Hammond marshaled all of the
urbanity, erudition, and sardonicism of Biddle, yet little or none of the
passion that served Biddle so ill and that magnifies the difficulty of
the task of a lost-cause revisionist. I refer in no way to racial attitudes
when I say that Hammond reads a great deal like U. B. Phillips. Both
writers sustained an admirable balance between commitment and the
illusion of detachment, and the commitment vitalized their efforts.
Admittedly, central banking does not match white supremacy as a gut
issue, but Hammond's long tenure at the Federal Reserve surely created
a concern for central banking far more intense than the usually detached and perhaps uninformed attitude most of us share.

Regarding Hammond's handling of the entrepreneurial theme, there
is no better place to start than with Amos Kendall. Most agree that
after Jackson, Kendall was the key man in the Bank War. And those
who consider the Bank War the prime issue of the thirties thus up-
grade Kendall's importance accordingly. Hammond's sketch of Kendall stressed laissez-faire principles and money-making practices.[14]
But however significant Kendall's role in the fall of the Bank—and
it *was* significant—his purist views did not determine Democratic
banking policy. As for Kendall's money-making, which came after
1845, one is tempted to paraphrase Schlesinger: "no amount of inference based on what Kendall was like after 1845 can be a substitute
for the facts before 1845." Similarly, the fact, noted by Hammond
with mock disapproval, that Blair made money from the *Globe* and
government printing tells us little about his politics. And so on with
the other Jacksonians paraded by Hammond in all their shameful ac-
quisitiveness, although in many cases the imputations of wealth are
retroactive.[15]

The entrepreneurial theme can be summarized: Jacksonians were as
deeply engaged in the rush for material gain as any political groups,
and the only possible qualititative difference lay in their shakier status
as more recent arrivals. Monopoly meant to them entrenched capital
which had to be dislodged so that they could get theirs. They shouted
anti-monopoly and laissez faire; they aimed to replace the fatcats then
holding the reins of economic power.

Who were these Jacksonian entrepreneurs? Not Andrew Jackson,
of course. Unfriendly historians have often cited his speculative ventures, especially before 1819, but President Jackson has never been
labeled a stock jobber, merely a ninny who allowed the stock jobbers

free rein. As for the others, Churchill Cambreleng was a New York City merchant, and Roger Taney owned a little, very little, stock in the Union Bank of Maryland. But politics engaged most of their attention, and they left the questionable delights of money-grubbing as a way of life to others.

Were these others Jacksonians? And equally important, if they were, did they run Jacksonian politics?

As to the first question, certainly the Jacksonian coalition of 1828 included many leading businessmen. Both the bandwagon character of Jackson's candidacy, and the fact that key economic issues remained submerged during the campaign, contributed to the creation of a haphazard alignment of political forces and partisans. There were Jacksonian entrepreneurs, and many of them remained lifelong adherents to the Democracy. Asa Clapp, a Portland, Maine, merchant and banker and reportedly the richest man in town, stayed with his party and probably considered himself an honest yeoman, Madeira wine notwithstanding. And to move across the mountains, finally, Robert J. Walker, the Mississippi Democrat, provides a fine example of flush-times entrepreneurial scrambling.

Both these men, and dozens of others, kept the Democratic faith. Many did not. In New York City not only were the monied men strongly anti-Jackson, but their disaffection became increasingly pronounced and arithmetically observable as the Jackson and Van Buren administrations ran their course.[16] A similar study of Boston's wealthy, made under my direction, confirmed the New York City findings. Since Massachusetts was National-Republican, then Whig territory, anti-Jacksonism there is no surprise. But the wealthies were decidedly more Whiggish than Boston at large (89 per cent were Whigs, while the average Whig voting percentage in Suffolk County was 63 per cent).[17] There were fewer defections from the Boston Democracy among 11 per cent who were wealthy than in New York, but probably because the overwhelming majority had already committed themselves against Jacksonism. In New York and Boston, defections among wealthy men from the Whig to the Democratic party were nonexistent.

On the second question posed, Jacksonian politics likewise fails to conform to the mold of the consensus historians. It should be clearly stated at the outset that the Jacksonians' reluctance to use the federal government as an active instrument in economic policy does not necessarily make them laissez faire advocates. The Jeffersonian inheritance included the view that the state legislature, where possible, should remain the locus of power. Jackson's constitutional scruples over the national bank and other aspects of the American System have come in for joshing by some historians apparently unable to believe that Jackson & Co. had not been secretly won over by the logic of Chief Justice Marshall's opinions. Jackson was serious.

Whatever the results of Jacksonian national policies, their intent was anything but laissez faire. Once more I refer to the banking issue, the most important political issue of the 1830's. After the removal of federal deposits from the Bank of the United States and the certainty that recharter would fail, the administration established the depository, or pet bank, system. From its start, Jacksonians sought statutory control over the banks, but for two years Whigs and Calhounites blocked adoption of a regulatory deposit act.[18] In 1836 a deposit act also containing Clay's proposal for distribution of the federal surplus to the states reached Jackson's desk. Jackson had opposed distribution, but he considered regulation of the pet banks enough reason to sign. Ultimately the Democrats under Van Buren decided to sever the cords between the federal government and the state banks. While the links existed, however, they sought government regulation in order to protect the public money.

In the states, where banking policy remained a constant preoccupation of legislatures, Democrats responded similarly. The Albany Regency, the best of the Democratic machines, produced the Safety Fund Act of 1829. The law provided insurance against bank failures and established the first state banking commission. The commissioners made periodic inspections of the state banks' books and could start court proceedings to close down mismanaged institutions. In 1838, New York adopted "free" banking, obviating the need for separate legislative charters in order to enter the banking business. Hammond called the law "one of the notable glories of the age of Jackson." [19] Maybe; but if so, like Lincoln, it now belongs to the ages, and not to the Jacksonians. New York Democrats resisted free banking throughout the 1830's. A legislature controlled by Whigs approved it in 1838, and many Democrats voted against it precisely because they wanted more regulatory provisions. Free banking was not unregulated banking, and if the Democrats had had their way it would have been even less of a laissez-faire innovation than it was.[20]

Each state had its own banking history, and local variables created different political challenges and responses. Yet a pattern of Democratic restrictions and restraints emerged, especially after the Panic of

1837. In Ohio the anti-bank Democratic faction became increasingly more influential, producing a curtailment of bank charters and attacks on existing institutions such as the Ohio Life Insurance and Trust Company. In the late 1830's, Democratic Governor Wilson Shannon called for a closely regulated state banking system, with such provisions as individual liability for holders of bank stock, restraints on investors' borrowing practices, and the suppression of small notes. When free banking came to Ohio in 1842, it brought with it many of the restrictions requested by Shannon earlier. Whigs repealed the law three years later, replacing it with a more moderate statute which retained important regulatory aspects.[21] The Ohio experience was representative of Democratic banking policy in its initial attempt to restrict bank chartering, and its subsequent acceptance of free banking with regulation.

When James K. Polk became governor of Tennessee in 1839, he could find no sufficient grounds to allow suspension of specie payments by his state's banks. "Like individual debtors," Polk sermonized, "they should meet their liabilities . . . as long as they are able to pay." If the legislature decided that suspension meant forfeiture of charters yet wished to recharter the banks, "the occasion may be a fit one to impose upon them such additional restrictions as the public safety may require .(. . as conditions of the continuance of their corporate privileges." [22]

Since its 1945 publication, Schlesinger's *Age of Jackson* has had its share of rough handling among historians. For a time, running down the book became a minor industry. Its one-sidedness, present-mindedness, selectivity, and its fame all made it a juicy target. The proscription seemed complete. The author (was he too proud to fight?) published only a short defensive letter in the *American Historical Review,* and he allowed the appearance recently of an unabridged paperback edition without a new apologetic introduction. Yet it must now be clear that I regard the book more appreciatively today than was the fashion a decade ago. I would not assign it to students as a single "text" to outline all we know, or all they should know about the Jacksonian period; but the volume remains, again in the words of J. R. Pole, "after twenty years, a work of extraordinary vitality and intelligence." [23]

Schlesinger caught much of the flavor of the Jacksonian era, especially the later, ill-fated Van Buren years. A reshuffling then took place in American politics, temporary and nonrevolutionary though it was, but one wide enough in scale to merit serious attention. When the Conservative Democrats balked over the sub-treasury, the Whigs received the last major addition of strength from dissident sections of the Democracy. Perhaps as important as the Democratic defections was the increasing identification of businessmen with the Whig party. This gave the parties after 1837 a greater class orientation, at least at the top of the pyramid. Van Buren also gained strength. From one end of the political spectrum, Locofocos and their allied groupings joined the Democrats, and from the other came the Calhoun states'-rights Southerners.[24]

From the ideologue's vantage point, the major American parties do not differ fundamentally. Yet to a greater degree than in most administrations, the major parties of the late Jacksonian period did present meaningful alternatives in the political process. The situation was admittedly anomalous, and it quickly disappeared. It was as if the political landscape opened up, revealing briefly the structure of a kind of politics that would call again at a later date.

Jacksonism was many things, and it changed over the years. Acceptance of this point need not force us back to 1945 in order to write positive glosses on Schlesinger. Jacksonian historiography will not nor cannot be the same as before the entrepreneurial-consensus critique. In particular, Meyers' view of Jacksonian ambivalence, Mc-Cormick's enlightening and sobering use of voting statistics, and Benson's exhortation to employ multivariate analysis of noneconomic influences on voting behavior provide exciting and exacting challenges for directing new work.[25] But whatever the new paths, or modified explorations of old ones, we should be extremely cautious before we banish the conflict-with-capital factor from Jacksonian politics. If we are not, we may fall into the same trap as the Civil War revisionists who, excluding the moral issue of slavery, ended by wondering what the struggle was all about.[26] The resulting negativism would all but kill further attempts at analysis.

NOTES

1. Arthur M. Schlesinger, Jr., *The Age of Jackson* (Boston, 1945).

2. See, for example, Alfred A. Cave, *Jacksonian Democracy and the Historians* (Gainesville, Fla., 1964); Charles Sellers, "Andrew Jackson versus the Historians," *Mississippi Valley Historical Review*, XLIV (March 1958), 615–634; John Higham, "The Cult of 'American Consensus,' Homogenizing Our History," *Commentary*, XXVII (February 1959), 93–100.

3. John Higham, "Beyond Consensus: The Historian as Moral Critic," *American Historical Reveiw*, LXVII (April 1962), 616; J. R. Pole, "The American Past: Is It Still Usable?," *Journal of American Studies*, I (April 1967), 73.

4. Schlesinger, *Age of Jackson*, p. 44.

5. Arthur Burr Darling, *Political Changes in Massachusetts, 1824–1848; A Study in Liberal Movements in Politics* (New Haven, 1925).

6. Harriet A. Weed, ed., *The Autobiography of Thurlow Weed* (Boston, 1884), p. 405.

7. Mark Haller, "The Rise of the Jackson Party in Maryland," *Journal of Southern History*, XXVIII (August 1962), 307–326; Donald B. Cole, "The Election of 1832 in New Hampshire," *Historical New Hampshire*, XXI (Winter 1966), 33–50; Charles McCool Snyder, *The Jacksonian Heritage: Pennsylvania Politics, 1833–1848* (Harrisburg, Pa., 1958).

8. Shaw Livermore, Jr., *The Twilight of Federalism: The Disintegration of the Federalist Party, 1815–1830* (Princeton, 1962), pp. 247–250.

9. Louis Hartz, *The Liberal Tradition in America: An Interpretation of American Political Thought Since the Revolution* (New York, 1955), pp. 89–113.

10. David Hackett Fischer, *The Revolution of American Conservatism: The Federalist Party in the Era of Jeffersonian Democracy* (New York, 1965).

11. George E. Baker, ed., *The Works of William H. Seward*, 5 vols. (Boston, 1884), I, 11.

12. Francis J. Grund, *Aristocracy in America: From the Sketch-Book of a German Nobleman*, Torchbook ed. (New York, 1959), p. 131.

13. Bray Hammond, *Banks and Politics in America: From the Revolution to the Civil War* (Princeton, 1957). For criticism of Hammond's view of politics and Bank War origins, see my article "Sober Second Thoughts on Van Buren, the Albany Regency, and the Wall Street Conspiracy," *Journal of American History*, LIII (June 1966), 19–40.

14. Hammond, *Banks and Politics*, pp. 332–334.

15. *Ibid.*, pp. 329–344.

16. Frank Otto Gatell, "Money and Party in Jacksonian America: A Quanti-

tative Look at New York City's Men of Quality," *Political Science Quarterly,* LXXXII (June 1967), 235–252.

17. Robert S. Rich, "Politics and Pedigrees: The Wealthy Men of Boston in the Age of Jackson," Unpublished M.A. Thesis (University of California at Los Angeles, 1969).

18. Charles Sellers, *James K. Polk, Jacksonian, 1795–1843* (Princeton, 1957), pp. 228ff.

19. Hammond, *Banks and Politics,* p. 573.

20. Gatell, "Sober Second Thoughts on Van Buren," pp. 26–28.

21. Francis P. Weisenberger, *The Passing of the Frontier, 1825–1850* (Columbus, 1941), pp. 328–362.

22. Robert H. White, ed., *Messages of the Governors of Tennessee,* 5 vols. (Nashville, 1952–), III, 281–282.

23. Pole, "Usable Past," p. 67.

24. William G. Carleton, "Political Aspects of the Van Buren Era," *South Atlantic Quarterly,* L (April 1951), 167–185.

25. Marvin Meyers, *The Jacksonian Persuasion: Politics and Belief* (Stanford, 1957); Richard P. McCormick, "New Perspectives on Jacksonian Politics," *American Historical Review,* LXV (January 1960), 288–301; Lee Benson, *The Concept of Jacksonian Democracy: New York as a Test Case* (Princeton, 1961).

26. Arthur M. Schlesinger, Jr., "The Causes of the Civil War: A Note on Historical Sentimentalism," *Partisan Review,* XVI (October 1949), 469–481.

Jacksonian Quantification: On Asking the Right Questions

EDWARD PESSEN

Twenty years ago I joined several colleagues in Richard B. Morris'
seminars in testing the validity of the labor thesis that had recently
been put forward by Arthur M. Schlesinger, Jr.[1] Our approach to the
problem was first to try to identify the working-class districts in such
cities as Philadelphia, New York, Boston, and Newark, and then to
consult the electoral data in order to determine the voting preferences
of the laboring poor. In showing that most workingmen appeared to
have voted against Andrew Jackson in most elections, we believed we
were refuting Mr. Schlesinger's labor thesis.[2]

His *Age of Jackson* had argued that Jacksonian Democracy owed
its success to the electoral support it received from urban working
classes as well as to its following among the nation's yeomanry. Other
features of the labor thesis were being challenged at the time by studies
that questioned the authenticity of several of the Democracy's self-
styled "labor" champions, Jackson's alleged sympathy for labor, and
the closeness of the ties between Jacksonian Democracy and organized
workingmen's groups.[3] Innocent as we were in the ways of statistical
procedure, our conclusions as to how workers voted were less than
definitive.[4] Yet it appeared that we had either refuted the labor thesis
in its entirety or at least addressed ourselves to answering every question it had raised. But we had overlooked one question. It happened to
be the most interesting and important question Mr. Schlesinger had
asked, and one which he had answered in the affirmative. The question was: "*Should* labor have supported Jackson?"

It is not hard to understand why so many of us have bypassed this problem and others like it. Such questions are extremely difficult to answer. Even to discuss them sensibly requires vast and detailed knowledge of the actual policies of a particular administration. The knowledge cannot be confined to measures directly related to labor or to the economic interests of labor. Workingmen, like men of other classes, are affected by policies that may be devoid of economic content. Only a crude economic determinism would insist that labor's true interest in a given political act be measured by its effect toward maximizing wages, minimizing hours, or optimizing conditions. Young scholars will understandably hesitate before tackling a job they may modestly doubt they have the erudition to handle.

Some of us may find such questions too likely to evoke a subjective response: honest men will never agree upon what was good for labor or for any other economic or social class. Some of us may be suspicious, too, of a historical study that seems to lack clinical detachment. In speaking of the past, ministers and moralists advise men what they ought to have done. Historians tell men what they did and—if with less certainty—why they did it and to what effect.

For whatever reasons, many Jacksonian scholars then and now have preferred to deal with questions that can be more readily answered by head counts.[5] Such projects are satisfying in a number of ways. They are relatively easy to do. They may take a lot of time and also help induce blindness, yet they are not mentally taxing, certainly not for that stage in which the researcher proceeds to tick off the evidence of whatever it is he is looking for. When the evidence is new, each additional piece of it adds to the sense of worth felt by the man accumulating it. For he knows that he is doing something no one else before him has ever done. Modest though his contribution may be, it is beyond argument a contribution. The data are hard, their usefulness certain. They are there to serve other historians, whatever their persuasion. Where insights or interpretations may have undeserved reputations in their own time and be dismissed later as subjective or wrongheaded, a table of objective evidence on the voting or other behavior of this or that class will stand impervious to the ravages of time, its value intact. And where the research designs have been sensible, empirical evidence has often provided answers of the highest historical value. Earl Hamilton's innovative discussion of the early modern world's "price revolution" was based on the list he compiled of the changing prices paid for certain goods by a few hospitals in Spain.

Fritz Redlich has said of the "new economic history"—that at times forbidding and esoteric blending of econometrics and traditional economic history devised a little over a decade ago by *enfants terribles* in and out of the Harvard Graduate School of Economics—that it not only measures but that it *comprehends* by measuring. This is not necessarily an indictment. Where the data speak clearly, someone obviously has had the sense to ask a good question.

Jacksonian issues have been illuminated in recent years by quantitative studies. There is nothing new in such studies, of course. Charles Beard did them. His contemporaries, Arthur C. Cole and Dixon Ryan Fox, relied heavily on them in their fruitful investigations of the Whig party in the South and the political parties of New York State in the Jacksonian era.[6] The something new in the work of such modern researchers as Charles G. Sellers, Jr., Grady McWhiney, John Vollmer Mering, Lee Benson, and Thomas B. Alexander and his associates, who have gone over the same ground examined by Cole and Fox, is that the modern men have gone over it much more painstakingly.[7] In a sense, the fundamental methodology of recent times continues to be what it was a half-century ago. Heads are still being counted, if in greater numbers and according to a system of classification that divides them into many more sub-groups than before. It would be carrying relativism too far to regard the contemporary methodology as merely a function of a transitory age preoccupied with the computer, an age whose ways are therefore doomed to be superseded. It seems clear that the modern method is not only different from but superior to the old. Some of its questions may be less sweeping than were older ones, but the answers are more firmly grounded in reality. Much of the most important new information we have acquired about the Jacksonian era since the end of World War II is the product of the new empiricism.

For an age many of whose scholars seem convinced that they have sharply repudiated Beard's simplistic equation of men's economic holdings with their political beliefs, we continue to show an amazing interest in the wealth and social status of party leaders. Detailed investigations have been conducted into the socio-economic backgrounds and positions of congressional representatives, national figures, top- and middle-grade major party leaders in the states, municipal candidates, and even municipal poll-watchers. As might have been expected, the evidence has revealed variations in the situation of party activists. Florida's top Whigs were somewhat wealthier than their Jacksonian counterparts. A similar distinction prevailed in Missouri. In the latter state large slaveowners were decisively Democratic, tavern keepers overwhelmingly so. The burden of the modern studies, however, is the marked similarity in status as well as the atypical wealth enjoyed by leaders of the Whig and Jacksonian parties.[8] The traditional belief that Jacksonian civil service appointees were typically commoners has also been exposed as a myth by a diligent empiricist.[9]

These modern disclosures demolish the old notion that the party of Clay was commanded by an aristocracy of wealth, in contrast to a Democracy led by plebeians. One more point scored against the old Progressive version of Jacksonian politics and its Schlesingerian supplement. If, however, the political beliefs and actions of individuals are not determined by their material situations, how much is our understanding of politics enhanced by new socio-economic information concerning the status of party leaders?

Not that such evidence is irrelevant. That the leaders of Caesar's party were neither of the patriciate nor the poor is important information. Insight into the nature of that or any other party is deepened by familiarity with the kind of social or economic types who composed it. (If Beard is passé, it is not because economic factors have lost their significance. Skepticism is due rather to his thin research, the *excessive* importance he attributed to wealth as a clue to political behavior, and his doctrinaire dedication to a particular interpretation of the significance of mercantile as against landed wealth.) While an individual's wealth may not determine his politics, the political behavior of a group whose members share a similar economic situation is influenced by that situation. Economic factors cannot be discounted as an influence on voting because many studies indicate that voters' denominational or other noneconomic affiliations seemed more decisive than economic factors in accounting for their voting behavior. That the correlation between a given group's religious characteristics and its political choice is greater than the correlation between its economic status and its voting habits does not preclude the possibility that the group's electoral preference was due in part to economic considerations in the minds of its members.

Socio-economic data on party leaders remain valuable. Yet they do not answer the most important questions about party: What was the nature of the party's *behavior?* What principles were revealed by the party's *actions?* What were the *consequences* of these actions?

Joel Silbey has painstakingly gathered evidence on the congressional votes cast by Whig and Democratic congressmen for the decade after 1841.[10] Silbey's work clearly shows, if it needed showing, that head counts can be applied to party actions as well as to the status of the actors. It is no criticism of his valuable contribution to note that it settles for reporting the congressional votes. Its modest attempt at historical evaluation is confined essentially to noting that party loyalty better than sectional interest explains the major party voting blocs that developed in response to the issues of the day.

The historical method that counts heads has been applied most widely to the study of voting behavior. We have studied the voting of the rich and the poor, and as a sign of our growing emancipation from Marx and Beard and our fascination with Freud and Jung, have lately taken to measuring the political choices of distinctive personality types. Lee Benson and his able graduate student, Ronald P. Formisano, breaking with the earlier preoccupation with the socio-economic status of voters, have drawn correlations between particular ethnic groups, religious denominations, and men of unique life style, on the one hand, and Whig or Democratic voting, on the other, for New York State and Wayne County, Michigan.[11] Richard P. McCormick's quantitative studies of voting have shown that Andrew Jackson's candidacy attracted no particularly mighty outpouring of voters to the polls. McCormick's investigation of New York and North Carolina elections during the Jacksonian era demonstrates that voters in these states did not vote by class: poorer voters were divided in their party preferences almost precisely as were their wealthier neighbors.[12] In a number of other states, certain counties in election after election reported exactly the same distribution of votes between the major parties despite changes in the socio-economic situation within the counties. The unchanging party voting percentages obviously downgrade the significance of voters' material conditions as an explanation of their electorial choices.

John Vollmer Mering and Donald B. Cole have used electoral statistics from Missouri and New Hampshire, respectively, to draw detailed portraits of the kind of county that was either drawn to or alienated by the Democracy. Economics had much to do with it, but the choice of party was not a simple function of a community's wealth or poverty. Closeness to rivers, ties with other communities, the presence of a number of churches, particularly those of evangelical tendency, a sizable population, an educated citizenry, a general atmosphere of vitality—these and not "aristocratic" leanings or wealth *per se* were the characteristic traits of anti-Jacksonian towns.[13] And, of course, a number of us, Cole included, have disclosed that workers showed no special attachment to the party of the Hero.

Rich men, on the other hand, were heavily anti-Jacksonian. It had been surmised that the more or less equal wealth enjoyed by the leaders of New York's Democratic and Whig parties indicated that New York's men of wealth were equally divided in their political preferences. Frank Otto Gatell has recently indicated that this was not so for New York City.[14] The overwhelming preference for Whiggery shown by rich men in the Metropolis by no means demonstrates that overwhelming fears of the Democracy accounted for it. Yet any correlation between wealth and Whig voting appears to confirm an earlier view of Jacksonian parties. On the other hand, New York City was not the whole country. According to Alexandra McCoy, one of Lee Benson's students, Wayne County's rich men were pro-Whig by a much smaller margin than were New York's plutocracy. In Michigan the evangelical religion of substantial men was found a much surer clue to their Whiggery than was their wealth.[15]

These studies of voting are for the most part of high value. It is in no sense a criticism of them to suggest, however, that they leave important things unsaid. That moralistic types opposed the Jacksonian party does not explain why they did so. Interestingly, in opposition to the explanation that the anti-Jacksonian voting of wealthy evangelicals was due more to their religious beliefs than to their social position, the leading student of the Protestant "Benevolent Empire" attributes the political position of its wealthy leaders to the Democracy's banking policy.[16] That moralistic anti-latitudinarians found the reputed Jacksonian affinity for drink and high living distasteful does tell us something about the *reputation* of the Democracy and of the mental set of some of its opponents. In my judgment it does not provide us with the most important information about the party.

A similar point can be made about almost all of the quantitative studies of voter behavior. They throw a useful if indirect light on the mood of the voter. They suggest the contemporary reputation of the parties. The latter information is by no means insignificant, since what men of a time think is so may be as important as the historical actuality. What the empirical studies do not do is to evaluate the actual performance of the party—precisely the supreme task of the historical craft.

An unfortunate consequence of overvaluing the affinity between a party and a given class of voters is the tendency to draw unwarranted conclusions from the disclosed relationship. That Jackson's—or any other—party won support from workers would not make it the "workers' party," even had the support in question been overwhelming. Workers or members of any other occupational category who might unite as a class behind a candidate might do so for the wrong reasons. Being human, voters are prone to misconstrue events. In an age of patent demagogy, the Democracy's claim that it championed the common man—seemingly confirmed by its rival's less than astute assertion that the Jacksonians were indeed a revolutionary *canaille*—could convince many voters that charge and countercharge were true, at least in part. In the face of such propaganda, have-nots—or men who believed themselves have-nots—could easily conclude that the maligned party was truly theirs. Yet neither florid rhetoric nor poor people's illusions would transform an opportunistic party into a radical one.

We do not yet know why voters vote as they do. All we know is that their motives are complex and that irrational factors seem to play a part.[17] Statisticians note that a correlation between voters of a particular characteristic and a given party does not establish a causal relationship.[18] Yet even if we could explain a voter's behavior we still should not have come any closer to understanding the performance of the party he votes for.

I hope I have not given the impression that what I call the head-count approach is in any sense a bad thing. My belief is that it has been widely used to answer questions that are not of the highest significance to the historian. In some cases it has served as a substitute for what should be the main activities of the historian's calling: the vivid narrative recounting of what happened and the discussion of why it happened and what its consequences were.

Paradoxically, while historians, like their co-workers in other scholarly fields, have grown increasingly aware of the complexity if not the unattainability of truth, a historical methodology has flourished whose unspoken assumption seems to be not only that truth exists "out there," but that it is not so elusive after all. We can somehow grasp it and do so by a quantitative approach. A nice example of human unwillingness to be influenced by theoretical assurances of hopelessness! Like the character in Samuel Beckett's *Waiting for Godot* who *knows* that everything is meaningless yet happily tries on new hats, the head-counters are practicing existentialists. More power to them. (Or should I say, to us?, for I have myself undertaken a quantitative study on the social backgrounds and origins of the Jacksonian era's wealthy men.) Most of us head-counters are doubtless well aware that if discrete truths can be achieved by empiricism, the larger Truth is as resistant to it as it is to other approaches.[19]

Rather than propose the setting aside of the method whose recent uses I have questioned, I would urge its continued refinement and ask its practitioners to give thought to possible new applications. Certainly our understanding of party behavior and its consequences would be enlarged if we had procedures whereby we could establish quantitatively the effects of party policy on the American population as a whole or on particular segments of it. Among other things we might learn better whether Jacksonian policies warranted labor support.

Perhaps the more imaginative among us might imitate our brethren of the new economic history. Where Fogel posited an America without railroads to test the validity of the thesis that stressed their indispensability to the ante-bellum economy, Jacksonian scholars could measure the hypothetical consequences of measures that were never enacted.[20] A bold spirit may yet carry our art into the age of surrealism, hypothetico-deductive models, and metahistory by writing a history of things that never were. What would connect so poetic an enterprise to the realm of reality would be its reliance on an analytic method that measured the likely consequences of a rejected historical proposal and compared them with the effects of policy that was actually followed.

In sum, the next task for quantitative history is a difficult and challenging one. Detailed information must be gathered on the *consequences of action* to complement the useful data so far accumulated on the *characteristics of the actors*. With that we shall have put to fuller and more significant use this new methodology, and enlarged our understanding of Jacksonian politics and other matters as well.

NOTES

1. Arthur M. Schlesinger, Jr., *The Age of Jackson* (Boston, 1945).
2. William A. Sullivan, "Did Labor Support Andrew Jackson?," *Political Science Quarterly,* LXII (December 1947), 569–580; Milton J. Nadworny, "New Jersey Workingmen and the Jacksonians," *Proceedings of the New Jersey Historical Society,* LXVII (July 1949), 185–198; Walter Hugins, *Jacksonian Democracy and the Working Class* (Stanford, 1960), pp. 203–218; and Edward Pessen, "Did Labor Support Jackson?: The Boston Story," *Political Science Quarterly,* LXIV (June 1949), 262–274.
3. Joseph Dorfman, "The Jackson Wage-Earner Thesis," *American Historical Review,* LIV (January 1947), 296–306; Richard B. Morris, "Andrew Jackson Strikebreaker," *ibid.,* LV (October 1949), 54–68; and Edward Pessen, "The Workingmen's Movement of the Jacksonian Era," *Mississippi Valley Historical Review,* XLIII (December 1956), 428–443.
4. Robert T. Bower observed that my own study had failed to note that Jackson's voting support in wards of low assessed valuation of property had steadily increased. "Note on 'Did Labor Support Jackson?: The Boston Story,' " *Political Science Quarterly,* LXV (September 1950), 441–444. Bower himself did not see that the Jackson vote also rose in wealthy wards. Using only the factor of assessed valuation, Bower failed to establish a significant correlation, let alone a causal relationship, between wards of low assessment and a preference for Jackson, to support his contention that the Boston evidence showed that labor did support Old Hickory.
5. Of course scholars have not forsaken other than quantitative approaches to history. Much of the most interesting modern work on the politics of the Jacksonian era has been the interpretive discussion of its issues. Friend and foe alike to Mr. Schlesinger's argument, and the men who recently have by-passed it and moved consideration of the subject to a new plateau, have engaged in a historical debate of high level, marked not least by its ability to command the interest of the nonspecialist. Examples of original and insightful analysis would include John William Ward, *Andrew Jackson: Symbol for an Age* (New York, 1955); Marvin Meyers, *The Jacksonian Persuasion* (Stanford, 1957); Glyndon G. Van Deusen, "Some Aspects of Whig Thought and Theory in the Jacksonian Period," *American Historical Review,* LXIII (January 1958), 305–322; Gene Wise, "Political 'Reality' in Recent American Scholarship: Progressives versus Symbolists," *American Quarterly,* XIX (Summer 1967), 303–328; Lynn L. Marshall, "The Strange Stillbirth of the Whig Party," *American Historical Review,* LXXII (January 1967), 445–468; Major L. Wilson, "The Concept of Time and the Political Dialogue in the United States, 1828–48," *American Quarterly,* XIX (Winter 1967), 619–644; Frank

Otto Gatell, "Sober Second Thoughts on Van Buren, the Albany Regency, and the Wall Street Conspiracy," *Journal of American History*, LIII (June 1966), 19–40; Richard H. Brown, "The Missouri Crisis, Slavery and the Politics of Jacksonianism," *South Atlantic Quarterly*, LXV (Winter 1966), 55–72; and Mary E. Young's essays on the Indian issue: "The Creek Frauds: A Study in Conscience and Corruption," *Mississippi Valley Historical Review*, XLVII (December 1955), 415–439; and "Indian Removal and Land Allotment: The Civilized Tribes and Jacksonian Justice," *American Historical Review*, LXIII (October 1958), 31–45. Of course the quantitative studies by Lee Benson and others contain their share of original and provocative analysis.

6. Charles A. Beard, *An Economic Interpretation of the Constitution of the United States* (New York, 1913); Arthur C. Cole, *The Whig Party in the South* (New York, 1914), Dixon Ryan Fox, *The Decline of the Aristocracy in the Politics of New York, 1801–1840* (New York, 1919).

7. Thomas B. Alexander, Kit C. Carter, Jack R. Lister, Jerry C. Oldshue, and Winfred G. Sandlin, "Who Were the Alabama Whigs?," *Alabama Review*, XVI (January 1963), 5–19; Thomas B. Alexander, Peggy Duckworth Elmore, Frank M. Lowery, Mary Jane Pickens Skinner, "The Basis of Alabama's Ante-Bellum Two-Party System," *ibid.*, XIX (October 1966), 243–276; Charles G. Sellers, "Who Were the Southern Whigs?," *American Historical Review*, LIX (January 1954), 335–346; Grady McWhiney, "Were the Whigs a Class Party in Alabama?," *Journal of Southern History*, XXIII (November 1957), 510–522; John Vollmer Mering, *The Whig Party in Missouri* (Columbia, Mo., 1967); and Lee Benson, *The Concept of Jacksonian Democracy: New York as a Test Case* (Princeton, 1961).

8. Among the studies that make these points are Arthur W. Thompson, *Jacksonian Democracy on the Florida Frontier* (Gainesville, Fla., 1961); Mering's and Benson's studies; Herbert Doherty, *The Whigs of Florida* (Gainesville, Fla., 1961); Alexander and associates, "Who Were the Alabama Whigs?"; McWhiney, "Were the Whigs a Class Party in Alabama?"; William D. Hoffman, *Andrew Jackson and North Carolina Politics* (Chapel Hill, 1958); Paul Murray, *The Whig Party in Georgia, 1825–1853* (Chapel Hill, 1948); Herbert Ershkowitz, "New Jersey Politics During the Era of Andrew Jackson, 1820–1837," Unpublished Ph.D. Dissertation (New York University, 1965); Edwin A. Miles, *Jacksonian Democracy in Mississippi* (Chapel Hill, 1960); Harry R. Stevens, *The Early Jacksonian Party in Ohio* (Durham, N.C., 1957); and Milton Henry, "Summary of Tennessee Representation in Congress from 1845 to 1861," *Tennessee Historical Quarterly*, X (June 1951), 140–148.

9. Sidney H. Aronson, *Status and Kinship in the Higher Civil Service: Standards of Selection in the Administrations of John Adams, Thomas Jefferson, and Andrew Jackson* (Cambridge, Mass., 1964).

10. Joel H. Silbey, *The Shrine of Party: Congressional Voting Behavior, 1841–1852* (Pittsburgh, 1967).

11. Benson, *Concept of Jacksonian Democracy*; Ronald P. Formisano, "The Social Bases of American Voting Behavior: Wayne County, Michigan, 1837–1852, as a Test Case," Unpublished Ph.D. Dissertation (Wayne State University, 1966).

12. Richard P. McCormick, "New Perspectives on Jacksonian Politics," *American Historical Review*, LXV (January 1960), 288–301; and McCormick, "Suffrage Classes and Party Alignments: A Study in Voter Behavior," *Mississippi Valley Historical Review*, XLVI (December 1959), 397–410. See also

Charles G. Sellers, "The Equilibrium Cycle in Two-Party Politics," *Public Opinion Quarterly*, XXIX (Spring 1965), 16–38.

13. Donald B. Cole, "The Presidential Election of 1832 in New Hampshire," *Historical New Hampshire*, XXI (Winter 1966), 32–50; Mering, *Whig Party*.

14. Frank Otto Gatell. "Money and Party in Jacksonian America: A Quantitative Look at New York City's Men of Quality," *Political Science Quarterly*, LXXXII (June 1967), 235–252.

15. Alexandra McCoy, "Political Affiliations of American Economic Elites: Wayne County, Michigan, 1844, 1860, as a Test Case," Unpublished Ph.D. Dissertation (Wayne State University, 1965).

16. Clifford S. Griffin, *Their Brothers' Keepers: Moral Stewardship in the United States, 1800–1865* (New Brunswick, N.J., 1960), pp. 55–57.

17. See Edward N. Saveth, "American History and Social Science: A Trial Balance," *International Social Science Journal*, XX, No. 2 (1968), 319–330, for its informed discussion and excellent notes on this and related issues. Richard Hofstadter has written that the "rationalistic bias," according to which political man votes in order to advance his economic interests as he understands them, "has very largely broken down in our own time . . . partly because of what has been learned through public opinion polling and depth psychology"; "Fundamentalism and Status Politics of the Right," *Columbia Forum*, VIII (Summer 1965), 24.

18. See V. O. Key, Jr., *A Primer of Statistics for Political Scientists* (New York, 1959).

19. For an informed discussion of the quantitative method in history, its achievements, possibilities, and limitations, see William O. Aydelotte, "Quantification in History," *American Historical Review*, LXXI (April 1966), 803–825.

20. Robert W. Fogel, *Railroads and Economic Growth: Essays in Economic History* (Baltimore, 1964).

A Case Study in Comparative History: Populism in Germany and America

KENNETH BARKIN

In a recent symposium on populism, J. Rogers Hollingsworth suggested that historians go beyond its leaders to study rank-and-file Populists for answers to the persistent and perplexing questions about the movement.[1] That course may well prove productive, and no doubt it should be pursued. But another line of inquiry which holds at least as great promise for enlarging our understanding of populism lies in the comparative approach. Bogged down as we are in disputes among the movement's interpreters about the radicalism of the time, and even about the social backgrounds of the interpreters themselves, this may be the correct moment to turn to a comparative approach. The kinds of fresh insights and suggestive questions that can be drawn from intelligent comparisons might well free us from the constrictions of the present terms of the debate over populism. Comparative history can also give meaning to events and currents that, from a more traditional focus, require no commentary.

Critics of the comparative approach complain that it neglects historical uniqueness while exaggerating superficial resemblances. But such objections are valid only in the case of inferior products; for the best comparative history, as both Marc Bloch and G. R. Elton have observed, draws attention to differences rather than similarities. Research in comparative history may ultimately enhance theories of America's uniqueness; more important, the *nature* of America's distinctiveness will be precisely defined. At the very least, the comparative method allows us to test the validity of traditional hypotheses. At its best it will offer a new perspective and save us from the distorted focus of the nineteenth-century nationalist school of historiography. In the specific case of populism it can enable us to separate what is unique about the American movement from what it shares with farm movements of other nations.

I

Two distinct interpretations now dominate American historical thinking about the Populist era. The older of the two, which in little more than a decade has taken on the aura of orthodoxy, was advanced by Richard Hofstadter in *The Age of Reform*.[2] Hofstadter viewed the Populists as a regressive social force, captivated by a nostalgia for an earlier, less complex age in which yeoman farmers prospered and industrial monopolies were still unknown. The Populists rejected their own times because of an obsessive fear of burgeoning plutocracy and a penchant for seeing hostile conspiracies everywhere. While recognizing the legitimate grievances of the farmers, Hofstadter emphasized the irrational motives behind their movement—though not to the extent charged by some of his critics.

In contrast, Norman Pollack tells us, "Populism was far more radical than is generally assumed. Had populism succeeded, it could have fundamentally altered American society in a socialist direction."[3] Pollack spurns the Hofstadter view as a typical product of the consensus-minded 1950's and, on the basis of considerable research in archival sources, claims that the farmers of the nineties made a penetrating critique of industrial America. Rather than being mired in the past, they sought to create a more humane capitalist order free of alienation.

On the surface it would appear that Hofstadter and Pollack offer diametrically opposed points of view. Yet I would suggest that their theories implicitly share a common foundation: a belief in the uniqueness of the American response to the crisis of the 1890's. Both treat the American situation in isolation—Hofstadter, because the American farmer was alone in his Protestantism, his medium-sized holdings, and his commercial ethos; and Pollack, because European agrarian movements tended toward reaction in stark contrast to the American.[4]

Yet it is clear that most Populist leaders did not regard their plight as particularly unique. They realized that neither the price decline of the nineties nor agrarian radicalism was confined to the North American continent. Populist writers frequently referred to the international dimensions of the crisis. The Omaha Platform of 1892 begins, "A vast conspiracy against mankind has been organized on two continents, and is rapidly taking possession of the world." In *The Populist Revolt,* John Hicks refers to an Alliance leader who saw problems in all agricultural nations, whether "high tariff or low tariff; monarchies, empires, or republics; single gold standard, silver standard, or double standard." [5] *Caesar's Column* is so cataclysmic because the dangers are threatening all of Western civilization, not just America.[6] Donnelly's novel is replete with references to the European situation. The keen social critic Henry Adams reported from England in 1893, "I expect troubled times for many years to come on all sides, especially in Europe and Asia. . . . In our country we shall follow more or less the path of the world outside." [7] Nor, I should add, did the German agrarian movement fail to express support for its American counterparts and for William Jennings Bryan, "the battler against capitalism." [8] Pursuing the comparative approach, it becomes clear that the agrarian movements in Germany and America represent two species within a common genus, and that any attribution to American populism of similarities with Marxism or radicalism, whether of the left or the right, is open to serious question.

It is the German experience of the 1890's that most closely parallels that of America. Nor is this coincidental, for the two nations bore remarkable similarities. Both contained a predominantly Protestant population with a sizable Catholic minority and a small urban Jewish community. According to W. W. Rostow, Germany and America began to industrialize and reached the stage of economic maturity at approximately the same time.[9] By the end of the century they had passed that delicate point at which industry surpasses agriculture in the generation of wealth, and farmers in both lands looked toward the future with great foreboding. Unlike in Great Britain and France, development in Germany and America centered on heavy industry rather than textiles. Both nations erected high industrial tariff barriers in the last quarter of the century and experienced the growth of enormous monopolistic enterprises. To match America's Rockefeller, Carnegie, and Harriman, Germany could boast of Krupp, Siemens, and Thyssen. The trends toward oligopoly and plutocracy were denounced by partisans of agriculture in Prussia's eastern provinces no less than in the Midwestern United States. Rapid urbanization accompanied industrial development, and in both nations led to a strong antipathy toward the city. In America this development was abetted by the alien character of the cities, while in Germany this purpose was served by the common belief that the cities were hotbeds of atheistic socialism. Thus it is no coincidence that William Jennings Bryan and Karl Oldenberg, an agrarian sympathizer at the University of Marburg, both came to the conclusion in the nineties that the countryside could exist without the city but that the converse was impossible.[10] Politically the two nations were alike in being governed under a federal system with a distribution of power between the central and local authorities. Frustrated by defeats on the national level, German and American farmers could turn to the states where their influence was more telling. Finally, the difference in the sizes of farms in the two countries should not be exaggerated—all of the German empire at its zenith could comfortably have fitted into Texas. Most squires cultivated estates no larger than three or four hundred acres, that is, not much bigger than the average holdings of a Kansas or Nebraska farmer.

Of course, significant differences existed between the two societies, and these differences led to distinctive responses by each agrarian movement. There were no American counterparts of the Prussian Junkers, from whose ranks the empire's political, administrative, and military elites were drawn. Nor could the most eminent Populists (let alone a Sockless Jerry Simpson or Mary Lease) rival them in social status. Throughout the nineteenth century, first Prussia's and later Germany's economic policies reflected the interests of these east-elbian estate owners. Free trade prevailed only so long as Germany exported grain. When prices fell in the seventies and cheap foreign grain began appearing on the German market, Bismarck obliged his Junker compatriots by introducing a modest tariff in 1879. In response to their entreaties he raised it fourfold during the next eight years. [11] After Bismarck's dismissal in 1890, however, the Junkers found that his successor, Leopold von Caprivi, and the young William II, showed greater interest in industrial progress than in the agricultural crisis.[12] As a result, despite their traditional social and political prerogatives, they faced the severe price decline of the early nineties as did the American farmers—without recourse to a benign central government.

A genuine gulf existed in the nineteenth century between German and American attitudes toward the proper role of the state. The laissez-faire philosophy permeating American thought never took firm hold in the land of Hegel and Friedrich List. With its strong patriarchal traditions, Germany led the revolt against liberal economics and the concept of the caretaker state. Economists from Britain and America flocked to Berlin to learn of the wonders of the state from the historical school. The American Economics Association was founded in 1885 in imitation of the state-oriented *Verein für Sozialpolitik*.[13] The German state played a considerable role in the nation's industrial development by financing mixed public-private enterprises, investing heavily in mining, and nationalizing the railroads. Encouraged by conservative social thinkers rooted in the mercantilist tradition, German political leaders shed the liberal dogma of mid-century and came to accept the necessity of state intervention to cope with the problems created by industrial capitalism.

Two further differences merit brief mention. After 1875, German production of grain no longer met the needs of a burgeoning population. As imports increased, the tariff issue assumed an urgency for the German farmer that did not arise in the United States, where the supply of grain always exceeded the demand. Second, class divisions were sharper and social mobility less common in Germany, obviating even the possibility of an anti-capitalist alliance between workers and farmers. In view of these dissimilarities, it is not surprising that German and American agrarian radicalism did not tread identical paths. What is striking are the close parallels.

II

In both nations, large segments of the farm community refused to embrace populism. Farmers in the old Granger states, Iowa, Illinois, and Indiana, as well as those in the mid-Atlantic area, voted for traditional parties in the nineties and demonstrated few signs of active discontent. Chester McArthur Destler and, more recently, Ray Scott have explained a similar passivity in Illinois in terms of the gradual abandonment of grain for livestock and dairy farming.[14] Often neglected is the increased value of truck farming in the prairie states between 1890 and 1900—in no major state did it rise less than 200 per cent, and in Indiana it increased by 320 per cent. In Germany, representatives of rural Oldenburg and Württemberg voted against even the most moderate demands of the German Farmers League. Cattle and pigs were the main sources of income in Oldenburg, and farmers there purchased huge quantities of grain for fodder and profited enormously from the fall in prices. Because their market lay in the mushrooming cities, they refused to ally with the Junkers in a struggle against urban Germany. The same holds true for Württemberg, where farmers geared their crops to the needs of nearby urban centers and found employment there for their sons during the winter. Friedrich Hartmann of the Württemberg People's party claimed that the relationship between agriculture and industry was so close in his state that a decline in the workers' standard of living would inevitably lead to rural depression.[15] This was also true of the Ruhr area and helps to explain the absence of militancy there.

Cooperatives were a common response to the hard times of farmers who had diversified or cultivated near urban markets. In both nations, farmers began organizing as never before for the purposes of buying, marketing, and borrowing. The number of dairy cooperatives rose sevenfold between 1890 and 1900 in America. Of the 10,803 associations listed by the Department of Agriculture in 1925, only one hundred had begun before 1890.[16] The same decade in Germany witnessed a 330 per cent growth in farmer associations, most of them in lending and purchasing.[17] Cooperatives were not the answer for all farmers, but for those who had geared their production to urban markets they often provided an adequate means to survive the crisis.

To the persistent question, "What motivated farmers to become Populists?," the comparative approach leads me to a conclusion similar to one reached by a journalist in 1892: "All the farmers want is more money . . . and the sooner they get it, the more reluctant they become to ride forty miles in a lumber wagon through the rain to hear Mrs. Lease and General Weaver make speeches." [18] Only the severe depression in agriculture can explain at once the upsurge in radicalism in the South, Midwest, and Germany. Farmers in these areas who joined a radical agrarian movement were alike in three specific ways: first, they were more heavily indebted than the more quiescent farmers; second, for whatever reason, their income depended almost solely on one nonperishable crop; third, their lands were situated great distances from urban industrial centers.

Whether one believes that interest rates in the Populist states were exorbitant or not, it is clear that farmers in these areas were severely burdened with debts.[19] Mortgages were held on the property of one of every two Kansans and every three Nebraskans. Per capita indebtedness amounted to $110 in Dakota, $126 in Nebraska, and $170 in Kansas. Nor is this surprising, for land values doubled in these states during the eighties, fostering a boom psychology and heavy speculative investments. When prices fell, those who intended to sell later at a huge profit, and even those whose investments were not speculative, found themselves in difficult straits. In the South, C. Vann Woodward tells us, "The farmer, former masters . . . along with former slaves and yeomen, had been reduced to a state of peonage to the town merchant. The lien system converted the Southern economy into a vast pawnshop." [20] The reason for indebtedness may have been different in the South, but the result was the same when cotton prices tumbled.

Contrary to Hofstadter's belief, the commercial ethos was not confined to the American farmer. The Junkers, experiencing unparalleled prosperity from the 1830's until the mid-seventies, gambled on its continuance by speculating in land. Between 1835 and 1864 the average one hundred Prussian estates exchanged hands more than twice each, the median length of ownership amounting to fourteen and a half years. One study of 4,771 estates showed 23,654 changes in ownership in a thirty-year period.[21] Relying on their political power to buoy up prices, the Junkers did not stop their investments even after the boom collapsed. When agrarian radicalism appeared on the scene, indebtedness averaged approximately 52 per cent of property value in the eastern provinces, compared with 22 and 24 per cent in the more tranquil provinces of Westphalia and the Rhineland. A breakdown of these statistics by the Prussian Statistical Bureau showed indebtedness to be proportional to the size of holdings; thus in West Prussia 73 per cent of the largest estates were indebted to 50 per cent of their value or more, as compared with 53 per cent for medium-sized holdings.[22] Since the estate-owning Junkers took the lead in the German agrarian movement, indebtedness ought not to be underestimated as a spur to radicalism.

It has become fashionable of late to concentrate on certain subtle and seemingly sophisticated causes of Populist militancy, such as the absence of community in the newly opened lands (a malady, one might add, that is more characteristic of the mid-twentieth century than the late nineteenth).[23] Certainly many threads of discontent converged in a movement as complex as populism. It should nevertheless be remembered that the level of Populist militancy was inversely proportional to the price of leading farm commodities, and that alienation seemed to reach tolerable proportions when prosperity returned. The central fact of rural life in the early nineties was an enormous decline in the real income of the farming population. According to one estimate, the farmers earned 18 per cent less in 1896 than in 1891. Their share of the national income dropped from 20.7 per cent in

1879 to 15.8 per cent in 1889.[24] Throughout the decade the terms
of trade favored the creditor, whose gain in purchasing power in
Georgia rose by more than 22 per cent.[25] Farmers on both continents
continually complained of selling at prices below their costs of
production.

Hardest hit by the depression were farmers whose incomes depended
almost solely on grain and cotton. An international economy in grain
had gradually developed in the last quarter of the century with the
spread of railroads and steamships. At once these technological innovations permitted the opening of new areas of cultivation and sharply
reduced the cost of transportation. These factors, combined with bumper
crops throughout the world in the years after 1891 and a world-wide
industrial depression, resulted in a supply greatly in excess of the
demand. Wheat sold at 49 cents a bushel in 1894, compared with an
average of more than 80 cents during the eighties. Cotton also dropped
to unprecedented lows—the selling price of the entire American crop
declined by more than $31 million a year for a five-year period during
which production rose by 25 per cent. In Germany, rye prices remained
32 marks per ton below the break-even point for three successive
years. It is therefore not surprising that militancy and wheat farming
tended to go together in Nebraska, or that populism in Virginia and
Florida was confined to cotton-growing districts.[26]

For a variety of reasons the farmers who became Populists could
not or did not choose to adapt to the problems created by the growth
of an international economy by diversifying their crops. All were, of
course, hampered by their sizable indebtedness from obtaining further
capital. Southern cultivators risked the loss of their only source of
capital by abandoning cotton. Merchants demanded that cotton remain
king in order to preserve their monopoly on the sale of foodstuffs.
In the far Midwest, the lack of capital and the nature of the soil
were primary hindrances to diversification. The Junkers, accustomed
to being bailed out of their difficulties by the state, relied on their
influence in Berlin to mitigate the effects of the depression.

Finally, the farmers who turned to radicalism were handicapped
by the distances their holdings lay from populated industrial centers.
The kinds of farming—dairy and vegetables—that prospered or at
least held their own during the nineties required a proximity to the
burgeoning urban markets. Only at great risk could a farmer whose
land was situated hundreds of miles from Chicago or Berlin invest
in perishable products that were costly to transport. He had virtually

no option of adapting to an industrially oriented economy. Ravaged by debts and unable to find a secure niche in a rapidly changing international economy, this farmer tended to gravitate toward militancy at the first sign of distress.

This emphasis on economic motivation is further confirmed by the fact that common hardships transcended traditional enmities in the countryside. In Germany, the age-old conflict between squire and peasant over land came to an end with the onslaught of the agricultural crisis.[27] Peasants in Prussia and Hesse, whose economic plight resembled that of the Junkers, joined their old foes in the Farmers League and sent militant agrarian representatives to the Reichstag. Of 250 local centers, the Farmers League boasted 109 in the peasant-populated districts of western Germany. Several peasant organizations, including the *Deutsche Bauernbund*, merged with the Junker-led group and adopted the rhetoric of anti-capitalism. This radical transformation in peasant political behavior occurred in spite of religious and social cleavages that set them apart from the squirarchy.

This departure from German tradition is paralleled in America by the rapprochement between black and white farmers in the South. What would certainly have appeared inconceivable a decade earlier occurred in the early nineties when back-country farmers rushed to Tom Watson's house to defend a black sympathizer.[28] The Populists actively courted black farmers not because of a shared alienation or a belief in racial equality, but on the basis of a common misery that might be overcome by a struggle in concert. Watson made his appeal to blacks in these very terms. "Gratitude may fail: so may sympathy and friendship and generosity and patriotism; but in the long run, self-interest always controls. Let it once appear plainly . . . that it is to the interest of the white man that the vote of the Negro should supplement his own, and the question of having that ballot freely cast and fairly counted, becomes vital to the white man. He will see that it is done." [29] As long as cotton prices remained below costs, the Southern black farmer could look to a party that would run and support black candidates for office against white opposition.

The problem with considering populism from other than an economic perspective is that the alternatives fail to explain not only the simultaneous rise of agrarian radicalism in America and Germany, but even the breadth of the movement within America. Kansas farmers may have been new to their lands and suffering from "a lost psychic continuity," as Hollingsworth suggests, but this cannot be said of

Southern populists or the Junkers, both of whom were no less militant. Similarly, although Midwestern farmers shared a common social status, the very opposite holds for Germany and for the South, where the most disparate rural classes came together. Both C. Vann Woodward and the historian of Virginia populism, William Sheldon, have pointed to the surprising number of socially prominent Southerners who left the Democratic party for the farmers movement.[30] Tom Watson himself came from a respectable slave-owning family with more than 1,300 acres of land. In Virginia, Sheldon writes, "The officers of the Farmers' Assembly were representatives of the best class of farmers in the state." Nor, as Walter Nugent has persuasively argued, can one isolate religion or ethnic identification as the most significant criterion in determining who became a Populist.[31] One is left, then, with explaining populism as the response of a particularly vulnerable segment of the rural population to a sustained decline in prices generated by technological innovation in the transportation industry.

The origins of the Populist movement and its evolution into a third political party is a familiar tale. The growth of the German Farmers League is not so well known, but it has several parallels with the American experience. The League came into existence in February 1893, after a year of increasing friction between the government and the farm community.[32] Chancellor Caprivi struck the first note of discord in December 1891 by incorporating a 15-mark reduction in grain duties into a tariff treaty with Austria-Hungary. Because prices were temporarily high and because of the long tradition of harmonious relations, agrarian representatives chose to go along with the chancellor, despite his seemingly excessive concern with industrial prosperity. More than half of the Conservatives in Parliament voted for the treaty, most of whom interpreted it as a move in foreign policy.[33] A year later a mood of rebelliousness swept German agriculture, culminating in the call of Ruprecht aus Ransern, a Silesian farmer, for the rural population to adopt the anti-government policies of the Social Democrats. The enraged Ransern wrote, "We must stop being and choosing liberals, ultramontains, or conservatives . . . we must join together in a great agrarian party and thereby seek to win, by more influence in Parliament and the legislature." [34] The estrangement of the farmers followed their realization that the Austrian treaty signaled a major departure in the state's attitude toward agriculture. By the winter of 1892 it became clear that further treaties with Rumania and Russia were being contemplated despite a sharp fall in grain prices. Caprivi's rhetoric about the priority of finding markets for German industrialists now had to be taken seriously, especially after he told the Reichstag, "It is my view that grain duties are a great burden to the nation, and one ought not speak of agricultural sacrifices, but sacrifices for agriculture." [35]

Responding to Ransern's plea, Germany's leading agrarian magnates met in Berlin in February 1893 to organize the Farmers League. With an initial membership of 169,000 that expanded to over 230,000 by 1900, the League commanded a staff of 112 employees in its Berlin headquarters. Its newspaper quickly reached a circulation of 130,000, and in the crucial year of tariff treaty renewal, 1902, the League distributed more than seven million pieces of literature.[36] In contrast to the grass-roots nature of American populism, the League, reflecting the hierarchical character of German society, was organized along elitist lines from the outset. Junkers occupied all positions of power and successsfully prevented the rank and file from exerting any significant influence over policy formation. From its inception, the League adopted a radical posture that, with the exception of the socialists, was unmatched on the German political scene. Within a few months of its founding, the League declared unrelenting war against Caprivi and international capitalism. Subsequently, the emperor was listed among the foes of German agriculture. This demagogic anti-capitalism emanating from the traditionally quiescent rural population shocked government leaders. Writing to a friend in March 1895, Caprivi noted, "In regard to the latter [the agrarian movement] the future is bleak, and it appears to me that a revolution by the agrarians is not impossible and for the moment more dangerous than one by the Social Democrats. If the agrarian agitation continues, who will stop it?" [37] In Bavaria the Minister of Finance warned the legislature that League activities endangered the foundations of order in the state.[38]

Similar to the American Populist movement, the Farmers League began as a militant pressure group outside of the formal political process. Six months before an election the League circulated its program to all candidates for office and demanded concurrence in writing from those seeking its support. The signators winning League approval received financial contributions as well as literature for distribution in their districts. The League sponsored its own nominees only in rural constituencies where all candidates refused to endorse its program. Despite numerous entreaties, it never fully endorsed a political party or contributed to party coffers. After 1898 the voting records of delegates elected with League support were examined periodically to ascertain whether they had worked to implement agrarian policies.

Because these tactics proved so successful, especially on the state level, German Populists, unlike their American counterparts, never found it necessary to establish a full-blown political party. With six major parties competing for votes in many constituencies, League endorsement often made the difference between victory and defeat for a candidate. The greater radicalism of German agrarians may in part be explained by the League's functioning as a vested interest group, a status that did not require the compromises inherent in formal political life. Twenty-five per cent of the delegates elected to the Reichstag in 1893—the year of the League's founding—had voluntarily obligated themselves to support League demands. In the next election the percentage rose to 30.[39] The League generally controlled between 33 and 40 per cent of the seats in the Prussian *Landtag* and could frequently claim a majority in the smaller agricultural states. At least three parties reflected the League's growing influence by adopting more sympathetic stands toward agriculture. After 1893 the Conservatives devolved into an agrarian interest group; subsequently all of their delegates endorsed League policies. Both the Catholic Center and National Liberals depended on peasant support in areas hard hit by the depression. To stave off voter defections, the candidates of the two parties moved to the right even when they refused to be obligated to the League.[40]

In Germany, as in America, the Populists found greater success on the state level. This was particularly true because of the enormous size of Prussia (three-fifths of the empire in land and population). When the government sought in 1894 to connect Prussia's eastern and western provinces by a series of canals, the League mobilized its supporters and sympathizers in the legislature against the proposed bill.[41] Freiherr Conrad von Wangenheim, the League's second president, made it clear that the canals would not be built until the Reichstag granted agrarian demands. Despite the emperor's personal intervention the bill was defeated, and suffered the same fate when it was reintroduced in 1899 and 1901. Having to rule both the empire and Prussia, a chancellor faced nothing but frustration if he lacked the trust of the agrarians; for they could use their power in Prussia to influence national policies —an option not open to the American Populists.

III

Perhaps the most striking parallel between German and American populism lies in the tendency of agrarians in both nations to share a remarkably similar world-view. Their anxieties and fears as well as their own self-image evidenced a common concern with their place in a rapidly changing, and for them, disintegrating world. Their policies sought to create a secure niche for agriculture, free from the vagaries of an international capitalist economy. In Germany and America the agrarian program revealed the farmers' loss of faith in an unrestrained free-market system.

Populists in the 1890's viewed the immediate future of their societies with great foreboding. History had somehow been switched onto the wrong track and was heading at breakneck speed toward disaster. A sense of imminent cataclysm pervaded their writings and was in part responsible for the urgency of their message. In *Caesar's Column,* Ignatius Donnelly clearly expresses his fear that, "these so-called wise men of the world have eaten away the walls of society in a thousand places, to the thinness of tissue paper, and the great ocean is about to pour in at every aperture." [42] Marked pessimism reigned in Germany where the groups loyal to the Wilhelmian empire (*staatserhaltende*) seemed to be in rapid decline.[43] Germany's leading bimetallist, Wilhelm von Kardorff, wrote in a vein similar to Donnelly, "I would consider it cowardly to leave my posts in such times, when the conviction increasingly overwhelms me that we are moving toward a terrible catastrophe without a chance of being saved." [44]

For agrarians the root of the problem lay in the spread of financial capitalism, and in the profit motive in particular. That they were petty capitalists themselves did not prevent them from opposing capitalism on a national or international scale. Small shopkeepers, after all, may despise department stores although they are in the same business and for the same reason. Suffering farmers did not bother about the inconsistencies of attitude that have troubled later scholars. What repeatedly emerges in the literature of German and American populism is the outrage at a system wherein physical labor can go unrewarded while speculators reap huge profits. Farmers viewed themselves as the basic productive group in society, yet found their position declining relative to the middlemen who, from their perspective, performed a secondary function at best. Paralleling the American farmer's distinction between the producer and nonproducer, League members in Germany distinguished between *schaffende* (creative) and *raffende* (exploitive) work. They demanded that the imperial government restrain the stock brokers and merchants, whose every success impaired the healthy fabric of society. Ultimately the League sought to destroy their function by isolating Germany from the world economy. In most American states middlemen were forbidden membership in the Alliance organizations.[45] Senator William Peffer of Kansas characterized them as men "who produce nothing, who add not a dollar to the nation's wealth, who fatten on the failures of other men, whose acquisitions are only what their fellows have lost." [46]

Apart from their sense of righteous indignation at what they saw as an unjust distribution of wealth, agrarians thought unrestrained capitalism disrupted a healthy social structure. Adolf Wagner, a professor at Berlin and a League supporter, warned that Germany was heading in the same direction as America—"a land of billionaires and plutocrats." Agricultural society, he observed, was based on concord, the integration of all parts into a holistic organism.[47] In contrast, industrial capitalism fostered divisiveness and class conflict. Should the rural population disappear, the German social structure would be nothing more than an oligarchy of wealthy capitalists and a large impoverished proletariat—unremitting civil war would be the result. Neither international bankers nor Marxian socialists could form a secure patriotic foundation for Germany. Thus national well-being and harmony depended upon the preservation of a prosperous farm community. In one form or another, Wagner's fears were shared by all militant agrarians.

While Germans sought to prevent this ominous polarization, American agrarians viewed plutocracy as a cancer already eating at the foundations of society. Scarcely an assembly of Populists passed without a condemnation of the eastern "money power." At the St. Louis convention a resolution augured the possibility of a farm population divided between European-type aristocrats and tenant farmers.[48] Agrarians were haunted by a common fear of the inevitable result of financial capitalism: the accumulation of wealth at the top and the disappearance of the medium-sized entrepreneur. The belief that only productive or creative work merited reward was clearly an attempt to get at the root of a system that threatened the farmers' very existence.

In the agrarian cosmology, England represented the pit from which the evil had originated and had come to hold sway. Denunciations of England became almost ritualistic in American Populist writings and speeches. The theme of an America trapped in a weblike financial system dominated by John Bull reached millions of farmers in the widely read *Coin's Financial School*.[49] Agrarians in both nations held up the fate of English agriculture as an example of what lay in store for the countryside in a mature capitalist society. In the plains states, where alien land ownership was common, the hostility toward England reached its peak.[50]

In Germany, Anglophobia did not reach the intensity it enjoyed in the United States, perhaps because England shared the villain's role with the Jews. For German agrarians, the Jews incarnated all the evils of capitalism in a way the English did not.[51] Jewish emancipation and assimilation coincided wth Germany's growing involvement in an international economy and the breakdown of a state-regulated social order. The Jews occupied a prominent position in German commerce and finance, which particularly impressed itself upon the German mind during the scandals accompanying the depression of 1873.[52] Moreover, the German farmer personally encountered Jews, unlike his American counterpart, as money-lenders and merchants. Thus the enmity that the American Populist divided among bankers, middlemen, and English financiers tended to coalesce in Germany around the Jews. The League was openly and avowedly anti-semitic, and its literature sought to play upon the latent anti-semitism of the peasants. An extreme example is a League editorial in 1895 which began, "It lies in the nature of the matter that agriculture and Jewry will be engaged in a life and death struggle until one lies lifeless or at least powerless on the ground." [53] The few anti-semites running for the Reichstag relied on the League's financial support and usually voted with the agrarians on social and economic questions.

Comparison with Germany makes American Populist anti-semitism appear anemic and relatively negligible. The concatenation of factors that led the German farmer to identify the Jew with capitalism was absent in this country. Jews were not dispersed through the countryside, nor were they associated with the stock exchange in the popular mind. America's commercial and industrial development, unlike Germany's, proceeded without the overly prominent participation of the Jews. Nevertheless, it is interesting to note that the few outbursts of anti-semitism resemble those of the League in that they are based not on religious or racial antipathy but on economic grounds. When Donnelly

had a character say, "There [in Europe] you know, the real government is now a coterie of bankers, mostly Israelites," or "The world is
today Semitized," he was writing in a language both familiar and congenial to German agrarians.[54]

Intrinsic to the so-called Catonist view of society, and also evident
in the two agrarian movements, is a belief in the indispensability of the
land population. Thus the old German aphorism *Hat das Bauer Geld,
hat's die ganze Welt,* which came into usage again in the nineties,
expressed a sentiment that echoed across the Atlantic. Leonidas Polk,
the President of the Southern Alliance, warned that, "retrogression in
agriculture means national decline, national decay, and ultimate and
inevitable ruin." [55] In 1896, Bishop Louis Fink of Kansas concluded
a pastoral letter with the question, "Are not the country population
and country occupation the very foundation of general prosperity?"

In Germany, where urbanization had been extremely rapid, agrarians created a romantic mythology about the cultivators of the soil.
They were repeatedly called the fountain of youth of the German
people, whose evanescence would ultimately lead to the nation's destruction.[56] After every war, agrarians argued, the peasants had been
the source of moral and physical renewal. Their good health and unquestioning patriotism made them indispensable for a strong army—
a necessity in a nation surrounded by hostile powers. Fearful of the
effects of rural depopulation, Graf Mirbach delivered a speech in the
Reichstag calling for strict regulation of internal migration. He proposed that rural emigration be limited to those having a job and adequate housing awaiting them.[57] Peter Spahn, an agrarian sympathizer
in the Center party, urged the government to move all army barracks
to rural areas to prevent farm boys from being seduced by the superficial charms of urban life during their military service.[58] Populists
charged the city with siring weak physical types as well as being the
spawning ground of alcoholism, prostitution, and mental disorders.
The more extreme agrarians claimed that they would not be satisfied
until the cities began losing population to the countryside.[59]

IV

Since agrarians in both nations shared a common apprehension about
the trend of the times, it should not be surprising that they looked
to the same agency for succor. "Government," Donnelly wrote, "national, state, and municipal—is the key to the future of the human

race." [60] This sentiment, widely held by American Populists, was also basic to the German farmer's approach to his problems. Adolf Wagner, the father of state socialism and editor of the *Staatssozialist,* urged his views on League members at their first convention in 1894. Very much in the manner of Donnelly, he asserted that economic liberalism had led to the current plight of the farmer, and that only resolute state action could forestall irreparable harm to the nation's welfare.[61] It is also remarkable how similar (sometimes down to small details) the specific demands of the two movements were. These parallels have not to my knowledge been commented upon elsewhere, but they are perhaps the best indication that German and American agrarian movements were of a common genus.

Almost every state and national Populist program in America included the call for a graduated income tax. The rural population recognized that industry and finance had come to generate greater wealth than the land, yet the land remained the primary source of governmental income. In the depression of the nineties it became imperative to shift this burden to those who had escaped it because of anachronistic tax laws. Congressmen from the South and West managed to pass a 3 per cent income tax in 1894, only to have it declared unconstitutional by the Supreme Court.

Even before the Farmers League, German agrarians were anxious to see the capitalists shoulder the lion's share of the tax burden. Between 1878 and 1886 four small states approved a graduated tax in response to pressure from the countryside. In 1891 Johannes Miquel, the Prussian Minister of Finance, desirous of currying favor with the agrarian-dominated Conservative party, introduced a plan to revise Prussia's whole tax structure.[62] The taxes on land and buildings were placed under the jurisdiction of local government, where the Junkers could exercise control over the rates. Miquel based the state's revenue on a graduated income tax rising from zero to 3 per cent. Agrarians sought to raise the maximum to 5 per cent but compromised with the government at 4. They were rewarded when Miquel allowed debts to be deducted from the calculation of taxable income. The minister avowed that his purpose was to "unburden the land in contrast to mobile capital." [63] Despite these genuine concessions, the Farmers League included a demand for further tax relief in its first published program.

Because of the farmer's belief that low prices resulted in part from the practices of cunning and unscrupulous speculators, American Populists demanded the termination of all trading in grain futures. The Chicago Board of Trade was considered a den of thieves, and it was commonly believed that Leopold Bloom, Benjamin Hutchinson, and Edward Pardridge amassed millions on the commodity market while the farmer barely covered his costs.[64] A bill introduced in Congress by William Hatch in 1892 sought to reduce or even eliminate trading in futures by imposing a 10 per cent tax on purchasers who did not take physical possession of their grain. With the backing of thirty farm organizations, the Hatch Bill passed the House and Senate, only to die because the session ended before the House could pass on several amendments. Frustrated at the national level, Populists turned to the states, where they managed to win several victories. This proved worthless, however, since none of the states housing major commodity exchanges passed restrictive legislation.

Again the Germans proved somewhat more successful. Under agrarian pressure, Caprivi convened a committee to investigate speculative practices on the stock exchange. The committee report recommended numerous reforms, but advised against the termination of futures trading.[65] While an anti-futures bill was being debated in 1896, a Jewish firm with the aid of two banks created a *cause célèbre* by seeking to corner the market in a certain grain. Responding to the ensuing public outcry, the Reichstag passed a stiff law that virtually ended the practice by regulating it to death. Nevertheless, futures trading continued under another name outside of the exchange for the next four years, and in 1900 agrarians reluctantly agreed to its necessity by scrapping the law in return for representation on the stock exchange's board of directors.

There is no need to stress the importance of bimetallism for the American Populist movement. It is clear that farmers viewed the gold standard as a major cause of their woes. They looked to a double standard to cheapen the dollars they paid to their creditors and to inflate the prices received for agricultural products. German bimetallism originated with the publication in 1875 of *Against the Grain* by Wilhelm von Kardorff, the leader of the German Free Conservative party. The next year it became the major demand of the newly formed Association of Tax and Economic Reform. The movement remained weak during the eighties because Bismarck eschewed this volatile issue in favor of increased grain tariffs. In the early nineties the bimetallists, joined by the Farmers League, won enough support in the Reichstag to force Caprivi to establish a committee on the currency question. The chancellor denounced the agrarians, who, he said, used the demagogic issues of anti-semitism and bimetallism to advance their cause.[66] With the backing of the League, Kardorff succeeded in getting a resolution through the Reichstag in February 1895 requesting the government to convene an international conference to discuss the world monetary situation. Three months later the agrarians engineered a bill recommending a national bimetallist policy through the two houses of the Prussian legislature.[67] Just prior to the gold strikes in South Africa and Alaska, Kardorff claimed that he was close to gaining a majority in the Reichstag willing to dethrone gold.

Before bimetallism became an obsession, American Populists, particularly in the South, placed their hopes in the sub-treasury plan.[68] This proposal called upon the federal government to establish a chain of warehouses where farmers could store their grain or cotton until the market price rose above the unfavorable levels of the harvest season. In addition, the state was to provide low-interest loans to farmers, accepting their goods as collateral. Farmers obviously intended to improve the position of the seller in relation to the buyer and the creditor. The Lubin plan, which also won the endorsement of several state alliances, depended upon the government's willingness to pay a premium to farmers for every ton exported to Europe.[69]

The German counterparts of these demands were the *Kornhausbewegung* and the Kanitz plan. The former, a replica of the sub-treasury plan apart from the loan provision, won many supporters in 1895 with the publication of *Kornhaus contra Kanitz* by O. Grass-Klanin.[70] A year later Prussia allocated three million marks for the construction of warehouses; Bavaria and Württemberg soon followed suit. Within three years the experiment was abandoned as a dismal failure. Local agrarian groups appointed farmers with little business experience to manage the depots. At harvest time farmers tended to sell their best grain for cash to repay debts, using the storage facilities only for the lower grades. Debts piled up quickly until the warehouses became an enormous liability for the states.

Count Kanitz submitted his proposal in April 1895, in the aftermath of the agrarian defeat over the Russian tariff treaty. His goal, to reverse the urban migration by assuring farmers an annual profit, exceeded anything sought by the Americans. He asked the state to establish an import monopoly for the purpose of selling grain at fixed prices in the domestic market.[71] The prices would be high enough to insure a substantial profit to cultivators of the four major grains. In

deference to sharp criticism, the Count subsequently agreed to discard
his prescribed levels in favor of the average selling price between the
years 1850 and 1890. Critics ridiculed the plan as socialism in behalf
of the Junkers, and even moderate partisans of agriculture were aghast
at what they considered a design to provide farmers with a guaranteed
annual income.[72] Kanitz's plan suffered a humiliating defeat, receiving
only forty-six votes. In 1895 it was reintroduced, and with a strong
League effort the number of supporters more than doubled. Nevertheless, the determined opposition of the chancellor and the Catholics,
even Catholic agrarians, who believed the plan more worthy of the
Social Democrats, doomed it to failure each time that Kanitz resub-
mitted it.[73]

Among the disparities in the history of American and German
populism, two stand out. Both Woodward and Hofstadter have pointed
to the absence of intellectual support for the agrarian cause, even
among the Mugwumps who shared the farmers' antipathy to financial
capitalism.[74] This was decidedly not true of the German experience,
and to some extent explains both the greater success and militancy of
the League. Professors from the leading universities endorsed League
demands and accepted invitations to address agrarian meetings.[75] They
sat on government committees, where their highly respected opinions
were heard by the empire's leading ministers and politicians. A whole
body of literature by academics eulogizing the rural way of life was
published in the 1890's, much of it in the form of articles for popular
weekly and monthly magazines.[76] To be sure, the gold standard and
capitalism had proponents among the professoriate, but they were
fighting an uphill battle.

The reasons for this divergence are not difficult to ascertain. To
American professors, still deeply imbued with laissez-faire principles, a
program demanding comprehensive state action in behalf of one
segment of society was heretical and unworthy of serious consideration.
In the German milieu, agrarian appeals to the state did not automatically evoke a negative response. In this sense, it is interesting to note
that the few American academics in sympathy with state intervention
(Frances Walker, E. Benjamin Andrews, Edmund James, Richard Ely,
and Arthur T. Hadley) either studied in Germany or read widely in
the writings of the historical school.[77]

The prestigious status of the Junkers is also relevant. An alliance
between state-employed professors and the empire's leading social class
did not face the obstacles that precluded cooperation between Populists

and intellectuals in America. The romantic and organic currents that permeated nineteenth-century German thought served to strengthen this alliance. A recurring theme in social philosophy was the soundness of a rural corporative society in contrast to the evils engendered by financial capitalism.[78] In a peculiar way, unification also enhanced the romanticization of the tillers of the soil by conservative academics. The Junkers and peasants received new plaudits after 1871 as the backbone of the army and the pillars of the new German empire. By the nineties some theorists came to fear that the youthful and fragile empire could not withstand the social polarization and discord accompanying industrial capitalism. Convinced that divisive class conflict would inevitably escalate with social and economic change, they saw in the strengthening of the agricultural population the only hope of preserving Bismarck's creation.[79]

The second major divergence centers on the efforts of American Populists to form a producers' alliance with labor against industry and finance. Such a combination was not possible in Germany. Even in America, farmer-labor cooperation failed miserably in the only instance in which it was realized.[80] What made it at all conceivable in America was the nonideological position of labor and the relatively modest social station of the Midwestern Populists. The Farmers League could hardly appeal to a class fully identified with Marxian socialism. From its vantage point, the mutual hostility to capitalism paled in importance before the workers' ostensible commitment to revolution and avowed atheism.[81] In addition, the workers were pitted against agriculture on the crucial tariff issue, for bread prices in Germany, unlike in America, depended upon the level of grain duties. If the Junkers had ventured to approach the Social Democrats, they would have been ridiculed as the employers of tenant farm labor. The orthodox Marxists of the nineties looked upon the decline of the agricultural population as an inexorable law of history.

V

At this point some reflections on populism are in order. Pollack points to the similar approach taken by Marx and American Populists toward capitalism as evidence of the latter's genuine left radicalism. Yet, as I have sought to show, a closer parallel lies with the Junkers, a group universally considered conservative if not reactionary. Where Pollack has gone astray is in his assertion that a critique of capitalism and advocacy of state-sponsored reform is necessarily left radical. This is simply not true. European romantic conservatives, deeply imbued with Christian social teachings, pointed to the evils of capitalism before Marx was born. As Karl Mannheim has written:

> It is generally believed that the socialists were the first to criticize capitalism as a social system; in actual fact, however, there are many indications that this criticism was initiated by the right-wing opposition and was then gradually taken over by the left opposition. . . . The abstractness of human relationships under capitalism which is constantly emphasized by Marx and his followers was originally the discovery of observers from the conservative camp.[82]

Standing at the threshhold of the industrial capitalist era, early nineteenth-century romantics were able to compare its characteristics with those of an earlier, and for them superior, social system. The result of their unique perspective was a perceptive and all-embracing critique, one that in its pessimism and fear of social disintegration resembles the one indigenously developed and later put forth by American Populists.[83] What distinguishes Marx from the conservatives is his positive attitude toward capitalism (despite its faults), and his belief that its triumph over feudalism is fundamentally progressive. His radicalism lies not in his critique but in his prediction that the evils of capitalism will magnify, leading to revolution and subsequently a more humane social order.

Nor can the Populists be considered left radicals because they were the first to call upon the state to play an active role in society. In a superficial sense this is radical, especially in the context of America in the nineties. But state intervention is not an end but a means—a tool with which one can effect desired social goals. It can be used to achieve quite conservative ends as in the case of Bismarck's social legislation. The crucial question is: "Would the implementation of Populist demands have moved America in the direction of socialism, as Pollack contends?" No more so, I believe, than the adoption of the League's program would have brought Germany closer to Marxian socialism. The central goal of socialists was a collectivist society based on the abolition of private property.[84] Marxists not only foresaw the evanescence of the independent entrepreneur, they welcomed it as a precondition for the realization of the socialist ideal. They did not share the concern of agrarians in both nations with increasing social polarization; this was simply confirmation of the master's predictions. Friedrich

Engels advised German socialists to leave the peasants to the anti-semites.

Genuine socialism was anathema to American Populists. At times they toyed with nationalizing property, but it was always the property of their enemies, the monopolies and large corporations.[85] In December 1889 the *Alliance Journal* denounced those elements in the Knights of Labor who "would destroy all ownership in land and divide the possessions of others among all other classes." [86] The American farmer became a Populist not to abolish private property but to prevent his own from being confiscated.

Populist policies were a blueprint to retard social change. They sought to regulate capitalism because the polarization that came in its wake threatened their economic existence. If their program had been adopted, it would have modified the ground rules of capitalism in order to permit the survival of the small and medium-sized independent entrepreneur in an age of flux. Populists, in good Jeffersonian fashion, believed that the self-employed man was indispensable to the successful functioning of American democracy. Peffer of Kansas, in the tradition of Southey, Coleridge, and Adam Müller (not Marx), deplored the replacement of the wagon-maker and blacksmith by the mechanic, who did "his work with . . . the same method that an inanimate implement does." [87]

American populism was both politically and socially conservative: it looked to the established state to realize its aims, and it resisted rather than encouraged the social consequences of an international capitalist economy. Nostalgia occupied a large place in Populist rhetoric, as did revolution in the slogans of the workers two generations later. Both sought to assure themselves of a secure place within a remodeled capitalist order. That was the thrust of the Populist program and was underscored by Tom Watson in 1891 when in clarifying his position he said, "Don't misunderstand me to be making war upon capital as such. I am but denouncing that capital which is used tyrannically. I recognize the fact that without capital there can be no progress." [88] Ultimately, they sought a more organic relationship between past and present in which transition occurred with less social dislocation.

I use the word "conservative" to describe them in a literal sense. American Populists were not potential right-wing radicals, as Hofstadter and others have vaguely intimated, and as was true of the German agrarians.[89] The League's crusade to end the depression de-

veloped into a thoroughgoing attack upon Germany's involvement in
an international capitalist economy. The Junker leadership of the
League sought to forestall any future threats to their economic position
(and indirectly to their social and political privileges) by urging a
policy of autarchy upon the nation. The profit motive was to be
tolerated in Germany only insofar as it promoted Junker prosperity
and supremacy. A government that openly encouraged increased participation in a world economy was held to be a tool of capitalists and
an enemy of sound national development. Thus the League did not
dissolve after grain tariffs were increased by 40 per cent in 1902; in
fact League delegates voted against the rise as insufficient to restore
agriculture to its rightful primacy in the economy. The new chancellor,
Bernhard von Bülow, claimed that the appetite of the agrarians grew
with eating.[90] In Bavaria the farmers denounced all interest on loans
as usurious and demanded its total abolition. As early as 1898, League
literature proclaimed the future of Germany to lie on the land, and
went on from there to assert that patriotism without anti-capitalism
was not possible. Virulent anti-semitism became a mask behind which
a genuinely radical critique of a modern capitalist society flourished.[91]

Three points are central to an understanding of why the Germans
edged toward radicalism and the Americans did not. First, the Junkers
felt more threatened and beleaguered by capitalism than the American
farmer because of their status as Prussia's traditional ruling elite; social
and political prerogatives as well as economic well-being were at stake.
Not only lower grain prices, but the challenge of vigorous new elites
spawned by financial and industrial capitalism determined the response
of German agrarian leaders to the crisis of the nineties. The League's
continued existence after the end of the depression indicates that economic aims (while primary) were not the League's sole *raison d'être*.
Second, Germany was more of a static society than America in the
early nineteenth century.[92] Late medieval patterns of thought and institutions survived because Germany had experienced neither an era of
expansive commercial capitalism nor a political revolution. As a result,
industrial capitalism struck with enormous impact, fostering a more
elemental reaction than in the United States.[93] Third, Germany was
still a young and insecure nation in the 1890's. In the public mind
unification and patriotism were closely identified with the rural population, a coupling that was reinforced by the avowed international
loyalties of the socialist working class. Thus, urbanization and indus-

trialization appeared to threaten the fabric of unity by weakening the rural social order.

Using the comparative method, it is difficult to view the two populisms of America and Germany as anything but distinctive variations on a common theme.

NOTES

1. J. Rogers Hollingsworth, "Populism: The Problem of Rhetoric and Reality," *Agricultural History*, XXXIX (April 1965).

2. Richard Hofstadter, *The Age of Reform* (New York, 1955), chaps. 1–3. Also see his essay "Free Silver and the Mind of 'Coin' Harvey," in *The Paranoid Style in American Politics and other Essays* (New York, 1964), pp. 238–317. On the historiography of populism, see Theodore Saloutos, "The Professors and the Populists," *Agricultural History*, XL (October 1966). It should be emphasized that this essay is confined to populism and the German Farmers League. Other agrarian movements are not considered.

3. Norman Pollack, *The Populist Response to Industrial America* (Cambridge, Mass., 1962), p. 12. For Pollack's more recent views, see "Fear of Man: Populism, Authoritarianism, and the Historian," *Agricultural History*, XXXIX (April 1965); and the introduction to *The Populist Mind* (Indianapolis, 1967). For his view of Hofstadter's interpretation, see "Hofstadter on Populism: A Critique of 'The Age of Reform,'" *Journal of Southern History*, XXVI (November 1960).

4. Hofstadter, *Age of Reform*, p. 44; Pollack, *Populist Response*, p. 3. Pollack maintains here that farmers turn toward the past only when there is an abrupt transformation from feudalism to industrial capitalism. I would argue that they merely become more radical when a gradual transition is lacking. The thrust of agrarian movements seems to be the same no matter how long or short the transition period is.

5. John Hicks, *The Populist Revolt* (Minneapolis, 1931), p. 54. Hofstadter quotes an Alliance leader to the same effect on page 50, but does not draw out its implications.

6. Ignatius Donnelly, *Caesar's Column* (Chicago, 1891). Thus Donnelly has the leading character assert, "It was a shame to have to use such instruments. But the whole world was corrupt to the very core . . ." (p. 162). On Donnelly, see Martin Ridge, *Ignatius Donnelly: The Portrait of a Politician* (Chicago, 1962).

7. *Letters of Henry Adams (1892–1918)*, ed. W. C. Ford (Boston, 1938), p. 33.

8. Alfred Vagts, *Deutschland und die Vereinigten Staaten in der Weltpolitik*, 2 vols. (New York, 1935), I, 519.

9. See the chart facing page 1 in W. W. Rostow, *The Stages of Economic Growth* (London, 1960). By 1914 both Germany and America had surpassed Great Britain as industrial powers.

10. Karl Oldenberg, *Deutschland als Industriestaat* (Göttingen, 1897).

11. On Bismarck's introduction of tariffs, see Helmut Böhme, *Deutschlands Weg zur Grossmacht* (Cologne, 1966); Ivo Lambie, *Free Trade and Protection in Germany* (Wiesbaden, 1963); M. Nitzsche, *Die handelspolitische Reaktion in Deutschland* (Stuttgart and Berlin, 1905); and Hans Rosenberg, *Grosse Depression und Bismarckzeit* (Berlin, 1967).

12. Caprivi defended his tariffs as necessary to expand Germany's industrial markets and thereby bring a halt to the sizable emigration. From 1890 to 1894 the emperor departed from precedent by showing no interest in agriculture and severely criticizing the Junkers for their lack of patriotism. During this period the agrarian movement branded him an enemy of German agriculture. Rudolf Arndt, ed., *Die Reden des Grafen Caprivi* (Berlin, 1894), p. 166; Graf von Waldersee, *Denkwürdigkeiten des General-Feldmarschalls Alfred Grafen von Waldersee*, ed. by H. O. Meissner, 3 vols. (Stuttgart, 1923), II, 306.

13. Joseph Dorfman, *The Economic Mind in American Civilization, 1865–1918* (New York, 1949), III, 205. The policies of the American Economic Association show that even in America a group could advocate state intervention without being radical left or radical at all.

14. Chester McArthur Destler, *American Radicalism, 1865–1901* (New London, 1946), pp. 105ff. Ray Scott, *The Agrarian Movement in Illinois, 1880–1896* (Urbana, Ill., 1962), p. 6. Also see Fred Shannon, *The Farmer's Last Frontier* (New York, 1945), p. 260.

15. *Verhandlungen des Reichstages . . . Stenographische Berichte* (Berlin, 1871–1938), 1893–1894, 1505–1508. Also see Heinz Haushofer, *Die deutsche Landwirtschaft im technischen Zeitalter* (Stuttgart, 1963), vol. V; Friedrich Aereboe, *Agrarpolitik* (Berlin, 1928); and A. Schäffle, *Ein Votum gegen den neuesten Zolltarif* (Berlin, 1901).

16. R. H. Elsworth, "Agricultural Cooperative Associations," *U.S. Department of Agriculture Technical Bulletin* No. 46 (Washington, D.C., 1928), pp. 3–6; Destler, *American Radicalism*, p. 104; Hofstadter, *Age of Reform*, p. 113.

17. S. Körte, ed., *Deutschland unter Wilhelm II*, 3 vols. (Berlin, 1913), II, 473. Wilhelm Treue, *Die deutsche Landwirtschaft zur Zeit Caprivis und ihr Kampf gegen die Handelsverträge* (Berlin, 1933), p. 29.

18. Hicks, *Populist Revolt*, p. 264.

19. In *Money at Interest: The Farm Mortgage on the Middle Border* (Ithaca, 1955), Allan Bogue makes a good case for declining interest rates in the Populist areas, but he does not deny that farmers in these areas were heavily indebted. Ultimately he is merely questioning their contention that interest rates were usurious.

20. C. Vann Woodward, *Tom Watson, Agrarian Rebel* (New York, 1938), pp. 129, 131. On indebtedness in America, see Shannon, *Farmer's Last Frontier*, pp. 303–307; Raymond C. Miller, "The Background of Populism in Kansas," *Mississippi Valley Historical Review*, XI (March 1925), 470; Nelson Dunning, ed., *The Farmers' Alliance History and Agricultural Digest* (Washington, D.C., 1891), p. 304; and Hallie Farmer, "The Economic Background of Frontier Populism," *Mississippi Valley Historical Review*, X (March 1924), 420.

21. J. K. Rodbertus, *Zur Erklärung und Abhülfe der heutigen Kreditnot des Grundbesitz* (Jena, 1876), table at end. On German indebtedness, see Theodor von der Goltz, *Geschichte der deutschen Landwirtschaft* (Stuttgart, 1902), II, 51, 132; Lujo Brentano, "Über eine zukünftige Handelspolitik des deutschen Reiches," *Schmollers Jahrbuch,* IX (1885), 16. The turnover in estates indicates both sales to the bourgeoisie as well as speculation.

22. *Die ländliche Verschuldung,* published by the Prussian Statistical Bureau (Berlin, 1902). From these statistics it can be seen that the Junkers suffered most severely from the price decline. Thus, although social and political considerations may have played a role in the League's formation, they were certainly quite secondary to economic motivation.

23. Hollingsworth, "Populism," p. 83. Both Hollingsworth and Pollack, the latter especially, take the liberty of reading back present-day ills into the Populist era. In Pollack's introduction to *The Populist Mind,* words like poverty, technology, participation, and transformation of values are used in reference to the Populists, although they all have a modern ring to them.

24. Shannon, *Farmer's Last Frontier,* p. 353; Charles Hoffman, "The Depression of the Nineties," *Journal of Economic History,* XVI (June 1956), 144.

25. Walter Nugent, *The Tolerant Populists* (Chicago, 1963), p. 68. On Georgia, see also Alex Arnett, *The Populist Movement in Georgia* (New York, 1922).

26. *Ibid.,* p. 65; Agricultural Yearbook (1899), pp. 764–765. For grain prices, see H. Farnsworth, "Decline and Recovery of Wheat Prices in the 90's," *Wheat Studies,* X (1934), 339–341. For German prices, see *Statistisches Jahrbuch für das Deutsche Reich;* also the large volume *Deutsche Landwirtschaft,* published by the Imperial Statistical Bureau in 1913.

27. Rosenberg, *Grosse Depression,* pp. 151–153. Rosenberg sees this transformation in traditional peasant political behavior as a direct result of the economic crisis.

28. Woodward, *Tom Watson,* chap. 13. On Populism and the Negro, see Jack Abramowitz, "The Negro in the Populist Movement." *Journal of Negro History,* XXXVIII (July 1953). Woodward believes that Watson was the first to treat Negro strivings seriously and to see them as an integral part of the Southern economy.

29. Quoted in Pollack, *Populist Mind,* p. 369.

30. William Dubose Sheldon, *Populism in the Old Dominion* (Princeton, 1935), pp. 32–35. Sheldon quotes a Virginian to the effect that the rowdy element was not present at Populist gatherings. On Watson's background, see Woodward, *Tom Watson,* p. 217. In "The Populist Heritage and the Intellectual," *American Scholar,* LIX (Winter 1959), Woodward says that populism in Virginia included the most aristocratic names in the state.

31. Nugent says, "Economic distress cut across lines of religion, of nationality, origins, or race, of previous political affiliation, even of occupation and of wealth and status." Nugent, *Tolerant Populists,* p. 235. He points out that immigrants played a significant role in the Kansas party from the outset.

32. The best work on the League is Hans-Jürgen Puhle, *Agrarische Interessenpolitik und preussischer Konservatismus* (Hannover, 1966). Also see Sarah Tirrell, *German Agrarian Politics After Bismarck's Fall* (New York, 1951); and T. Nipperdey, "Interessenverbände und Parteien in Deutschland vor dem ersten Weltkrieg," *Politische Vierteljahresschrift,* No. 2 (1961).

33. *Sten. Ber.* (1890–1892), p. 3376. The faction that voted for the treaty lost power in 1892 when the party adopted a new program.

34. Otto von Kiesenwetter, *Zehn Jahre wirtschaftspolitischen Kampfes* (Berlin, 1903), pp. 16–22; Puhle, *Agrarische Interessenpolitik,* p. 33.

35. *Sten. Ber.,* vol. 128 (1892–1893), 1085. As a result of statements such as this, Caprivi was termed a "Schweinhund" in the agrarian press.

36. Pauline Anderson, *The Background of Anti-English Feeling in Germany, 1890–1902* (Washington, D.C., 1939), p. 140. Puhle rightly observes that the League was the first mass movement on the right in Germany.

37. Max Schneidewin, "Briefe des toten Reichskanzlers von Caprivi," *Deutsche Revue,* XLVII (1922), 146.

38. Wilhelm Gerloff, *Die Finanz- und Zollpolitik des Deutschen Reiches* (Jena, 1913), p. 383.

39. Puhle, *Agrarische Interessenpolitik,* p. 215.

40. Nipperdey, "Interessenverbände und Parteien," p. 273. In the voting on the Russian tariff treaty of 1894, the major difference between supporters and opponents was not so much party as the rural or urban character of the delegate's district. The Center party found that its peasant support dwindled if it did not vote with the League, while its working-class vote remained constant.

41. The best work on the Canal is Hannelore Horn, "Der Kampf um den Bau des Mittellandkanals," *Staat und Politik,* VI (1964).

42. Donnelly, *Caesar's Column,* p. 46. Elsewhere he says, "The condition of the world has, however, steadily grown worse and worse . . ." (p. 99). The sense of imminent doom in the writings of Donnelly and Mary Lease is well described in Frederic Jaher, *Doubters and Dissenters* (Glencoe, Ill., 1964).

43. In the minds of agrarians, the workers and capitalists were not reliable enough to defend the nation's interest. The chairman of the League said an army made up of stockbrokers could not take a house of cards. *Allgemeine Zeitung,* 96 Jg. N. 49 (February 19, 1894). Graf von Kanitz, the leading agrarian in the Reichstag, was quite pessimistic. He warned, "The signs of present times are very distinct; decline of agriculture and the small businessman, depopulation of the land; capital accumulation in big cities and the rise of Social Democracy as a result of big city growth. . . . If agriculture does not become more prosperous, this development with all of its disruptive effects will continue." Kanitz, *Die Festsetzung von Mindestpreisen* (Preussisch-Holland, 1894).

44. Fritz Hellwig, *Carl Freiherr von Stumm-Halberg* (Heidelberg, 1936), p. 462.

45. All middlemen were considered nonproducers by Kansas Populists. Nugent, *Tolerant Populists.* p. 237. According to Saloutos, the Southern Alliance excluded merchants, clerks, and most shopkeepers from membership, and even believed they were physically inferior specimens of manhood—a concept very close to German agrarian views of middlemen. Saloutos, *Farmer Movements in the South, 1865–1933* (Berkeley, 1960), pp. 76, 78, 84.

46. Quoted in Pollack, *Populist Mind,* p. 99.

47. Adolf Wagner, *Agrar- und Industriestaat* (Jena, 1901); *Grundlegung der Politischen Ökonomie,* 2 vols. (Leipzig, 1892–1894); see my article in the June 1969 issue of the *Journal of Modern History,* "Adolf Wagner and German Industrial Development." For the tendency of German thinkers to associate concord with rural society, see Ralf Dahrendorf, *Society and Democracy in Germany* (Garden City, 1967).

48. Dunning, *The Farmers' Alliance History,* pp. 130–131; Donnelly, *Caesar's Column,* p. 97. The preamble to the Omaha Platform is one long diatribe against plutocracy.

49. See Hofstadter's essay on "Coin" Harvey mentioned in note 2.

50. Nugent, *Tolerant Populists*, p. 48. Lease continually denounced England in her speeches.

51. On German anti-semitism in this period, see Puhle, *Agrarische Interessenpolitik*, chap. 3; P. J. Pulzer, *The Rise of Political Anti-Semitism in Germany and Austria* (New York, 1964); Paul Massing, *Rehearsal for Destruction* (New York, 1949); and George Mosse, *The Crisis of German Ideology* (New York, 1964).

52. This is well documented in Rosenberg, *Grosse Depression*, chap. 3.

53. Puhle, *Agrarische Interessenpolitik*, p. 130.

54. Recently there has been a dispute among American historians about the scope and depth of anti-semitism in the Populist movement. That Donnelly's book is at least implicitly anti-semitic seems to me beyond doubt. Saloutos is correct, however, in wondering if anti-semitism was not more apparent in the Eastern universities in the nineties. I tend to agree with John Higham's point in "Anti-semitism in the Gilded Age," *Mississippi Valley Historical Review*, XLIII (March 1957), wherein he points to the international upswing accompanying the depression of the early nineties. I would limit this upswing to political anti-semitism, for the social variety seems to be independent of economic conditions.

55. Jaher, *Doubters and Dissenters*, p. 138; Scott, *Agrarian Movement in Illinois*, p. 63.

56. *Sten. Ber.* (1893–1894), vol. 182, 2934–2942; *Ist eine Erhöhung der landwirtschaftlichen Schutzzölle notwendig?*, published by Das Volksverein für das katholische Deutschland (1901); Wagner, *Agrar- und Industriestaat*. The League's first program began, "German agriculture is the first and most important business, the most solid support of the German Empire."

57. The League went further than Mirbach and requested that local officials be given the power to refuse the right of internal migration from the rural areas.

58. *Sten. Ber.* (1902), vol. 182, 2913–2918. The same idea was proffered by Professor Karl Oldenberg, "Landarbeitermangel und Abhilfe." *Zeitschrift für Agrarpolitik*, V (February 1907), 85. In the American context, regulation of internal movement seems quite reactionary, yet in Prussia such controls existed well into the nineteenth century.

59. Kanitz and Wangenheim looked forward to the day when agriculture could pay its labor force as much as industry. The rhetoric about a balance between agriculture and industry was, in effect, a demand for huge state subventions for agriculture.

60. Donnelly, *Caesar's Column*, p. 115. Donnelly and the Populists were coming to the same conclusion as the American Economics Association. For the influence of German thought on American thinking, see Joseph Dorfman, "The Role of the German Historical School in American Economic Thought," *American Economic Review*, XLV (1955), 17–28.

61. Wagner, *Grundlegung*, I, 57–63; *Sozialismus, Sozial Demokratie, Katheder- und Staatssozialismus* (Berlin, 1895); *Die Strömungen in der Sozialpolitik und der Katheder- und Staatssozialismus* (Berlin, 1912).

62. Hans Herzfeld, *Johannes von Miquel*, 2 vols. (Detmold, 1938), pp. 224ff; Von der Goltz, *Deutschen Landwirtschaft*, p. 286; Aereboe, *Agrarpolitik*, pp. 386–388.

63. Walter Geiger, *Miquel und die Preussiche Steuerreform 1890/1893* (Göppingen, 1934), p. 19; Karl Kröger, *Die Konservativen und die Politik Caprivis* (Rostock, 1937), p. 20.

64. Cedric Cowing, *Populists, Plungers, and Progressives* (Princeton, 1965),

pp. 5–29. Louisiana and California passed anti-futures laws. Southerners in Congress were hesitant about a national anti-futures law, believing this was a matter best left to the states. Most probably, the death of the bill was not accidental, although Cowing does not pursue this.

65. Ulrich Teichmann, *Die Politik der Agrarpreisstützung* (Cologne, 1955), p. 215ff.

66. *Sten. Ber.* (1893–1894), I, 1452. Unusual for a German chancellor, Caprivi repeatedly denounced the League for its demagogical use of anti-semitism and bimetallism.

67. Vagts, *Deutschland und die Vereinigten Staaten,* I, 504–508; Siegfried von Kardorff, *Wilhelm von Kardorff* (Berlin, 1936), p. 328; Hellwig, *Carl Freiherr von Stumm-Halberg,* pp. 460–464; Wagner, *Bimetallismus und Handelsverträge* (Berlin, 1894). Kardorff claimed to be in close touch with American bimetallists, especially the senators from Nevada.

68. Hicks, *Populist Revolt,* p. 189ff; "The Sub-Treasury: A Forgotten Plan for the Relief of Agriculture," *Mississippi Valley Historical Review,* XV (December 1928), 355–373.

69. Theodore Saloutos, "The Agricultural Problem and 19th-Century Industrialization," *Agricultural History,* XXII (July 1948), 173.

70. O. Grass-Klanin, *Kornhaus contra Kanitz* (Stettin, 1895); Teichmann, *Die Politik der Agrarpreisstützung,* p. 227.

71. Kanitz, *Sten. Ber.* (1894), vol. 135, 2090ff; Alexander Gerschenkron, *Bread and Democracy in Germany* (Berkeley, 1943), p. 53.

72. Many opponents believed that Kanitz's plan contravened Germany's tariff treaties and was therefore impossible to execute. The conservative professor Gustav Schmoller calculated that the plan was equivalent to a tariff of 115 for wheat, 83 for rye, and 78 for barley; that is, between 100 and 300 per cent higher than the tariff rates agreed upon in the treaty with Russia. Gustav Schmoller, "Einige Worte zum Antrag Kanitz," *Schmollers Jahrbuch,* XIX (1895).

73. The views of the Center party are contained in a speech by Karl Bachem, *Sten. Ber.* (1893–1894), III, 2108–2114.

74. Woodward, "The Populist Heritage and the Intellectuals"; Hofstadter, *Age of Reform,* p. 92ff. America is fortunate that the farmers did not form a mass base for the anti-modernism of the eastern Mugwumps.

75. Among those supporting the agrarians were Adolf Wagner and Max Sering at Berlin, Karl Oldenberg at Marburg, Karl Diehl at Freiburg, and Ludwig Pohle at Leipzig. Wagner toured the country speaking in behalf of agrarian demands in 1901, and Sering spoke annually to an assembly of Junkers on agriculture's plight. See my forthcoming book, *The Controversy over German Industrialization, 1890–1902.*

76. There is a bibliography of such articles in my book. Among the popular journals were *Die Woche, Die Zukunft,* and *Deutsche Monatschrift.*

77. Dorfman, *Economic Mind,* p. 206.

78. See Dahrendorf, and R. H. Bowen, *German Theories of the Corporate State* (New York, 1947).

79. Wagner, *Verhandlungen des Vereins für Sozialpolitik,* vol. 76 (1897), 441ff; *Agrar- und Industriestaat;* Ludwig Pohle, *Deutschland am Scheidewege* (Leipzig, 1902). All of these theorists argued that the bonds of unity were quite weak in Germany and that any added pressure or reason for conflict could tear the nation apart.

80. Certainly it is worth noting the farmers' sympathetic attitude toward

labor in the United States; but its importance has recently been exaggerated. Both Destler and Scott have declared the alliance in Illinois an unmitigated failure. Not a single candidate was elected by the alliance, and the treasury remained empty. What allowed the alliance to be even conceivable was the fact that America exported grain. If grain had been imported, labor and agriculture would have been natural rivals over grain tariffs, as in Germany. Destler, *American Radicalism*, p. 211; Scott, *Agrarian Movement in Illinois,* p. 88.

81. The League did talk in terms of a producers' alliance, similar to the Americans, with those elements of the working class not bound to Social Democracy. Nothing materialized from this rhetoric.

82. Karl Mannheim, "Conservative Thought," in P. Kecskemeti, ed., *Essays on Sociology and Social Psychology* (London, 1953), p. 90; C. Schmitt-Dorotic, *Politische Romantik* (Munich, 1919). More recently Raymond Williams has written, "Marx, for instance, was to attack capitalism, in his early writings, in very much the language of Coleridge, of Burke, and—of Cobbett." *Culture and Society* (New York, 1958), p. 20.

83. The Populist critique also resembles the romantic one in its frequent reference to Christian social teachings. In "Religion in the Alliance," the Reverend Isom Langley wrote, "Is that government Christian which creates millionaires and palaces on the one hand and miserable homes on the other?" Dunning, *Farmers' Alliance History*, p. 314. Donnelly says, "The old tender Christian love is gone . . ." It is unimaginable that a socialist would have used those words. At the Ocala convention, Polk expressed his fear that America was departing from its Christian moorings. Henry Demarest Lloyd's *Wealth Against Commonwealth*, widely read by the Populists, received its best reviews from religious periodicals. Destler, *Henry Demarest Lloyd and the Empire of Reform* (Philadelphia, 1963), p. 356.

84. George Lichtheim, *Marxism* (New York, 1961), p. 49.

85. The League also mentioned the need to nationalize the coal mines of the Ruhr. Since railroads were already state owned in Germany, this did not become an issue.

86. Saloutos, *Farmer Movements in the South*, p. 105. I have seen no evidence that the farmers desired the nationalization of all land, or even of farm land—a demand that all European socialists shared. Pollack does not seem to distinguish what is basic to European socialism from what it shares with movements having quite contrary aims.

87. Quoted in Pollack, *Populist Mind*, p. 83. This kind of anguish about the passing of the artisan was endemic in conservative writings in the nineteenth century. It is to be found in the writings of Ruskin, Schmoller, and all those whose ideal social order lay in the past.

88. *Ibid.*, p. 434. Nugent has, in my opinion, come to the soundest conclusion about this question: "The majority of them therefore accepted industrialization but condemned monopoly, accepted banking and finance but condemned usury and financial sleight of hand, . . . welcomed enterprise but condemned speculation." *Tolerant Populists*, p. 238. Destler also has written, "To the Populists, as noted above, collectivist methods were simply a legitimate means of restoring free enterprise and small competitive capitalism." Destler, *American Radicalism*, p. 224.

89. Hofstadter is less guilty of this accusation than Victor Ferkiss or Peter Vierick.

90. Bülow found that no matter how many concessions he made to agriculture, he could not satisfy the agrarians. In the end he resigned when they

helped to defeat a tax increase, part of which added to the burden of the farmers.

91. The thesis that rabid anti-semitism is often a mask for attacks on the state and the whole social and economic order was put forth by Hannah Arendt in *The Origins of Totalitarianism* (New York, 1951), Part II.

92. Until 1807 Prussia was legally a caste society. Social mobility and the unrestrained profit motive were not common in preindustrial Germany. It should be remembered that Germany had no merchant marine, no colonies, no slave or rum trade. The guild system survived well into the nineteenth century.

93. German thought in the nineteenth century, whether of the left or right, is marked by a strong hostility to the whole system of industrial capitalism. H. Rosenberg has written that Germans reacted to the depression of 1873 not by blaming their stock broker but by laying the blame on capitalism itself. Liberalism and the independent middle class, the staunchest supporters of capitalism, were both weak in Germany.

Index

A Note on the Contributors

SYDNEY E. AHLSTROM is professor of church history and American history at Yale University. He holds a doctorate from Harvard University. His writings include *The American Protestant Encounter with World Religions* (1963) and *Theology in America* (1967).

KENNETH BARKIN is assistant professor of history at the University of California, Riverside. He attended Brooklyn College and Brown University. He is the author of *The Controversy over German Industrialization* (1970).

HERBERT J. BASS, the editor of this volume, is professor of history at Temple University. He attended Boston University and the University of Rochester. He has written *"I Am a Democrat": The Political Career of David Bennett Hill* (1961) and edited *Readings in American History* (1963) and *America's Entry into World War I* (1964).

ROBERT H. BREMNER is professor of history at The Ohio State University, from which he also received the doctorate. He is the author of *From the Depths: The Discovery of Poverty in the United States* (1956) and *American Philanthropy* (1960).

GEORGE H. DANIELS, associate professor of history at Northwestern University, received his graduate education at the University of Iowa.

He has written *American Science in the Age of Jackson* (1968) and edited *Darwinism Comes to America* (1968).

DOUGLAS F. DOWD is the author of *Modern Economic Problems in Historical Perspective* (1962) and *Thorstein Veblen* (1958), and editor of *America's Role in the World Economy* (1966). He holds both undergraduate and graduate degrees from the University of California, and is professor of economics at Cornell University.

LAURENCE EVANS, a graduate of the University of Maine and of Johns Hopkins University, is professor of history at the State University of New York, Binghamton. He wrote *United States Policy and the Partition of Turkey, 1914–1924* (1965) and was a co-editor of the volumes of *Foreign Relations of the United States* for the years 1943, 1944, and 1945.

LAWRENCE M. FRIEDMAN is professor of law at the Stanford University School of Law and holds undergraduate and law degrees from the University of Chicago. He is the author of *Contract Law in America: A Social and Economic Case Study* (1965) and *Government and Slum Housing: A Century of Frustration* (1968), and co-editor of *Law and the Behavioral Sciences* (1969).

FRANK OTTO GATELL is associate professor of history at the University of California at Los Angeles. He holds degrees from City College of New York and Harvard. He has written *John Gorham Palfrey and the New England Conscience* (1963) and co-edited *American Negro Slavery: A Modern Reader* (1968).

PHILIP J. GREVEN, JR., is author of *Four Generations: Population, Land, and Family in Colonial Andover, Massachusetts* (1970). He attended Harvard and Columbia, and is associate professor of history at Rutgers University.

DAVID D. HALL is associate professor of history and American studies at Yale University. He attended both Harvard and Yale. He has compiled *The Antinomian Controversy, 1636–1638: A Documentary History* (1968).

ROBERT JAY LIFTON is Foundations' Fund Research Professor of Psychiatry at the Yale University School of Medicine. He attended Cornell University and New York Medical College. Among his books are *Thought Reform and the Psychology of Totalism: A Study of "Brainwashing" in China* (1961), *Death in Life: Survivors of Hiroshima* (1967), and *Revolutionary Immortality: Mao Tse-tung and the Chinese Cultural Revolution* (1968).

THOMAS J. McCORMICK, associate professor of history at the University of Pittsburgh, is a graduate of the University of Cincinnati and the University of Wisconsin. He is the author of *China Market: America's Quest for Informal Empire, 1893–1901* (1967).

SAMUEL T. McSEVENEY is an assistant professor of history at Brooklyn College, where he did his undergraduate work. He also attended the University of Connecticut and the University of Iowa. He has written several articles that utilize quantification methods.

ALLEN R. MILLETT is associate professor of history at The Ohio State University, from which he also holds his graduate degrees. He wrote *The Politics of Intervention: The Military Occupation of Cuba, 1906–1909* (1968).

RODERICK NASH is associate professor of history at the University of California, Santa Barbara. He holds degrees from Harvard and the University of Wisconsin. Among his publications are *Wilderness and the American Mind* (1967), *The American Environment* (1968), and *Grand Canyon of the Living Colorado* (1969).

EDWARD PESSEN is professor of history in the Graduate Center, City University of New York and at Staten Island Community College of the City University. His degrees are from Columbia University. His work in the Jacksonian period includes *Jacksonian America: Society, Personality, and Politics* (1969), *Most Uncommon Jacksonians* (1967), and *New Perspectives on Jacksonian Parties and Politics* (1969).

CHARLES ROSENBERG is the author of *The Cholera Years: The United States in 1832, 1849, and 1866* (1962) and *The Trial of the Assassin Guiteau: Psychiatry and Law in the Gilded Age* (1968). A graduate of Wisconsin and Columbia, he is professor of history at the University of Pennsylvania.

MORTON ROTHSTEIN is professor of history at the University of Wisconsin. His degrees are from Brooklyn College and Cornell University. He has written a number of articles in economic history.

JOEL H. SILBEY is professor of history at Cornell University. He attended Brooklyn College and the University of Iowa. He wrote *The Shrine of Party: Congressional Voting Behavior 1841–1852* (1967), and edited *The Transformation of American Politics, 1840–1860* (1967).

DAVID B. TYACK is associate professor of education and history at Stanford University. He received both his bachelor's degree and doctorate from Harvard. Among his books are *George Ticknor and the Boston Brahmins* (1967), *Turning Points in American Educational History* (1967), and *Nobody Knows: Black Americans in the Twentieth Century* (1970).

RUDOLPH J. VECOLI is professor of history and director of the Center for Immigration Studies at the University of Minnesota. A graduate of the Universities of Connecticut, Pennsylvania, and Wisconsin, he has written *The People of New Jersey* (1965).

RICHARD C. WADE is professor of history at the University of Chicago. He holds degrees from the University of Rochester and Harvard University. Among his works are *The Urban Frontier: The Rise of Cities in the West, 1790–1830* (1959), *Slavery in the Cities: The South, 1820–1860* (1964), and *Chicago: Growth of a Metropolis* (1970).

HAROLD D. WOODMAN is associate professor of history at the University of Missouri. He attended Roosevelt University and the University of Chicago. He has written *King Cotton and His Retainers* (1967) and edited *Slavery and the Southern Economy* (1967) and *Conflict or Consensus in American History* (1966).

ROBERT ZEMSKY, associate professor of American civilization at the University of Pennsylvania, is a graduate of Whittier College and Yale University. His book on the politics of eighteenth-century Massachusetts, in part a statistical analysis of political data, will be published soon.